CW00919242

Intelligent Methods and Alternative Economic Models for Sustainability

Latifa Dekhici
University of Sciences and Technology of Oran Mohamed-Boudiaf, Algeria

Khaled Guerraiche
LDREI Laboratory, Higher School of Electrical Engineering and Energy of Oran, Algeria

Rabia Azzemou
University of Sciences and Technology of Oran Mohamed-Boudiaf, Algeria

Jihène Jlassi
Higher Institute of Industrial Management of Sfax, University of Sfax, Tunisia

A volume in the Advances in Finance, Accounting, and Economics (AFAE) Book Series

Published in the United States of America by
    IGI Global
    Business Science Reference (an imprint of IGI Global)
    701 E. Chocolate Avenue
    Hershey PA, USA 17033
    Tel: 717-533-8845
    Fax: 717-533-8661
    E-mail: cust@igi-global.com
    Web site: http://www.igi-global.com

Library of Congress Cataloging-in-Publication Data

Names: Dekhici, Latifa, 1979- editor.
Title: Intelligent methods and alternative economic models for
  sustainability / edited by Latifa Dekhici, Khaled Guerraiche, Rabia
  Azzemou, Jihène Jlassi Mabrouk.
Description: Hershey, PA : Business Science Reference, [2024] | Includes
  bibliographical references and index. | Summary: "The book delves into a
  wide array of topics, encompassing both intelligent methods and
  innovative economic models. By synergizing these two areas, the book
  aims to provide a comprehensive overview that offers practical solutions
  for promoting sustainability across various sectors"-- Provided by
  publisher.
Identifiers: LCCN 2023055078 (print) | LCCN 2023055079 (ebook) | ISBN
  9798369314180 (hardcover) | ISBN 9798369314197 (ebook)
Subjects: LCSH: Sustainable development--Technological innovations. |
  Intelligent agents (Computer software)
Classification: LCC HC79.E5 I51786 2024 (print) | LCC HC79.E5 (ebook) |
  DDC 338.9/27--dc23/eng/20231207
LC record available at https://lccn.loc.gov/2023055078
LC ebook record available at https://lccn.loc.gov/2023055079

This book is published in the IGI Global book series Advances in Finance, Accounting, and Economics (AFAE) (ISSN: 2327-5677; eISSN: 2327-5685)

British Cataloguing in Publication Data
A Cataloguing in Publication record for this book is available from the British Library.

All work contributed to this book is new, previously-unpublished material.
The views expressed in this book are those of the authors, but not necessarily of the publisher.

For electronic access to this publication, please contact: eresources@igi-global.com.

Advances in Finance, Accounting, and Economics (AFAE) Book Series

ISSN:2327-5677
EISSN:2327-5685

Editor-in-Chief: Ahmed Driouchi, Al Akhawayn University, Morocco

MISSION

In our changing economic and business environment, it is important to consider the financial changes occurring internationally as well as within individual organizations and business environments. Understanding these changes as well as the factors that influence them is crucial in preparing for our financial future and ensuring economic sustainability and growth.

The **Advances in Finance, Accounting, and Economics (AFAE)** book series aims to publish comprehensive and informative titles in all areas of economics and economic theory, finance, and accounting to assist in advancing the available knowledge and providing for further research development in these dynamic fields.

COVERAGE

- Auditing
- Public Finance
- Health Economics
- Microeconomics
- Fiscal Policy
- International Economics
- Comparative Accounting Systems
- Theoretical Issues in Economics, Finance, and Accounting
- Economics Geography
- Entrepreneurship in Accounting and Finance

IGI Global is currently accepting manuscripts for publication within this series. To submit a proposal for a volume in this series, please contact our Acquisition Editors at Acquisitions@igi-global.com or visit: http://www.igi-global.com/publish/.

Titles in this Series

For a list of additional titles in this series, please visit:
www.igi-global.com/book-series/advances-finance-accounting-economics/73685

Revolutionizing the Global Stock Market Harnessing Blockchain for Enhanced Adaptability
Nuno Geada (ISCTE, University Institute of Lisbon, Portugal) Rohit Sood (Lovely Professional University, India) and Ajay Sidana (Amity International Business School, Amity University, Noida, India)
Business Science Reference • copyright 2024 • 285pp • H/C (ISBN: 9798369317587) • US $295.00 (our price)

Six Sigma DMAIC and Markov Chain Monte Carlo Applications to Financial Risk Management
Vojo Bubevski (Vojo Bubevski Consulting, UK)
Business Science Reference • copyright 2024 • 299pp • H/C (ISBN: 9798369337875) • US $255.00 (our price)

Artificial Intelligence Approaches to Sustainable Accounting
Maria C. Tavares (ISCA, University of Aveiro, Portugal) Graça Azevedo (University of Aveiro, Portugal) José Vale (ISCAP, Polytechnic Institute of Porto, Portugal) Rui Marques (University of Aveiro, Portugal) and Maria Anunciação Bastos (ISCA, University of Aveiro, Portugal)
Business Science Reference • copyright 2024 • 312pp • H/C (ISBN: 9798369308479) • US $275.00 (our price)

Impact of Digitalization on Reporting, Tax Avoidance, Accounting, and Green Finance
Ahmad Alqatan (Arab Open University, Kuwait) Khaled Hussainey (University of Portsmouth, UK) Mounira Hamed (University of Tunis El Manar, Tunisia) and Kameleddine Benameur (American University of Kuwait, Kuwait)
Business Science Reference • copyright 2024 • 358pp • H/C (ISBN: 9798369316788) • US $270.00 (our price)

For an entire list of titles in this series, please visit:
www.igi-global.com/book-series/advances-finance-accounting-economics/73685

701 East Chocolate Avenue, Hershey, PA 17033, USA
Tel: 717-533-8845 x100 • Fax: 717-533-8661
E-Mail: cust@igi-global.com • www.igi-global.com

To the researchers whose relentless pursuit of knowledge drives us to a better world
To all those who tirelessly strive for a more sustainable and equitable world.

Table of Contents

Khadidja ElKobra Belbachir, University of Science and Technology of Oran Mohamed-Boudiaf, Algeria
Redouane Tlemsani, University of Science and Technology of Oran Mohamed-Boudiaf, Algeria

Detailed Table of Contents

> *Marwa Mallek, Faculty of Economics and Management of Sfax, Tunisia*
> *MohamedAli Elleuch, Faculty of Economics and Management of Sfax,*
> *Tunisia*
> *Yosra Akouri, Higher Institute of Biotechnology of Sfax, Tunisia*

Hospital pharmacies are in contact with a large number of suppliers. The selection of the latter is an important task that has a crucial impact on the performance of the pharmacy sustainable supply chain. Studies, constituting a reference on the subject, have looked into the criteria for evaluating suppliers as well as the multidimensional aspect of the problem. The pharmaceutical supply chain is complex, and pharmaceutical companies must overcome the most common challenges to efficiently get patients the medicines they need. This paper looks at a multidimensional classification of suppliers of medical devices. First, the authors used the multi-criteria method of decision support AHP (analytics hierarchy process) for the choice of suppliers in the pharmacy with contradictory criteria. Subsequently, the authors developed a hybrid approach coupling the AHP method and the GP (goal programming) model to solve a problem dealing with the selection of suppliers in a sustainable supply chain under a set of constraints.

> *Dharmbir Prasad, Asansol Engineering College, India*
> *Rudra Pratap Singh, Asansol Engineering College, India*
> *Rahul Kumar, Asansol Engineering College, India*
> *Ranadip Roy, Sanaka Educational Trust's Group of Institutions, India*
> *Azizul Islam, Asansol Engineering College, India*
> *Md. Irfan Khan, IAC Electricals Pvt. Ltd., India*

The demand for renewable energy resources has increased significantly in recent years due to environmental concerns. The hybrid energy system is proposed as a solution to meet this demand. In this work, the HOMER software is used to design and optimize a hybrid model for electricity and hydrogen coproduction. The proposed model consists of various green energy resources such as solar PV, wind for hydrogen production. The system includes a green hydrogen storage facility while excess electricity is produced from renewable sources. The cost of energy production is found to be $0.08/kWh, which is competitive with conventional fossil fuel-based energy generation. In addition, the system has a lower environmental impact, with a 72% reduction in CO_2 emissions as compared to regular energy production methods.

Chapter 3

    Sabyasachi Pramanik, Haldia Institute of Technology, India

Innovative technologies including geothermal desalination, anaerobic digestion, microbial fuel cells, and internet of things integration may be able to aid with the combined challenges of wastewater treatment and energy sustainability. Anaerobic digestion converts organic waste into biogas, a renewable energy source that may be used to produce heat and electricity. Microbial fuel cells (MFCs) use the metabolic processes of microbes to convert organic materials into electricity, allowing for the simultaneous treatment of wastewater and the generation of renewable energy. Geothermal desalination reduces the need for fossil fuels and uses heat from geothermal sources to turn brackish or salty water into freshwater, which is less harmful to the environment. IoT connection allows geothermal desalination systems and bioenergy from wastewater processes to collect, monitor, control, and optimise data in real-time.

Chapter 4

    Imad Eddine Khiloun, SIMPA Laboratory, University of Science and Technology of Oran Mohamed-Boudiaf, Algeria
    Karima Belmabrouk, University of Science and Technology of Oran Mohamed-Boudiaf, Algeria
    Latifa Dekhici, University of Science and Technology of Oran Mohamed-Boudiaf, Algeria

This book chapter provides a concise yet comprehensive exploration of supply chain optimization through a multi-agent approach. Spanning historical foundations to contemporary intelligent methodologies, the literature review examines communication, collaboration, and coordination methods between agents. The analysis reveals achievements and challenges, emphasizing the pivotal role of intelligent agents in enhancing decision-making and adaptability. The chapter serves as a valuable resource for researchers and practitioners, offering insights into the dynamic landscape of supply chain management within the context of multi-agent systems. Through this exploration, the chapter contributes to shaping the future of resilient and efficient supply chain networks.

Pollution has taken a big toll on the environment. It touched the air that causes health diseases for living things, including humans. Among the transportation problems, especially the routing problems, vehicles are responsible for the pollutants' emissions, such as NOx and PM. Plus, CO_2 vehicle emissions result in an increase in global warming. This research presents the development of the bi-objective eco-routing problem with constraints that optimize the tradeoff between the total gaze emissions and the total travel distance and proposes an UNSGA-II approach to solve it. The objective is to study the performance of the proposed method under a fixed and variable speed environment and its impact on the emission gazes and distance. Experiments show that the UNSGA-II offers a promising solution, ensures the best set of distribution routes with minimum emissions can be achieved under varying speeds, and the initialization algorithm accelerates its convergence and guarantees population diversity.

Although numerous risk mitigation strategies have been developed for specific types of risks in supply chain risk management (SCRM), there is a lack of concrete and generic frameworks for an integrated network SCRM process. Consequently, it is often challenging to trace the process by which conclusions are drawn from previous research studies. The main goal is to create a framework that includes articulating SCRM issues, ranking risk variables, and creating mitigation strategies. Using the "scenario method" offers a comprehensive perspective that is displayed in a single table and helps identify different options. The extended supply chain's potential tools are used to create a unique framework for scenario building in risk mitigation plans in this research. The research demonstrates the importance of the framework and how it may help organizations implement strong strategies based on compelling scenarios through a thorough case study.

Chapter 7

Ghania Khensous, École Normale Supérieure d'Oran, Algeria
Amal Boumedjout, École Normale Supérieure d'Oran, Algeria
Kaouter Labed, École Normale Supérieure d'Oran, Algeria

Artificial intelligence has emerged as a transformative force across numerous sectors, and its impact on education is no exception. In recent years, AI has gained prominence in the field of education; revolutionizing the way we teach, learn, and administer educational processes. From personalized learning experiences to intelligent tutoring systems, AI has the potential to reshape the future of education, making it more accessible, adaptive, and effective than ever before. The future of learning and teaching will be shaped by the convergence of innovative technologies, data-driven methodologies, and personalized learning experiences. Therefore, the authors explore the dynamic landscape of artificial intelligence in education; this book chapter discusses mainly: AIED areas, AIED applications, learning about AI as well as preparing for AI.

Chapter 8

Jihen Jlassi, Higher Institute of Industrial Management of Sfax, Tunisia
Mohamed Ali Daly Elleuch, Higher Institute of Industrial Management
of Sfax, Tunisia
Ines Rekik, Higher Institute of Industrial Management of Sfax, Tunisia
Marwa Mallek, University of Economic Science and Management of
Sfax, Tunisia

The travelling salesman problem (TSP) is the challenge of finding the shortest yet most efficient route for a person to take given a list of specific destinations. It is an optimization problem in the fields of computer science and operations research. There are obviously a lot of different routes to choose from, but finding the best one the one that will require the least distance or costs, several researchers have spent decades trying to optimize the modeling and the resolution. In some real cases, the classical problem is not able to model the existing problem in a given company. In this paper, we propose models for the TSP, that can be used with linear or quadratic service time functions, and that embeds novel improved lower and upper bounds. With proposed models, the authors consider exponentially many sub-tour eliminations, capacities, and demands constraints, which are separated dynamically. The main purpose is to help the transport manager to select the optimal distribution circuit that optimizes various objectives.

Chapter 9

Sarâh Benziane, University of Science and Technology of Oran Mohamed-Boudiaf, Algeria

This chapter explores the intersection of intelligence, innovation, and sustainability in shaping economic trajectories. It delves into the transformative power of intelligent approaches, guided by technological advancements, data-driven insights, and adaptive policies, to drive economic innovation. The chapter emphasizes the imperative of aligning economic paradigms with sustainability principles, envisioning a future where prosperity is not only economically robust but also environmentally responsible and socially inclusive. Through an examination of case studies, emerging trends, and the role of artificial intelligence, the chapter aims to provide a comprehensive overview of how intelligent economic practices can pave the way for sustainable and resilient futures. It invites readers to consider the critical interplay between intelligence and sustainability in the pursuit of economic prosperity that harmonizes with the needs of both current and future generations.

Chapter 10

Khadidja ElKobra Belbachir, University of Science and Technology of Oran Mohamed-Boudiaf, Algeria
Redouane Tlemsani, University of Science and Technology of Oran Mohamed-Boudiaf, Algeria

For decades, researchers in the field of machine learning have been trying to raise the features of systems and develop methods and approaches, but they often suffer from a scarcity of data in various machine learning fields. For this and due to the urgent need in our research that we have developed in the field of online handwriting recognition, we had to create a special data set for the Arabic language characters written simultaneously on a graphical tablet. In this work, we created a data set called "Noon" in university neighbourhood laboratories and used its first version in research work that was published in international refereed journals. The construction details have gone through phases, which will be presented in the following sections in this chapter.

Preface

In the face of a world overwhelmed by environmental challenges, the need for sustainability has reached a critical juncture. This multidimensional concept demands a delicate equilibrium between environmental preservation, economic viability, and social equity. Navigating this intricate terrain necessitates innovative solutions that bridge the present and the future. The urgency is palpable as we grapple with the repercussions of unsustainable practices.

Sustainability demands innovative solutions to bridge the gap between the needs of the present and the aspirations of future generations. Intelligent Methods and Alternative Economic Models for Sustainability recognizes the pressing need for transformative strategies that navigate the intricate intersections of environmental, economic, and social considerations. The established linear "take-make-dispose" model has proven unsustainable, necessitating a paradigm shift towards regenerative systems. Amid these challenges, the book identifies a critical gap—intelligent methodologies and alternative economic models that can pave the way for a sustainable future are often scattered in disparate fields, lacking a cohesive exploration. As such, the urgency lies in blending these disparate strands into a comprehensive tapestry to guide solutions for sustainability across diverse sectors.

In today's world, the urgency of sustainability has become increasingly apparent as we confront a myriad of environmental, economic, and social challenges. Climate change, resource depletion, and social inequities are just a few of the issues that underscore the need for transformative action. Against this backdrop, the topic of "Intelligent Methods and Alternative Economic Models for Sustainability" occupies a pivotal position in contemporary discourse.

At a time when the consequences of unsustainable practices are becoming more pronounced, there is a growing recognition of the need for innovative solutions that can reconcile economic development with environmental stewardship and social equity. The traditional linear model of production and consumption, characterized by its "take-make-dispose" approach, is no longer tenable in the face of finite resources and ecological limits. Consequently, there is a palpable shift towards circular economy principles and regenerative systems that seek to minimize waste, maximize resource efficiency, and promote sustainable livelihoods.

Moreover, advancements in technology, particularly in the realms of big data analytics, artificial intelligence, and the Internet of Things (IoT), offer unprecedented opportunities to catalyze sustainability efforts. These intelligent methods hold the promise of optimizing complex systems, enhancing decision-making processes, and unlocking new avenues for innovation. By harnessing the power of data-driven insights and predictive analytics, organizations and policymakers can make more informed choices that align with sustainability objectives.

Furthermore, alternative economic models are gaining traction as viable pathways towards sustainability. From community-based initiatives to corporate social responsibility practices, there is a growing realization that economic prosperity must be pursued in harmony with social and environmental well-being. Concepts such as the triple bottom line and inclusive growth are reshaping the discourse on economic development, emphasizing the need to measure success not just in terms of financial returns but also in terms of social impact and environmental stewardship.

In this context, the topic of "Intelligent Methods and Alternative Economic Models for Sustainability" emerges as a timely and relevant contribution to global efforts towards a more sustainable future. By exploring innovative approaches and highlighting successful case studies, this edited volume seeks to inform and inspire stakeholders across sectors to embrace sustainability as a guiding principle in their decision-making processes. In doing so, it aims to catalyze a collective shift towards a more resilient, equitable, and prosperous world for present and future generations.

The book transcends theoretical discourse, offering real-world insights into successful sustainability initiatives. This comprehensive approach caters not only to researchers in computer sciences, economics, and sustainability but also empowers policymakers with actionable strategies and engages the broader public, fostering awareness and understanding of sustainability issues that impact us all.

Through studies, theoretical insights, and practical applications, this volume offers a comprehensive exploration of the possibilities and pathways towards a sustainable future.

We invite readers to reflect on the pressing challenges of our time and the transformative potential of intelligent methods and alternative economic models in shaping a more sustainable world. Together, let us embark on a quest for knowledge, innovation, and action as we strive to build a future that is not only sustainable but also prosperous and equitable for all.

This volume brings together a diverse array of scholars, researchers, and practitioners who have dedicated themselves to advancing knowledge and fostering sustainable development. Through a comprehensive examination of alternative economic models, big data analytics, intelligent methodologies, and technological innovations, this book seeks to provide a cohesive framework for addressing the multifaceted challenges of sustainability.

The chapters within this volume span a wide range of topics, from evaluating supplier performance in sustainable supply chains to modeling green hydrogen and electricity coproduction systems. We delve into utilizing wastewater for sustainable energy generation, exploring the role of artificial intelligence in education, and innovating prosperity through intelligent economic paradigms.

Chapter 1 is "The Evaluation of Supplier Performance for Sustainability in the Pharmaceutical Supply Chain: A Case Study of Hedi Jaballah Hospital in Tunisia." In this chapter, the focus is on evaluating the performance of suppliers within the pharmaceutical supply chain to enhance sustainability. The study employs the Analytics Hierarchy Process (AHP) method for supplier selection and then integrates it with the Goal Programming (GP) model to address sustainability considerations. Through a case study conducted at Hedi Jaballah Hospital in Tunisia, the chapter explores the complexities of supplier evaluation and decision-making processes within the pharmaceutical supply chain, highlighting the importance of sustainable practices in healthcare settings.

Chapter 2 is "Modeling of Green Hydrogen and Electricity Coproduction System for Techno-eco-environmental Analysis of Sustainable Microgrid." This chapter delves into the design and optimization of a hybrid energy system for coproducing green hydrogen and electricity. Utilizing the HOMER software, the study examines the integration of various renewable energy sources such as solar PV and wind for hydrogen production. Through techno-eco-environmental analysis, the chapter evaluates the cost-effectiveness and environmental impact of the proposed system, highlighting its potential to reduce CO_2 emissions and promote sustainable energy generation within microgrid settings.

Chapter 3 is "Utilizing Waste Water for Sustainable Energy Generation via IoT-Integrated Technologies." Addressing the dual challenges of wastewater treatment and energy sustainability, this chapter explores innovative technologies such as anaerobic digestion and microbial fuel cells (MFCs) integrated with the Internet of Things (IoT). By harnessing the metabolic processes of microbes and geothermal desalination, these technologies offer potential solutions for simultaneous wastewater treatment and renewable energy generation. The chapter emphasizes the role of IoT in real-time data monitoring and optimization, highlighting its potential to enhance sustainability outcomes in wastewater management.

Chapter 4 is "A Literature Review on Supply Chains Optimization Using Multi Agents Communication and Collaboration." This chapter offers a comprehensive exploration of supply chain optimization through a multi-agent approach. From historical foundations to contemporary intelligent methodologies, the literature review examines communication, collaboration, and coordination methods between agents.

It highlights the pivotal role of intelligent agents in enhancing decision-making and adaptability within supply chain management, contributing valuable insights for researchers and practitioners alike.

Chapter 5 is "A Novel Optimization Model for the Bi-objective Eco-Routing Problem." Focusing on transportation-related pollution, this research presents a novel optimization model for the bi-objective eco-routing problem. By optimizing the tradeoff between emissions and travel distance, the chapter proposes an UNSGA-II approach to address the environmental impact of vehicle emissions. Through experiments, the study demonstrates the effectiveness of the proposed method in achieving optimal distribution routes with minimal emissions, thereby contributing to sustainable transportation solutions.

Chapter 6 is an "Essential Guide to Supply Chain Risk Management with Strategic Prospective Tools." This chapter addresses the challenge of supply chain risk management (SCRM) by proposing a comprehensive framework for integrated network SCRM processes. By utilizing the "scenario method" and extended supply chain tools, the chapter offers insights into articulating SCRM issues, ranking risk variables, and creating mitigation strategies. Through a case study, it demonstrates the effectiveness of the framework in developing robust risk mitigation plans, contributing to resilient and efficient supply chain networks.

Chapter 7 explores the "Role of Artificial Intelligence in Education." This chapter explores the transformative role of artificial intelligence (AI) in reshaping education. From personalized learning experiences to intelligent tutoring systems, AI has the potential to revolutionize teaching and learning processes. By examining AI applications and preparing for AI integration in education, the chapter underscores the dynamic landscape of educational technology and its implications for future learning environments.

Chapter 8 is about modelling and resolution of a distribution problem considering environmental criteria a case study of a Tunisian company. This chapter addresses the challenge of optimizing distribution routes while considering environmental criteria. By proposing models for the Travelling Salesman Problem (TSP) that embed novel improved lower and upper bounds, the chapter aims to help transport managers select optimal distribution circuits that minimize environmental impact. Through a case study conducted at a Tunisian company, the study demonstrates the effectiveness of the proposed models in optimizing distribution routes with environmental objectives.

Chapter 9 is "Innovating Prosperity: Intelligent Approaches and Economic Paradigms for Sustainable Futures." This chapter explores the intersection of intelligence, innovation, and sustainability in shaping economic trajectories. By delving into intelligent economic practices guided by technological advancements and adaptive policies, the chapter emphasizes the imperative of aligning economic paradigms with sustainability principles. Through case studies and emerging trends, it provides insights into how intelligent economic approaches can contribute to sustainable and resilient futures.

Chapter 10 is "Introducing the Ultimate NOUN Dataset for Online Handwritten Alphabet Recognition." This chapter presents the development of a specialized dataset for online handwritten alphabet recognition, focusing on the Arabic language. By addressing the scarcity of data in machine learning fields, the chapter introduces the "Noon" dataset, created through research conducted in university laboratories. Through detailed construction phases, the chapter highlights the importance of datasets in advancing research in online handwriting recognition and machine learning applications.

Each contribution offers unique insights and practical solutions that contribute to the collective effort towards a sustainable future. We extend our sincere gratitude to all the contributors whose expertise and dedication have made this volume possible. Their commitment to advancing knowledge and fostering sustainable development is truly commendable.

Furthermore, we would like to express our appreciation to the anonymous reviewers for their invaluable feedback and insightful suggestions, which have greatly enhanced the quality and rigor of this publication without forgetting the team at IGI Global for their support and guidance throughout the publication process. Their commitment to excellence and dedication to disseminating cutting-edge research have been instrumental in bringing this project to fruition.

In conclusion, we hope that this edited volume serves as a valuable resource for scholars, researchers, policymakers, practitioners, and students alike, inspiring continued exploration, innovation, and collaboration in the dynamic field of sustainability. May the insights contained within these pages spark new ideas, provoke critical inquiry, and pave the way for a more sustainable and resilient future for all.

Latifa Dekhici
University of Sciences and Technology of Oran Mohamed-Boudiaf, Algeria

Khaled Guerraiche
LDREI Laboratory, Higher School of Electrical Engineering and Energy of Oran, Algeria

Rabia Azzemou
University of Sciences and Technology of Oran Mohamed-Boudiaf, Algeria

Jihène Jlassi
Higher Institute of Industrial Management of Sfax, University of Sfax, Tunisia

Chapter 1

Evaluation of Supplier Performance for Sustainability in the Pharmaceutical Supply Chain:
A Case Study of Hedi Jaballah Hospital in Tunisia

Marwa Mallek
Faculty of Economics and Management of Sfax, Tunisia

MohamedAli Elleuch
Faculty of Economics and Management of Sfax, Tunisia

Yosra Akouri
Higher Institute of Biotechnology of Sfax, Tunisia

ABSTRACT

Hospital pharmacies are in contact with a large number of suppliers. The selection of the latter is an important task that has a crucial impact on the performance of the pharmacy sustainable supply chain. Studies, constituting a reference on the subject, have looked into the criteria for evaluating suppliers as well as the multidimensional aspect of the problem. The pharmaceutical supply chain is complex, and pharmaceutical companies must overcome the most common challenges to efficiently get patients the medicines they need. This paper looks at a multidimensional classification of suppliers of medical devices. First, the authors used the multi-criteria method of decision support AHP (analytics hierarchy process) for the choice of suppliers in the pharmacy with contradictory criteria. Subsequently, the

DOI: 10.4018/979-8-3693-1418-0.ch001

authors developed a hybrid approach coupling the AHP method and the GP (goal programming) model to solve a problem dealing with the selection of suppliers in a sustainable supply chain under a set of constraints.

INTRODUCTION

Background and Research Motivation

The efficient use of resources and the search for an optimal system from pharmaceuticals to services and patients stimulates logistical thinking in hospital pharmacies. The difficulties of optimizing flows and stocks lead pharmacists to find difficult balances and to discover new avenues to facilitate the supply chain and seek refined solutions to these new problems (Mille., 2008). In this context, logistics allows the hospital to have a good circulation of pharmaceutical products, reduce stocks, limit waste and provide better inventory monitoring (Hamidi & Bouzembrak.,2020). On the other hand, the increase in hospital expenditure leads to worrying social security deficits. This requires a reduction in hospital expenses. Spending on pharmaceutical products represents a significant portion of total spending on which it seems possible to act quickly. The concept of hospital management consisting of planning several criteria (social, economic, technical and political, etc...). The criteria formulated can be quantitative or qualitative in nature. The obligation to control contradictory objectives is therefore in itself an additional and sufficient reason to undertake steps to reorganize the logistics chain. These issues confirm the need to restructure the flow of pharmaceutical products which deserve to be analyzed and evaluated using multi-objective methods. Pharmaceutical supply management can make a significant contribution to the performance of a hospital center, particularly through the presence of the right products at the right time to support the provision of services. Hospital logistics represents a complex multi-criteria process which is characterized by a diversity of needs, criteria, products as well as distribution channels. The main mission of this logistics is to control and optimize physical flows from suppliers to pharmacies. It is an essential tool for reorganizing pharmaceutical supply chain processes.

Literature Review

The sustainable supply chain is an important field of study that has given rise to a very abundant literature (Ramezankhani et al., 2018 and Hald & Mouritsen., 2018). There is no universal definition of this term. We quote below some definitions, taken from the scientific literature. Regarding the role played by a sustainable supply chain in the transformation process of a product, some authors;

Lee &Billington (1993), Rota-Frantz et al.(2001), Londe & Masters (1994) equate a sustainable supply chain to a network of facilities that performs the functions of raw material supply, processing of these raw materials into components and then into finished products, and distribution of the finished products to the customer.

Tayur et al.(1999) define a logistics chain for a given product as a system of subcontractors, producers, distributors, retailers and customers between which material flows are exchanged in the direction of suppliers to customers and material flows information in both directions.

Logistics is a relatively new discipline in hospital pharmacies. The supply sector, however, is only a small part of the work to be done. In addition, it is clear that pharmaceutical supply chains must go beyond the level of stewardship to engage in a radical overhaul in order to integrate logics of flow optimization, cost reduction and risk management (Nathalie., 2004).

Pharmaceutical logistics is a process that aims to make available to patients as efficiently as possible, the pharmaceutical products that will be administered to them, under conditions that guarantee safety and traceability while respecting the many regulations surrounding pharmaceutical products and their dispensation. The hospital pharmacy represents a non-negligible part of the expenses of a health establishment. It is an integral part of hospital logistics activities which support the care of patients. The pharmacy should not be seen as "isolated" in the hospital, but as the central link in the pharmaceutical supply chain whose goal is to make pharmaceutical products available to the patient (Nicolas and Charles.,2013). The pharmaceutical supply chain is faced with multiple and important challenges. It has become increasingly complex and is now subject to many specific constraints such as compliance with good production and distribution practices, traceability, transport and storage conditions, cost control, control stocks and shortages, expiry dates, regulation of drug prices, etc. (Chrifi et al., 2015).

A sustainable supply chain exists when at least two organizations are working on the completion of a given product. If and only if this association is deliberately managed with a view to maximizing its performance, then we can speak of sustainable supply chain management. As with the term "the sustainable supply chain", the scientific community has proposed several definitions of sustainable supply chain management.

According to Thomas & Griffin (1996), sustainable supply chain management is the management of the flow of goods and information both within and between locations such as retail outlets, distribution centers and production and assembly. According to Tan (2003), sustainable supply chain management encompasses the management of supplies and goods from the suppliers of raw materials to the finished product. Sustainable supply chain management focuses on how companies use processes, technology and capability to improve the competitiveness of their suppliers. According to Dominguez & Lashkari (2004), the interest of Supply Chain Management (SCM) is to facilitate sales by correctly positioning the products in the right quantity, in the right place, and when there is a need and finally at the lowest cost. The main objective of SCM is to efficiently allocate generation, distribution, and transmission and information resources in the presence of conflicting objectives, with the aim of achieving the level of service demanded by customers at the lowest cost. Chiu and Kremer (2013) studied two different scenarios for product design stage to increase supply chain performance namely centralised and decentralised supply chains. Divsalar et al. (2020) proposed a SCOR based model for evaluating supply chain performance of medical equipment companies using lean, agile, resilient and green (LARG) framework. Khan et al. (2023) identified and prioritized factors for pharmaceutical supply chain performance improvement in Pakistan. Ishizaka et al. (2023) evaluated the performance of five suppliers in the pharmaceutical industry by employing a hybrid methodology.

The proper functioning of a pharmaceutical company depends on the efficient circulation of certain flows. We can classify them as physical flows, information flows. In hospitals, the flow of information passes mainly by fax and by telephone and the physical flows pass via the establishment pharmacy.

Pharmaceutical supply chains ensure the manufacture of pharmaceutical products, their supply to pharmacies and their delivery to customers. These chains focus on customer satisfaction and quality of service so that customers become repeat buyers.

Any pharmaceutical company must constantly ensure the proper management of its stocks.

To accompany good optimization of its stock makes it possible to avoid out of stock, to reduce storage costs, to be reactive to orders from its customers. As a pharmacist, you will have to make strategic decisions. However, this is not an easy exercise knowing that it is necessary to take into account many parameters. To help you in your task, consider using decision support tools.

A decision support tool aims to guide pharmacists towards the most appropriate choice of suppliers. There are several management decision support tools. This tool allows you to review the different options available to achieve an objective. Each of them can be decomposed into new solutions. There are methods that will serve as a tool to help select the best solution among the solutions obtained by multi-criteria approaches. They are widely used to solve supplier selection problems.

Yousefi et al. (2016) proposed a robust dynamic DEA to identify sustainable suppliers. Considering business and environmental factors, Yu et al. (2016) proposed a transportation distance method considering supplier selection and also proposed an incentive mechanism to encourage policy makers to make more environmentally friendly decisions. Su et al. (2016) used a hierarchical gray DEMATEL method to analyze criteria in an environment with incomplete information. Govindan et al. (2019) proposed the ELECTRE-based method to effectively address the problem of third-party reverse logistics provider selection. Thanh and Lan (2022) considered the triple bottom line, a fuzzy analytical hierarchical process (FAHP) approach dealing with supplier selection in the food processing industry.

The contribution presented in this study concerns a hybrid approach between fuzzy multi-criteria analysis and mathematical modeling for a problem of selection of drug suppliers within a Tunisian hospital.

SELECTION OF HOSPITAL SUPPLIERS' PROBLEM

The pharmaceutical sector is one of the critical sectors in any country and plays a vital role in the well-being of society (Sabouhi et al., 2018). We have taken the pharmaceutical companies in Tunisia as the case for the present study. Indeed, Tunisia is one of the African countries that can boast of having a pharmaceutical industry. However, Growth in the Tunisian pharmacy industry is estimated at 40% within two years. The growth of this sector follows the implementation of privatization phases accompanied by a more adequate tax and regulatory framework at the beginning of the 1990s. Coverage of market needs in pharmaceutical products through local production thus increased from 14% in 1990 to over 52% in 2019 (Sinta., 2021). The Tunisian pharmaceutical products market is divided into two sectors:

- A hospital sector (hospital) marked by the predominance of pharmaceutical products in Tunisia and whose distribution to public structures is exclusively ensured by the central pharmacy.
- A pharmacy sector (Officinal) whose distribution is monopolized by the PCT only at the level of imported products and only at the level of distribution to suppliers.

The problems of supplier selection are one of the strategic decisions that have a considerable impact on the performance of hospital pharmacy in Tunisia. With the evolution of manufacturing systems, this decision becomes more and more critical. For pharmacists, the problem of choosing suppliers consists in determining the ranking of suppliers. Pharmaceutical hospital logistics within the HediJaballah Hospital in Tunisia, which aims to efficiently deliver pharmaceutical products from the supplier to the pharmacy depot, is one such supporting process. The pharmacy-supplier type relationship, the search for quality of service, as well as the response time to a request are innovative concepts in the hospital. Like many companies and organizations, the hospital must integrate the principles of cost reduction and quality of care. One of the elements of quality lies in a good organization of the sustainable supply chain. Hospitals have for more than ten years been the place of major transformations. HediJaballah Hospital has to manage different flows of unequal importance. As for the pharmaceutical flows, they cannot suffer from the risk of ruptures because of their nature, which can be vital for the life of the patient. HediJaballah Hospital introduce characteristics that distinguish the management issues they pose and can be the source of very interesting scientific investigations. Indeed, the hospital has its own internal chain which must be integrated to take advantage of the full integration potential of the external chain, the final use remaining the main area of uncertainty in the management of supplies.

Supply managers at HediJaballah Hospital, generally deal with several suppliers but often have to decide to choose one of them. The selection of the latter thus becomes a strategic decision which has a crucial impact on the performance of the hospital. Currently, the selection of hospital suppliers is done via tenders, essentially economic databases. The selection of these is based on a single type of criteria. But, when making this choice, we often need to take several criteria into account simultaneously. The hospital is in contact with a large number of suppliers. The selection of pharmaceutical suppliers is therefore an important function often carried out by the purchasing department of the hospital. This selection, multi-criteria by nature, includes both qualitative and quantitative, subjective and objective criteria. In most cases, in order to select the best suppliers, it is necessary to make a compromise between these criteria, some of which may be contradictory. Several models in the literature have focused on the multi-criteria decision-making process.

DECISION SUPPORT

Decision support is very much in demand by organizations in the event that they are faced with problems of choice and evaluation (Seuring., 2013). However, faced with a selection problem, the user of the method must make a choice of criteria to use, which is rarely enlightened except by his experience. In our work we are interested in the processes of selection of suppliers in the HediJaballah Hospital for pharmaceutical products whose objective is decision support in choosing the best suppliers. In the present work we relied, firstly, on the AHP method presented by Thomas L. Saaty, in order to apply it to a multidimensional choice of suppliers with a set of contradictory criteria. This multi-criteria classification approach was applied to prioritize pharmaceutical product suppliers for the case of a hospital in Hedi Jaballah. Next, we will define the principle of this method.

The Principle of the AHP Method

The AHP method is a multi-criteria analytical approach for decision support. It is fundamentally based on complex calculations using matrix algebra.

Setting:
C: [C_j] where j= 1, ..., m represents the number of criteria;
A: [A_i] where i= 1, ..., n is the number of alternatives;
P_i: represents the total priority value of each alternativei;
P_{ij}: represents the weight of each alternative i linked to the criterionj;
W_j: represents the importance weights of each criterionj;
C_{ij}: represents the relative weight of each alternative i linked to criterion j.

Mathematical Formulation

In the application of the AHP, the relative importance or the weight of the criteria are determined after consultation with the experts or the organization of interviews or group meetings. At this level the criteria should be compared in pairs separately using a qualitative or quantitative assessment approach. In general, a nine-point numerical scale, called the Saaty scale, is recommended for comparisons. In our case, the use of the AHP method involves eight steps:

Step 1: Determining the relative weight of the criteria by comparing the criteria in pairs, the pairwise comparisons are made by subjectively comparing the pairs of criteria. Subsequently, values on a scale of 1 to 9, which represent the degree of importance of an attribute in relation to another attribute, are assigned (Table 1).

Next, we filled the data into a square matrix with melements, where mis the number of decision criteria. In addition, this matrix must contain the total of each column, which is calculated based on the following formula:

Table 1. Saaty scale

Weight	Verbal judgment of preference
1	Equal importance
3	Moderate importance
5	High importance
7	Very high importance
9	Extreme importance or absolute importance
2,4,6,8	Used for intermediate judgments compared to those listed above

$$S_j = \sum_{j=1}^{m} C_{ij}, \forall i = 1, \ldots, n \qquad (1)$$

Where S_j is the sum of the importance values of each criterionj.

Step 2: Normalization of comparisons between criteria jaccording to the following formula:

$$n_{ij} = \frac{C_{ij}}{S_j}, \forall i = 1, \ldots, n \qquad (2)$$

Where S_j is the normalized value of each criterion j.

Step 3: Calculation of the weights of the normalized values on each line according to the following equations:

$$W_j = \frac{\sum_{j=1}^{m} n_{ij}}{m}, \forall i = 1, \ldots, n \qquad (3)$$

Where S_j is the weight of the normalized values of each criterionj.

Step 4: Determine the relative weights of the alternatives based on criteria. The procedure for comparing the alternatives is identical to that relating to the criteria. The results are stored in a square matrix for each k to m-element scenario where m is the number of alternatives. The number of matrices is equal to the number of criteria.

Step 5: Normalization of the comparisons between the alternatives with respect to each decision criterion.

Step 6: Fill in the performance matrix where the performance of the alternatives should be identified for each criterion and the data should be written in the performance matrixP $= [P_{ij}]$.

Step 7: Determine the total value for the priority of each alternative, while the weight of each alternative linked to each criterion with the weight of each criterion, Then we calculate their sum:

$$P_i = \sum_{j=1}^{m} P_{ij} \times w_j, \forall i = 1, \ldots, n \qquad (4)$$

Where, P_{ij} represents the weight of each alternative i linked to criterion j and $\sum_{j=1}^{m} P_{ij} = 1$.

Table 2. The randomized index

Matrix size	3	4	5	6	7	8	9	10
IR	0.58	0.90	1.12	1.24	1.32	1.41	1.45	1.49

Step 7: Alternate Ranking. The best alternative is the one for which the sum of the multiplications between the weight of each alternative and the weight of each criterion has the highest value.

In this hierarchical classification approach, it is also possible to check the consistency of our approach by calculating the coherence or consistency ratio (CR). The latter constitutes an acceptance test of the weights of the various criteria. This step aims to detect any inconsistencies in the comparison of the importance of each pair of criteria. The coherence ratio CR is calculated as follows: $CR = \dfrac{CI}{RI}$ With CI, the consistency index and RI, a randomized index. The consistency index is calculated as follows:

$$CI = (\lambda \max - n) / (n-1)$$

λ max: maximum eigenvalue; n :number of criteria. The randomized index is a value that depends on the size of the matrix (Table 2).

The Principle of the Goal Programming Method

The multi-objective model of Goal Programming (GP) is widely used and accepted by researchers because of its adaptability and its effectiveness in providing the most appropriate solutions to decision makers. Therefore, the GP model provides legitimacy to its users for their decisions where several contradictory and immeasurable criteria are involved.

Setting:

– δj_+ Positive deviation of the solution x from the goal gj.
– $\delta j-$ Negative deviation of the solution x from the goal gj.
– CI (x):Constraint system of the problem.
– fj (x):Evaluation of the solution x with respect to the criterion Cj.

ᴹathematical Formulation

Indeed, the principle of the GP model is the minimization of the absolute distance between the level of achievement and the level of aspiration that decision-makers introduce through the goal values (gj) with respect to each criterion (Cj) In this model, decision makers seek to find an alternative (Ai) closest to their profile established by each goal (gj). For each criterion (Cj).

If the level of achievement is greater than the level of aspiration (gj, then this results in the GP model as a positive deviation (deviation) $\delta j+$ ᵍreater than 0;

If the level of achievement is lower than the level of aspiration (gj, then this is reflected by a negative deviation δj- ᵍreater than 0;

If the level of achievement is equivalent to the level of aspiration (gj, then this translates to $\delta j-_= \delta j+=^0$. Thus, the goal of the GP model is that the positive deviations ($\delta j+$) ₐⁿd negative values (δj-) a_r^e as close as possible to 0. The GP model is formulated as follows:

$$MinZ = \sum_{j=1}^{n}\left(\delta_j^+ + \delta_j^-\right) \qquad (5)$$

Under constraints:

$$f_j(x) + \delta_j^- - \delta_j^+ = g_j, \forall j = 1,....,n \qquad (6)$$

$$C_l(x) \qquad (7)$$

$$\delta_j^- \geq 0 et \delta_j^+ \geq 0 \forall j = 1,....,n \qquad (8)$$

SUSTAINABLE PHARMACEUTICAL SUPPLY CHAIN

The main objective of this chapter is to develop a multi-criteria approach to decision support for solving supplier selection problems in pharmaceutical supply chains. Indeed, we consider the case where the Hedi hospital pharmacy Jaballah, in charge of the evaluation and classification of a set of m suppliers rated A^i., i = 1, . . ., m . The suppliers are evaluated while taking into consideration both subjective (qualitative) and objective (quantitative) C_j conflicting criteria noted, j = 1, . . ., n, under a set of constraints. This section discusses the presentation of our hybrid approach combining the multi-criteria evaluation of suppliers based on the AHP method and the integration of a set of constraints with the GP model.

Application of the AHP Method

In our case we start with the starting point of the use of this method we identify the problems. The objective is to optimize and choose the best criteria and alternatives. The multidimensional classification of six suppliers (A1: All-paramedical company, A2: Mayer biomedical, A3: Adhe -els, A4: PCT, A5: MEDIS SFAX, A6: Medical Eagle) was carried out according to seven criteria, namely: C1: Deadline delivery, C2: Late delivery, C3: Product quality, C4: Packaging quality, C5: Labeling quality, C6: capacity and C7: Experience. The first step in the AHP approach is to formulate the comparison matrix for each pair of criteria. Consultation with the purchasing manager at HediJaballah Hospital was essential to set the comparison coefficients for each pair of criteria according to the Saaty scale. The involvement of the purchasing manager, and possibly of his collaborators, is essential at this level because they are best placed to assess the relative importance of the criteria two by two. Table 3 consolidates the evaluation set of alternatives and criteria.

These seven supplier classification criteria have different units of measurement. This leads us to normalize the initial data so as not to bias the calculation of the scores used to classify suppliers. The data thus transformed are shown in Table 4.

The calculation of the eigenvalues as well as the eigenvector associated with the largest eigenvalue made it possible to identify the following weighting coefficients for eight evaluation matrices. Before proceeding with the calculation of the weighted scores, it is essential to test the consistency of the comparisons by pairs at the level of the matrix and this through the calculation of the consistency ratio CR. The consistency ratio is clearly less than 1, which confirms the consistency of the judgments at the level of the matrix. The calculation of the scores of the different suppliers and their multi-criteria classification are presented in Table 5.

In the final stage of the AHP method, the general weights are computed with respect to the overall criteria (Table 6).

The analysis of the results shows that the best supplier is the F4 with a score of 25.8%, followed by the F2 supplier with a score of 18.4% and in third place the F5 supplier with a performance of 17.3%. . It should be noted that this score represents the performance of each supplier, simultaneously, according to all the evaluation criteria. Using this AHP scoring approach for each provider, Hedi Jaballah Hospital can prioritize pharmaceutical suppliers. Once the multi-criteria evaluation is carried out, we now move on to optimizing the choice of suppliers according to

Table 3. Evaluation of alternatives and criteria

Evaluation of suppliers according to criterion N° 1							Evaluation of suppliers according to criterion N° 2						
	A1	A2	A3	A4	A5	A6		A1	A2	A3	A4	A5	A6
A1	1	9	1/3	1/3	1/3	5	A1	1	1/3	1/3	1/3	1/3	1/5
A2	1/9	1	1/3	1/3	1/5	5	A2	3	1	1/5	1/3	5	5
A3	3	3	1	1/3	5	5	A3	3	5	1	1/3	1/3	7
A4	3	3	3	1	7	7	A4	3	3	3	1	7	7
A5	3	5	1/5	1/7	1	9	A5	3	1/5	3	1/7	1	9
A6	1/5	1/5	1/5	1/7	1/9	1	A6	5	1/5	1/7	1/7	1/9	1

Evaluation of suppliers according to criterion N° 3							Evaluation of suppliers according to criterion N° 4						
	A1	A2	A3	A4	A5	A6		A1	A2	A3	A4	A5	A6
A1	1	1/5	1/3	7	1/3	5	A1	1	1/5	1/3	7	1/3	5
A2	5	1	5	1/3	1/5	1/5	A2	5	1	5	1/3	1/5	1/5
A3	3	1/5	1	1/3	1/5	7	A3	3	1/5	1	1/3	1/5	7
A4	1/7	3	0	1	7	7	A4	1/7	3	3	1	7	7
A5	3	5	5	1/7	1	5	A5	3	5	5	1/7	1	5
A6	1/5	5	1/7	1/7	1/5	1	A6	1/5	5	1/7	1/7	1/5	1

Evaluation of suppliers according to criterion N° 5							Evaluation of suppliers according to criterion N° 6						
	A1	A2	A3	A4	A5	A6		A1	A2	A3	A4	A5	A6
A1	1	1/3	1/5	7	1/3	5	A1	1	1/3	1/7	3	1/3	5
A2	3	1	5	1/3	5	1/5	A2	3	1	5	9	5	5
A3	5	1/5	1	1/3	7	7	A3	7	1/5	1	3	3	5
A4	1/7	3	3	1	7	7	A4	1/3	1/9	1/3	1	7	7
A5	3	1/5	1/7	1/7	1	9	A5	3	1/5	1/3	1/7	1	3
A6	1/5	5	1/7	1/7	1/9	1	A6	1/5	1/5	1/5	1/7	1/3	1

Evaluation of suppliers according to criterion N° 7							Assessment of criteria							
	A1	A2	A3	A4	A5	A6		C1	C2	C3	C4	C5	C6	C7
A1	1	1/3	1/3	1/3	1/3	5	C1	1	1/5	1/3	1/9	1/3	1/3	1/3
A2	3	1	1/3	9	5	1/5	C2	5	1	1/3	1	1/3	7	9
A3	3	3	1	1/3	7	7	C3	3	3	1	9	9	9	9
A4	3	1/9	3	1	9	9	C4	9	1	1/9	1	1/5	1/3	1/5
A5	3	1/5	1/7	1/9	1	7	C5	3	3	1/9	5	1	7	1/3
A6	1/5	5	1/7	1/9	1/7	1	C6	3	1/7	1/9	3	1/7	1	1/3
							C7	3	1/9	1/9	5	3	3	1

Table 4. Standardization of evaluation matrices

Evaluation of suppliers according to criterion N° 1							Evaluation of suppliers according to criterion N° 2						
	A1	A2	A3	A4	A5	A6		A1	A2	A3	A4	A5	A6
A1	0.10	0.42	0.07	0.15	0.02	0.16	A1	0.06	0.03	0.04	0.15	0.02	0.01
A2	0.01	0.05	0.07	0.15	0.01	0.16	A2	0.17	0.10	0.03	0.15	0.36	0.17
A3	0.29	0.14	0.20	0.15	0.37	0.16	A3	0.17	0.51	0.13	0.15	0.02	0.24
A4	0.29	0.14	0.59	0.44	0.51	0.22	A4	0.17	0.31	0.39	0.44	0.51	0.24
A5	0.29	0.24	0.04	0.06	0.07	0.28	A5	0.17	0.02	0.39	0.06	0.07	0.31
A6	0.02	0.01	0.04	0.06	0.01	0.03	A6	0.28	0.02	0.02	0.06	0.01	0.03

Evaluation of suppliers according to criterion N° 3							Evaluation of suppliers according to criterion N° 4						
	A1	A2	A3	A4	A5	A6		A1	A2	A3	A4	A5	A6
A1	0.08	0.01	0.03	0.78	0.04	0.20	A1	0.08	0.01	0.02	0.78	0.04	0.20
A2	0.41	0.07	0.44	0.04	0.02	0.01	A2	0.41	0.07	0.35	0.04	0.02	0.01
A3	0.24	0.01	0.09	0.04	0.02	0.28	A3	0.24	0.01	0.07	0.04	0.02	0.28
A4	0.01	0.21	0.00	0.11	0.78	0.28	A4	0.01	0.21	0.21	0.11	0.78	0.28
A5	0.24	0.35	0.44	0.02	0.11	0.20	A5	0.24	0.35	0.35	0.02	0.11	0.20
A6	0.02	0.35	0.01	0.02	0.02	0.04	A6	0.02	0.35	0.01	0.02	0.02	0.04

Evaluation of suppliers according to criterion N° 5							Evaluation of suppliers according to criterion N° 6						
	A1	A2	A3	A4	A5	A6		A1	A2	A3	A4	A5	A6
A1	0.08	0.03	0.02	0.78	0.02	0.17	A1	0.07	0.16	0.02	0.18	0.02	0.19
A2	0.24	0.10	0.53	0.04	0.24	0.01	A2	0.21	0.49	0.71	0.55	0.30	0.19
A3	0.41	0.02	0.11	0.04	0.34	0.24	A3	0.48	0.10	0.14	0.18	0.18	0.19
A4	0.01	0.31	0.32	0.11	0.34	0.24	A4	0.02	0.05	0.05	0.06	0.42	0.27
A5	0.24	0.02	0.02	0.02	0.05	0.31	A5	0.21	0.10	0.05	0.01	0.06	0.12
A6	0.02	0.51	0.02	0.02	0.01	0.03	A6	0.01	0.10	0.03	0.01	0.02	0.04

Evaluation of suppliers according to criterion N° 7							Assessment of criteria							
	A1	A2	A3	A4	A5	A6		C1	C2	C3	C4	C5	C6	C7
A1	0.08	0.03	0.07	0.03	0.01	0.17	C1	0.04	0.02	0.16	0.00	0.02	0.01	0.02
A2	0.23	0.10	0.07	0.83	0.22	0.01	C2	0.19	0.12	0.16	0.04	0.02	0.25	0.45
A3	0.23	0.31	0.20	0.03	0.31	0.24	C3	0.11	0.35	0.47	0.37	0.64	0.33	0.45
A4	0.23	0.01	0.61	0.09	0.40	0.31	C4	0.33	0.12	0.05	0.04	0.01	0.01	0.01
A5	0.23	0.02	0.03	0.01	0.04	0.24	C5	0.11	0.35	0.05	0.21	0.07	0.25	0.02
A6	0.02	0.52	0.03	0.01	0.01	0.03	C6	0.11	0.02	0.05	0.12	0.01	0.04	0.02
							C7	0.11	0.01	0.05	0.21	0.21	0.11	0.05

Table 5. Confirmation of consistency of judgments

	AI/C1	AI/C2	AI/C3	AI/C4	AI/C5	AI/C6	AI/C7	Cj / Cj
λmax	7.73	9.44	10.55	11.17	11.36	11.83	10.86	10.48
CI	0.35	0.69	0.91	1.03	1.07	1.17	0.97	0.58
R	1.24	1.24	1.24	1.24	1.24	1.24	1.24	1.32
RC	0.28	0.55	0.73	0.83	0.86	0.94	0.78	0.44

Table 6. Multi-criteria classification of pharmaceutical suppliers

	C1	C2	C3	C4	C5	C6	C7	Wi	laughed
A1	0.006	0.009	0.074	0.016	0.028	0.006	0.007	0.146	5,000
A2	0.003	0.028	0.063	0.012	0.030	0.021	0.026	0.184	2,000
A3	0.009	0.036	0.044	0.009	0.029	0.011	0.024	0.162	4,000
A4	0.014	0.060	0.090	0.022	0.034	0.008	0.030	0.258	1.000
A5	0.006	0.030	0.088	0.017	0.017	0.005	0.010	0.173	3,000
A6	0.001	0.012	0.029	0.006	0.015	0.002	0.011	0.077	6,000

	AI/C1	AI/C2	AI/C3	AI/C4	AI/C5	AI/C6	AI/C7	Cj / Cj
Validation	≤ 1	≤ 1	≤ 1	≤ 1	≤ 1	≤ 1	≤ 1	≤ 1

capacity constraints using the GP. Indeed, the results found can also serve as a basis for setting up an optimization of the selection of suppliers according to the Goal Programming model.

Application of the Goal Programming Model

The objective in the application of the Goal Programming model is to apply a multi-objective method of choosing pharmaceutical suppliers, through multi-objective mathematical programming and under a set of constraints. Optimization requires the choice of suppliers who come closest to the wishes of the decision-maker upstream of the decision-making process, in order to satisfy the objectives to be achieved. We devote this section to our second hybrid approach combining the results of the AHP method and the GP model with a set of constraints. The objective is double, on the

Decision variables		
X_i	: Binary value equal to 1 if supplier *i* is selected and 0 otherwise;	
Y_{j1}	: Positive variable that indicates positive deviations from the objective **j**;	
Y_{j2}	: Positive variable that indicates negative deviations from the objective **j**.	

one hand, to show its applicability under the constraints and on the other hand, to carry out a comparison with the preceding approach using the AHP method.

The application of the AHP-GP approach is essentially based on the results obtained. We propose a program taking into account simultaneously several objectives in a problem of the most satisfactory intra-user choice.

Box 1.

The formulation of the AHP-GP model is as follows:

$$\text{Min } Z = \sum_{j=1}^{8} \left(\mathbf{Y_{j1}} + \mathbf{Y_{j2}} \right)$$

Subject to

$$\sum_{i=1} a_{ij} \times X_i - Y_{j1} + Y_{j2} = 1 \, \forall j \in \{1,\ldots,7\} \tag{10}$$

$$\sum_{i=1} C_i \times X_i - Y_{81} + Y_{82} = B \tag{11}$$

$$X_i \in \{0,1\}, \, \forall i \in \{1,\ldots,6\} \tag{12}$$

$$Y_{j1}, Y_{j2} \geq 0, \, \forall j \in \{1,\ldots,8\} \tag{13}$$

Equation (9) identifies the goal function that aims to minimize the weighted total goal deviations. Equation (10) describes the objectives of the problem and also calculates the positive and negative deviations. Equation (11) guarantees that the choice of selected suppliers capable of meeting these needs (B) taking into account the capacity of each supplier (C_i). Equation (12) describes the binary decision variables and equation (5) is the inequality constraint.

Figure 1. Lindo solver status

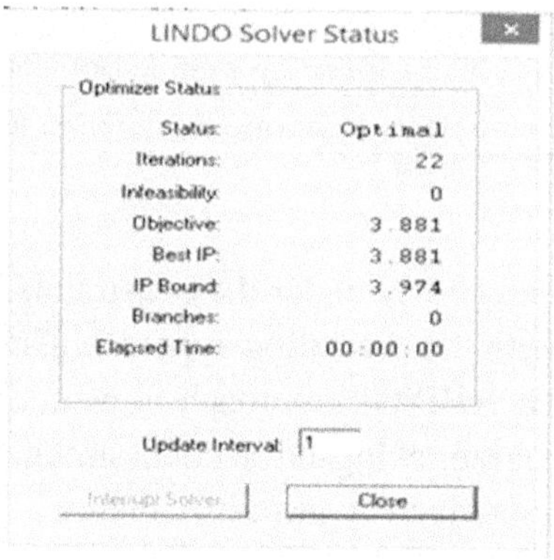

The area of IT devoted to finding solutions that improve the organization is called operational research, optimization or even decision-making. We are now able to determine, more quickly than ever, the best results to solve our problem. Lindo software (Linear Interactive and Discrete Optimization) is an operational search engine that allows real-time decision making. Lindo is a software used to solve linear, integer and quadratic optimization models. One of Lindo 's features is that it offers tools that can help with the analysis of models using the simplex algorithm.

First, we prepared the model in the form required by the Lindosoftware .Before Lindo offers us a first report on the optimal solution, he gives us the state of the problem expressed by the following Fig 1.

This preliminary report tells us that:

- **Status**: optimal; it informs us about the status of the current solution. It can be Optimal (optimal), Feasible (feasible), Infeasible (not feasible) or Unbounded (unbounded).
- **Iterations**: 22: indicates the number of iterations needed to solve the problem (using the revised version of the Simplex method).
- **Infeasibility**: **0: Indicates the amount of violation in the constraints.**
- **Objective**: 3.881: This is the objective function value relative to the current solution.
- **Best IP**: 3.881: This is the best value of the objective function.
- **IP Bound**: 3.974: This is the objective function bound for this solution.
- **Branches**: 0: This is the number of integer variables &quot ; branches on &quot ; by Lindo .
- **Elapsed Time**: 00:00:00: This is the time elapsed before the resolver is invoked (this time is variable even for the same example).

Figure 2. Inputs and outputs of the proposed model by Lindo

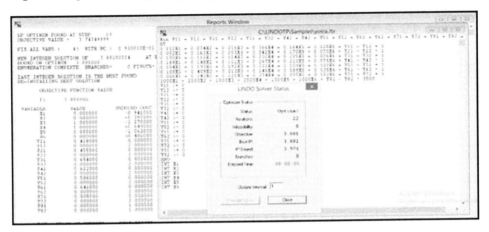

The results report obtained by the Lindo software contains information on the optimal solution. In the following figure, the first column shows the different decision variables. Their values are given in the second column.

We find that suppliers 3 and 4 are chosen to optimize the sustainable supply chain of Hedi Jaballah Hospital.

CONCLUSION

We have presented in this paper the application of the optimal choice of pharmaceutical suppliers combining the AHP method and the GP model. The approach mainly comprises two phases respectively an evaluation phase and a multi-criteria analysis which consists in finding the preferences of the suppliers according to a set of contradictory criteria. The evaluation presented is based on the AHP method. Then the GP model is used to optimize the choice of suppliers. This model integrates a priori the preferences of the suppliers. The proposed model is limited to expert-based decisions of organizations, future studies can involve stakeholders such as policy makers and validate the model from the multi-stakeholder perspective.

REFERENCES

Chiu, M. C., & Kremer, G. E. O. (2013). An investigation on centralized and decentralized supply chain scenarios at the product design stage to increase performance. *IEEE Transactions on Engineering Management*, *61*(1), 114–128. doi:10.1109/TEM.2013.2246569

Chrifi, H., Echchatbi, A., & Cherkaoui, A. (2015). Modélisation de la chaîne logistique pharmaceutique marocaine: vers l'intégration du facteur risque. Xème Conférence Internationale, Tanger, Maroc.

Divsalar, M., Ahmadi, M., & Nemati, Y. (2020). A SCOR-based model to evaluate LARG supplychain performance using a hybrid MADM method. *IEEE Transactions on Engineering Management*, *69*(4), 1101–1120. doi:10.1109/TEM.2020.2974030

Dominguez, H., & Lashkari, R. S. (2004). Model for integrating the supply chain of an appliance company: A value of information approach. *International Journal of Production Research*, *42*(11), 2113–2140. doi:10.1080/00207540410001666297

Govindan, K., Kadzi ´nski, M., Ehling, R., & Miebs, G. (2019). Selection of a sustainable third-party reverse logistics provider based on the robustness analysis of an outranking graph kernel conducted with ELECTRE I and SMAA. *Omega*, *85*, 1–15. doi:10.1016/j.omega.2018.05.007

Hald, K. S., & Mouritsen, J. (2018). The evolution of performance measurement systems in a supply chain: A longitudinal case study on the role of interorganisational factors. *International Journal of Production Economics*, *205*, 256–271. doi:10.1016/j.ijpe.2018.09.021

Hamidi, N., & Bouzembrak, A. (2020). *La chaine logistique et la gestion des stocks d'une entreprise Cas: ENIEM* [Doctoral dissertation, Université Mouloud Mammeri].

Ishizaka, A., Khan, S. A., Kheybari, S., & Zaman, S. I. (2023). Supplier selection in closed loop pharma supply chain: A novel BWM–GAIA framework. *Annals of Operations Research*, *324*(1-2), 13–36. doi:10.1007/s10479-022-04710-7

Khan, S. A., Gupta, H., Gunasekaran, A., Mubarik, M. S., & Lawal, J. (2023). A hybrid multi-criteria decision-making approach to evaluate interrelationships and impacts of supply chain performance factors on pharmaceutical industry. *Journal of Multi-Criteria Decision Analysis*, *30*(1-2), 62–90. doi:10.1002/mcda.1800

La Londe, B. J., & Masters, J. M. (1994). Emerging logistics strategies: Blueprints for the next century. *International Journal of Physical Distribution & Logistics Management*, *24*(7), 35–47. doi:10.1108/09600039410070975

Lee, H. L., & Billington, C. (1993). Material Management in Decentralized Supply Chains. *Operations Research, 41*(5), 835–847. doi:10.1287/opre.41.5.835

Mille, F. (2008). Systèmes de détection des interactions médicamenteuses: points faibles & propositions d'améliorations (Doctoral dissertation, Université Pierre et Marie Curie-Paris VI).

Nathalie Sampieri-Teissier. (2004). *Enjeux et limites d'une amélioration des pratiques logistiques dans les hôpitaux publics français. Logistique & management*. Taylor & Francis.

Nicolas, P., & Charles, D. (2013). *Le contrôle de gestion logistique hospitalier. Comptabilité sans frontières*. The French Connection.

Ramezankhani, M. J., Torabi, S. A., & Vahidi, F. (2018). Supply chain performance measurement and evaluation: A mixed sustainability and resilience approach. *Computers & Industrial Engineering, 126*, 531–548. doi:10.1016/j.cie.2018.09.054

Rota-Frantz, K., Thierry, C., & Bel, G. (2001). Gestion des flux dans les chaînes logistiques (Supply Chain Management). *Performances Industrielles et Gestion Des Flux*. Hermes Science-Lavoisier Paris.

Sabouhi, F., Pishvaee, M. S., & Jabalameli, M. S. (2018). Resilient supply chain design under operational and disruption risks considering quantity discount: A case study of pharmaceutical supply chain. *Computers & Industrial Engineering, 126*, 657–672. doi:10.1016/j.cie.2018.10.001

Seuring, S. (2013). A review of modeling approaches for sustainable supply chain management. *Decision Support Systems, 54*(4), 1513–1520. doi:10.1016/j.dss.2012.05.053

Sinta, T. (2021). *Tunisia: the ambitions of the pharmaceutical industry*. African News Agency. https://www.africanewsagency.fr/tunisie-les-ambitions-du-sec teurpharmaceutique/?lang=en

Su, C. M., Horng, D. J., Tseng, M. L., Chiu, A. S. F., Wu, K.-J., & Chen, H.-P. (2016). Improving sustainable supply chain management using a novel hierarchical grey-DEMATEL approach. *Journal of Cleaner Production, 134*, 469–481. doi:10.1016/j.jclepro.2015.05.080

Tan, K. (2003). *Sur l'évaluation de performances des chaînes logistiques* [Doctoral dissertation, Institut National Polytechnique de Grenoble-INPG].

Tayur S., Ganeshan R., & Magazine M. (1999). *Quantitative models for supply chain management*. Kluwer AcademicPublishers.

Thanh, N. V., & Lan, N. T. K. (2022). A new hybrid triple bottom line metrics and fuzzy MCDM model: Sustainable supplier selection in the food-processing industry. *Axioms*, *11*(2), 57. doi:10.3390/axioms11020057

Thomas, D. J., & Griffin, P. M. (1996). Coordinated supply chain management. *European Journal of Operational Research*, *94*(1), 1–15. doi:10.1016/0377-2217(96)00098-7

Yousefi, S., Shabanpour, H., Fisher, R., & Saen, R. F. (2016). Evaluating and ranking sustainable suppliers by robust dynamic data envelopment analysis. *Measurement*, *83*, 72–85. doi:10.1016/j.measurement.2016.01.032

Yu, F., Xue, L., Sun, C., & Zhang, C. (2016). Product transportation distance-based supplier selection in sustainable supply chain network. *Journal of Cleaner Production*, *137*, 29–39. doi:10.1016/j.jclepro.2016.07.046

Chapter 2

Modeling of Green Hydrogen and Electricity Coproduction System for Techno–Eco–Environmental Analysis of Sustainable Microgrid

Dharmbir Prasad
iD https://orcid.org/0000-0002-9010-9717
Asansol Engineering College, India

Rudra Pratap Singh
iD https://orcid.org/0000-0001-7352-855X
Asansol Engineering College, India

Rahul Kumar
Asansol Engineering College, India

Ranadip Roy
iD https://orcid.org/0000-0003-2111-2581
Sanaka Educational Trust's Group of Institutions, India

Azizul Islam
Asansol Engineering College, India

Md. Irfan Khan
IAC Electricals Pvt. Ltd., India

ABSTRACT

The demand for renewable energy resources has increased significantly in recent years due to environmental concerns. The hybrid energy system is proposed as a solution to meet this demand. In this work, the HOMER software is used to design and optimize a hybrid model for electricity and hydrogen coproduction. The proposed model consists of various green energy resources such as solar PV, wind for hydrogen production. The system includes a green hydrogen storage facility while excess electricity is produced from renewable sources. The cost of energy production is found to be $0.08/kWh, which is competitive with conventional fossil

DOI: 10.4018/979-8-3693-1418-0.ch002

fuel-based energy generation. In addition, the system has a lower environmental impact, with a 72% reduction in CO2 emissions as compared to regular energy production methods.

INTRODUCTION

Future energy needs can be significantly reduced by using green hydrogen, which is produced from sustainable resources like solar and wind. The economics of green hydrogen are slightly complicated, mainly due to the significant disparity in the fundamental costs and supply of RE sources. Depending on global climate goals, the development of industry-specific initiatives, energy-efficiency measures, direct electrification and the deployment of carbon-capture technology, the annual demand for hydrogen by 2050 might range from 150 to 500 million metric tons (as shown in Figure 1) (PwC, 2023).

India is one among the fastest-growing economies in the world, with a rapidly increasing demand for energy. It has set goals to achieve Net Zero by 2070 and energy independence by 2047 (Ministry of Science & Technology, 2023). Its energy transition is focused on maximizing the usage of RE across all economic sectors in order to meet this goal. A potential substitute for facilitating this shift is green hydrogen. In addition to replacing fossil fuels in industry and providing clean transportation, hydrogen can also be used for decentralized power generation, aviation and maritime transportation. Standards for environmentally friendly hydrogen generation in the nation have been released by the Ministry of New and Renewable Energy (2023). In the case of electrolysis-based production, the non-biogenic greenhouse gas

Figure 1. Hydrogen demand projection across the world

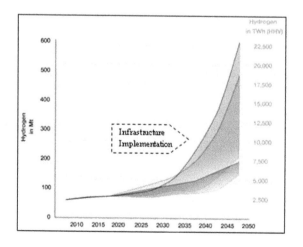

emissions resulting from water treatment, electrolysis, gas purification, drying, and compression of hydrogen shall not exceed 2 kg of carbon dioxide equivalent per kg of hydrogen (kg CO2 eq/kg Hydrogen), averaged over the previous 12 months. In this way, the United Nations SDG7 of 'affordable and clean energy' may also be achieved through hydrogen development (Osman et al., 2022).

The microgrid require assembling of distributed energy resources for resiliency in the form of energy security, including generation, storage and loads. It serves energy to different types of consumers including household, business hub and industrial unit. Since, traditional fossil fuel-based energy sources are responsible for environmental pollution and climate change and thus there is a growing need for sustainable and green sources. The net-zero approach in microgrid contains both electricity and hydrogen production by switching from primarily fossil fuel-based energy to RE with zero carbon emissions. In recent times, the RE resources like solar, wind and biomass have gained popularity because of their low environmental impact and cost-effectiveness. Hybrid RE systems, which combine multiple energy resources, have been proposed as a solution to meet the increasing demand for energy in a sustainable and efficient manner. These systems utilize a combination of resources like solar PV, wind turbines and biomass to generate electricity and hydrogen, which can be used for various applications.

In this study, rest of the paper is organized in following sequence: initially, study objective; then, background review. Thereafter, mathematical formulation, site potential evaluation, RE system modeling, results discussion and finally concluded.

STUDY OBJECTIVE

The purpose of this study is to find the optimal combination of resources and components that can provide a sustainable and cost-effective solution for electricity and hydrogen production. The study also evaluates the environmental impact of the system by reducing CO_2 emissions compared to conventional energy production methods. In the present work, following are the undertaken objectives:

$$OF= min\{(LCOE, LCOH) \text{ and } CO_2\} \tag{1}$$

RESEARCH BACKGROUND REVIEW

The term green energy refers to energy produced from natural resources that are replenished more quickly than they are used up e.g., the sun and the wind sources.

There are multiple ways for RE based coproduction of electricity and green hydrogen. Following are few highlights on recent aligned works:

(i). Renewable energy integration: Even in the early stages of the RE expansion, a number of nations have seen a deceleration in the deployment of variable RE due to system integration issues or a period of severe curtailment in energy generation. RE system integration is already a significant challenge and has been for some time. However, there multiple studies have been carried out to address these challenges; few such recent researches are presented as below:

Zhang et al., (2020) study suggested that the economic model evaluates the cost, characteristics and performance of electricity and electric power generation in terms of lithium-ion batteries combination and hydrogen storage capacity. In order to inject hydrogen into natural gas systems that are powered by excessive wind energy, a new gas security management strategy is developed in this study (Zhao et al., 2020). With the coordinated operation of tightly coupled infrastructures in mind, it provides four gas security indices for the IEGS measuring gas security. This article proposed a multi-renewable to hydrogen production method to enhance the green H2 production efficiency for renewable-dominated HFSs (Zhang et al., 2021). Further, the resources aimed to create a zero-emissions energy system in the park by combining solar PV, wind, power-to-gas and carbon capture to reduce emissions, create hydrogen/natural gas and diversify carbon sources (Jia et al., 2023). Another study, presented optimization strategies for renewable energy microgrids that combine rules and regulations to improve hybrid performance (Huangfu et al., 2023). Next, HassanzadehFard et al., (2023) studied have shown that using waste energy, especially waste electricity, can reduce energy costs by 18%. Shahverdian et al. (2023) optimized a solar-geothermal cogeneration system for power, hydrogen and freshwater production, achieving high-efficiency to generate freshwater and economic benefits. In its continuation, a method for solving problems such as gas-electric boilers effectively reduce costs, while the combination of electricity and gas eliminates the use of electricity, but still increases costs (Yan et al., 2023). Thereafter, a method to improve the revenue and stability of HESS is presented. The simulations suggested that economic gain align is align to the use of RE and the reduction of carbon emissions (Han et al., 2023).

(ii). Hydrogen production analysis: The hydrogen production model provides understanding of process design assumptions and cost analysis methodology for microgrid distributed (forecast/filling station) facilities. Following literatures have covered hydrogen production analysis:

Eisapour et al. (2021) demonstrated a flexible hybrid energy installation for the Shiraz Elam Campus that integrates renewable energy such as electricity and heat. The results shown reduced emissions, cost savings and highlighted the importance of smart energy systems for the continued growth of the school. Then, a study suggested that RE research and optimization and microgrid systems offer efficient and environmental solutions: solar, wind, diesel generators, batteries and hydrogen storage to generate 2/3 renewable energy and reduce CO_2 (Akarsu & Genç, 2022). Alkaline electrolyzer, high pressure HS tank with compressor and proton exchange membrane fuel cell stack make up the proposed integrated HESS concept in (Li et al., 2022). The findings demonstrate that the HESS responds more quickly than the conventional BESS in the microgrid, laying a strong theoretical framework for a later integration of wind-PV-HESS-BESS. Further, a study demonstrated the importance of renewable energy systems together with hydrogen technology in solving energy problems related to optimization, production process, problem solving skills and safety (Khan et al., 2022). A two-stage development system for renewable energy systems is proposed to account for cost of living, energy independence and hydrogen impact (He et al., 2022a). Next, a research was designed in school to create an integrated zero-emissions energy system that reduces emissions while producing hydrogen and natural gas using solar photovoltaic, wind power distribution, power-to-gas and carbon capture technologies (He et al., 2022b). A research described zero energy management and optimization of urban buildings using renewable energy, water pumps and hydrogen taxis (Liu et al., 2022). Furthermore, a study evaluated off-grid hybrid renewable systems with battery/hydrogen storage. The end result is that hydrogen can reduce emissions, albeit at a higher cost (Kilic & Altun, 2022). A study found that, EVs have advantages over hydrogen cars, combining hybrid energy storage for carbon neutral buildings and transportation with new energy vehicles, improving design and reducing emissions and costs (Fan et al., 2022). Then, a study recommended provision of solar, wind and hydrogen storage to stabilize and reduce peak demand. This smart system connected various devices and uses controls to save energy, reduce CO2 and minimize energy reuse (Behzadi et al., 2023). Thereafter, a study examined the use of HSS in RE. Coproduction can improve HSS outcomes by emphasizing the importance of performance metrics for improvement (Luo et al., 2023). Another study described HMES, combining RE and hydrogen to improve sustainability. It uses hot water and hydrogen storage tanks to generate electricity while emphasizing cost reduction and risk management to complete the project (Zhang et al., 2023). In another study, optimization methods are used to reduce the energy and total cost of renewable energy to provide reliable electricity and heat for business needs (Azad & Shateri, 2023). Then, a similar research presented a multi-purpose optimization strategy for renewable energy H-RE-CCHP planning for sustainability and facilitation (Wang et al., 2023). In a research, which is having fuel oxidizer and biomass gasification wind power and low hydrogen content of syngas; together outperformed biomass based SOFCs by improving B-point energy efficiency and environmental impact (Hai et al., 2023). In Texas energy research to replace coal and natural gas with cost-effective N-RHES that combined nuclear, wind, solar and green hydrogen to meet energy needs and promote clean business (Bryan et al., 2023). An electric thermal energy storage system runs on an electricity price control mechanism. A 20 MW rated steam turbine is powered by a 45 GWh thermal energy storage system that is charged using power from a 1600 MW grid link with cheaper wholesale grid electricity low-cost wholesale grid electricity (Bachmann, 2023).

(iii). Eco-environment sustainability of microgrid: The eco-environment sustainability analysis is crucial for long-term energy storage and flexible power generation solutions to support highly fluctuating RE networks. In order to assess the characteristics of energy technologies, it considers costs, environmental benefits, risks, uncertainties and availability time frames. In this context, few recent studies are briefed as follows:

More energy efficient and new technologies reduce fuel consumption, emissions, and costs and increase the share of renewable energy (Akhtari & Baneshi, 2019). Further, the energy model for buildings in Spain from 2030 to 2050 combines solar, wind and hydrogen technologies using geospatial optimization for low-cost decarbonisation of energy consumption (Maestre et al., 2022). Another study optimized PV-hydrogen hybrid systems to be carbon neutral to maximize profits from photovoltaic physics models and government subsidies and is useful to policymakers, business owners and investors (Yang et al., 2023). Then, a group of researchers evaluated a hybrid RE system comprising PV, batteries, fuel cells, electrolysers and hydrogen. Their study presented the configurations compared to NPC and COE and simulates optimization in the Moroccan climate (Jurado et al., 2023). In (Di et al., 2023), the study examined, from a techno-economic perspective, the capabilities of an off-grid MES that is designed to meet the energy needs of novel refueling stations, capable of supplying electricity for fast charging EVs and hydrogen for fuel cell EVs.

MATHEMATICAL FORMULATION

During the day, PV panels are in charge of converting solar energy into electricity; but, at night, they are unable to produce energy. Equation (2) is used by HOMER Pro to determine how much electricity a set of flat-plate PV panels produces (Eisapour et al., 2021),

$$P_{pv} = Y_{pv} f_{pv} \left(\frac{\bar{G}_T}{\bar{G}_{T\_stc}} \right) \left[1 + \alpha_p \left(T_c - T_{c\_stc} \right) \right] \tag{2}$$

where, Y_{pv} (kW): PV array rated capacity, f_{pv} (%): derating factor, $\overline{G}_T$ (W/m^2): solar radiation intensity on the PV array, $\overline{G}_{T\_stc}$ (W/m^2):, αp (%/o^C): temperature coefficient of the panels, Tc (°C): cell temperature and $Tc_{\_stc}$ (°C): temperature of the PV cell under STC.

At the height of the rotor, wind turbines are able to capture wind energy. The following equation (3) is used to determine the wind speed at the rotor's corresponding elevation above the ground (Li and others, 2022),

$$V_{hub} = V_{anem} \frac{\ln\left(\frac{z_{hub}}{z_0}\right)}{\ln\left(\frac{z_{anem}}{z_0}\right)} \tag{3}$$

where, V_{anem} (m/s): wind speed at anemometer height, z_{hub} (m): hub height of the turbine, z_0 (m): surface roughness length and z_{anem} (m): height of the anemometer.

Following realization of the wind speed at the hub height, the wind turbine power output is formulated by (4) (Li et al., 2022).

$$P_{wtg} = \left(\frac{\rho}{\rho_0}\right) P_{wtg\_stp} \tag{4}$$

where, ρ: real air density, $\rho0$: air density at STC, $Pwt_{g\_stp:}$ power output at standard condition,

In applications requiring stand-alone power requirements, diesel generators are employed as a backup power source. Equation (5) is used in this model to compute the diesel generator's electric efficiency (Kilic & Altun, 2022),

$$\eta = \frac{P_{GEN}}{\rho_D V_D LHV_D} \tag{5}$$

where, P_{GEN} (W): diesel generator power, ρD (kg/m3$^)$: diesel fuel density, VD (m3$^{/}$h): volumetric fuel flow rate and LHVD (J/kg): fuel lower heating value.

Hydrogen is created by an electrolyzer using extra power in the system, and it is then stored in a tank to be used by the fuel cell later on as needed. It is possible to model an electrolyzer by using the empirical current-voltage relations presented in (6) (Kilic & Altun, 2022),

$$V = V_{rev} + \left(\frac{r_1 + r_2 T}{A} \right) I + s \log \left\{ \left(\frac{t_1 + t_1/T + t_3/T^2}{A} \right) + 1 \right\}$$

(6)

where, V_{rev}: reversible voltage, $r(\Omega m^2)$: ohmic resistance parameter, s and t: overvoltage coefficients, A (m²): area of electrode and T: temperature.

The system's converted costs, including the initial capital cost, O&M expenses, replacement costs and fuel costs, are displayed in the objective function of the NPC optimization. Mathematically, the NPC is represented as (7) (Wang et al., 2023),

$$NPC(i,n) = \sum_{t=0}^{n} \frac{C_t}{(1+i)^t}$$

(7)

where, i (%): real discount rate, n (year): project's lifetime, t (year): year of operation and C_t ($): total cost in a year.

By using the formula (8) (Wang et al., 2023), the real discount rate is expressed,

$$i = \frac{i'-f}{i+f}$$

(8)

where, i': expected inflation rate and f: nominal discount rate.

According to Wang et al. (2023), CRF is a function of the project's duration and the discount rate, which can be calculated using (9),

$$CRF(i,n) = \frac{i(1+i)^n}{(1+i)^n - 1}$$

(9)

The annualized value of the total NPC is the whole annualized cost. Using (10) (Wang et al., 2023), HOMER determines the overall annualized cost,

$$C_{an\_t} = CRF(i,n) \times NPC$$

(10)

The COE provides an indication of the LCOE production and is a key indicator of the financial viability of the project, which can be formulated using (11) (Wang et al., 2023),

$$COE = \frac{C_{an\_t}}{E_t}$$

(11)

Table 1. Results for resource assessment for coproduction of electricity and hydrogen at site

Month	CI	DR (kWh/m²/day)	T (ºC)	V_{WT} (m/s)
January	0.613	4.310	17.440	3.830
February	0.618	5.010	21.720	3.690
March	0.605	5.690	27.260	4.040
April	0.592	6.200	31.490	4.880
May	0.547	6.020	32.060	5.350
June	0.427	4.760	30.190	5.750
July	0.384	4.240	28.580	5.660
August	0.385	4.090	28.110	5.140
September	0.423	4.120	27.390	4.540
October	0.533	4.510	25.490	3.470
November	0.590	4.280	21.480	3.520
December	0.621	4.150	17.630	3.810

SITE POTENTIAL EVALUATION

The study area for exploring green hydrogen production using Homer Pro encompasses the Chhota Bainan region of West Bengal. It is a small village located in the Nadia district of West Bengal (co-ordinates *viz.,* latitude: 22°59.2' N and longitude: 87°51.3' E). The regions possess unique characteristics and abundant renewable resources that make them suitable for study and implementing green hydrogen production unit. This region is known for its plane land, which can potentially be utilized for setting up solar and wind farms. The abundance of sunlight and consistent wind patterns in the area provide favorable conditions for RE generation. With the feasibility infrastructure and technological access has the potential to become a hub for green hydrogen production. The proposed site has significant energy demands and is currently reliant on conventional energy sources, which contribute to environmental degradation and carbon emissions. Exploring green hydrogen production in these regions can lead to a sustainable transition and help achieve climate goals by reducing greenhouse gas emissions and promoting the use of clean energy. Solar and wind energy resource access for green hydrogen production is abundant at site, which are illustrated as follows:

(i). Solar energy resource: The results of solar resource data, which shows the amount of solar radiation received by a surface horizontal to the ground, is important for assessing the solar energy potential of a site and its designing. Monthly average

Figure 2. Site resource characteristics of results for coproduction of electricity and hydrogen

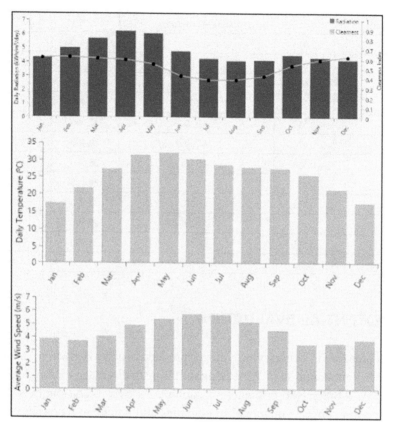

GHI data of the study location over 22 year period is obtained from NASA-POWER database. Table 1 and Fig. 2 shows the monthly average GHI data for Bongan. The minimum GHI value for Bongan occurred in August is 4.090 kWh/m² /day; whereas, the maximum GHI values occurred in April is 6.200 kWh/m² /day.

(ii). Temperature resource: A graph of temperature resource data, which shows the temperature variations at a site over time, is important for assessing the performance and efficiency of RE systems that are sensitive to temperature changes, such as solar panels and batteries. Monthly average temperature over 30 year period is shown in Table 1 and Fig. 2. The minimum monthly average air temperature value for Bongan occurred in January is 17.440°C. Whereas, the maximum monthly average air temperature occurred in May is 32.060°C.

(iii). Wind resource: A chart of wind resource data, which shows the wind speed and direction variations at a site over time, is important for assessing the potential

Figure 3. Flow chart for coproduction modeling of electricity and green hydrogen production

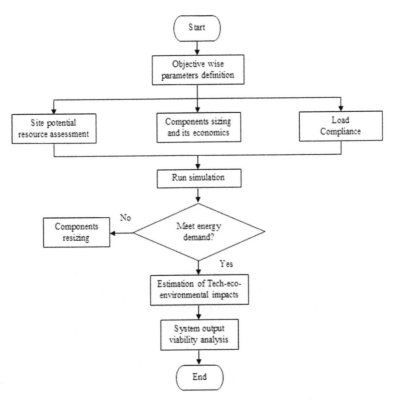

of wind energy at the site and designing an appropriate wind energy system for the site. Table 1 and Figure 2 shows the monthly mean wind speed data over 30 years at 50 m height for the proposed site. The maximum monthly mean wind speeds occurred in June with a value of 5.75 m/s.

INTEGRAL RE SYSTEM MODELING

The software requires hourly electric load demand, resources, components, and their cost and economic data as input to simulate and optimize. The optimizer utilizes a derivative-free algorithm to catch the least cost combination for the system components that satisfies electric loads per hour and user-defined constraints when it searches from an infinite space of component sizes until user-defined convergence criteria are found. Finally, the eco-environment sensitivity analysis is performed to assess the impacts of alterations in input parameters that are not controlled. The flow chart

Figure 4. Schematic for hybrid RE system integration model

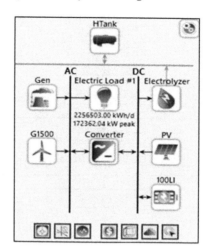

corresponding to its execution is presented in Figure 3. The HOMER is widely-used software for simulating and modelling off-grid and grid-connected power systems. The software is particularly helpful in designing the hybrid RE systems that can meet thermal and electrical loads through a combination of components such as PV module, WT, diesel generators, electrolyzers, battery storage, hydrogen storage and fuel cells. The system modelling block diagram is shown in Figure 4.

(i). Solar power generation: The use of generic flat PV systems has become growingly popular due to their versatility and ease of installation. It can be mounted on various surfaces including concrete, metal, and even shingles. Additionally, they can be used in both residential and commercial settings, providing a reliable and cost-effective source of electricity. Generic flat PV refers to a type of PV module that is designed to be installed on flat surfaces such as roofs or walls. These modules are made up of layers of semiconductor materials that absorb sunlight and convert it into electricity. Once installed, these systems require little upkeep other than occasional cleaning to ensure optimal performance. Furthermore, their modular design allows for easy expansion, making it easy to increase energy production as needed. Its capacity sizing features have been presented in Table 2 and Figure 5.

(ii). Wind power generation: A wind turbine is a device that converts the kinetic energy of wind into electrical power. The turbine consists of blades that rotate when wind blows over them, which in turn spins a generator to produce electricity. WTs come in various sizes and designs, ranging from small turbines used to power homes or small communities to large utility-scale turbines used in wind farms to generate electricity on a larger scale. The advantages of WTs are that they produce electricity without emitting greenhouse gases or other pollutants, they have low operating cost

Table 2. Capacity sizing features of PV and wind power generation

SI.	PV power generation	Value	SI.	WT power generation	Value
1	Derating factor (%)	80	7	Capital cost ($)	3000000
2	Capital cost ($/kW)	2500	8	Replacement cost ($)	3000000
3	Replacement cost ($/kW)	2500	9	O&M cost ($/year/kW)	30000
4	O&M cost ($/year/kW)	10	10	Hub height (m)	80
5	Lifetime (year)	25	11	Lifetime (years)	20
6	Power capacity (kW)	0-1000	12	Power rating (MW)	1.5

compared to other energy sources, and they have the potential to provide stable source of electricity in areas with consistent wind resources. However, WTs also have some limitations, such as their intermittent power output, that can be affected by changes in wind speed and direction, along with the potential for noise and visual impacts on local communities. In this study, the proposed model has WT turbine with the following features cited in Table 2 and Figure 5.

(iii). Battery energy storage: Li-ion batteries are known for their high energy density, which means they can store a large amount of energy in a relatively small volume. They are also lightweight, which makes them ideal for portable applications. However, they can be expensive and require careful management to avoid overcharging or overheating. It is typically composed of multiple battery cells. Overall, a 100 kWh Li-ion battery represents a significant advancement in battery technology, enabling a wide range of applications that were previously impossible or impractical. Its technical parameters are given in Table 3 and Figure 6.

Figure 5. Power output characteristics for solar and wind power generation

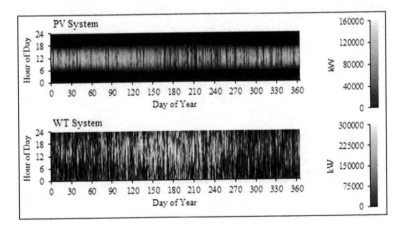

Table 3. Features of battery storage and power conversion system

Sl.	Battery storage	Value	Sl.	Power converter	Value
1	Nominal voltage (V)	6	7	Capital cost ($)	300
2	Nominal capacity (kWh)	100	8	Replacement cost ($)	300
3	Nominal capacity (Ah)	167	9	O&M cost ($/year/kW)	0
4	Round-trip efficiency (%)	90	10	Inverter efficiency (%)	95
5	Maximum charge current (A)	167	11	Inverter lifetime (year)	15
6	Maximum discharge current (A)	500	12	Capacity (kW)	107816
7	String size	1	13	Rectifier capacity (%)	100
8	Initial state of charge (%)	100	14	Rectifier efficiency (%)	95
9	Minimum state of charge (%)	20	15	Mean power output (kW)	20189
10	Minimum storage life (year)	5	16	Hours of Operation (hours/year)	3747

(iv). Power conversion system: The switch to renewable energy makes it more difficult to provide electricity reliably in present days while satisfying government ambitions to minimize carbon emissions. As a result, the demand for energy storage technology is rising. Any efficient energy storage system must have a power conversion system. The PCS acts as an interface between the DC batteries and the power grid. Its techno-economic parameters are summarized in Table 3 and Figure 6.

(v). Electrolyzer for hydrogen production: An electrolyzer is a device that uses electricity to split water or other electrolytes into their constituent elements, typically hydrogen and oxygen. Electrolysis is achieved by passing an electric current through

Figure 6. Daily operating characteristics for battery storage and power conversion system

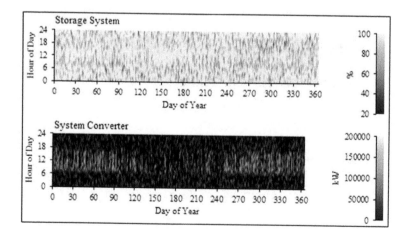

Table 4. System modelling parameters of electrolyzer for hydrogen production

Sl.	Properties	Value	Sl.	Properties	Value
1	Rated capacity (kW)	10.0	5	Capacity factor (%)	32.3
2	Total input energy (kWh/year)	28260	6	Total Production (kg/year)	609
3	Hours of operation (hour/year)	2826	7	Specific Consumption (kWh/kg)	46.4
4	Minimum output (kg/hour)	0	8	Maximum Output (kg/hour)	0.215

the water, which causes the water molecules to break down into hydrogen and oxygen ions. The ions are then attracted to electrodes of opposite charge, where they combine to form hydrogen gas at the negative electrode (cathode) and oxygen gas at the positive electrode (anode). These are used in various applications, including hydrogen production for fuel cells, industrial gas production and energy storage. Its system modelling parameters of electrolyzer for hydrogen production is given in Table 4 and Figure 7. Hydrogen produced by electrolysis is considered a clean energy source because it produces no harmful emissions and can be produced using renewable energy sources such as solar and wind power.

(vi). Fossil fuel based power generation: A fossil fuel based diesel genset is a type of generator set that is designed to automatically adjust its output to match the specific power needs of an electrical system. This type of generator is equipped with advanced control systems that constantly monitor the power demands of the connected load and adjust the generator's output accordingly. One of the key benefits of an autosize genset is that it can help to improve overall energy efficiency and reduce fuel consumption, as it only generates the amount of power that is actually

Figure 7. Daily hydrogen production and diesel generator operating characteristics

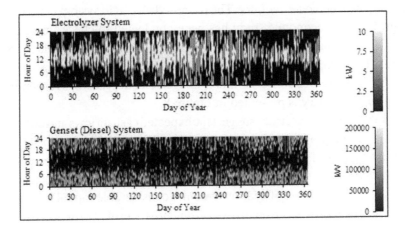

Table 5. Capacity sizing features of fossil fuel based diesel generator

Sl.	Properties	Value	Sl.	Properties	Value
1	Fuel curve intercept (L/hr)	2787	10	Minimum runtime (minute)	0
2	Fuel curve slope (L/hr/kW)	0.236	11	Replacement ($)	500
3	Fuel lower heating (MJ/kg)	43.2	12	O&M ($/hour)	0.030
4	Fuel density (kg/m³)	820	13	Fuel price ($/L)	1.00
5	Fuel carbon content (%)	88	14	CO emissions (g/L fuel)	16.5
6	Fuel sulfur content (%)	0.4	15	Unburned HC emissions (g/L fuel)	0.72
7	Minimum load ratio (%)	25	16	Particulates emissions (g/L fuel)	0.1
8	Life time (hours)	15000	17	Fuel sulphur to PM emissions (%)	2.2
9	Initial capital ($)	500	18	NOx emissions (g/L fuel)	15.5

needed at any given time. Daily operating features of diesel generator is presented in Table 5 and Figure. 7. This can be particularly useful in situations, where power demand varies widely over time, such as in remote or mobile applications.

RESULTS AND DISCUSSION

In order to create a workable system, HOMER model tools were used to economically optimize, and set up hybrid RE system, as well as assess its technological viability. Initially, the electric needs of Chhota Bainan, West Bengal 713427, India are met with 190,000 kW of diesel generator capacity. It is proposed to add 140,834 kW of PV, 246,100 kWh of battery capacity and 289,500 kW of wind generation capacity. In this study, the investment has a payback of 5.92 years and an IRR of 15.6%. Corresponding results to the study is illustrated below:

(i). Economic outcome analysis: The proposed microgid system is not connected to the grid, and its economic study has been conducted to check implementation viability. Cost summary of different components used in the production of the electricity. The components used in generation are genset, wind turbine, lithium-ion battery, PV plate, power converter and hydrogen electrolyzer. Corresponding cash flow and cost summary is presented in Figure 8.

The cash flow characteristics suggest the expected cash inflows and outflows over the lifetime of the project (as presented in Figure 9), which can help stakeholders evaluate the financial feasibility and profitability of investments in renewable energy.

(ii). Technical observations: In order to overcome technological obstacles early on, the exploitation and use of hydrogen require considerable capital investments; as a result, financial subsidies from the government are needed to support the growth

Figure 8. Characteristics of cash flow and cost summary of the system

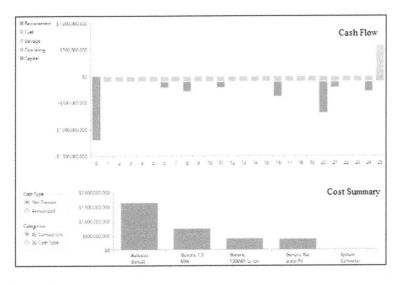

of enterprises. Table 6 and Figure 10 signify electricity-hydrogen production and characteristics of the percentage of energy demand fulfilled by various RE sources.

(iii). Environment sustainability analysis: Clean and renewable energy must replace fossil fuels as the main energy source in order to create an eco-environment. Because global warming's negative impacts will be avoided, reducing carbon dioxide emissions will benefit the environment. In this study, coproduction of green hydrogen and electricity using RE would significantly contribute towards sustainable microgrid. In this context, corresponding result is presented in Table 7. The monthly hydrogen production through electrolyser is portrayed in Figure 11.

Figure 9. Comparative characteristics for cash flow over project lifetime

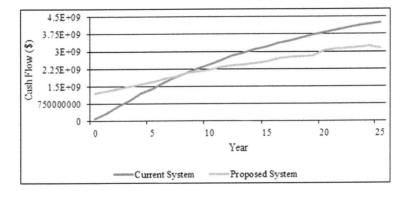

Table 6. Results for hydrogen production using RE available

Sl.	Properties	Value
1	Excess electricity (%)	26.8
2	Unmet electrical load (kWh/year)	0
3	Capacity shortage (kWh/year)	0
4	Renewable fraction (%)	59
5	Maximum renewable penetration (kWh/year)	1178
6	Hydrogen production by electrolyzer (kg/year)	609
7	Hydrogen production reformer (kg/year)	0
8	LCOH ($/year)	399,224

CONCLUSION

The results of this study can have significant implications for the energy sector, as they provide insights into the feasibility and cost-effectiveness of hybrid RE systems for electricity and hydrogen production. These systems can help reduce the dependence on fossil fuels and promote sustainable energy production. The present analysis of Chhota Bainan region in West Bengal reveals that it has a significant potential for RE generation, especially through solar and wind sources. The annual average solar radiation of the region is 4.54 kWh/m²/day and the average wind speed is 4.78 m/s, which makes it a favorable location for developing hybrid RE systems. Based on the HOMER simulation results, the most efficient system with the lowest energy cost of $0.295 kWh for West Bengal. This scenario includes a hybrid renewable model, which can meet the annual load and generate excess electricity for 609 kg/year green hydrogen production. The system has a simple payback period of around 5.92 years and can produce around 70% of the total electricity from renewable sources.

Figure 10. Characteristics for coproduction of electricity and green hydrogen

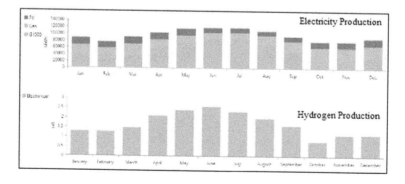

Figure 11. Monthly hydrogen production characteristics

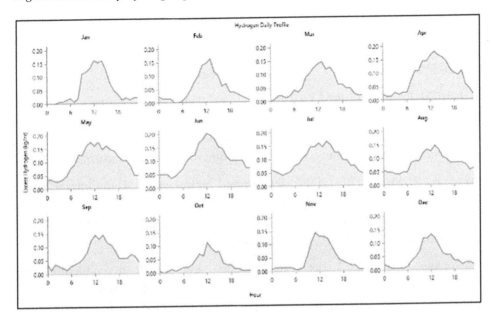

Developing hybrid renewable energy systems can help meet the energy demand of the region, reduce carbon emissions and promote sustainable development.

Table 7. Emission reduction by the proposed green hydrogen with hybrid RE system

Sl.	Properties	Value
1	Carbon dioxide (kg/year)	230,244,112
2	Carbon monoxide (kg/year)	1,451,332
3	Unburned hydrocarbons (kg/year)	63,331
4	Particulate matter (kg/year)	8,796
5	Sulfur dioxide (kg/year)	563,813
6	Nitrogen oxides (kg/year)	1,363,372
7	Hydrogen production reformer (kg/year)	0
8	LCOH ($/year)	399,224

REFERENCES

Akarsu, B., & Genç, M. S. (2022). Optimization of electricity and hydrogen production with hybrid renewable energy systems. *Fuel, 324*, 124465. doi:10.1016/j. fuel.2022.124465

Akhtari, M. R., & Baneshi, M. (2019). Techno-economic assessment and optimization of a hybrid renewable co-supply of electricity, heat and hydrogen system to enhance performance by recovering excess electricity for a large energy consumer. *Energy Conversion and Management, 188*, 131–141. doi:10.1016/j.enconman.2019.03.067

Azad, A., & Shateri, H. (2023). Design and optimization of an entirely hybrid renewable energy system (WT/PV/BW/HS/TES/EVPL) to supply electrical and thermal loads with considering uncertainties in generation and consumption. *Applied Energy, 336*, 120782. doi:10.1016/j.apenergy.2023.120782

Bachmann, O. (2023). Large scale low-cost green hydrogen production using thermal energy storage and polymer electrolyte membrane electrolysis systems. *IET Renewable Power Generation, 17*(4), pp.775-793. (Bachmann, 2023)

Behzadi, A., Alirahmi, S. M., Yu, H., & Sadrizadeh, S. (2023). An efficient renewable hybridization based on hydrogen storage for peak demand reduction: A rule-based energy control and optimization using machine learning techniques. *Journal of Energy Storage, 57*, 106168. doi:10.1016/j.est.2022.106168

Bryan, J., Meek, A., Dana, S., Sakir, M. S. I., & Wang, H. (2023). Modeling and design optimization of carbon-free hybrid energy systems with thermal and hydrogen storage. *International Journal of Hydrogen Energy, 48*(99), 39097–39111. doi:10.1016/j.ijhydene.2023.03.135

Di Micco, S., Romano, F., Jannelli, E., Perna, A., & Minutillo, M. (2023). Techno-economic analysis of a multi-energy system for the co-production of green hydrogen, renewable electricity and heat. *International Journal of Hydrogen Energy, 48*(81), 31457–31467. doi:10.1016/j.ijhydene.2023.04.269

Eisapour, A. H., Jafarpur, K., & Farjah, E. (2021). Feasibility study of a smart hybrid renewable energy system to supply the electricity and heat demand of Eram Campus, Shiraz University; simulation, optimization, and sensitivity analysis. *Energy Conversion and Management, 248*, 114779. doi:10.1016/j.enconman.2021.114779

Fan, G., Liu, Z., Liu, X., Shi, Y., Wu, D., Guo, J., Zhang, S., Yang, X., & Zhang, Y. (2022). Two-layer collaborative optimization for a renewable energy system combining electricity storage, hydrogen storage, and heat storage. *Energy, 259*, 125047. doi:10.1016/j.energy.2022.125047

Hai, T., El-Shafay, A. S., Alizadeh, A. A., Dhahad, H. A., Chauhan, B. S., Almojil, S. F., Almohana, A. I., & Alali, A. F. (2023). Comparison analysis of hydrogen addition into both anode and afterburner of fuel cell incorporated with hybrid renewable energy driven SOFC: An application of techno-environmental horizon and multi-objective optimization. *International Journal of Hydrogen Energy*.

Han, F., Zeng, J., Lin, J., & Gao, C. (2023). Multi-stage distributionally robust optimization for hybrid energy storage in regional integrated energy system considering robustness and nonanticipativity. *Energy*, *277*, 127729. doi:10.1016/j. energy.2023.127729

HassanzadehFard, H., Tooryan, F., & Dargahi, V. (2023). Standalone hybrid system energy management optimization for remote village considering methane production from livestock manure. *International Journal of Hydrogen Energy*, *48*(29), 10778–10796. doi:10.1016/j.ijhydene.2022.12.085

He, J., Wu, Y., Wu, M., Xu, M., & Liu, F. (2022a). Two-stage configuration optimization of a novel standalone renewable integrated energy system coupled with hydrogen refueling. *Energy Conversion and Management*, *251*, 114953. doi:10.1016/j.enconman.2021.114953

He, J., Wu, Y., Yong, X., Tan, Q., & Liu, F. (2022b). Bi-level optimization of a near-zero-emission integrated energy system considering electricity-hydrogen-gas nexus: A two-stage framework aiming at economic and environmental benefits. *Energy Conversion and Management*, *274*, 116434. doi:10.1016/j.enconman.2022.116434

Huangfu, Y., Tian, C., Zhuo, S., Xu, L., Li, P., Quan, S., Zhang, Y., & Ma, R. (2023). An optimal energy management strategy with subsection bi-objective optimization dynamic programming for photovoltaic/battery/hydrogen hybrid energy system. *International Journal of Hydrogen Energy*, *48*(8), 3154–3170. doi:10.1016/j. ijhydene.2022.10.133

Jia, K., Liu, C., Li, S., & Jiang, D. (2023). Modeling and optimization of a hybrid renewable energy system integrated with gas turbine and energy storage. *Energy Conversion and Management*, *279*, 116763. doi:10.1016/j.enconman.2023.116763

Jurado, F., Mezrhab, A., Moussaoui, M. A., & Vera, D. (2023). Cost and size optimization of hybrid solar and hydrogen subsystem using HomerPro software. *International Journal of Hydrogen Energy*.

Khan, T., Yu, M., & Waseem, M. (2022). Review on recent optimization strategies for hybrid renewable energy system with hydrogen technologies: State of the art, trends and future directions. *International Journal of Hydrogen Energy*, *47*(60), 25155–25201. doi:10.1016/j.ijhydene.2022.05.263

Kilic, M., & Altun, A. F. (2022). Dynamic modelling and multi-objective optimization of off-grid hybrid energy systems by using battery or hydrogen storage for different climates. *International Journal of Hydrogen Energy*.

Li, J., Li, G., Ma, S., Liang, Z., Li, Y., & Zeng, W. (2022). Modeling and Simulation of Hydrogen Energy Storage System for Power-to-Gas and Gas-to-Power Systems. *Journal of Modern Power Systems and Clean Energy*.

Liu, J., Zhou, Y., Yang, H., & Wu, H. (2022). Net-zero energy management and optimization of commercial building sectors with hybrid renewable energy systems integrated with energy storage of pumped hydro and hydrogen taxis. *Applied Energy*, *321*, 119312. doi:10.1016/j.apenergy.2022.119312

Luo, L., Cristofari, C., & Levrey, S. (2023). Cogeneration: Another way to increase energy efficiency of hybrid renewable energy hydrogen chain–A review of systems operating in cogeneration and of the energy efficiency assessment through exergy analysis. *Journal of Energy Storage*, *66*, 107433. doi:10.1016/j.est.2023.107433

Maestre, V. M., Ortiz, A., & Ortiz, I. (2022). Transition to a low-carbon building stock. Techno-economic and spatial optimization of renewables-hydrogen strategies in Spain. *Journal of Energy Storage*, *56*, 105889. doi:10.1016/j.est.2022.105889

Ministry of New and Renewable Energy. (2023). *India rolls out green hydrogen production standards*. Live Mint. https://www.livemint.com/industry/energy/india-rolls-out-green-hydrogen-production-standards-11692426710928.html

Ministry of Science & Technology. (2023). *National Green Hydrogen Mission*. MST. https://www.india.gov.in/spotlight/national-green-hydrogen-mission

Osman, A. I., Mehta, N., Elgarahy, A. M., Hefny, M., Al-Hinai, A., Al-Muhtaseb, A. A. H., & Rooney, D. W. (2022). Hydrogen production, storage, utilisation and environmental impacts: A review. *Environmental Chemistry Letters*, *20*(1), 1–36. doi:10.1007/s10311-021-01322-8

PwC. (2023). *The green hydrogen economy: Predicting the decarbonisation agenda of tomorrow*. PwC. https://www.pwc.com/gx/en/industries/energy-utilities-resources/future-energy/green-hydrogen-cost.html

Shahverdian, M. H., Sedayevatan, S., Hosseini, M., Sohani, A., Javadijam, R., & Sayyaadi, H. (2023). Multi-objective technoeconomic optimization of an off-grid solar-ground-source driven cycle with hydrogen storage for power and fresh water production. *International Journal of Hydrogen Energy*, *48*(52), 19772–19791. doi:10.1016/j.ijhydene.2023.02.062

Wang, Y., Song, M., Jia, M., Li, B., Fei, H., Zhang, Y., & Wang, X. (2023). Multi-objective distributionally robust optimization for hydrogen-involved total renewable energy CCHP planning under source-load uncertainties. *Applied Energy, 342,* 121212. doi:10.1016/j.apenergy.2023.121212

Yan, R., Wang, J., Huo, S., Qin, Y., Zhang, J., Tang, S., Wang, Y., Liu, Y., & Zhou, L. (2023). Flexibility improvement and stochastic multi-scenario hybrid optimization for an integrated energy system with high-proportion renewable energy. *Energy, 263,* 125779. doi:10.1016/j.energy.2022.125779

Yang, G., Zhang, H., Wang, W., Liu, B., Lyu, C., & Yang, D. (2023). Capacity optimization and economic analysis of PV–hydrogen hybrid systems with physical solar power curve modeling. *Energy Conversion and Management, 288,* 117128. doi:10.1016/j.enconman.2023.117128

Zhang, H., Wang, J., Zhao, X., Yang, J., & Bu sinnah, Z. A. (2023). Modeling a hydrogen-based sustainable multi-carrier energy system using a multi-objective optimization considering embedded joint chance constraints. *Energy, 278,* 127643. doi:10.1016/j.energy.2023.127643

Zhang, K., Zhou, B., Or, S. W., Li, C., Chung, C. Y., & Voropai, N. (2021). Optimal coordinated control of multi-renewable-to-hydrogen production system for hydrogen fueling stations. *IEEE Transactions on Industry Applications, 58*(2), 2728–2739. doi:10.1109/TIA.2021.3093841

Zhang, Y., Hua, Q. S., Sun, L., & Liu, Q. (2020). Life cycle optimization of renewable energy systems configuration with hybrid battery/hydrogen storage: A comparative study. *Journal of Energy Storage, 30,* 101470. doi:10.1016/j.est.2020.101470

Zhao, P., Gu, C., Hu, Z., Xie, D., Hernando-Gil, I., & Shen, Y. (2020). Distributionally robust hydrogen optimization with ensured security and multi-energy couplings. *IEEE Transactions on Power Systems, 36*(1), 504–513. doi:10.1109/TPWRS.2020.3005991

Chapter 3
Utilizing Waste Water for Sustainable Energy Generation via IoT-Integrated Technologies

Sabyasachi Pramanik
https://orcid.org/0000-0002-9431-8751
Haldia Institute of Technology, India

ABSTRACT

Innovative technologies including geothermal desalination, anaerobic digestion, microbial fuel cells, and internet of things integration may be able to aid with the combined challenges of wastewater treatment and energy sustainability. Anaerobic digestion converts organic waste into biogas, a renewable energy source that may be used to produce heat and electricity. Microbial fuel cells (MFCs) use the metabolic processes of microbes to convert organic materials into electricity, allowing for the simultaneous treatment of wastewater and the generation of renewable energy. Geothermal desalination reduces the need for fossil fuels and uses heat from geothermal sources to turn brackish or salty water into freshwater, which is less harmful to the environment. IoT connection allows geothermal desalination systems and bioenergy from wastewater processes to collect, monitor, control, and optimise data in real-time.

DOI: 10.4018/979-8-3693-1418-0.ch003

INTRODUCTION

Treatment of wastewater is essential for both human safety and environmental health. The facilities purify the water and maintain its purity, but they need energy, which raises the cost of operation and contributes to carbon emissions. Anaerobic digestion, microbial fuel cells, and geothermal desalination are a few examples of sustainable energy sources that researchers are investigating. The incorporation of IoT into various processes for improved efficiency and environmental advantages is also covered in this chapter. Utilizing microorganisms to break down organic material in wastewater without the need of oxygen, anaerobic digestion creates biogas as a byproduct. Through this process, organic waste is transformed into biogas, a sustainable energy source for the creation of both power and heat. Anaerobic digestion is used in wastewater treatment facilities to manage organic waste and recover useful energy, which lessens the need for non-renewable resources (Llácer-Iglesias et al., 2021).

Microbial Fuel Cells (MFCs) are an innovative technology that has promise for producing sustainable energy from wastewater. They create electricity by harnessing the metabolic processes of microorganisms, enabling continuous power production. MFCs have the ability to provide simultaneous pollution removal and energy recovery in wastewater treatment systems. For use in actual applications, research strives to enhance MFC performance and scalability. Geothermal desalination is a cutting-edge technique that transforms brackish or saltwater into freshwater by combining geothermal energy with desalination procedures. This strategy addresses freshwater shortages while simultaneously producing renewable energy, resulting in high energy efficiency and decreased dependency on fossil fuels (Chandrasekhar et al., 2020).

By providing real-time monitoring, data gathering, and analysis of parameters in anaerobic digestion, MFCs, and geothermal desalination systems, IoT technology increases the efficiency of bioenergy production. Operators can optimise energy output and water treatment efficiency, detect problems, and monitor process variables remotely (Boopathi & Myilsamy, 2021; Haribalaji et al., 2021; Sampath et al., 2022). IoT-based control and automation systems provide better operational management, lower energy use, and predictive maintenance, which reduces costs and helps the environment. In order to generate sustainable energy from wastewater, this chapter examines anaerobic digestion, microbial fuel cells, and geothermal desalination methods. The advantages and difficulties of incorporating IoT for effective resource utilization and resource optimization are covered. The future of wastewater treatment and resource recovery may be more sustainable and energy-efficient if these improvements are understood (Karn et al., 2021).

Due to rising energy needs and environmental concerns, it is essential to develop and apply novel methods for the sustainable energy production from wastewater. We can lessen our influence on the environment and support a low-carbon economy by using energy potential in wastewater treatment procedures. With less dependence on outside energy sources, lower operating costs, and reduced carbon emissions, this strategy provides a solution to balance energy use in wastewater treatment facilities. Diversifying the energy mix via sustainable wastewater energy production lessens reliance on fossil fuels and its negative effects on the environment. By decentralizing production and lowering sensitivity to outside interruptions, it also provides energy security and resilience. The use of IoT in the production of bioenergy from wastewater has opportunities for improving system efficiency and resource use. According to Guo et al. (2019), this data-driven strategy promotes proactive decision-making, early identification of operational abnormalities, and focused optimization techniques, all of which lead to an increase in energy efficiency and cost-effectiveness.

Technology breakthroughs, cost-effectiveness, scalability, and regulatory frameworks are all necessary for sustainable energy production from wastewater. For acceptance and long-term sustainability, stakeholder participation, governmental backing, and public awareness are essential. The convergence of IoT, geothermal desalination, microbial fuel cells, anaerobic digestion, and microbial fuel cells offers a viable route to wastewater management that is both ecologically responsible and energy efficient. These technologies may minimize environmental effects, operating costs, and support a sustainable energy future by converting wastewater treatment facilities from energy consumers to energy producers (Aftab et al., 2020).

For the preservation of the environment, public health, and the well-being of communities, wastewater treatment and energy sustainability are essential. While energy sustainability reduces non-renewable energy usage and supports renewable and clean energy alternatives, wastewater treatment eliminates hazardous contaminants. Addressing these issues and establishing a sustainable future need an understanding of these factors. For a number of reasons, including environmental protection, public health, resource recovery, circular economy, energy efficiency, and lowering carbon footprints, wastewater treatment is crucial. (Anitha et al., 2023; Boopathi, 2023c, 2023b; Koshariya et al., 2023a; Palaniappan et al., 2023; Sathish et al., 2023) Untreated wastewater may affect aquatic ecosystems, contaminate water bodies, reduce oxygen levels, and have a detrimental influence on biodiversity. Safe discharge is guaranteed, water resources are safeguarded, ecosystems are preserved, and ecological equilibrium is maintained. Poor wastewater treatment may also endanger the public's health since it can harbor microbes and pathogens that can lead to illnesses that are transmitted via the water. Wastewater treatment supports a sustainable, circular civilization by removing important resources including energy, nutrients, and water (Meneses-Jácome et al., 2016).

Utilizing technology like energy recovery systems, cutting-edge aeration methods, and renewable energy integration to optimize energy sustainability may lower energy needs, operating costs, decrease greenhouse gas emissions, and fight climate change. The Sustainable Development Goals of the United Nations, which place a high priority on access to clean water and sanitation as well as the promotion of cheap, clean energy, depend on energy sustainability and wastewater treatment (Radeef & Ismail, 2021).

Wastewater has enormous bioenergy potential for generating sustainable energy and is a result of home, industrial, and agricultural activity. It has organic material from food scraps, agricultural runoff, and human waste that may be turned into renewable energy sources. A commonly used process called anaerobic digestion decomposes organic material without the need of oxygen, reducing complex chemicals to simpler ones and producing biogas. As long as there is organic matter available, microbial fuel cells (MFCs) can continuously produce power from wastewater. According to Liu et al. (2013), hydrothermal carbonization (HTC) transforms organic matter into hydrochar, a sustainable energy source with fewer carbon emissions.

Algae may be grown in nutrient-rich wastewater, which can be utilized as a feedstock for biofuels. Sludge-to-Energy systems reduce volume, save disposal costs, and recover energy from organic material by converting wastewater sludge into heat, electricity, or biofuels. Bioenergy may be produced from wastewater, decreasing reliance on fossil fuels, greenhouse gas emissions, and fostering a circular economy. By converting organic waste into renewable energy sources through technologies like anaerobic digestion, microbial fuel cells, hydrothermal carbonization, algae cultivation, and sludge-to-energy, environmental problems can be solved, energy sustainability can be achieved, and a resource-efficient, circular society can be promoted (Chandrasekhar et al., 2020).

In this chapter, cutting-edge technologies for wastewater treatment and energy production are discussed, including anaerobic digestion, microbial fuel cells, geothermal desalination, and IoT integration. Organic matter is converted into biogas by anaerobic digestion and energy by MFCs. Geothermal desalination turns saltwater into freshwater, eliminating the need for fossil fuels and having less of an adverse effect on the environment. Real-time data gathering, monitoring, control, and optimization are made possible through IoT integration.

DIGESTIVE ANAEROBIC

Without the need of oxygen, a biological process called anaerobic digestion decomposes organic material to create biogas. It involves a variety of microbes cooperating to break down complicated molecules into simpler ones. The concept, associated microorganisms, and the creation and composition of biogas are all covered in this section.

The Basis and Mechanism of Anaerobic Digestion

Under anaerobic digestion, complex organic substances including carbohydrates, lipids, proteins, and cellulose are broken down via biochemical processes by bacteria that can survive under anoxic conditions. According to Mohanakrishna et al. (2016) and Pant et al. (2010), anaerobic digestion occurs in four stages: hydrolysis, acidogenesis, acetogenesis, and methanogenesis.

- The first step in the breakdown of complex organic molecules into simpler ones is called hydrolysis. Hydrolytic bacteria produce extracellular enzymes that break down big molecules into sugars, amino acids, and fatty acids.
- Acidogenesis is the process by which acidogenic bacteria convert the byproducts of hydrolysis into volatile fatty acids (VFAs), organic acids, alcohols, and gases such as carbon dioxide and hydrogen.

Acetogenic bacteria produce acetic acid, hydrogen, and carbon dioxide as a result of the conversion of VFAs and intermediate products, which is essential for the creation of methane, the main precursor.

- The process of methanogenesis, which produces biogas from acetic acid and hydrogen, is the last step of anaerobic digestion. Methanogenic archaea use the products of acetogenesis to produce methane and carbon dioxide.

Microorganisms Involved in Organic Matter Degradation

An intricate microbial community made up of numerous microbial species collaborates in anaerobic digestion to break down organic materials. According to Chen et al. (2008) and Ward et al. (2008), the major microbial groupings include hydrolytic bacteria, acidogenic bacteria, acetogenic bacteria, and methanogenic archaea. By dissolving complex substances, hydrolytic bacteria create enzymes for proteins, carbohydrates, and lipids. Acidogenic bacteria convert the substances generated during hydrolysis into VFAs, alcohols, and organic acids, allowing for flexible metabolization. For the generation of precursors for methane creation, acetogenic bacteria convert VFAs and intermediates into acetic acid, hydrogen, and carbon dioxide. For maximum action in delicate conditions, methanogenic archaea—organisms that create methane via anaerobic digestion—need a steady pH and temperature.

Production and Composition of Biogas

Biogas, a combination of gases including methane, carbon dioxide, and other gases, is created during anaerobic digestion. Various elements, including feedstock, operational circumstances, and microbial community, affect the composition. Methane makes about 50–75% of biogas, along with 25–50% carbon dioxide and trace quantities of other gases. Methane is a useful renewable energy source that helps to reduce greenhouse gas emissions. Microorganisms aid in the processes of hydrolysis, acidogenesis, acetogenesis, and methanogenesis during anaerobic digestion, which turns organic waste into biogas (Ahring, 2003; Batstone et al., 2002). For optimal production and efficient use of this renewable energy source, it is essential to comprehend the concept, procedure, microorganisms, and composition of biogas. Successful projects employ anaerobic digestion to provide power, heat, and operate wastewater treatment facilities.

Through the use of combined heat and power (CHP) systems or biogas-fired generators, electricity may be produced from biogas, improving the energy efficiency of industrial operations as well as space and water heating. Additionally, it may be used to generate direct heat, heat buildings, dry crops, and heat industrial processes, all of which help to promote energy sustainability and lessen reliance on fossil fuels. Wastewater treatment and energy generation may be combined with anaerobic digestion, which can be incorporated into wastewater treatment facilities to enhance treatment procedures and recover energy. In order to handle wastewater, the municipal of Oslo in Norway built an anaerobic digestion facility. This facility generates biogas, which is then converted to biomethane and utilized as a sustainable fuel for municipal buses, lowering greenhouse gas emissions and fostering the circular economy.

Thames Water, a supplier of water and wastewater services in the UK, creates biogas from sewage sludge and food waste using anaerobic digestion plants. Energy self-sufficiency, cost savings, and the achievement of renewable energy goals are all facilitated by the use of this biogas for power production, treatment facilities, and grid excess (Angelidaki et al., 2003; Gujer & Zehnder, 1983; Van Lier et al., 2001). In Wisconsin, the Milwaukee Metropolitan Sewerage District has created a cutting-edge anaerobic digestion system that generates biogas from food scraps, fats, oils, and grease. This plant produces extra heat for on-site operations and nearby companies in addition to renewable power for approximately 2,500 residences.

In wastewater treatment facilities, anaerobic digestion generates power and heat, among other economic and environmental advantages. By turning garbage into useful resources, this strategy lowers greenhouse gas emissions, supports energy sustainability, and promotes a circular economy. Projects using anaerobic digestion provide effective wastewater treatment and energy recovery, helping to meet renewable energy goals and advance a sustainable future.

(MFCS) MICROBIAL FUEL CELLS

Microbial Fuel Cells are a promising technology that uses microbial metabolism to turn organic material into power. As a promising decentralized and environmentally friendly energy system, they combine organic matter degradation and electricity production to provide a novel approach to sustainable energy generation and wastewater treatment (Chen et al., 2008; Mohanakrishna et al., 2016; Ward et al., 2008).

Microbial Fuel Cell Principles

Extracellular electron transfer is used in microbial fuel cells to transport electrons from the oxidation of organic materials to an electrode and generate an electric current for use in a variety of applications (Chandrasekhar et al., 2020; Pant et al., 2010).

Microbial fuel cell components

Figure 1 depicts the elements of microbial fuel cells for the creation of energy and the transport of electrons.

- Anode: The anode is the electrode where organic material is oxidized. In order to improve electron transport, it is often composed of conductive

Figure 1. Components of microbial fuel cells

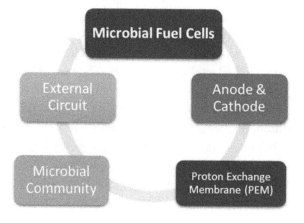

material like carbon cloth or graphite and coated with a catalyst like platinum or carbon nanotubes.

- Cathode: Reduction processes take place at the cathode electrode. Typically, it is formed of a substance like platinum or graphite that catalyses the reduction of oxygen. At the cathode, oxygen serves as an electron acceptor, joining with protons and electrons to create water.
- Proton Exchange Membrane (PEM): The PEM divides the fuel cell's two compartments by sitting in between the anode and the cathode. Protons may go through the PEM without combining the anode and cathode compartments. It makes it possible to produce a proton gradient, which propels the flow of electrons from the anode to the cathode.
- Microbial population: To carry out the oxidation of organic materials and transmit electrons to the anode, microbial fuel cells depend on a diversified microbial population. These microorganisms, also known as electrogenic bacteria, have special metabolic properties and build biofilms on the anode surface. Geobacter, Shewanella, and Pseudomonas species are a few examples of electrogenic bacteria that are often utilized.
- External Circuit: By connecting the anode and cathode, the external circuit enables the flow of electrons produced during microbial metabolism. Through the circuit, the electrons power external devices or recharge batteries.

Microbial Fuel Cells' Operational Principles

By oxidizing the organic stuff in the fuel, such as wastewater, microbial fuel cells produce electrons and protons. Electrogenic bacteria near the anode electrode help in the transport of electrons there. A proton gradient is produced by proton migration, which happens when protons move across the proton exchange membrane. At the cathode, oxygen is reduced, becoming water when it interacts with protons and electrons. The reduction process completes the electron transport route and produces an electric current that may power equipment or power storage.

Benefits and Uses of Microbial Fuel Cells

Microbial fuel cells (MFCs) provide renewable energy generation, low-energy sensors for sensor networks, and sustainable waste management in addition to sustainable energy production. They generate electricity from organic waste, which lessens reliance on traditional energy sources and enables long-term operation without the need for additional power sources.

Microbial fuel cells use the metabolic processes of microbes to turn organic material into energy. They function by extracellular electron transfer and have uses in sensor networks, bioenergy recovery, wastewater treatment, and the production of renewable energy. In mediator-based and mediator-less designs, MFCs provide environmentally responsible energy systems and environmental stewardship.

Energy Production through Microbiological Metabolism

Through metabolic processes, microorganisms break down chemical substances and release electrons as byproducts. Electrogenic bacteria transmit electrons directly to electrode surfaces, which is important for power production in MFCs (Liu et al., 2013; Pant et al., 2012). Organic matter oxidation, electron transfer, proton migration, electron acceptance at the cathode, and electricity generation all contribute to the energy production of MFCs. Organic material is oxidized by microorganisms in the anode chamber, releasing electrons and protons (H+). Protons go via the electrolyte or proton exchange membrane while electrons are transferred by electrogenic bacteria employing cytochromes. The electron transfer route is finished by an electron acceptor, such as molecular oxygen or another, creating water or reduced molecules.

MFC Configuration Types

MFCs may be divided into two categories according on whether a mediator is present or not:

Chemical mediators, such as ferricyanide or neutral red, are used in mediator-based systems to promote electron transport between bacteria and electrodes. These technologies increase transfer rates and broaden the selection of electrogenic microorganisms. Specialized outer membrane proteins or nanowires are used in mediator-less systems to make direct contact, which simplifies operation and lowers costs. Microbial fuel cells (MFCs) use chemical intermediaries for the transport of electrons while producing power via microbial metabolism. The two primary arrangements are mediator-based systems, which rely on chemical intermediaries, and mediator-less systems, which rely on direct electron transfer between bacteria and electrodes. Understanding these combinations is essential for improving MFC performance and investigating their potential use in wastewater treatment and sustainable energy production.

Applications of MFCs in the Production of Bioenergy and Wastewater Treatment

Especially in the fields of wastewater treatment and bioenergy generation, microbial fuel cells (MFCs) have shown considerable promise in a variety of applications. The special capacities of MFCs provide various benefits in these areas.

Water Treatment: By simultaneously treating wastewater and producing energy, MFCs provide a novel method of wastewater treatment. The MFC's microbes use the organic stuff in the wastewater as fuel, which encourages the breakdown of contaminants. MFCs provide energy recovery and nutrient removal in wastewater treatment, lowering energy demand and powering plants or grids, among other advantages of employing them in wastewater treatment. They enable microbial metabolism, transforming nutrients into less hazardous forms, and provide decentralised, sustainable, energy-efficient treatment in off-grid or distant sites.

MFCs provide a novel method for producing bioenergy by swiftly transforming organic matter into electricity. The bioenergy potential of MFCs comprises the following: By oxidizing organic matter, MFCs produce renewable electricity, making it possible for devices and batteries to be powered. They promote sustainable waste management by converting organic waste into biofuel. For off-grid populations, agricultural activities, and remote sensing systems, MFCs provide decentralized energy options.

MFCs combine energy production and wastewater treatment, encouraging resource recovery and environmental sustainability as benefits of MFC technology. They lessen their dependency on fossil fuels by using renewable resources like organic matter or wastewater. MFCs are appropriate for distant or off-grid applications because to their cheap running costs and energy recovery.

DESALINATION GEOTHERMAL

Geothermal energy is used in geothermal desalination to desalinate brackish or saltwater. This sustainable energy source uses heat that is naturally produced by the decay of materials like uranium, thorium, and potassium to extract heat from the Earth's crust. Conduction and convection processes are used to move the heat to the Earth's surface (Goosen et al., 2010; Gude, 2018; Kiaghadi et al., 2017). There are three primary categories of geothermal energy:

- High-Temperature Geothermal Energy: In areas where the Earth's crust is relatively thin, hot fluids and steam may rise closer to the surface, producing this form of geothermal energy. Geothermal resources that reach temperatures of 150 °C (302 °F) or above are ideal for steam turbine power production.
- Medium-Temperature Geothermal Energy: These resources have temperatures between 176°F and 302°F (80°C to 150°C). They may be used to direct heating tasks like district heating and space heating.

Low-temperature geothermal resources are those that have temperatures under 80°C (176°F). They are appropriate for several uses, such as desalination, water heating, and greenhouse heating.

Desalination Using Geothermal Energy

Geothermal energy may be utilized for desalination in areas with a limited supply of water, offering long-term solutions to the rising need for freshwater.

- Heat Source for Desalination: Thermal desalination and membrane-based desalination are two types of desalination technologies that may both use geothermal energy as a heat source. The heat produced may be utilized to make steam or as thermal energy for desalination.
- Thermal desalination methods: Multi-effect distillation (MED) and multi-stage flash (MSF) are two examples of thermal desalination systems that may make use of geothermal energy. These procedures include heating saltwater using geothermal energy to create steam, which is subsequently condensed to make freshwater.
- Hybrid Systems: To build hybrid systems, geothermal energy may be combined with other desalination methods. Reverse osmosis (RO) and geothermal heat, for instance, may be used to increase the desalination process' effectiveness while using less energy and enhancing system performance.

Geothermal desalination has advantages for the environment over conventional desalination techniques. It lessens reliance on fossil fuels and cuts down on greenhouse gas emissions brought on by desalination operations that need a lot of energy.

- Regional Suitability: Geothermal desalination is most suited for places with geothermal resources and water constraint, such as geothermal hot spots close to coastal areas. It offers a viable and accessible local alternative for the generation of freshwater.

For desalination applications, geothermal energy is a viable heat source, particularly when there are limited resources and water shortages. It may be incorporated with other technologies or employed in thermal procedures. Efficiency, cost-effectiveness, and environmental sustainability are all goals of research. Direct techniques and indirect approaches are the two basic categories.

Methods of Direct Geothermal Desalination

These techniques directly drive the desalination process using geothermal heat. According to these techniques, heat transfer takes place when geothermal fluid or steam comes into direct contact with the salty water (Gude, 2016; Kaczmarczyk et al., 2022). The two often used direct techniques are:

- Multi-Stage Flash (MSF) Desalination: MSF is a thermal desalination method that depends on salty water evaporating under decreased pressure. Freshwater is produced by condensing the steam that is produced by geothermal heat. The procedure involves a number of chambers or stages where the pressure is progressively reduced, resulting in the steaming of the water. Water is more easily evaporated and condensed at each cycle because each stage runs at a lower pressure and temperature. The residual brine is then separated from the freshwater that was collected during the condensation process.

Another thermal desalination method that makes use of geothermal heat is Multi-Effect Distillation (MED). Multiple evaporator units—referred to as effects—are stacked in sequence in MED. Every effect runs at a lower temperature and pressure than the one before it. Steam is produced using the geothermal heat and then transferred via the evaporator units. In each consequence, the steam warms the salt water, which causes it to evaporate. Multiple stages of evaporation and condensation are made possible by the fact that the vapour generated in one action serves as the heating source for the next. Condensation produces freshwater, which is collected as the brine is released.

Methods of Indirect Geothermal Desalination

Through the use of a heat exchanger, geothermal energy is used in these techniques to indirectly offer a heat source. Instead of coming into direct contact with the salty water, geothermal fluid or steam transfers heat to a secondary working fluid that is then employed in the desalination process. The two often used indirect techniques are:

- Reverse osmosis (RO) desalination: This membrane-based desalination technique uses a semi-permeable membrane to separate freshwater from salt water. Geothermal heat is utilized in indirect geothermal desalination to warm a secondary working fluid, such as a heat transfer fluid or a vapor compressor system. The temperature of the saline water supply before it reaches the reverse osmosis system is then raised using this heated fluid or vapor. By lowering water viscosity and promoting membrane performance, the increased temperature aids in increasing the effectiveness of the reverse osmosis procedure.

- Mechanical Vapor Compression (MVC) Desalination: This desalination method compresses vapor to raise its temperature and pressure. In indirect geothermal MVC, steam is produced from geothermal heat and mechanically compressed using a fan or a compressor. The salty water is subsequently heated by the compressed vapor, which causes it to evaporate. The leftover brine is released while the vapor is then condensed to create freshwater.

Saline water desalination processes use geothermal energy, including direct and indirect approaches. Availability of resources, required capacity, and application needs all influence the decision. In terms of efficiency, cost-effectiveness, and system complexity, each technique offers benefits and drawbacks. Enhancing performance and profitability for sustainable freshwater demand is the goal of research and development.

Combining Multiple-Effect Distillation (MED) and Reverse Osmosis (RO) with Geothermal Heat

Reverse osmosis (RO) and multiple-effect distillation (MED) desalination techniques may be efficiently combined with geothermal heat to improve overall performance. Let's look at how various techniques combine geothermal heat:

Multiple-Effect Distillation Using Geothermal Heat

Geothermal heat may be used as the main energy source in MED desalination to create steam for the evaporation process. A heat exchanger is where the geothermal fluid or steam is channeled so that it may heat the saline water supply. The MED system produces more freshwater because of the accelerated evaporation of water brought on by the greater temperature.

- Greater Efficiency: Geothermal heat offers MED a steady and dependable supply of energy. The geothermal fluid's high temperature enables quick and effective water evaporation in each effect, increasing freshwater output per unit of energy input.
- Enhanced Heat Recovery: The MED system can successfully recover and repurpose geothermal heat. The hot brine created by the condensation of steam in each effect may be utilized to heat the saline water supply in the next effects, further increasing energy efficiency.
- Lower Operating Costs: Compared to conventional fossil fuel-based energy, geothermal energy is a more affordable source of heat. Desalination can

be done more cheaply by using geothermal energy in MED, which lowers operational expenses.

Reverse Osmosis (RO) With Geothermal Energy

A membrane-based desalination method called reverse osmosis may gain from the incorporation of geothermal heat. Through the preheating of the saline water supply in this instance, geothermal heat is indirectly exploited to increase the efficiency of the RO process (Aghababaie et al., 2015; Xu et al., 2015; Yaqoob et al., 2021).

- Geothermal heat increases the temperature of the saline water supply, lowers water viscosity, and increases desalination efficiency, all of which enhance membrane performance. This lowers the need for energy, leading to energy savings and increased effectiveness. Higher temperatures also deter scaling and fouling, resulting in longer membrane lifetime and less frequent maintenance.

Geothermal Desalination Advantages in Terms of Cost- and Energy-Efficiency

In comparison to conventional desalination techniques, geothermal desalination has a number of advantages in terms of energy efficiency and cost-effectiveness: geothermal energy is a renewable and environmentally friendly solution for desalination, reducing reliance on fossil fuels and promoting sustainable freshwater production. It provides geothermal power generation synergy, high energy efficiency, reduced operational costs, localized and decentralized production, and synergy with both, maximizing resource utilization and cost-effectiveness. Desalination is becoming more economically feasible in areas with a wealth of geothermal resources.

Reverse osmosis desalination and multiple-effect distillation provide energy efficiency and cost-effectiveness when combined with geothermal heat. Geothermal energy offers a dependable, renewable source of heat that cuts down on energy use, operational expenses, and dependency on fossil fuels. Geothermal desalination is a practical method for producing freshwater, particularly in areas with a lack of water and rich resources. Desalination technologies are being improved via research and development in order to be widely used and have a sustainable water future.

CASE STUDIES OF EFFECTIVE GEOTHERMAL DESALINATION INITIATIVES

The Caribbean's Nevis Geothermal Desalination Plant

In order to alleviate the water shortage, the Caribbean island of Nevis has constructed a geothermal desalination plant. The project combines geothermal energy production with desalination, which uses leftover heat from the power plant. Geothermal fluid is removed from the subsurface reservoir to produce steam, which is then sent to the power generating unit to produce clean, renewable energy and desalinate water. The island's reliance on imported water is decreased by the desalination plant, which creates freshwater by repeatedly evaporating saltwater. By using renewable energy for both power generation and desalination, this successful example of integrating geothermal power generation with desalination lowers greenhouse gas emissions and highlights the advantages of waste heat for sustainable freshwater production (Kaczmarczyk et al., 2022; Kiaghadi et al., 2017).

Alaska's Akutan Geothermal-Powered Desalination Facility

Due to the shortage of freshwater resources, the island town of Akutan in Alaska has water scarcity. In order to solve this problem, a desalination facility driven by low-temperature geothermal resources was created. Reverse osmosis desalination uses waste heat while the ORC power production system produces energy. Through the removal of salt and contaminants, freshwater fit for drinking and other purposes is created. By eliminating reliance on expensive and ecologically hazardous water transport methods, the geothermal-powered desalination plant increases water security and self-sufficiency. The experiment shows that geothermal energy may be used to desalinate water in isolated areas with little access to freshwater resources.

Florida, USA: Green Cove Springs Geothermal Desalination Pilot Plant

Geothermal desalination for brackish water treatment has been successfully demonstrated at the Green Cove Springs Geothermal Desalination Pilot Plant in Florida. In the pilot plant, brackish water is heated before it enters the reverse osmosis (RO) system using a hybrid system that combines geothermal energy with RO desalination. This procedure lowers the energy needed to produce freshwater while increasing RO efficiency. The pilot plant offers important insights into energy efficacy, financial viability, and environmental sustainability while demonstrating the promise of geothermal desalination for brackish water treatment. Geothermal energy and desalination technology combination demonstrates the possibility for sustainable and green methods of freshwater production.

INTEGRATION OF IOT IN WASTEWATER BIOENERGY PROCESSES

The Internet of Things (IoT) is a network of linked systems, sensors, and gadgets that interact and share data online. With the improvement of operational effectiveness, resource optimization, and real-time monitoring and control, it has gained traction in the wastewater treatment industry. According to Boopathi, 2023a, Harikaran et al., 2023, Reddy et al., 2023, and Samikannu et al., 2023, IoT is a key factor in the transformation of energy generating systems in wastewater treatment facilities. Figure 2 depicts the integration of IOT in bioenergy from wastewater processes.

- Real-time monitoring and data collection: The Internet of Things (IoT) makes it possible to gather data in real-time from a variety of sensors placed all around the wastewater treatment facility. These sensors are capable of detecting variables including pH levels, temperature, dissolved oxygen levels, organic matter concentrations, and gas generation. Operators may learn more about how the anaerobic digestion process, microbial fuel cells, or any other bioenergy generating technologies installed into the plant are doing by regularly monitoring these metrics.
- Process Optimization and Control: The Internet of Things (IoT) makes it possible to use cutting-edge analytics and control algorithms to enhance the efficiency of bioenergy producing processes. Real-time sensor data

Figure 2. Integration of IOT in wastewater bioenergy processes

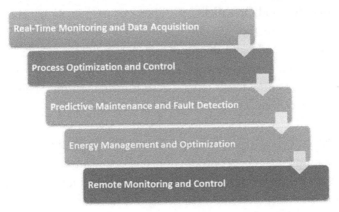

paired with machine learning algorithms may find patterns and correlations, enabling more accurate parameter management and energy production optimization. For instance, the Internet of Things (IoT) may maximize the generation of biogas by adjusting the rate at which organic matter is fed into anaerobic digesters (Boopathi, Balasubramani, et al., 2023; Gowri et al., 2023; Janardhana et al., 2023; Sathish et al., 2023; Yupapin et al., 2023).

- Predictive Maintenance and Fault Detection: The Internet of Things (IoT) makes it easier to do predictive maintenance by continually checking the state of the equipment and identifying future faults or failures. The analysis of sensor data and use of predictive analytics algorithms enable maintenance professionals to spot early indications of equipment deterioration or anomalies. As a result, preventative maintenance is possible, downtime is reduced, and the overall effectiveness of the bioenergy producing systems is maximized.

- Energy Management and Optimization: The Internet of Things (IoT) may be integrated with energy management systems to optimize energy production and consumption in wastewater treatment facilities. To make wise choices about energy consumption, storage, and grid interaction, real-time data on energy output from bioenergy processes, energy demand from different plant activities, and energy pricing may be employed. According to Boopathi (2019, 2021, 2022a, 2022c, 2022b, 2022d), this integration provides effective energy management, cost savings, and perhaps the involvement of wastewater treatment facilities in demand response programs.

- Remote Monitoring and Control: IoT makes it possible to remotely monitor and manage devices that produce bioenergy. Remote access to real-time data and parameter control by operators enables effective administration and troubleshooting without requiring on-site physical presence. This remote accessibility improves operational flexibility, speeds up problem-solving and decision-making, and decreases reaction times.

- Data Analytics and Optimization: Advanced data analytics and optimization can be done with the vast amounts of data that IoT devices generate. In order to find trends, optimize process parameters, forecast energy output, and boost overall effectiveness, machine learning algorithms may analyze both historical and current data. These information may help with resource allocation decisions and continuously improve processes.

Integration of IoT into wastewater bioenergy operations has advantages for increasing sustainability, energy production, and operating cost reduction. Resource management is improved and sustainable energy is generated as a result of the shift to smart, data-driven operations.

Components and IoT in Wastewater Treatment Working Process

In order to allow data collecting, monitoring, control, and optimization, IoT in wastewater treatment needs the integration of many components and devices (Boopathi, Siva Kumar, et al., 2023; Kumara et al., 2023; Selvakumar et al., 2023; Vanitha et al., 2023). An overview of the main elements and the operation of IoT in wastewater treatment is provided below:

Devices and Sensors

- Sensors: An array of sensors are used by IoT systems to detect and gather data on variables including pH levels, temperature, dissolved oxygen, flow rates, turbidity, and chemical concentrations. The influent, primary treatment, secondary treatment, and effluent phases of the wastewater treatment process are all possible deployment locations for these sensors.
- Data Loggers: Over time, data loggers gather and store sensor data. They are essential to continuous data gathering because they make it possible to gather real-time data for analysis and management.
- Actuators: In the wastewater treatment plant, actuators are used to control and regulate a number of processes, such as altering valves, pumps, or aeration systems. They get instructions from the IoT system based on algorithms for data analysis and optimization.

Figure 3. Components and IoT in wastewater treatment working process

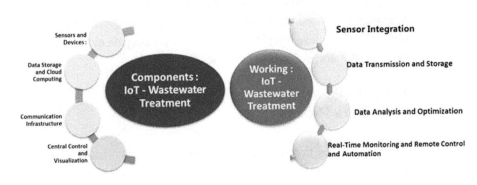

Communication Facilities

- Network connection: In order to communicate data from sensors to the main control system, IoT systems depend on network connection. Both conventional (Ethernet) and wireless (Wi-Fi, cellular, or satellite) communication methods may be used to accomplish this.
- Gateway Devices: Gateway devices serve as a bridge between the central control system and the sensors. They gather information from several sensors and send it to remote or local servers for archiving and analysis.

Cloud computing and data archiving

- Data Storage: The wastewater treatment plant's sensor data is kept in databases or cloud storage platforms. These databases make it possible to store, retrieve, and analyze historical data securely.
- Cloud Computing: Cloud platforms provide computing power and resources for machine learning, optimization techniques, and data analysis. Based on the gathered data, they allow sophisticated analytics and immediate decision-making.

Visualisation and Central Control

- Central Control System: The central control system serves as the IoT network's brain, processing and analyzing data so that it can be utilized to make choices and manage different parts of the wastewater treatment process.
- Data Analysis and Algorithms: To gain insights, spot trends, and optimize process parameters, advanced analytics algorithms, such as machine learning and artificial intelligence approaches, are used to the obtained data.
- Visualization Tools: Graphical user interfaces (GUIs), like as dashboards, provide a simple way to show data trends, process conditions, and performance indicators. Through these interfaces, operators may keep an eye on the system, examine the data, and come to wise conclusions.

Microbial Fuel Cells With IoT Support for Real-Time Data Processing

Microorganisms are used by microbial fuel cells (MFCs) to turn organic material into power. According to Babu et al. (2023), Boopathi, Arigela, et al. (2023), and Subha et al. (2023), MFCs may improve their performance and efficiency by incorporating IoT technology. IoT may be used in MFCs in the following ways:

- Sensor Integration: The Internet of Things (IoT) makes it possible to integrate different sensors into MFCs in order to gather real-time data on variables like voltage, current, temperature, pH levels, and microbial activity. These sensors provide useful information for analysis and control by continually monitoring the MFC's functionality and state.
- Data Transmission and Storage: Through wired or wireless connectivity, the gathered sensor data is sent to a central control system or cloud platform. This information is safely kept for future analysis and is accessible from a distance for management and monitoring needs.
- Data Analysis and Optimization: IoT makes it possible to apply sophisticated analytics algorithms to the data that has been gathered. It is possible to analyze trends, find connections, and improve MFC performance using machine learning algorithms. Understanding how microorganisms behave, increasing the effectiveness of electricity production, and improving operational conditions may all be aided by this approach?
- Real-Time Monitoring and Alerts: IoT makes it possible to monitor MFCs in real-time and get alerts when they are performing poorly. Any deviations from the required parameters may result in warnings or notifications, enabling operators to respond quickly to resolve problems and improve the operation of the system.
- Remote Control and Automation: MFCs may be automated and controlled remotely via IoT. Based on real-time data and analysis, operators may change parameters like organic matter content or aeration rates. This option for remote control improves operational effectiveness and enables rapid reactions to optimize electricity production and microbial activity.

Microbial fuel cells for the production of bioenergy may now be better understood, optimized, and controlled in real-time thanks to the integration of IoT in MFCs.

Systems for Geothermal Desalination That Use IoT-Based Automation and Control

Geothermal heat sources are used to power the desalination process in geothermal desalination systems, turning saltwater or brackish water into freshwater. According to Anitha et al., 2023, Boopathi, Arigela, et al., 2023, and Jeevanantham et al., 2023, IoT technology may be very useful in automating and managing these systems to maximize energy use and operational efficiency. IoT may be used in geothermal desalination in the following ways:

- Sensor Integration: The Internet of Things (IoT) makes it possible to integrate sensors to track vital geothermal desalination system characteristics including temperature, pressure, flow rates, and salt levels. In order to help operators make wise choices, these sensors give real-time data on the system's performance and ambient circumstances.

- Remote Monitoring and Control: The Internet of Things (IoT) enables operators to access real-time data and control parameters from a central control system or via mobile apps. This allows for remote monitoring of geothermal desalination systems. This remote accessibility makes it easier to operate systems effectively, diagnose issues, and tweak operational settings for the best results.

- Geothermal desalination systems may use IoT-based algorithms and analytics to optimize energy use. Adjusting operational parameters, such as flow rates, temperature differences, and heat transfer rates, may be done by analyzing real-time data on energy consumption, heat exchange efficiency, and environmental variables. In addition to maximizing energy efficiency, this optimization also lowers operating expenses.

- Problem diagnosis and Maintenance: The Internet of Things (IoT) offers continuous monitoring of system parameters, which enables early problem diagnosis in geothermal desalination systems. Operators may get warnings or messages when operational conditions deviate from standard ones, allowing them to quickly plan maintenance tasks and spot possible problems. To improve maintenance schedules and save downtime, predictive maintenance algorithms may also be used.

- Integration with Energy Management Systems: Geothermal desalination systems and energy management systems may be integrated via IoT. Better coordination between energy production, storage, and desalination processes is made possible by this integration. To maximize energy use and cost-effectiveness, demand response initiatives and real-time energy pricing may be used.

Geothermal desalination systems may increase operational effectiveness, energy optimization, remote monitoring, and maintenance by leveraging IoT-based control and automation. The sustainability and efficiency of geothermal-powered desalination processes are improved by this connection.

JOB STUDY

Control and automation in geothermal desalination systems using IoT capabilities

IoT was effectively used to geothermal desalination, energy production, and district heating at Iceland's Reykjanes Geothermal Power Plant. In addition, the facility uses waste heat from the production of power to desalinate saltwater using geothermal energy. According to many studies (Jeevanantham et al., 2023; Koshariya et al., 2023b; Reddy et al., 2023; Saha1 et al., 2022; Samikannu et al., 2023), the system's performance was greatly enhanced by the incorporation of IoT technology.

IoT Implementation

- Sensor Integration: The Reykjanes Power Plant's geothermal desalination system uses a variety of sensors to track vital indicators including temperature, pressure, flow rates, salt levels, and energy use. For the system to collect data in real time, these sensors are positioned in carefully chosen locations.
- Data Collection and Transmission: Through a dependable IoT network, the sensor data is gathered and delivered to a central control system. The network guarantees rapid and secure data delivery, enabling ongoing oversight and management.
- Remote Monitoring and Control: Operators have access to real-time data gathered from the sensors through the IoT-enabled central control system. Operators may make educated judgments about system parameters, energy consumption, and efficiency while remotely monitoring the geothermal desalination system's performance.
- Data Analysis and Optimization: To analyze trends, find correlations, and improve the performance of the geothermal desalination system, advanced analytics algorithms are used to the acquired data. The prediction and optimization of energy consumption, heat transfer rates, and operating parameters are made possible by machine learning approaches.
- Energy Optimization and Cost-Effectiveness: The Internet of Things-based automation and control allow for the geothermal desalination system to use energy more efficiently. Energy price data and real-time data on production and consumption are analyzed to change operational parameters to maximize energy efficiency and minimize operating expenses.

Geothermal desalination at Reykjanes Power Plant is improved by the incorporation of IoT technology, which has several advantages.

- Greater Operational Efficiency: System performance and energy consumption have been optimized by operators thanks to real-time monitoring and management of the geothermal desalination system. Improved freshwater production efficiency has resulted from changes to operating settings based on real-time data analysis.

- Energy Optimization: By using real-time data on energy use and price, the IoT-enabled system has permitted the optimization of energy usage. Costs were reduced as a consequence of this optimization, which also increased sustainability.

- Remote Monitoring and Maintenance: Geothermal desalination systems may now be monitored remotely, reducing the requirement for on-site presence and enabling effective monitoring, troubleshooting, and maintenance procedures. Early defect identification and preventative maintenance have reduced downtime and made sure everything is running smoothly.

- Enhanced Sustainability: The geothermal desalination process is now more sustainably run as a result of the inclusion of IoT technology. The facility has produced freshwater in a way that is both more ecologically friendly and economically feasible by optimizing energy use and lowering operating expenses.

IoT has the potential to improve the effectiveness, performance, and sustainability of geothermal-powered desalination operations, as shown by the Reykjanes Power Plant's successful use of IoT-enabled control and automation in its geothermal desalination system. This case study highlights the useful advantages of IoT integration in geothermal desalination systems, showing how it has a favorable effect on freshwater production and resource optimization.

CONCLUSION

The combined difficulties of wastewater treatment and energy sustainability may be addressed with the help of cutting-edge technologies including geothermal desalination, anaerobic digestion, microbial fuel cells, and IoT integration. Organic material is transformed into biogas by anaerobic digestion, a sustainable energy source that may be utilized to generate power and heat. Microbial fuel cells (MFCs) allow for the simultaneous treatment of wastewater and production of renewable energy by using microorganisms' metabolic activities to turn organic materials into electricity. By converting salty or brackish water into freshwater using heat from geothermal sources, geothermal desalination lessens the need for fossil fuels and has a less negative effect on the environment. Geothermal desalination systems and bioenergy from wastewater processes can gather, monitor, regulate, and optimize data in real-time thanks to IoT connectivity.

Case studies like the Reykjanes Geothermal Power Plant show how these technologies may be successfully implemented, leading to increased operational efficiency, energy optimization, remote monitoring, and maintenance, as well as cost-effectiveness and sustainability. A more sustainable and resilient future may be achieved by combining sustainable energy generation from wastewater with cutting-edge technology to effectively treat wastewater, produce bioenergy, and provide freshwater.

REFERENCES

Aftab, S., Shah, A., Nisar, J., Ashiq, M. N., Akhter, M. S., & Shah, A. H. (2020). Marketability Prospects of Microbial Fuel Cells for Sustainable Energy Generation. *Energy & Fuels*, *34*(8), 9108–9136. doi:10.1021/acs.energyfuels.0c01766

Aghababaie, M., Farhadian, M., Jeihanipour, A., & Biria, D. (2015). Effective factors on the performance of microbial fuel cells in wastewater treatment–a review. *Environmental Technology Reviews*, *4*(1), 71–89. doi:10.1080/09593330.2015.10 77896

Ahring, B. K. (2003). Perspectives for anaerobic digestion. *Advances in Biochemical Engineering/Biotechnology*, *81*, 1–30. doi:10.1007/3-540-45839-5_1 PMID:12747559

Angelidaki, I., Ellegaard, L., & Ahring, B. K. (2003). Applications of the anaerobic digestion process. *Advances in Biochemical Engineering/Biotechnology*, *82*, 1–33. doi:10.1007/3-540-45838-7_1 PMID:12747564

Anitha, C., Komala, C. R., Vivekanand, C. V., Lalitha, S. D., Boopathi, S., & Revathi, R. (2023, February). Artificial Intelligence driven security model for Internet of Medical Things (IoMT). *Proceedings of 2023 3rd International Conference on Innovative Practices in Technology and Management, ICIPTM 2023*. IEEE. 10.1109/ICIPTM57143.2023.10117713

Babu, B. S., Kamalakannan, J., Meenatchi, N., M, S. K. S., S, K., & Boopathi, S. (2023). Economic impacts and reliability evaluation of battery by adopting Electric Vehicle. *IEEE Explore*, 1–6. doi:10.1109/ICPECTS56089.2022.10046786

Batstone, D. J., Keller, J., Angelidaki, I., Kalyuzhnyi, S. V., Pavlostathis, S. G., Rozzi, A., Sanders, W. T., Siegrist, H., & Vavilin, V. A. (2002). The IWA Anaerobic Digestion Model No 1 (ADM1). *Water Science and Technology : A Journal of the International Association on Water Pollution Research*, *45*(10), 65–73. doi:10.2166/wst.2002.0292

Boopathi, S. (2019). Experimental investigation and parameter analysis of LPG refrigeration system using Taguchi method. *SN Applied Sciences, 1*(8), 892. doi:10.1007/s42452-019-0925-2

Boopathi, S. (2021). Improving of Green Sand-Mould Quality using Taguchi Technique. *Journal of Engineering Research*. doi:10.36909/jer.14079

Boopathi, S. (2022a). An experimental investigation of Quench Polish Quench (QPQ) coating on AISI 4150 steel. *Engineering Research Express, 4*(4), 45009. doi:10.1088/2631-8695/ac9ddd

Boopathi, S. (2022b). Cryogenically treated and untreated stainless steel grade 317 in sustainable wire electrical discharge machining process: A comparative study. *Environmental Science and Pollution Research International, 30*(44), 1–10. doi:10.1007/s11356-022-22843-x PMID:36057706

Boopathi, S. (2022c). Experimental investigation and multi-objective optimization of cryogenic Friction-stir-welding of AA2014 and AZ31B alloys using MOORA technique. *Materials Today. Communications, 33*, 104937. doi:10.1016/j.mtcomm.2022.104937

Boopathi, S. (2022d). Performance Improvement of Eco-Friendly Near-Dry Wire-Cut Electrical Discharge Machining Process Using Coconut Oil-Mist Dielectric Fluid. *Journal of Advanced Manufacturing Systems*. doi:10.1142/S0219686723500178

Boopathi, S. (2023a). An Investigation on Friction Stir Processing of Aluminum Alloy-Boron Carbide Surface Composite. In *Materials Horizons: From Nature to Nanomaterials* (pp. 249–257). Springer. doi:10.1007/978-981-19-7146-4_14

Boopathi, S. (2023b). Deep Learning Techniques Applied for Automatic Sentence Generation. In Promoting Diversity, Equity, and Inclusion in Language Learning Environments (pp. 255–273). IGI Global. doi:10.4018/978-1-6684-3632-5.ch016

Boopathi, S. (2023c). Internet of Things-Integrated Remote Patient Monitoring System: Healthcare Application. In *Dynamics of Swarm Intelligence Health Analysis for the Next Generation* (pp. 137–161). IGI Global. doi:10.4018/978-1-6684-6894-4.ch008

Boopathi, S., Arigela, S. H., Raman, R., Indhumathi, C., Kavitha, V., & Bhatt, B. C. (2023). Prominent Rule Control-based Internet of Things: Poultry Farm Management System. *IEEE Explore*, (pp. 1–6). IEEE. doi:10.1109/ICPECTS56089.2022.10047039

Boopathi, S., Balasubramani, V., & Sanjeev Kumar, R. (2023). Influences of various natural fibers on the mechanical and drilling characteristics of coir-fiber-based hybrid epoxy composites. *Engineering Research Express*, 5(1), 15002. doi:10.1088/2631-8695/acb132

Boopathi, S., & Myilsamy, S. (2021). Material removal rate and surface roughness study on Near-dry wire electrical discharge Machining process. *Materials Today: Proceedings*, 45(9), 8149–8156. doi:10.1016/j.matpr.2021.02.267

Boopathi, S., Siva Kumar, P. K., & Meena, R. S. J., S. I., P., S. K., & Sudhakar, M. (2023). Sustainable Developments of Modern Soil-Less Agro-Cultivation Systems. In Human Agro-Energy Optimization for Business and Industry (pp. 69–87). IGI Global. doi:10.4018/978-1-6684-4118-3.ch004

Chandrasekhar, K., Kumar, G., Venkata Mohan, S., Pandey, A., Jeon, B. H., Jang, M., & Kim, S. H. (2020). Microbial Electro-Remediation (MER) of hazardous waste in aid of sustainable energy generation and resource recovery. *Environmental Technology & Innovation*, 19, 100997. doi:10.1016/j.eti.2020.100997

Chen, Y., Cheng, J. J., & Creamer, K. S. (2008). Inhibition of anaerobic digestion process: A review. *Bioresource Technology*, 99(10), 4044–4064. doi:10.1016/j.biortech.2007.01.057 PMID:17399981

Goosen, M., Mahmoudi, H., & Ghaffour, N. (2010). Water Desalination using geothermal energy. *Energies*, 3(8), 1423–1442. doi:10.3390/en3081423

Gowri, N. V., Dwivedi, J. N., Krishnaveni, K., Boopathi, S., Palaniappan, M., & Medikondu, N. R. (2023). Experimental investigation and multi-objective optimization of eco-friendly near-dry electrical discharge machining of shape memory alloy using Cu/SiC/Gr composite electrode. *Environmental Science and Pollution Research International*, 0123456789(49), 1–19. doi:10.1007/s11356-023-26983-6 PMID:37126160

Gude, V. G. (2016). Geothermal source potential for water desalination - Current status and future perspective. *Renewable & Sustainable Energy Reviews*, 57, 1038–1065. doi:10.1016/j.rser.2015.12.186

Gude, V. G. (2018). Geothermal Source for Water Desalination-Challenges and Opportunities. *Renewable Energy Powered Desalination Handbook: Application and Thermodynamics*, 141–176. doi:10.1016/B978-0-12-815244-7.00004-0

Gujer, W., & Zehnder, A. J. B. (1983). Conversion processes in anaerobic digestion. *Water Science and Technology*, 15(8–9), 127–167. doi:10.2166/wst.1983.0164

Guo, Z., Sun, Y., Pan, S. Y., & Chiang, P. C. (2019). Integration of green energy and advanced energy-efficient technologies for municipal wastewater treatment plants. *International Journal of Environmental Research and Public Health, 16*(7), 1282. doi:10.3390/ijerph16071282 PMID:30974807

Haribalaji, V., Boopathi, S., & Asif, M. M. (2021). Optimization of friction stir welding process to join dissimilar AA2014 and AA7075 aluminum alloys. *Materials Today: Proceedings, 50*, 2227–2234. doi:10.1016/j.matpr.2021.09.499

Harikaran, M., Boopathi, S., Gokulakannan, S., & Poonguzhali, M. (2023). Study on the Source of E-Waste Management and Disposal Methods. In *Sustainable Approaches and Strategies for E-Waste Management and Utilization* (pp. 39–60). IGI Global. doi:10.4018/978-1-6684-7573-7.ch003

Janardhana, K., Anushkannan, N. K., Dinakaran, K. P., Puse, R. K., & Boopathi, S. (2023). Experimental Investigation on Microhardness, Surface Roughness, and White Layer Thickness of Dry EDM. *Engineering Research Express, 5*(2), 025022. doi:10.1088/2631-8695/acce8f

Jeevanantham, Y. A., A, S., V, V., J, S. I., Boopathi, S., & Kumar, D. P. (2023). Implementation of Internet-of Things (IoT) in Soil Irrigation System. *IEEE Explore*, (pp. 1–5). IEEE. doi:10.1109/ICPECTS56089.2022.10047185

Kaczmarczyk, M., Tomaszewska, B., & Bujakowski, W. (2022). Innovative desalination of geothermal wastewater supported by electricity generated from low-enthalpy geothermal resources. *Desalination, 524*, 115450. doi:10.1016/j.desal.2021.115450

Karn, A. L., Pandya, S., Mehbodniya, A., Arslan, F., Sharma, D. K., Phasinam, K., Aftab, M. N., Rajan, R., Bommisetti, R. K., & Sengan, S. (2021). An integrated approach for sustainable development of wastewater treatment and management system using IoT in smart cities. *Soft Computing*, 1–17. doi:10.1007/s00500-021-06244-9

Kiaghadi, A., Sobel, R. S., & Rifai, H. S. (2017). Modeling geothermal energy efficiency from abandoned oil and gas wells to desalinate produced water. *Desalination, 414*, 51–62. doi:10.1016/j.desal.2017.03.024

Koshariya, A. K., Kalaiyarasi, D., Jovith, A. A., Sivakami, T., Hasan, D. S., & Boopathi, S. (2023a). AI-Enabled IoT and WSN-Integrated Smart Agriculture System. In *Artificial Intelligence Tools and Technologies for Smart Farming and Agriculture Practices* (pp. 200–218). IGI Global. doi:10.4018/978-1-6684-8516-3.ch011

Koshariya, A. K., Kalaiyarasi, D., Jovith, A. A., Sivakami, T., Hasan, D. S., & Boopathi, S. (2023b). AI-Enabled IoT and WSN-Integrated Smart. *Practice, Progress, and Proficiency in Sustainability*, 200–218. doi:10.4018/978-1-6684-8516-3.ch011

Kumara, V., Mohanaprakash, T. A., Fairooz, S., Jamal, K., Babu, T., & B., S. (2023). Experimental Study on a Reliable Smart Hydroponics System. In *Human Agro-Energy Optimization for Business and Industry* (pp. 27–45). IGI Global. doi:10.4018/978-1-6684-4118-3.ch002

Liu, Y., Liu, H., Wang, C., Hou, S. X., & Yang, N. (2013). Sustainable energy recovery in wastewater treatment by microbial fuel cells: Stable power generation with nitrogen-doped graphene cathode. *Environmental Science & Technology*, *47*(23), 13889–13895. doi:10.1021/es4032216 PMID:24219223

Llácer-Iglesias, R. M., López-Jiménez, P. A., & Pérez-Sánchez, M. (2021). Hydropower technology for sustainable energy generation in wastewater systems: Learning from the experience. *Water (Basel)*, *13*(22), 3259. doi:10.3390/w13223259

Meneses-Jácome, A., Diaz-Chavez, R., Velásquez-Arredondo, H. I., Cárdenas-Chávez, D. L., Parra, R., & Ruiz-Colorado, A. A. (2016). Sustainable Energy from agro-industrial wastewaters in Latin-America. *Renewable & Sustainable Energy Reviews*, *56*, 1249–1262. doi:10.1016/j.rser.2015.12.036

Mohanakrishna, G., Srikanth, S., & Pant, D. (2016). Bioprocesses for waste and wastewater remediation for sustainable energy. In *Bioremediation and Bioeconomy* (pp. 537–565). Elsevier. doi:10.1016/B978-0-12-802830-8.00021-6

Palaniappan, M., Tirlangi, S., Mohamed, M. J. S., Moorthy, R. M. S., Valeti, S. V., & Boopathi, S. (2023). Fused Deposition Modelling of Polylactic Acid (PLA)-Based Polymer Composites. In Development, Properties, and Industrial Applications of 3D Printed Polymer Composites (pp. 66–85). IGI Global. doi:10.4018/978-1-6684-6009-2.ch005

Pant, D., Singh, A., Van Bogaert, G., Irving Olsen, S., Singh Nigam, P., Diels, L., & Vanbroekhoven, K. (2012). Bioelectrochemical systems (BES) for sustainable energy production and product recovery from organic wastes and industrial wastewaters. *RSC Advances*, *2*(4), 1248–1263. doi:10.1039/C1RA00839K

Pant, D., Van Bogaert, G., Diels, L., & Vanbroekhoven, K. (2010). A review of the substrates used in microbial fuel cells (MFCs) for sustainable energy production. *Bioresource Technology*, *101*(6), 1533–1543. doi:10.1016/j.biortech.2009.10.017 PMID:19892549

Radeef, A. Y., & Ismail, Z. Z. (2021). Bioelectrochemical treatment of actual carwash wastewater associated with sustainable energy generation in three-dimensional microbial fuel cell. *Bioelectrochemistry (Amsterdam, Netherlands), 142*, 107925. doi:10.1016/j.bioelechem.2021.107925 PMID:34392137

Reddy, M. A., Reddy, B. M., Mukund, C. S., Venneti, K., Preethi, D. M. D., & Boopathi, S. (2023). Social Health Protection During the COVID-Pandemic Using IoT. In *The COVID-19 Pandemic and the Digitalization of Diplomacy* (pp. 204–235). IGI Global. doi:10.4018/978-1-7998-8394-4.ch009

Samikannu, R., Koshariya, A. K., Poornima, E., Ramesh, S., Kumar, A., & Boopathi, S. (2023). Sustainable Development in Modern Aquaponics Cultivation Systems Using IoT Technologies. In *Human Agro-Energy Optimization for Business and Industry* (pp. 105–127). IGI Global. doi:10.4018/978-1-6684-4118-3.ch006

Sampath, B., Pandian, M., Deepa, D., & Subbiah, R. (2022). Operating parameters prediction of liquefied petroleum gas refrigerator using simulated annealing algorithm. *AIP Conference Proceedings, 2460*(1), 70003. doi:10.1063/5.0095601

Sathish, T., Sunagar, P., Singh, V., Boopathi, S., Sathyamurthy, R., Al-Enizi, A. M., Pandit, B., Gupta, M., & Sehgal, S. S. (2023). Characteristics estimation of natural fibre reinforced plastic composites using deep multi-layer perceptron (MLP) technique. *Chemosphere, 337*(June), 139346. doi:10.1016/j.chemosphere.2023.139346 PMID:37379988

Selvakumar, S., Adithe, S., Isaac, J. S., Pradhan, R., Venkatesh, V., & Sampath, B. (2023). A Study of the Printed Circuit Board (PCB) E-Waste Recycling Process. In Sustainable Approaches and Strategies for E-Waste Management and Utilization (pp. 159–184). IGI Global.

Subha, S., Inbamalar, T. M., Komala, C. R., Suresh, L. R., Boopathi, S., & Alaskar, K. (2023, February). A Remote Health Care Monitoring system using internet of medical things (IoMT). *Proceedings of 2023 3rd International Conference on Innovative Practices in Technology and Management, ICIPTM 2023.* IEEE. 10.1109/ICIPTM57143.2023.10118103

Van Lier, J. B., Tilche, A., Ahring, B. K., Macarie, H., Moletta, R., Dohanyos, M., Hulshoff Pol, L. W., Lens, P., & Verstraete, W. (2001). New perspectives in anaerobic digestion. *Water Science and Technology, 43*(1), 1–18. doi:10.2166/wst.2001.0001 PMID:11379079

Vanitha, S. K. R., & Boopathi, S. (2023). Artificial Intelligence Techniques in Water Purification and Utilization. In *Human Agro-Energy Optimization for Business and Industry* (pp. 202–218). IGI Global. doi:10.4018/978-1-6684-4118-3.ch010

Ward, A. J., Hobbs, P. J., Holliman, P. J., & Jones, D. L. (2008). Optimisation of the anaerobic digestion of agricultural resources. *Bioresource Technology, 99*(17), 7928–7940. doi:10.1016/j.biortech.2008.02.044 PMID:18406612

Xu, B., Ge, Z., & He, Z. (2015). Sediment microbial fuel cells for wastewater treatment: Challenges and opportunities. *Environmental Science. Water Research & Technology, 1*(3), 279–284. doi:10.1039/C5EW00020C

Yaqoob, A. A., Ibrahim, M. N. M., Umar, K., Parveen, T., Ahmad, A., Lokhat, D., & Setapar, S. H. M. (2021). A glimpse into the microbial fuel cells for wastewater treatment with energy generation. *Desalination and Water Treatment, 214*, 379–389. doi:10.5004/dwt.2021.26737

Yupapin, P., Trabelsi, Y., Nattappan, A., & Boopathi, S. (2023). Performance Improvement of Wire-Cut Electrical Discharge Machining Process Using Cryogenically Treated Super-Conductive State of Monel-K500 Alloy. *Iranian Journal of Science and Technology. Transaction of Mechanical Engineering, 47*(1), 267–283. doi:10.1007/s40997-022-00513-0

Chapter 4
Literature Review on Supply Chains Optimization Using Multi–Agents Communication and Collaboration

Imad Eddine Khiloun
SIMPA Laboratory, University of Science and Technology of Oran Mohamed-Boudiaf, Algeria

Karima Belmabrouk
iD https://orcid.org/0000-0003-1157-1274
University of Science and Technology of Oran Mohamed-Boudiaf, Algeria

Latifa Dekhici
iD https://orcid.org/0000-0002-9581-6488
University of Science and Technology of Oran Mohamed-Boudiaf, Algeria

ABSTRACT

This book chapter provides a concise yet comprehensive exploration of supply chain optimization through a multi-agent approach. Spanning historical foundations to contemporary intelligent methodologies, the literature review examines communication, collaboration, and coordination methods between agents. The analysis reveals achievements and challenges, emphasizing the pivotal role of intelligent agents in enhancing decision-making and adaptability. The chapter serves as a valuable resource for researchers and practitioners, offering insights into the dynamic landscape of supply chain management within the context of multi-agent systems. Through this exploration, the chapter contributes to shaping the future of resilient and efficient supply chain networks.

DOI: 10.4018/979-8-3693-1418-0.ch004

INTRODUCTION

We live in a world where supply chains form the backbone of our global economy, and their optimization is crucial for ensuring not only economic efficiency but also environmental responsibility.

In recent years, the concept of supply chain optimization has evolved beyond traditional approaches, thanks to advancements in technology. One such innovative paradigm that holds immense promise is the integration of multi-agent communication and collaboration into supply chain management.

Within these pages, we will delve into the intricacies of how intelligent agents, akin to entities with unique capabilities, can reshape the dynamics of supply chains. Our focus is not merely on efficiency but on a greener, more sustainable approach to supply chain orchestration. As the global community increasingly recognizes the imperative for environmental responsibility, the concept of green supply chains emerges as a beacon of hope.

The goal is clear: to unravel the potential within multi-agent systems for optimizing supply chains, steering them towards a path of environmental consciousness. The narrative unfolds against the backdrop of a world that demands more than just efficiency, it yearns for supply chains that actively contribute to sustainability goals.

Through these pages, using the multi-agent communication and collaboration, we will unravel the potential to redefine traditional supply chain practices. As we delve into the state of the art, we'll navigate the evolving landscape where intelligent agents orchestrate a harmonious flow of information, driving optimization and innovation throughout the supply chain.

SUPPLY CHAINS

A supply chain is the intricate network of activities and entities involved in the creation, production, distribution, and delivery of goods or services. It encompasses all the steps from the origin, like raw material extraction or manufacturing, to the final consumption by end users. This network includes various stages such as procurement, production, transportation, warehousing, and retail. In essence, a supply chain represents the entire journey a product or service takes from conception to reaching the hands of consumers, involving multiple stakeholders like suppliers, manufacturers, distributors, retailers, and end consumers. The goal of effective supply chain management is to optimize these processes for efficiency, cost-effectiveness, and timely delivery, while also considering factors like sustainability and ethical practices (Lu, 2011).

Supply Chain Steps

The supply chain network can be divided into several steps:

1) Supplier Selection and Sourcing: Identification and selection of suppliers who provide the necessary raw materials or components for the production process.
2) Procurement: Negotiation of contracts and agreements with selected suppliers to acquire the required raw materials or components.
3) Manufacturing: Transforming raw materials into finished goods through the manufacturing or production process.
4) Quality Control: Ensuring the quality of the manufactured products before moving forward in the supply chain.
5) Packaging and Labeling: Packaging the finished goods appropriately for protection during transportation and labeling them for identification.
6) Warehousing and Distribution: Storing the finished products in warehouses, managing inventory, and distributing products to various locations.
7) Order Processing: Receiving and process orders from retailers or end customers, which includes checking pricing, discounts, and product availability in inventory.
8) Inventory Allocation: Allocating inventory based on the orders received, ensuring that products are available for shipment.
9) Order Confirmation: Confirming orders with customers, providing details such as shipping dates and tracking information.
10) Transportation: Using various modes of transportation (trucks, planes, ships, trains) to move products from distribution centers to their final destinations.
11) Retailing: Products are made available to consumers through retailers, either physical stores or online platforms.
12) Sales Transactions: Consumers purchase the products through sales transactions at retail outlets.
13) Customer Delivery: Delivering the product to the end customer, either directly from the distribution center or through retailers.
14) After-Sales Support: Providing support services, such as warranties or maintenance, to customers after the sale.

Supply Chains Problems and the Need for the Optimization

In the intricate landscape of modern supply chains, a myriad of challenges poses significant hurdles to the seamless flow of goods and services. These challenges span from logistical intricacies and fluctuating market demands to environmental concerns and ethical considerations. The dynamic nature of these challenges necessitates a

Figure 1. Supply chain entities and their roles

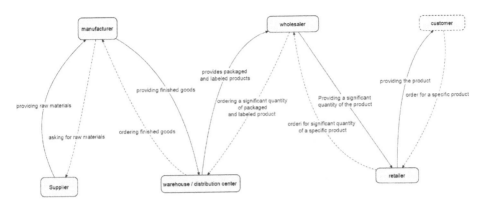

strategic approach to not only mitigate risks but also to optimize the entire supply chain. Amidst these challenges, the imperative for sustainability stands out as a paramount concern. The traditional linear supply chain models often fall short in addressing the environmental and social impacts of operations. In an era where environmental consciousness is increasingly vital, the need to align supply chain practices with sustainability principles becomes imperative (Mujkić et al., 2018).

Modern supply chains face some serious challenges and problems that need to be solved in order to optimize and to manage the whole supply chain network, including: 1) Supply Chain Disruptions: events such as natural disasters, geopolitical tensions, and global pandemics can disrupt the flow of goods and materials. These disruptions can lead to delays in production, shortages, and increased costs. 2) Inventory Management Issues: poor inventory management can result in overstocking or stockouts. Overstocking ties up capital and warehouse space, while stockouts can lead to missed sales opportunities and dissatisfied customers. 3) Demand Forecasting Challenges: accurate demand forecasting is essential for optimal inventory levels. Fluctuating consumer demand, seasonality, and unforeseen market trends can make accurate predictions challenging. 4) Supplier Relationship Management: ineffective communication with suppliers, lack of transparency, and reliance on a limited number of suppliers can lead to issues such as delayed deliveries, quality problems, and increased vulnerability to supply chain disruptions. 5) Globalization Complexity: global supply chains involve coordination across different countries, each with its own regulations, customs procedures, and logistics challenges. Cultural differences and varying legal frameworks can complicate operations. 6) Transportation Challenges: transportation bottlenecks, rising fuel costs, and inefficient logistics can result in delays, increased costs, and environmental concerns. Last-mile delivery challenges in urban areas add an additional layer of complexity. 7) Data Security and Cybersecurity Risks: the increasing reliance on digital technologies makes supply chains vulnerable to cyber threats. Data breaches can compromise sensitive information, disrupt operations, and erode customer trust. 8) Sustainability and Environmental Concerns: growing awareness of environmental issues puts pressure on companies to adopt sustainable practices. Balancing economic goals with environmental responsibility can be challenging and requires strategic planning. 9) Regulatory Compliance: navigating complex and evolving regulatory environments, including customs regulations, trade tariffs, and environmental standards, can be demanding and may result in compliance-related issues. 10) Talent Shortages and Skills Gap: the supply chain industry is facing a shortage of skilled professionals. The rapid evolution of technology requires a workforce with expertise in data analytics, automation, and other advanced technologies. 11) Lack of End-to-End Visibility: limited visibility across the entire supply chain can lead to inefficiencies and difficulties in identifying and resolving issues promptly. Real-time data and analytics are crucial for enhancing visibility (Timothy, 2023).

The interplay between the problems faced by modern supply chains and the growing emphasis on sustainability creates a compelling case for optimization. Optimization in this context involves the strategic reconfiguration of supply chain processes to enhance efficiency, reduce waste, and minimize environmental impact. It is about finding a delicate balance where economic objectives align seamlessly with ecological and social responsibility. Efforts to optimize modern supply chains must take into account the entire life cycle of a product, from raw material extraction to manufacturing, distribution, and eventual disposal. This holistic perspective ensures that each phase of the supply chain contributes to, rather than detracts from, the overarching goal of sustainability.

In the pursuit of optimization, technological advancements play a pivotal role. Innovations such as data analytics, artificial intelligence, and the Internet of Things provide tools to enhance visibility, streamline processes, and make data-driven decisions. These technologies empower supply chain managers to identify inefficiencies, predict disruptions, and implement proactive measures. Furthermore, collaboration across the supply chain ecosystem becomes instrumental. Close collaboration with suppliers, manufacturers, distributors, and other stakeholders fosters a shared commitment to sustainability goals. It also facilitates the exchange of best practices and the implementation of collective strategies to address challenges.

Multi-Agent Systems as a Representation for the Supply Chain

In the intricate web of the supply chain, a multitude of stakeholders plays vital roles: suppliers, manufacturers, distributors, logistics providers, wholesalers, retailers, and customers. It becomes imperative to establish an efficient framework for collaboration

Figure 2. The characteristics of intelligent agents (Brenner et al., 1998)

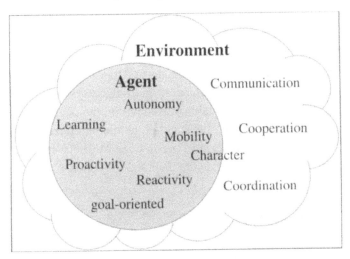

and communication among these entities to effectively manage and optimize the supply chain. Multi-agent systems offer a viable solution for handling the inherent complexity of communication between these diverse entities (Karunananda & Perera, 2016). Considering the supply chain's inherently distributed nature, characterized by numerous entities, it can be conceptualized as a multi-agent system. In this paradigm, each entity is represented as a distinct agent, as noted by (Terrada et al., 2020). This perspective prompts an exploration of intelligent agents' technology as a preliminary step before delving into the intricacies of multi-agent systems.

Accordin to (Chowdhary, 2020), agents are entities that take perception or input from the environment using its sensors, then perform actions on the environment using its effectors, they are reactive and proactive, reactive means that they can react or respond to the changes of the environment, proactive means that they have plans, and they can perform actions in order to achieve their future goals.

Intelligent agents have some other common characteristics such as autonomy, proactivity, reactivity, having a specific goal, the ability to communicate with other agents or programs, figure II.2 (Brenner et al., 1998) shows the characteristics of intelligent agents.

A multi-agent system comprises multiple agents, each possessing distinct goals, knowledge, and perspectives on the world. The system's objective is to facilitate communication and collaboration among these agents, enabling them to achieve individual, collective goals or both of them. In scenarios where organizations or individuals have diverse or conflicting objectives and proprietary information, multi-agent systems become indispensable for managing their interactions (Chowdhary, 2020).

Within the context of the supply chain, every entity (suppliers, manufacturers, distributors, retailers, etc.) is conceptualized as an autonomous agent. Each agent harbors its unique goals, preferences, and environmental outlook, inevitably leading to potential conflicts. For instance, a retailer and a manufacturing facility may simultaneously order the last available product from a supplier, creating a conflict within the supply chain. In such instances, multi-agent systems prove invaluable, demonstrating their capability to establish efficient communication and coordination among supply chain entities (e.g., the supplier, retailer, and manufacturing facility in our example). This functionality aims to eliminate conflicts, enhance information sharing, and empower agents to execute their actions concurrently.

LITERATURE REVIEW

In a multi-agent system designed to optimize the supply chain, the necessity of communication, collaboration, and coordination among agents is paramount. And there are some key reasons why these elements are crucial:

1) Efficient Decision-Making: collaborative decision-making is enhanced through communication and coordination. Agents can jointly analyze data, evaluate options, and make decisions that align with the overall goals of the supply chain, leading to more efficient outcomes.

2) Optimized Order Fulfillment: efficient collaboration ensures that orders are fulfilled optimally. For instance, manufacturers can coordinate with distributors and retailers to align production schedules with demand forecasts, reducing lead times and improving customer satisfaction.

3) Enhanced Visibility: communication and coordination contribute to increased visibility into the entire supply chain network. This transparency allows agents to anticipate potential issues, share insights, and collectively work towards optimizing the overall performance of the supply chain.

4) Reduction of Bullwhip Effect: the bullwhip effect may also be considered as a huge problem in the modern supply chains that needs to be solved, the bullwhip effect is a phenomenon in supply chains where small fluctuations or variations in consumer demand can be amplified when they move upstream towards the suppliers, for example, if a supply chain that contains a manufacturer, a distributor and a retailer, let's assume that a retailer experienced a sudden increase in customer demand for a particular product due to a temporary promotion or one of the holidays or national days, as a result to the customer increased demand, the retailer will increase the quantity of his demand for that specific product from the distributor in order to ensure that the product

will always be available, the distributor may interpret this increased order as a signal of sustained higher demand from customers while in reality it's just a short-term spike, the problem here is that the distributor inventory will be in excess, and it's difficult to sell the product, in that situation, small variations in the customer demand (downstream part of the supply chain) results in amplified fluctuations in the distributor's inventory or even the manufacturer's inventory (upstream part of the supply chain) leading to some problems, because the actual end-customer demand does not match the inflated orders they received (Tombido & Baihaqi, 2022). Agents can share accurate demand information, reducing the likelihood of exaggerated order variations.

5) Increased Efficiency and Productivity: collaboration and coordination lead to streamlined processes and reduced inefficiencies. Agents working in concert can optimize production schedules, minimize idle time, and enhance overall productivity throughout the supply chain.

6) Information Sharing: effective communication allows agents to share crucial information such as inventory levels, production schedules, and demand forecasts. This shared knowledge enhances the overall visibility of the supply chain, enabling better decision-making.

7) Adaptability to Changes: the supply chain environment is dynamic, with factors like demand fluctuations and unexpected disruptions. Continuous communication enables agents to adapt and respond swiftly to changes in the market, ensuring the supply chain remains agile.

8) Resource Optimization: collaboration among agents facilitates the optimization of resources across the supply chain. For example, suppliers can adjust production based on real-time demand communicated by retailers, minimizing excess inventory and reducing costs.

9) Conflict Resolution: coordination is essential to mitigate conflicts that may arise due to conflicting goals or resource constraints. Agents need to coordinate their actions to resolve conflicts efficiently, ensuring the smooth operation of the supply chain.

A lot of researches have been conducted employing a multi-agent communication and collaboration for the optimization and management of supply chains. Presented here is a literature review encompassing various studies on this subject with criticism of some research.

Petri Nets for the Collaboration Between Agents

A petri net is a graph that contains places and transitions, a place may contain some tokens. Places represent the states of the system, tokens represent the entities or resources and transitions represent the actions or events that cause state change or interactions between entities. Each place can send one token or more throughout one transition or more with arcs, each arc has the capacity to carry a specific weight (number of tokens). A place can only be linked to a transition (with an arc) and vice versa. A transition is enabled if each of its input places has at least one token, an enabled transition can fire at any time, when fired the token from the input places will move to the output places. The net marking is the distribution of tokens toward their places (Cheung, 2014).

Petri nets can be used in the context of supply chain, let's consider that there are agents in our system: suppliers, manufacturers, distributors, retailers, petri nets can facilitate the communication of goods and information between them. Places can represent different states or locations, like: warehouses, retail stores, manufacturing facilities ...etc. Tokens can represent the goods or information that is going to be transferred from a place to another, like products, orders, ...etc. Transitions can represent any actions within the system, like order placement (the retailer will request a product or a specific quantity of products), in this case the token is the order, the transition is the action (order placement) that will place that order (token) from the retailer (place 1) to the manufacturing facility (place 2). The transactions can be triggered by an external event or by the agent itself after a certain condition. The fact that an agent can send an information or a data or a product as a token to another agent by a specific transition restricted by some conditions, this whole process is considered as a communication between the two agents and this communication is managed by petri nets rules. In the petri net representation, it is not necessary that the agent is represented by one place, the agent may be represented by multiple places or even one place can represent multiple agents. There are many cases that can occur in the petri net: a) sequence: a transition will occur only after the other has taken place, for example the order placement transition comes before the order fulfillment transition. b) conflict: when multiple transitions compete for the same token, for example: let's say a token represents a product and transition 1 is (order fulfillment), transition 2 is (stocking product in the inventory), the 2 transitions will compete against each other for the same token, in the petri net, if there is a conflict, then only one transition will fire at a given time, the others will remain blocked. c) concurrency: multiple transitions can occur at the same time, that means that multiple actions can happen without any synchronization. d) synchronization: all input places need to have at least one token in order for the transition to fire.

In the study that has been done by (Khosravifar, 2013), petri nets have been used as a communication and collaboration technique between agents in a multi-agent system, they addressed two types of communication, negotiation and persuasion, they have created a negotiation environment in order to allow the initiation of the negotiation session between agents, the petri net that has been used in the negotiation

Figure 3. Negotiation session using petri nets (Khosravifar, 2013)

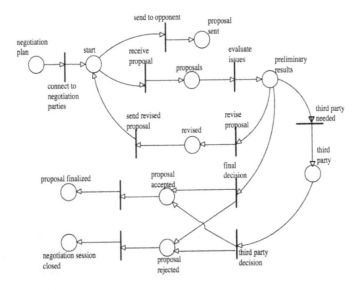

session allows agents to send a proposal to other agents, that proposal represents the agent's own perspective and specific goals that it want to achieve, that goal may contradict or complement the objectives of other agents, therefore, the agent can also receive proposals from other agents and evaluate them, eventually, the proposal may be accepted or rejected, if the conflicting agents reach a deadlock, a third party will be needed to resolve the conflict, in the petri net representation, states were represented with places, for example: the "proposal sent" is a state that clarify that the proposal has been sent from the first agent to the others, while actions were represented with transitions, for example: "send to opponent action".

Criticism

While Petri nets have been widely used in modeling and analyzing systems, including multi-agent systems, they are not without criticism, especially in the context of collaboration between agents in a multi-agent system, Firstly, they have limited expressiveness in capturing complex communication and collaboration scenarios in multi-agent systems. They may struggle to represent intricate relationships, dynamic information exchanges, and nuanced decision-making processes that are common in AI-driven collaborative environments, and we can observe that in the example that has been shown in the study, the scenario was too simplified compared to a real world example of a supply chain network. Petri nets may oversimplify the representation of agent behaviors, especially when agents exhibit intricate reasoning, learning, or adaptive capabilities. Representing the full spectrum of AI agent behaviors in a Petri net model can be challenging. Secondly, Petri nets may face challenges in representing dynamic changes in communication patterns and collaboration structures. In dynamic multi-agent systems, where agents may join or leave the system dynamically, Petri nets may lack the flexibility to adapt quickly to such changes.

Beliefs-Desires-Intensions Architecture in the Multi-Agent System

In the research that has been done by (Jabeur et al., 2017), they stated that the majority of the other techniques had used a centralized agent or module, this agent collects data and analyses it to make some specific plans, these plans can serve the individual as well as the collective goals of each logistics object and the goal of that agent is to find a way to facilitate the communication between LOs, they used a Beliefs-desires-intensions (BDI) architecture, Beliefs: stands for the agent's perception of the state of the world, for example: in the supply chains, the agent which is responsible for product storage has its own point of view of the current state of the world: location of warehouses, state of the products (which one needs to be stored rapidly and which one can wait). Desires: stands for the agent's goals or objectives that it want to achieve. Intentions: stands for the plans or actions that the agent choose to do to achieve its desires. The BDI architecture facilitates the communication between agents by allowing them to share and reason about their beliefs, desires and intentions. In this research, there is no centralized agent that make decisions, each agent is responsible for making decisions based on his own BDI architecture, these decisions can be a result of individual desires or collective desires. The proposed architecture is divided into several components:

1) The governance logistics component decides the agent behavior (individual or collaborative, it tries to reconcile individual and collective goals) and analyses the result of its actions to update the governance rules.

2) The individuality logistics component (ILC) allows the agent to apply the BDI that serves to achieve the agent's own goals, according to this architecture, the logistic object will be listening to communications from other LOs and if it received new information, it will update the individual beliefs of the agent using the revision function and the individual desires will also be updated according to the new beliefs using the option generation function.

3) The collective logistics component (CLC) does the same work as the ILC but it updates the collective beliefs and desires instead of the individual ones.

4) compromised logistics has a risk management function as well as an action generation function that updates the intentions according to the individual

desires and/or the collective desires, these intentions are used to make an action plan.

Each agent is going to have two plans, an individual plan (IP) and a collective plan (CL), if the IP is included in the CP then the action plan is going to be the IP.

If the IP and CP are consistent ie: if there is a similarity between actions from IP and actions from CP (the execution of these actions leads to the same sub-goals) or there is a complimentary between them (we need to execute one of them to be able to execute the other) then the action plan includes the IP, similar plans and complementary plans.

If the IP and CP are inconsistent ie: there is a conflict between actions from IP and CP, then the agent needs to solve it with the argumentation theory for example.

Criticism

One of the primary criticisms of the decentralized architectures that has been used in this study is the inherent difficulty in achieving effective coordination among autonomous agents. Without a central authority, ensuring that agents work together towards common goals can be challenging, leading to potential inefficiencies and conflicts. In addition to that, As the number of agents in a decentralized system grows, scalability becomes a significant concern. Coordinating many agents without a central coordinating mechanism can result in increased communication overhead and complexity. Moreover, this decentralized architectures imply that agents have limited or no access to global knowledge. This lack of a centralized repository of information can hinder decision-making processes, especially in scenarios where global context is crucial for effective collaboration.

There are plenty of researches that use a centralized architecture for the multi-agent system, In the research that has been done by (Jaimez-González & Luna-Ramírez, 2012), they used a multi agent system architecture to manage supply chains where agents work collaboratively to achieve this goal, they established a system that contains six agents, five of them represent the supply chain components: supply manager, production manager, inventory manager, sales manager, delivery manager and the last one is responsible for the coordination between the five agents and the transactions with other systems and companies, this architecture is considered as a centralized approach, where a specific agent will be in charge of the collaboration, communication, and coordination between the supply chain entities.

Negotiation for Conflict Resolution in Multi-Agent Systems

Negotiation involves a collective effort among a group of entities to reach a consensus on a particular matter that is mutually acceptable to all parties involved (Um et al., 2010), therefore, we can't talk about negotiation without mentioning the agreement technologies, agreement technologies' purpose is to solve conflict between agents and to reach an agreement between them, in order to solve the conflict, (Sierra et al., 2011) have addressed five key features that need to be verified: 1) Semantics: by semantics, we mean the ontologies and terms used by each agent, since agents are some sort of software developed by different software providers, they probably have different communication languages and different ontologies, therefore, in order to solve the conflict between them we need to allow communication between them, we need to find a way so that they can understand each other's ontologies and semantics. 2) Norms: by norms, we mean the rules that govern our multi-agent system, these rules and norms will certainly help each agent to know its own privileges and they can be useful to avoid conflicts in the first place. 3) Organizations: organization mean distributing specific roles to each agent in the system and ensuring a strictly organized communication protocols. 4) Trust: just like human societies use the reputation system to decide whether to interact with a specific entity, organization or person, that system can be used with agent, where past experiences have an impact on which agent is more trusted, having communication with an agent that has a good reputation will certainly avoid conflicts. 5) Negotiation: all the previously mentioned points can be used to avoid conflict, but they can't solve it, negotiation is the only way to solve conflicts between agents and to make them able to reach a mutual agreement.

According to (Li & Kokar, 2013), Agent Communication Language (ACL) is a protocol that is used to enable agent's communication in a multi-agent system, this protocol ensures the availability of some keys points cited by Sierra et al, when it comes to semantics, ACLs use well defined ontologies as well as a formal language to set a common ground between agents, this language can be a standardized language like XML, JSON, RDF or it may be a custom language made specifically for a particular multi-agent system, another important thing is the norms of the communication, ACLs use a set of protocols of communication and define the role of each agent in the communication process to avoid conflict between agents as much as possible, ACLs also ensure the organization of the communication environment as well as the organization of the communication itself, for that ACLs set various types of messages, including requests, responses, queries, notifications, and commands, even the structure of the message is defined, including headers, metadata, and content, in addition to all of that, powerful security mechanisms are used to ensure a secure communication.

Negotiation is one of the most used methods of communication between agents in a multi-agent system, many architectures have been proposed as a negotiation system between agents.

In the research that has been done by (Um et al., 2010), a new negotiation algorithm has been introduced to serve in the supply chain management with a trading agent, agents have been created using the Java Agent Development Framework (JADE) which is an open source software that helps in creating and developing a multi-agent system using the java programming language, while the simulation has been performed using JADE and Eclipse, experimentation show that this approach gave better results than the Kasbah system, which is a famous web service, or we can also call it a multi-agent system that helps users to create agents that buy and sell goods or services on their behalf, benefit/cost ratio has been used as a measure of evaluation in order to compare the methods performances.

In the research that has been done by (Cui-hong, 2011), a Supply Chain Management Negotiation System Based on Ontology has been developed, ontology refers to a formal and explicit specification of the concepts, relationships, and properties within a specific domain, it provides a structured representation of knowledge that enables consistent and meaningful communication between agents in the system, throughout using a common vocabulary, it helps to eliminate lack of interoperability between systems, the proposed architecture includes four sets of modules, each one of them contains a couple of sub-modules: policy module (contains ontology, database, knowledge base, data acquisition tool), knowledge management module (contains knowledge acquire, knowledge accumulate, knowledge innovation, knowledge communion and knowledge action), task module (contains the supply, demand, and production) and interface modules, each sub-module contains some agents which are related to its domain, the system consists of four types of proxies: structure agents, contract management agents, knowledge management agents, and negotiation agents, structure agents aim to organize the work and coordination, negotiation agents include two components: the bargaining agent and the creator of the bid generator.

In the research that has been done by (Terrada et al., 2020), practices and issues of the supply chain management have been identified, existing solutions have been analyzed, and a multi-agent negotiation platform has been established in order to manage supply chains. Their architecture involves two types of agents, the first type is the supervising agent which has a global view of the supply chain, the second type is a set of agents that represent supply chain actors, these actors are: suppliers, manufacturers, dispatchers and retailers, end customers are not included in this architecture, agents communicate using the ACL (agent communication language) massages. Agents need to interact with each other in order to achieve their individual and collective goals, even if they are designed in a completely different way, the multi-agent system allows separately developed agents to enable the ensemble of agents to function beyond the capabilities of any singular agent, in the study of (Saberi & Makatsoris, 2008), they proposed a model based on beer game four echelons, first, echelons in the context of supply chains means each entity involved in the supply chain (supplier tier 1, supplier tier 2, manufacturer, distributor, wholesaler, retailer), the beer game four echelons is a simulation that demonstrates the challenges and dynamics of supply chain management, four echelons are involved in this game: supplier, distributor, retailer, customer, in the proposed model, they assumed that there are multiple entities at the customer echelon, but only one entity at the others, each echelon is represented by an agent, the JADE framework has been used to create the multi-agent system, each agent has its own internal control and a mailbox, a forecasting agent is used to decide the quantity and the time of orders for the retailer and the distributor based on Economic Order Quantity EOQ which is an equation that takes into consideration: demand rate, ordering costs and holding costs in order to calculate the best order quantity and timing to keep costs low, without using the EOQ there may be an excess or shortage of inventory, because the quantity and the timing of orders are not relevant.

Criticism

Some negotiation methods may struggle to efficiently handle complex environments with a large number of agents and intricate interactions. As the complexity increases, the negotiation process may become time-consuming and computationally intensive. Moreover, Certain negotiation methods can be sensitive to the initial conditions or starting points of the negotiation process. This sensitivity might result in varying outcomes based on the initial negotiation parameters, leading to potential inconsistencies.

And the most important problem with the traditional negotiation systems is the shared ontologies between agents, shared ontologies aim to provide a common understanding of terms and concepts among negotiating agents. However, semantic misunderstandings can occur if agents interpret shared concepts differently. Variations in the interpretation of terms may lead to miscommunication and hinder the negotiation process, moreover, negotiation methods may not always consider the social context in which agents operate. Human-like social cues and conventions, which play a significant role in real-world negotiations, may not be fully incorporated into certain negotiation models. which leads us to a new type of negotiation that may be able to use the natural language instead of some simplified ontologies, and which we can call, an intelligent negotiation.

Intelligent Negotiation by Harnessing the Power of Large Language Models

Since natural language has proven its tremendous ability of communication between humans, making it easier for them to collaborate and coordinate with each other, it can help agents to be more efficient because they can use it to understand the ideas of other agents and to express their own beliefs in an understandable manner (Russell & Norvig, 2010).

To enable agents to communicate using natural language, the utilization of natural language processing techniques becomes imperative. This method leverages deep learning to construct Large Language Models (LLMs), endowed with the capacity to generate text resembling human language. Given that these LLMs share a common ontology, they can serve as a means of communication and negotiation between agents within a multi-agent system (Talebirad & Nadiri, 2023).

Accoring to (Sarigil & Koklu, 2022), Natural Language Processing (NLP) is a subfield of artificial intelligence (AI) that focuses on enabling computers to understand, interpret, and generate human language in a way that is both meaningful and contextually relevant. NLP involves the interaction between computers and natural language, allowing machines to comprehend, analyze, and respond to text or speech data. Here are the key components and processes involved in Natural Language Processing:

1) Tokenization: tokenization is the process of breaking down a text into individual units, typically words or phrases (tokens). This step is fundamental for further analysis, as it establishes the basic building blocks of the language.

2) Part-of-Speech Tagging (POS): POS tagging involves categorizing each token in a sentence into its grammatical parts of speech, such as nouns, verbs, adjectives, and adverbs. This information is crucial for understanding the syntactic structure and meaning of a sentence.

3) Parsing: parsing involves analyzing the grammatical structure of a sentence to determine its syntactic relationships. This process helps in creating a parse tree that represents the hierarchical structure of the sentence.

4) Named Entity Recognition (NER): NER identifies and classifies entities within a text, such as names of people, organizations, locations, dates, and more. This is essential for extracting meaningful information and understanding the context of the text.

5) Lemmatization: lemmatization is a linguistic process used in natural language processing to reduce words to their base or root form, known as the lemma. Unlike stemming, which involves cutting off prefixes or suffixes to obtain a word stem, lemmatization considers the context and meaning of words. It

employs a comprehensive vocabulary and morphological analysis to ensure that the resulting lemma is a valid word. For example, the lemma of "running" is "run," and the lemma of "better" is "good." Lemmatization is valuable in tasks such as text analysis and information retrieval where understanding the actual meaning of words is crucial.

6) Word vectorization: or word embedding, is a technique that represents words as numerical vectors in a multi-dimensional space. Each word is assigned a unique vector, and the spatial relationships between these vectors capture semantic similarities between words. Popular word vectorization models, such as Word2Vec, GloVe, and FastText, are trained on large datasets to learn the contextual relationships and meanings of words. This vector representation enables machines to understand the semantic relationships between words, making it particularly useful in natural language processing tasks like sentiment analysis, document clustering, and language translation.

7) Stemming: stemming is a text normalization technique that involves reducing words to their base or root form by removing prefixes or suffixes. The goal of stemming is to simplify words to their common linguistic root, even if the resulting stem is not a valid word. For instance, stemming would reduce both "running" and "runner" to the stem "run." While stemming is a simpler and computationally less expensive process compared to lemmatization, it may result in stems that are not actual words. Stemming is often applied in information retrieval, search engines, and text mining to reduce the dimensionality of the data and improve computational efficiency.

8) Stop words: they are common words that are often excluded from text analysis because they are deemed to carry little meaningful information. These words include articles, prepositions, and other frequently occurring words like "the," "and," "is," and "in." Removing stop words from text data helps reduce noise and focus on more meaningful content during analysis. While stop words are generally disregarded in tasks like sentiment analysis or document clustering, they may be relevant in certain contexts. For instance, in search queries, stop words might carry significance, and their exclusion could lead to misinterpretation.

9) Generation of Human-Like Text: advanced NLP models, such as Large Language Models (LLMs) created through deep learning, have the capability to generate human-like text. These models, like GPT-3, are trained on massive amounts of diverse text data and can generate coherent and contextually relevant language.

Natural Language Processing (NLP) and Large Language Models (LLMs) share an intricate relationship that has redefined the landscape of language understanding and generation. LLMs, such as GPT-3 (Generative Pre-trained Transformer 3) and BERT

(Bidirectional Encoder Representations from Transformers), represent a significant evolution in NLP. These models, often pre-trained on massive and diverse datasets, harness the power of deep learning to grasp the intricate patterns and contextual relationships within language. Unlike traditional rule-based NLP models, LLMs excel in capturing the nuances of human expression and understanding context. LLMs operate by representing words and phrases as vectors in high-dimensional spaces, fostering a more sophisticated understanding of language semantics. They are capable of contextual understanding, meaning they consider the entire context of a sentence or passage when processing language, enabling them to generate human-like text that goes beyond simplistic rule-based approaches. The advent of LLMs has propelled NLP to new heights, setting benchmarks in various language understanding tasks and paving the way for applications like sentiment analysis, language translation, and chatbots that generate coherent and contextually relevant responses. While LLMs bring unprecedented capabilities to NLP, their deployment also raises challenges and ethical considerations. Issues such as bias in language models, the responsible use of powerful language generation, and the potential for misinformation have become focal points of discussion. The synergistic interplay between NLP and LLMs reflects a dynamic field where advancements in language understanding and generation continually reshape the possibilities and responsibilities associated with processing natural language in the digital age (Makridakis et al., 2023; Talebirad & Nadiri, 2023). Large Language Models (LLMs), serve as formidable assets within the context of multi-agent systems, functioning not only as language models but also as powerful communication and interaction tools. In the realm of multi-agent systems, where autonomous entities collaborate and coordinate to achieve common goals. Very powerful LLMs have been developed in recent years including the Generative Pretrained Transformer (GPT) models (GPT-4 and GPT-3.5) and they show the ability to solve complex problems as autonomous entities which makes them considered as candidates to be used as language models for autonomous agents in a multi-agent system (Talebirad & Nadiri, 2023).

In addition to that, their ability to communicate with humans effectively and to express their responses in a simple yet comprehensible manner may allow them to express a good performance in communication in a multi-agent system.

Criticism

While Large Language Models (LLMs) are often considered promising candidates for communication and negotiation, it is essential to note that possessing such capabilities doesn't guarantee proficient negotiation skills. Firstly, models like GPT-3.5 and GPT-4 may exhibit effective communication when interacting with a single entity, typically a human. However, their proficiency in simultaneous communication with multiple entities remains uncertain. Secondly, existing GPT models have a tendency to align with the viewpoints of the humans they interact with rather than engaging in negotiation. This inclination has been observed, as highlighted by (Zhang et al., 2023). Despite LLMs demonstrating robust problem-solving abilities as independent entities, their performance in communication and collaboration within multi-agent systems remains ambiguous.

CONCLUSION

In conclusion, the exploration of supply chain optimization through a multi-agent approach has unveiled a rich landscape of communication, collaboration, and coordination methods within the realm of multi-agent systems. The literature review presented a comprehensive overview of both traditional and cutting-edge intelligent techniques employed in the optimization of supply chain processes. The historical context revealed the evolution of methodologies, showcasing the progression from conventional optimization strategies to the integration of intelligent agents in supply chain management. Early approaches laid the foundation, emphasizing the significance of coordination and collaboration, while recent advancements have harnessed the power of deep learning and natural language processing to enhance decision-making and adaptability. As we navigate the intricacies of supply chain optimization through a multi-agent lens, it is evident that the journey is dynamic and ongoing. Future research directions should address the identified challenges, exploring innovative solutions to enhance the efficiency, resilience, and sustainability of supply chain networks.

REFERENCES

Brenner, W., Zarnekow, R., & Wittig, H. (1998). Fundamental Concepts of Intelligent Software Agents. Springer. doi:10.1007/978-3-642-80484-7

Cheung, K. (2014). *Petri Nets*.

Chowdhary, P. (2020). *Fundamentals of Artificial Intelligence*. Springer. doi:10.1007/978-81-322-3972-7

Cui-hong, H. (2011). *Automated negotiation model of supply chain management based on multi-agent* (p. 180).

Jabeur, N., Al-Belushi, T., Mbarki, M., & Gharrad, H. (2017). Toward Leveraging Smart Logistics Collaboration with a Multi-Agent System Based Solution. *Procedia Computer Science, 109,* 672–679. doi:10.1016/j.procs.2017.05.374

Jaimez-González, C., & Luna-Ramírez, W.-A. (2012). *Towards a Multi-Agent System Architecture for Supply Chain Management., 58,* 207–219.

Karunananda, A., & Perera, L. C. M. (2016). Using a multi-agent system for supply chain management. *International Journal of Design & Nature and Ecodynamics, 11*(2), 107–115. doi:10.2495/DNE-V11-N2-107-115

Khosravifar, S. (2013). Modeling Multi Agent Communication Activities with Petri Nets. *International Journal of Information and Education Technology (IJIET),* 310–314. doi:10.7763/IJIET.2013.V3.287

Li, S., & Kokar, M. (2013). *Agent Communication Language.* doi:10.1007/978-1-4614-0968-7_5

Lu, D. (2011). *Fundamentals of supply chain management.* Ventus Publishing Aps.

Makridakis, S., Petropoulos, F., & Kang, Y. (2023). Large Language Models: Their Success and Impact. *Forecasting, 5*(3), 536–549. doi:10.3390/forecast5030030

Mujkić, Z., Qorri, A., & Kraslawski, A. (2018). Sustainability and Optimization of Supply Chains: A Literature Review. *Operations and Supply Chain Management: An International Journal, 11,* 186–199. doi:10.31387/oscm0350213

Russell, S. J., & Norvig, P. (2010). *Artificial intelligence a modern approach.*

Saberi, S., & Makatsoris, H. (2008). *Multi agent system for negotiation in supply chain management.*

Sarigil, Ş., & Koklu, M. (2022). *NATURAL LANGUAGE PROCESSING TECHNIQUES.*

Sierra, C., Botti, V., & Ossowski, S. (2011). Agreement Computing. *Kunstliche Intelligenz, 25*(1), 57–61. doi:10.1007/s13218-010-0070-y

Talebirad, Y., & Nadiri, A. (2023). *Multi-Agent Collaboration: Harnessing the Power of Intelligent LLM Agents.*

Terrada, L., El Khaili, M., & Hassan, O. (2020). Multi-Agents System Implementation for Supply Chain Management Making-Decision. *Procedia Computer Science, 177,* 624–630. doi:10.1016/j.procs.2020.10.089

Zhang, H., Du, W., Shan, J., Zhou, Q., Du, Y., Tenenbaum, J. B., Shu, T., & Gan, C. (2023). *Building Cooperative Embodied Agents Modularly with Large Language Models* (arXiv:2307.02485). arXiv.

Chapter 5

A Novel Optimization Model for the Bi–Objective Eco–Routing Problem

Amel Mounia Djebbar

iD https://orcid.org/0000-0002-4295-2080
Oran Graduate School of Economics, Algeria

Sabrina Delhoum
Oran Graduate School of Economics, Algeria

ABSTRACT

Pollution has taken a big toll on the environment. It touched the air that causes health diseases for living things, including humans. Among the transportation problems, especially the routing problems, vehicles are responsible for the pollutants' emissions, such as NOx and PM. Plus, CO2 vehicle emissions result in an increase in global warming. This research presents the development of the bi-objective eco-routing problem with constraints that optimize the tradeoff between the total gaze emissions and the total travel distance and proposes an UNSGA-II approach to solve it. The objective is to study the performance of the proposed method under a fixed and variable speed environment and its impact on the emission gazes and distance. Experiments show that the UNSGA-II offers a promising solution, ensures the best set of distribution routes with minimum emissions can be achieved under varying speeds, and the initialization algorithm accelerates its convergence and guarantees population diversity.

DOI: 10.4018/979-8-3693-1418-0.ch005

INTRODUCTION

On a global scale, pollution of the environment is a big issue. In fact, various pollutants present in the air, cause serious problems for the environment, human health, animals, and plants. Those problems are mostly caused by transportation logistic activities. Consequently, a competitive economic environment should require strategic and operational decisions for companies in order to optimize and manage their logistics processes more efficiently. According to the previous studies (Hickman et al., 1999; Naderipour et Alinaghian, 2016; Cheng et al., 2021), green logistics has emerged as a solution to the transportation problem, reducing vehicle emissions such as particulate matter (PM), nitrogen oxides (NO_x), and carbon dioxide (CO_2). The environment witnesses increasing serious pollution, especially NO_x, and PM, because these pollutants are fine particles (Dong et al., 2020; Sun et Apland, 2019), and light hydrocarbons that affect the air quality. NO_x is a primary pollutant principally produced by vehicle exhaust in the vicinity of arterial roads. Among them, the principal components are NO and NO_2 grouped together as NO_x (Matsumoto et al., 2006). Particularly formed during combustion processes, as in vehicle engines, they can cause respiratory problems such as asthma. Nitrogen dioxide emissions may also cause other health problems like cancer and low lung function (Atkinson et al., 2013). Road traffic is responsible for more than half of the emissions. Furthermore, while CO_2 is not considered a pollutant, it is the major greenhouse gas (GHG) emitted by vehicles and the primary contributor to the recent global warming. Thus, if no additional measures have been considered, road transport emissions will increase in the next years. Among the most crucial operational decisions is about cleaning and environmental protection. On this basis, integrating the routing problem that is an important topic in supply chain and operations research, while considering environmental and economic aspects can potentially reduce long-term costs, increase decision-making cohesion across the supply chain, and benefit the world population at large by lowering the damage to the environment. Routing problems appear in various uses in real life, such as distribution of petroleum products, distribution of industrial gases, delivery of goods to companies or individuals, tours of care, sales tours, and delivery of goods to retail stores, garbage collection and disposal, etc., and frequently implicate high costs. Optimizing multiple objectives routing problems can reflect more clearly the decision-making in transportation. Hence, the multi-objective model makes it possible to deal with the environmental aspect and the economic aspect at the same time. On other hand, have you constantly questioned in what way Amazon delivers thousands of packages every day? or how does Jumia bring your order to your door? When we have a list of places to visit, how do these massive corporations, or any other enterprise that handles goods transportation, deliver to multiple locations in the shortest amount of time while minimizing pollution emissions? The magic lies in the theoretical complexity associated with the incorporation of environmental aspects into transport activities; this type of question falls under the umbrella of Vehicle Routing Problems (VRP). In simple terms, it asks: "What are the optimal routes for vehicles to take to reach a particular group of customers?" A variant of the VRP is the Green VRP (GVRP).

Considering environmental aspects while planning transportation, particularly in the routing problem, is a probable solution to our problem. This latter is generally modeled as an optimization issue with a single objective that minimizes CO_2 emissions. In this article, we also explored the environmental aspect by considering additional objectives that minimize the pollutants' emissions and GHG and we simulated it in the form of a Multi-objective Optimization Problem (MOP) (Coello et al., 2007; Deb, 2001; Dhaenens et al., 2010). The objective is to obtain solutions that give a good compromise between the different objectives. Therefore, our contribution is to propose a new model called a Bi-objective Eco-Routing Problem (BERP) for optimizing simultaneously CO_2, PM, and NO_x emissions and the total traveling distance. The BERP consists of n vehicles positioned at a depot to provide m customers with discrete amounts of goods. The main objectives are to determine the optimum delivery route with minimum: CO_2, PM, NO_x emissions, and the total traveling distance with homogenous vehicles to deliver a group of clients. The result of the BERP is a several of routes that all begin and end at the depot, and satisfy the constraints, which are, all the clients are delivered only once, the vehicle capacity is not violated; the load of each customer, and not more than the quantity of the overall vehicles.

We developed an Upgraded Non-dominated Sorting Genetic Algorithm (UNSGA-II) from the original algorithm (Deb et al., 2002) with genetic operators to cope and solve our optimization problem. This well-known method is considered a good method to generate approximation sets for multi-objective problems.

The principal contributions of our work are distilled into the following: 1) this paper proposes the BERP, which is a variant of the GVRP that takes into consideration, the green logistics aspects. The solution of the BERP will provide us with a green and non-polluted environment in different aspects. 2) By considering a multi-objective problem, we can distinguish many previous works in this area. To our knowledge, there are no studies that treat three emitted gazes in multi-objective GVRP. This work not only takes into account CO_2 emissions but also incorporates pollutants such as PM and NO_x in the first objective function. The second treats the distance traveled. 3) In addition, we present a meta-heuristic to resolve our problem. 4) The algorithm is conducted with fixed and variable speed constraints to study the behavior of BERP.

Below is how the remain for this study is presented: The following section examines the literature on the GVRP variants in their two categories: single and multi-objective optimization problems. The definition of the problem and mathematical modeling are described in Section 3. In Section 4, the specifics of the UNSGAII for solving BERP are given. Moreover, results of the experiment using the benchmark are implemented with relevant discussions in Section 5. In section 6, conclusions are provided.

LITERATURE REVIEW

The VRP is an optimization-related issue that seeks to find the best route in order to satisfy a set of clients subject to constraints. This problematic is well-known to be an NP-hard (Lenstra and Kan, 1981). Among the objectives to be optimized, the rate of carbon emissions may be influenced by different factors, such as load, distance, fuel efficiency (i.e., the quantity of fuel utilized per kilometer or traveling distance), speed, traffic congestion, and road gradient (Elhedhli and Merrick, 2012; Osvald and Stirn, 2008; Poonthalir and Nadarajan, 2018; Suzuki, 2011).

This section starts with an overview of the important studies on multi-objective and single problems separately.

Single-Objective Optimization Problem

To cover diverse situations in green logistics emerging areas, especially the fundamental issue with transportation, the VRP has been extended to include other variants such as the Green VRP (Erdoğan and Miller-Hooks, 2012).

For instance, the subsequent research was done on GVRP, taking into consideration environmental aspects in their objective function were published. According to prior studies, researchers calculated the emissions produced by vehicles during transportation and provided several models for estimating carbon emissions and fuel consumption by considering a few pivotal and readily accessible factors. (Figliozzi, 2010) examined the reduction of emissions of VRPTW and fuel consumption, where the quantity of emissions depends on travel speed and on the departure time of every node. He took into account capacity constraints, time windows, and travel time. Moreover, the work of (Xiao et al., 2012) is an expansion of the VRP problem called Time Depend VRP (TDVRP); they applied a load-dependent function in order to minimize the fuel consumption rate. This problem has also been explored in (Naderipour et Alinaghian, 2016) where they presented a new model for the minimization, measurement, and evaluation of CO, NO_x, and CO_2 founded on the MEET approach (Hickman et al., 1999) in the open TDVRP in which the road circulation of congested regions such as city centers are regarded. This problem can be resolved by developing an adapted particle swarm metaheuristic. In addition, Maden and his colleagues (Maden et al., 2010) treated a vehicle scheduling and routing problem that incorporates time windows. In their model, the speed is dependent on traveling time. To solve the problem, they implemented an algorithm that minimizes the overall trip time. In the same context, a model that deems different constraints such as CO_2 emissions, fuel, and time travel is described by (Jabali et al., 2012). For CO_2 emissions, they designed a framework with a time-dependent VRP. Other studies, like (Sim, 2017), have developed a transportation model, that minimizes carbon emissions. (Soysal et imen, 2017) have translated the fuel consumption of a vehicle into emissions. An additional complete research was carried out by (Xiao et Konak, 2017), who proposed a mathematical formulation to solve a VRP. Their objective function included the total CO_2 emissions with and without payloads and the overall weighted tardiness penalty.

In (Li et al., 2018), they evoked another variant of VRP which used heterogeneous fixed fleet VRP that aims to decrease carbon production and fuel consumption. They proposed a split-tabu search method using the best split scheme. As well as (Sun et al., 2019), his work focused on a green delivery and pickup problem with heterogeneous vehicles. Their aim is to decrease carbon emissions using a set partitioning algorithm, a case study of a group of clients, and a number of products that were resolved at an acceptable time. In another work, (Olgun et al., 2021) studied the GVRP that incorporates simultaneous delivery and pickup. They modeled the problem and solved it with a hyper-heuristic method that included variable neighborhood and local search heuristics. That goal was to minimize fuel consumption, which was proportional to greenhouse gas emissions costs, while satisfying customer pickup and delivery demands simultaneously.

A number of authors have recognized another variant called "Pollution Routing Problem" (PRP) that consists of generating a series of routes to serve the clients and defining the speed of each vehicle off every route fragment. The primary goal of the PRP is to reduce the quantity of fuel used, along with other criteria such as minimizing travel distance, minimizing travel time, and minimizing the cost of GHG emissions (Bektaş and Laporte, 2011).

Multiobjective Optimization Problem

The literature review shows a few extensive multi-objective studies of routing problems. So far, studies on green and low-carbon logistic systems have remained a topic of current interest in the academic field (Gharaei et al., 2019). Let's start with a comprehensive analysis-based review of the literature that was done by Malladi and Sowlati (Malladi and Sowlati, 2018), where they examined the sustainability aspects of inventory routing problems and found that most of the environmental objectives in multi-objective models aim to minimize total emissions.

In other studies, (Abdullahi et al., 2021) proposed a weighted sum and a symbol of an epsilon-constraint model that integrates sustainability dimensions. To resolve the sustainable routing problem, they hybridized a biased randomized savings heuristic with an iterated greedy local search heuristic. The effects of the three factors were measured in relation to the cost of vehicles, CO_2, and accident risk. In the study (Molina et al., 2014), the authors suggested a multi-objective methodology founded on the Tchebycheff model for vehicle problems with a distinct vehicle. An algorithm was developed based on the C&W savings heuristic to minimize the three objective functions that are the total internal costs, the CO_2 emissions, and the emission of air pollutants such as NO_x. In (Long et al., 2019), the authors dealt with two types of Prize Collecte VRP (PCVRP) where the quantity of vehicles is fixed (PCVRP-P) or not (PCVRP-NP). For the resolution of the PCVRP-P problem, they proposed a Pareto method that integrates local search in genetic algorithm, and then they designed a decomposition strategy to solve the PCVRP-NP problem with the decomposition of it into different PCVRP-P problems.

Another research where they developed a novel mathematical formulation for the bi-objective cold-chain with a view to minimize carbon emissions for location-routing problems (Leng et al., 2020). Their primary objective consisted of several parts including carbon emission and fuel consumption costs and the second objective is the total waiting time clients and vehicles. (Xu et al., 2019) treated the GVRP, including soft time windows and time-varying vehicle speeds. The problem was presented as a mixed integer non-linear programming (MIP) model that includes a fuel consumption. Their model considered the vehicle load, the capacity, and the time-varying speed to be able to take into account the traffic congestion. They implemented an improved NSGA with adaptive and greedy strategies for GVRP.

To minimize carbon emission, overall cost, and client discontent, (Niu et al., 2021) investigated a bi-objective VRP with stochastic demands. To solve it, they proposed a Membrane Inspired Multi-Objective Algorithm (MIMOA). They concluded that compared to other classical multi-objective evolutionary methods, MIMOA is more effective in solving the problem. In the use of a bi-objective problem, (Tan et al., 2006) treated the VRPTW with objective to minimize the route's distance and the quantity of vehicles. (Jozefowiez et al., 2009) suggested an evolutionary methodology for the CVRP that decreased the overall distances traveled and also the route imbalance. In the same context, a reliable PRP that includes cross-dock selection when a minimum of single cross dock is utilized to process and transport the goods is presented by (Tirkolaee et al., 2020). They created a linear program with two objectives model with two goals: maximizing supply reliability and minimizing total cost, which includes routing costs and pollution. They used MOSA and NSGA-II in the resolution of the problem.

Another research paper solved the PRP by focusing on two goals: minimizing CO_2 emissions and overall travel distance. They suggested an original method to resolve the PRP using a multi-factorial algorithm. Their suggested strategy's viability was demonstrated by the faster convergence and superior solutions (Rauniyar et al., 2019).

Based on the above-reviewed literature, the following interpretations can be made: 1) most of them only consider a single objective such as cost, CO_2 emission and disregard the multi-objective; 2) the other emitted gazes by vehicles besides the CO_2 weren't considered despite its important environmental impact. Furthermore, our work didn't take into account only CO_2 emissions, but also incorporated pollutants emissions like PM and NO_x in the objective function; 3) the BERP model suggested in this research is to optimize two objectives, especially considering the gazes emissions. The best set of distribution routes are guaranteed by an UNSGA-II, and an initialization heuristic is created to accelerate its convergence and guarantee population variety.

PROBLEM DEFINITION AND FORMULATION

The principal contribution of our work is to minimize CO_2, NO_x, and PM as three important pollutants emitted from vehicles. Therefore, we propose in this section a new bi-objective environmental-routing problem for MOP that simultaneously optimizes total travel distance and environmental objectives.

MOP

The principal aim of a MOP is to find solutions within a given decision space by optimizing (minimize or maximize) m objectives (Deb, 2001; Coello et al., 2007). In fact, a feasible solution must satisfy both a number of constraints and variables bounds imposed by the problem. Mathematically, it's described as a set of m objective functions $f = (f_1, f_2, ..., f_m)$, a set X of feasible solutions in the decision space, and a set Z of feasible points in an objective space $Z = f(X)$. A solution $x = (x_1, x_2, ..., x_n)$ is a vector that contains n decision variables. For each solution $x \in X$, there exists a point $z \in Z$, denoted by $f: X \rightarrow Z$ with $z = f(x) = (f_1(x), f_2(x), ..., f_m(x))$. Multi-objective optimization algorithms utilize the notion of dominance to define that one solution x is better than other solution x_0. This occurs if two conditions hold:

The solution x is better than x_0 in all objectives.

The solution x is strictly superior to x_0 in at least one objective.

If any of the conditions are violated, solution x does not dominate solution x_0. A solution $x \in X$ is baptized Pareto-optimal when no other decision-space solution dominates it. The complete set of non-dominated vectors is the Pareto Front.

Optimization Model For Berp

The BERP is defined over a complete graph $G = (N, A)$, where $N = \{0, 1, 2, ..., n\}$ is a set of nodes, 0 corresponds to the depot, and the others correspond to the customers. $A = \{(i, j): i, j \in N, i \neq j\}$ is the arcs that link all the customers in N. Each customer $i \in N$ has a known demand $q_i > 0$, while the depot is assumed to have a zero demand. There is a fleet $K = \{1, 2, ..., k\}$ of identical vehicles with a capacity $Q_k > 0$. $d_{ij} \geq 0$ is the distance between i and j. The vehicles begin their route at the depot and come back at the end. All customers' demands must be satisfied. A set of routes that can be denoted by a binary variable x_{ijk}, i.e. $x_{ijk} = 1$ when a vehicle k, travels between nodes i and j and $x_{ijk} = 0$ otherwise. Based on the fundamental vehicle routing model problem, the new environmental consideration added that concerns the amount of CO_2, PM, and NO_x emitted from each vehicle. In the following, we provide the mixed integer program formulation of the BERP, which is an NP-hard problem, and we define the two primary objectives to optimize it. The environmental aspect is adapted from several studies (Enmon, 2015; Pradhananga et al., 2014).

$$\text{Minimizing } f_1 = \sum_{k \in K} \sum_{i \in N} \sum_{j \in N} x_{ijk} * d_{ijk} \tag{1}$$

$$
\begin{aligned}
\text{Minimizing } f_2 = &\sum_{k \in K} \sum_{i \in N} \sum_{j \in N} x_{ijk} * [(572.12 + 0.075052v^2 - 8.3102v + \frac{2619.7}{v}) \\
&+ \left(3.71975 + 0.00035318v^2 - 0.045401v + \frac{24.975}{v}\right) \\
&+ \left(0.301755 + 0.00002819v^2 - 0.00065055v + 3.6311/v\right)
\end{aligned}
\tag{2}
$$

Constraints of the model are as follows:

$$\sum_{i=1}^{N} \sum_{k=1}^{K} x_{ijk} = 1, j = 1,...,N \tag{3}$$

$$\sum_{j=1}^{N}\sum_{k=1}^{K}x_{ijk} = 1, \ i=2,\ldots,N \tag{4}$$

$$\sum_{i=1}^{N}x_{i0k} = 1, \ \forall k \in K \tag{5}$$

$$\sum_{j=1}^{N}x_{0jk} = 1, \ \forall k \in K \tag{6}$$

$$\sum_{i=1}^{N}x_{iuk} - \sum_{j=1}^{N}x_{ujk} = 0, \ \forall k \in K, \ \forall u \in N \tag{7}$$

$$x_{ijk}=1, \ y_{jk}=y_{ik}+q_i, \ \forall k \in K, \ \forall i,j \in N \tag{8}$$

$$y_{0k}=0, \ \forall k \in K \tag{9}$$

$$0 \leq y_{jk} \leq Q_k, \ \forall k \in K, \ \forall j \in N \tag{10}$$

Where,

y_{ik}: load of vehicle k while visiting node i,

v: speed of vehicle.

The first objective function Eq. (1), represents the economic dimension that aims to minimize the traveling distance, and the second objective function, Eq. (2), estimates the environmental dimension by assuming that delivery vehicles use diesel fuel and is composed of three parts. The first section computes the CO_2 emission factor, while the second and third sections compute the NO_x and PM emission factors, respectively. The total emissions of each routing solution are represented by the total emissions from every traveled arc in the road network. Constraint (3) and constraint (4) ensure that every client is only visited once, and that each vehicle entering a location must leave it. Constraints (5) and (6) ensure that each vehicle is used to serve at most one route. Constraint (7) ensures the route's continuity. Constraint (8), (9), and constraint (10) ensure that no vehicle can be overloaded.

RESEARCH METHODS

This section gives a thorough explanation of the BERP optimization proposed model, which is the extended model of the classical vehicle routing problem by optimizing two objectives; the first one is the minimization of CO_2, PM, and NOx emissions; the second objective is the minimization of the overall traveling distance. These objectives are important to ensure a clean and green environment in transportation activities, especially when considering coordination between the economic and environmental aspects. We have developed an UNSGA-II algorithm to treat the BERP with environmental considerations. The NSGA-II seems to be a promising method and it has been shown to be among the widely applied evolutionary algorithms and a very efficient heuristic for resolving multi-objective problems (Zhou et al., 2011; Haddadene et al., 2016; Gharaei et al., 2019; Liu et al., 2019; Li and He, 2020) in terms of the quality of the solutions. Previous research also shows that NSGA-II surpasses a Pareto-archive evolution method considering the diversity of solutions found and the convergence close to the Pareto-optimal (Knowles et Corne, 1999). Also, the NSGA-II method is an improved NSGA that was among the first evolutionary algorithms used (Srinivas et Deb, 1994). To overcome the shortcomings of NSGA, the NSGA-II method (Deb et al., 2002) introduced a fast non-dominant sorting method and a selection operator.

The NSGA-II uses two routines, called the ranking and the crowding distance, to sort solutions. The first determines how many solutions in the population are dominated by each solution. A Pareto front is defined according to equal solution rankings. The new solutions is generated by adding non-dominated solutions beginning from the initial ranked non-dominated front. When the total non-dominated solutions surpass the population size, not all the solutions are accepted, especially the inferior ranked non-dominated solutions. This step is applied using a sorting procedure according to the crowded comparison based on the crowding distance.

Fast Non-Dominant Sorting

This step consist of defining two variables for each solution p in the first population P; n_p represent the total of results that dominate p, and S_p is a set that contain solutions that p dominates. When $n_p = 0$, no solution will belong to the first front and will be put into a set F_1 and the rank of the p will be $p_{rank} = 1$. After that, each solution $s \in S_p$ in F_1 satisfying $n_s = 1$ in a separate set F_2 and s will belong to the

Algorithm 1: *Fast non-dominant sorting pseudo-code*

1	Initialization $n_p \leftarrow 0$, $S_p \leftarrow \phi$
2	for each $p \in P$
3	for each $q \in P$
4	if p dominates q
5	then $S_p = S_p \cup \{q\}$
6	else if q dominates p
7	then $n_p = n_p + 1$
8	if $n_p = 0$
9	then $F_i = F_i \cup \{p\}$
10	$i = 1$
11	while $F_i \neq \phi$
12	$R = \phi$
13	for each $p \in F_i$
14	for each $p \in S_p$
15	$n_q = n_q - 1$
16	if $n_q = 0$
17	then $R = R \cup \{q\}$
18	$i = i + 1$
19	$F_i = R$

second front and $s_{rank} = 2$. The algorithm will stop until the ith front is empty. Here, the use of the UNSGA-II comes to enhance the original NSGA-II approach. The improvement concerns the fast non-dominant sorting algorithm, which result a significant minimization of time of computation burden. Algorithm1 provides the fast non-dominat sorting algorithm's steps.

Crowding Distance

Depending on the crowding distance and the rank, all the selected solutions are affected a crowding distance value. This value between two solutions is compared on the same front, and the result that has the maximum value will be selected.

For each solution in a front, the Euclidian distance is used to calculate the crowding distance based on their m objectives. The solutions within the boundary take unlimited distance affectations since they are still selected. To calculate the crowding distance, we used: *I[i].m* represents the mth objective function value of

Algorithm 2: *Crowding distance calculation pseudo-code*

1	Obtain the number of solutions in set I: $l = |I|$
2	**For each** i, set the initial crowding distance value to zero: $I(i_d) = 0$
3	Sort the individuals using each objective value m: $I = sort(I, m)$
4	Ensure that the boundary points are selected: $I(1)_d = I(l)_d = \infty$
5	**For** $i = 2$ **to** l-1
6	Calculate the crowding distance: $I(i_d) = I(i_d) + abs\,(I[i + 1].m - I[i - 1].m)\,/\,(f_m^{max} - f_m^{min})$

the ith solution in the set I. f_m^{max} and f_m^{min} that represent maximal and minimal values of the mth objective function, respectively (see Algorithm 2).

Optimization By NSGA-Ii

In this article, the UNSGA-II for our bi-objective environmental- routing problem builds an initial population P0 representing a set of initial solutions. The number of these solutions indicates the size of the population. Each solution is a group of routes, each route is made up of nodes to visit and must start and end at the depot, see Figure 1.

Figure 1. An example of solution representation

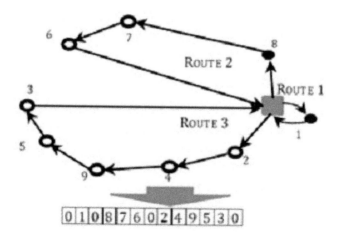

Algorithm 3: *Initialization phase of UNSGAII*

INPUT: Data file	
OUTPUT: solution of route	
1	Let $k = 0$, k number of vehicles
2	Let *vect* vector that contains all node
3	**while** node have been marked
4	Initialize a route with 0
5	$k = k+1$
6	A node i is randomly selected from *vect*
7	Insert this node i at the actual route
8	Mark the node
9	**for** (All unassigned node) **do**
10	sort all the node according to their distance with the node i
11	Insert the node at the route
12	Mark the node
13	**if** the capacity constraint is not satisfied
14	**then** the node is rejected
15	**Break**
16	**end for**
17	Insert node 0 at the route
18	**end while**
19	Evaluate Eq. (1) and Eq. (2) for each solution

The choice of the first solutions is an important step because it influences the result of the remainder framework. The details of the main steps of the Initialization Algorithm are given in Algorithm 3.

The next steps are to generate the offspring population P'; it consists of different genetic operators, so here, we opted for the application of the Order Crossover (OX) and Exchange Mutation (EM) operators because it is largely used in the literature by genetic algorithms for VRP problems (Karakatič and Podgorelec, 2015). First, the OX chooses two points randomly from P1 and P2, so, they will be divided into three parts each. The middle parts are inserted in the new solutions C1 and C2 from P1 and P2 respectively. To complete C1 and C2, we swept starting with the third part of P2 and P1 respectively in a circular manner (Karakatič and Podgorelec, 2015; García-Nájera et al., 2015; Zhu, 2003; Prins, 2004; García Nájera and Bullinaria, 2011), the applied operator is adapted to our problem.

Secondly, the EM operator corresponds to simply exchanging two random nodes inter-route (Berger and Barkaoui, 2004; García Nájera and Bullinaria, 2011; Karakatič and Podgorelec, 2015). We repeat the operators' iterations until the solution resultants are equal to the dimensions of the final population. After each operator's application (order crossover and exchange mutation), if the solution obtained doesn't satisfy the problem constraints, it will be rejected and we will reiterate the operators until we find the best solution. At this point, an offspring population P' is created. After, we combine P_0 and P' into a mating pool P of size $2*N$. Finally, according to the ranking of Pareto fronts, the sorted solutions are evaluated. The next population (size is N) contains the best solutions obtained by applying the tournament selection of the first P_0 solutions; this selection has a principal part in enhancing the average quality of the population, then transferring the best solution to the next generation. We select the solution that has the lowest front rank if the two solutions are from different fronts. In the opposite case, the highest crowding distance solution is selected.

The algorithm will terminate if the iteration number surpasses the maximum value given as an input parameter. Figure 2 illustrates the diagram of the proposed UNSGA-II approach and the pseudo-code is shown in Algorithm 4.

RESULTS AND DISCUSSIONS

This section describes and analyzes the experiments' findings that aim to have a clear and promising solution produced by the UNSGA-II of the previous section to optimize the proposed bi-objective model. Our goal here is to fulfill all customers' requests while minimizing the compromise between the pollutant emissions and the distance traveled. For the experiments, we used a dataset composed of 36 instances from Augerat and al. (www.bernabe.dorronsoro.es/vrp), called the instances A-B, the difference between these instances is the distribution of the customer locations for each set. These criteria are used to make this selection: instances with coordinates generated randomly within a value of 100 to have feasible solutions and reasonable execution times. For our input, we have made some changes to the files. Each file includes a set of clients and a depot, together with the coordinates x and y for each customer, the demand related to each node, the number of vehicles, their total capacities, and their numbers. All of the vehicles are homogeneous. The number of clients is between 31 and 80. Figure 3 describes respectively the distribution of nodes of the instance A-n32-k5 from set A and the instance B-n31-k5 from set B. Clients in data set A are positioned at random. However, the clients are clustered in data set B. The depot in the two instances is an outlying spot. Clustered instances are characterized as a set of clusters that integrate a number of nodes. In the same

Figure 2. Diagram of UNSGA-II

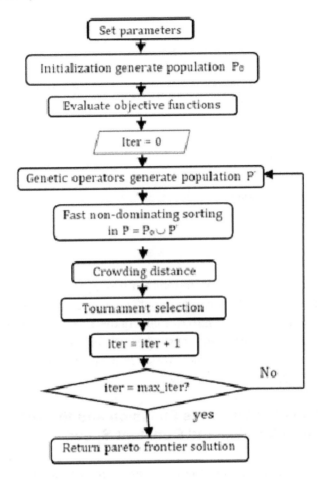

cluster, the customers have the same distance measure to each other. For the solution formulation, the demand of the customers is important because it changes from one customer to another in the cluster. In instances with randomly positioned clients, the distance and demand provide more flexibility in the search process for a solution.

We assume that the distance d_{ij} is equal to Euclidean distance between the locations of two different customers. We study two types of vehicle speed on trips: a constant speed of 40 km/h and a varying speed. By our assumption, all the existing vehicles are powered by conventional diesel. Our approach has been implemented in C++. All tests were run on a computer with an Intel Core (TM) i5-2330 processor at 2.6 GHz and the operating system, Microsoft Windows 8, using RAM of 4.00 GB.

It is clear that UNSGA-II has better results for all the data sets used, and the obtained total emissions gazes (teg) and the total distance (td) details are illustrated in

Algorithm 4: *The UNSGAII pseudo-code*

INPUT: Size of population N, maximal iterations, OX p probability and EM q probability	
OUTPUT: Set of solutions	
1	Initialize population of solutions P_0
2	Evaluate Eq. (1) and Eq. (2) for each solution
3	**while** iteration < maximal iterations do
4	tournament selection
5	Create an offspring P' from P_0 by performing order crossover with a probability of p and exchange mutation with a probability of q
6	Create the mating pool P of size $2*N$ by combining P' and P_0
7	Select the best population (N solutions) from P_0 based on crowding distance and the non-domination rank (Pareto front)
8	**end while.**

Tab. 1–2. The first objective f_1 is the total emissions gazes, and the second objective f_2 is the total distance, which has an initial value different for each instance and is enhanced over the iterations. The best values of the different parameters in UNSGA-II are obtained after several iterations, where the population size is 800, and there have been 150 iterations. The order crossover and exchange mutation probabilities are taken as 0.1 and 0.85 respectively.

Comparison of Total Gazes Emission and the Total Distance With Varying and Constant Speed

Table 1 and Table 2 compare the total gazes' emissions, and the total distance with both constant speed and varying speed, we report a column gap (%), which is respectively, the relative gap between the total gazes emission found between

Figure 3. Example of Instances from set A and set B

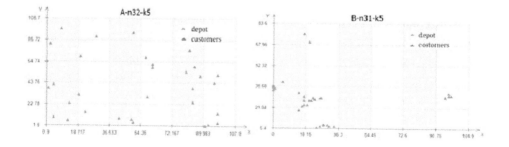

constant speed and varying speed, and the relative gap between the total distance found between constant speed and varying speed. The results obtained for the data sets contribute to a decrease in the total gazes emission when varying speed is used compared to constant speed. A 10.03% from data set A and 7.97% from data set B decrease in the total gaze's emission is realized using varying speed but only 1.99% in total distance from instances A and 1.88% from data set B. Since the vehicle, with a constant speed equal to 40km/h, emits more gazes during travel, so through the entire distance, there is excessive combustion of diesel. Hence, up to 10% less of gaze's footprints with the average varying speed equal to 30km/h is inferior to constant speed. The results specify the total emission gazes under a constant and varying speeds environment with speed varying between a minimum and maximum speed limit of 10 and 50 respectively. To derive the comparison of constant and varying speed emission gaze rates, the algorithm is run with the objective f1 taken as the emission gazes, and the corresponding non-dominated solution got for the emission gazes is displayed. It is observed that, as emission gazes are less, it is possible to serve more demands of customers with a lower number of vehicles and a substantial decrease in the total distance can be achieved. A positive percentage deviation is obtained for practically all data instances, which signifies the effectiveness of the varying speed. The results indicate that UNSGA-II is effective and very competent. It is also noticed that although the total distance obtained using varying and constant speeds is nearly the same, the gazes emitted don't need to be the same. It is dependent on the road conditions, traffic conditions, and the load of the vehicle, the vehicle's velocity, and several other factors, which are influential in the gaze's emission calculation. For example, if the route distance of 0 2 4 9 5 3 0 is 23.82 and the route distance of 0 4 5 9 3 2 0 is also 23.82, it is not necessary that both travel and emit the same amount of gazes as it may vary with the speed, vehicle load, and other factors.

To show the structural difference between the routes obtained with constant and varying speeds for the data set A-n32-k5, which is plotted and illustrated in Figure 4. It can be observed that the routes found for constant and varying speed are distinct, and the route taken by the vehicle differs because of the low speed, which consumes less diesel.

Pareto Optimal Front

The problem is modeled as a bi-objective optimization problem to minimize both total gazes emission and total distance. The challenge is to determine the route with the UNSGA-II total gazes emission for the obtained total distance. Objective f_1 is set as UNSGA-II and the algorithm is run for a specified maximum number of

Table 1. Results of randomly distributed customers

Data set	Solutions with constant speed			Solutions with varying speed			Gap (%)	
	Teg	Td	speed	Teg	Td	Avg. speed	teg	Td
A-n32-k5	2935.14	797.64	40	2737.23	797.68	29.50	7,23	-0,01
A-n33-k5	2529.86	687.50	40	2303.59	680.63	29.20	9,82	1,01
A-n33-k6	2758.37	749.60	40	2703.58	756.35	29.08	2,03	-0,89
A-n34-k5	2969.57	806.99	40	2709,78	800.65	31,60	9,59	0,79
A-n36-k5	3092.89	840.50	40	2798,52	826.87	31.82	10,52	1,65
A-n37-k5	3364.74	914.38	40	2509,73	741.54	28.12	34,07	23,31
A-n37-k6	3707.1	1007.42	40	3484.86	1029.66	30.95	6,38	-2,16
A-n38-k5	2951.15	801.99	40	2705.74	788.50	29.55	9,07	1,71
A-n39-k5	3275.89	890.24	40	2962.24	875.24	29.25	10,59	1,71
A-n39-k6	3273.32	889.53	40	2953.55	878.25	30.16	10,83	1,28
A-n44-k6	3744.61	1017.62	40	3369.87	995.68	31.47	11,12	2,20
A-n45-k6	3812.74	1036.13	40	3447.21	1011.86	29.68	10,60	2,40
A-n45-k7	4527.75	1230.44	40	4283.61	1239.08	30.61	5,70	-0,70
A-n46-k7	3709.29	1008.02	40	3344.97	981.70	30	10,89	2,68
A-n48-k7	4377.74	1189.67	40	4051.20	1188.98	29.54	8,06	0,06
A-n53-k7	4020.14	1092.49	40	4021.97	1172.12	29.45	-0,05	-6,79
A-n55-k9	4417.36	1200.44	40	3967.56	1164.43	31.56	11,34	3,09
A-n80-k10	7923.58	2153.27	40	7025.71	2061.96	30	12,78	4,43
Average	3743,96	1017,44	40,00	3410,05	999,51	30,09	10,03	1,99

iterations. The best routes are stored in the archive. The route that archives f_1 with total gazes emission is taken as the non-dominated solution.

Therefore, there are no published results to compare the performance of the suggested UNSGA-II, hence to derive the comparison between the total gaze's emission and the total distance for two different speeds (constant and variable speed) objective f_1 is based on the total gaze's emission and the total distance is obtained.

Impact of Speed Intervals on Emission Gazes and Total Distance

The speed variation results in a substantial decrease in the total gaze emitted and the total distance despite that total distance is not linked directly to the speed. It is essential to analyze the influence of various speed intervals on the total gaze

Table 2. Results of clustered distributed customers

Data set	Solutions with constant speed			Solutions with varying speed			Gap (%)	
	teg	Td	speed	teg	Td	Avg. speed	teg	Td
B-n31-k5	2501.66	679.83	40	2290,82	676.75	32.18	9,20	0,46
B-n34-k5	2917.26	792.78	40	2716.9	797.37	29.78	7,37	-0,58
B-n35-k5	3575.61	971.69	40	3590.42	975.71	28.69	-0,41	-0,41
B-n38-k6	3019.58	820.585	40	2872.72	817.81	30.65	5,11	0,34
B-n39-k5	2091.16	568.28	40	1914.57	565.69	30.08	9,22	0,46
B-n41-k6	3136.39	852.33	40	2864	846.21	29.44	9,51	0,72
B-n43-k6	2839.67	771.69	40	2660.91	780.94	30.77	6,72	-1,18
B-n44-k7	3488	947.88	40	3231.48	941.71	29.09	7,94	0,66
B-n45-k5	2852.86	775.277	40	2774.46	776.18	31	2,83	-0,12
B-n45-k6	2717.65	738.53	40	2770.55	736.997	29.96	-1,91	0,21
B-n50-k7	2814.41	764.83	40	2612.98	772.05	29.42	7,71	-0,94
B-n50-k8	5016.76	1363.33	40	5346.02	1355.53	29.89	-6,16	0,58
B-n51-k7	3802.22	1033.27	40	3519.20	1039.81	29.59	8,04	-0,63
B-n52-k7	2837.83	771.19	40	2680.68	786.74	30.37	5,86	-1,98
B-n56-k7	3709.29	1008.02	40	2582.99	757.87	31.04	43,60	33,01
B-n57-k7	4309.13	1171.03	40	3930.52	1153.55	30.41	9,63	1,52
B-n57-k9	6183.46	1680.38	40	5640.36	1666.54	29.57	9,63	0,83
B-n78-k10	4995.24	1357.48	40	4556.32	1346.24	29.76	9,63	0,83
Average	3489,34	948,24	40	3253,11	932,98	30,09	7,97	1,88

emitted values. Experiments are conducted to find the relationship between various

Figure 4. Routes obtained for constant and varying speed for A-n32-k5

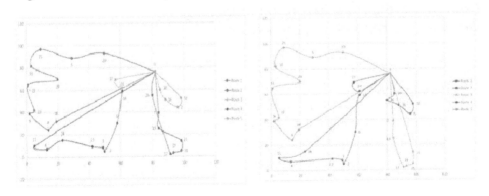

speed intervals and total emitted gaze and the two objective functions. To study the speed's behavior, two categories of speed are considered; constant speed and varying speed, the constant speed is fixed to *40*, the varying speed is taken in the range of *[10-50]* with the average varying speed for all iteration. The maximum speed is taken not to exceed *50*. In the tables 1-2, we considered two categories of speeds where the mean speed for each travel from node i to node j, where $i, j \in N$ is taken at random in varying speeds, and its impact on the two kinds of instances A and B is studied and the results are recorded. To study the total gaze emission details under varying speeds, the algorithm is run to get the best solution obtained from *150* iterations of each instance of the data set. According to this research, there is a positive correspondence between speed and the total emitted gazes.

It shows that, however variable speed decreases total produced gazes, the speed variation should not be greater to realize the benefits from the emitted gazes. In addition, it is hard to get the UNSGA-II at this rate as there is a frequent requirement for diesel or the time is insufficient for the vehicle to serve successive customers. Hence, the algorithm performs poorly when the varying speed is taken randomly with a 28.69 km/h difference. Though minimum emitted gaze's can be realized with varying speeds for A-n33-k5 and B-n39-k5, to derive a better routing plan, proper selection of speed interval is important. As seen from the results, varying speeds are able to get better gazes emitted minimization for most of the data instances. It is useful to observe that the average expected emitted gazes increases when the average expected speed increase and it is also noted that the interval of increase/decrease in speed has an impact on the total gazes' emission rate. Nevertheless, when we compare constant and varying speed, varying speed outperform fixed speed for the two objectives. Figure 5 shows that the gaze's emission and the distance is increasing when the quantity of vehicles increases with a large number of customers. In addition, under varying speeds, in data set B, gazes emitted (3489.34) is less than in data set A (3743.96). Both instances A and data sets B show a significant decrease in the emitted gazes from constant to varying speed.

Comparing the Results From Minimizing Distance vs. Minimizing Emissions

Figure 6 shows two comparisons of distance and emission constituents. While many researchers try to resolve routing problems with primary objectives such as total distance minimization or waiting time minimization, our research came to confirm the impact of an added objective that takes care of environmental issues that need to be treated to have a green and clear environment. Although few studies only consider CO_2 emissions, we incorporate pollutants such as PM and NO_x into the

Figure 5. Comparison between customers and vehicles for the two objective functions with varying speed

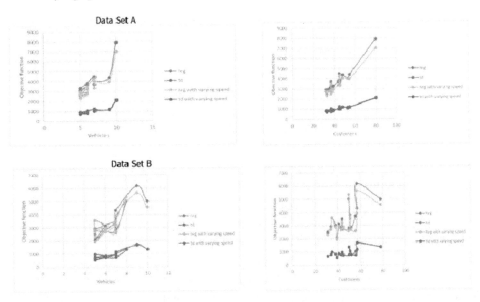

objective functions in this article, and the effect of factors such as vehicle speed can be influential in emitted gaze reduction.

Figure 6. Comparing emissions and distances with constant and varying speed optimization for two objectives

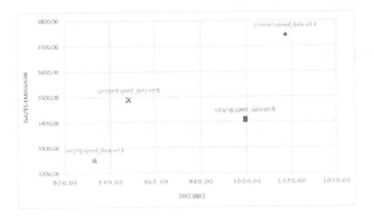

CONCLUSION

It is crucial to preserve a clean, green environment for upcoming generations by incorporating environmental aspects into transport activities, which makes the GVRP a popular area of research. The BERP is expressed as bi-objective MIP. It incorporates CO_2 emissions, PM and NO_x pollutant emissions calculation algorithms that take into account a vehicle's load, capacity, and the transportation distance. It requires considerable computing time for the generation of solutions. The first goal includes CO_2 emissions, as well as PM and NO_x pollutant emissions. The second objective consists of the total distance. An UNSGA-II procedure has been developed to solve our BERP efficiently. We summarized our contributions into three points. First, a bi-objective optimization problem BERP that intends to minimize both emitted gazes and the total distance is introduced and is modeled using a mixed-integer program. Second, an UNSGA-II with genetic operators is utilized to resolve the problem, and the results are compared to prove the efficacy of the algorithm. In addition, the results showed that the load node, vehicle capacity, and crowding distance have significant effects on the Pareto front, carbon dioxide emission, particulate matter and nitrogen oxide emissions, and travel distance. Third, to analyze the behavior of BERP, speed is used as a constant and variable constraint. The corresponding gaze emission and total distance are computed and examined in experiments using two separate data sets. Under varying speed environments, there is a significant improvement in emitted gazes. A better route is achieved with varying speeds. The extensive results of the experiments show that, considering minimization, the pollutants can reduce emissions by 10% on average. Other factors influencing the variation in gaze emissions are also recognized and analyzed in this study. The upcoming research in this regard will be based on adding different constraints to the proposed model, like considering time windows, multiple depots, and heterogeneous fleets. On the other hand, we treated the impact of road gradient and traffic congestion, which are very effective on gaze emissions.

REFERENCES

Abdullahi, H., Reyes-Rubiano, L., Ouelhadj, D., Faulin, J., & Juan, A. A. (2021). Modelling and multi-criteria analysis of the sustainability dimensions for the green vehicle routing problem. *European Journal of Operational Research*, 292(1), 143–154. doi:10.1016/j.ejor.2020.10.028

Atkinson, R., Barregård, L., Bellander, T., Burnett, R., Cassee, F., De Oliveira Fernandes, E., Forastiere, F., & Forsberg, B. (2013). *Review of evidence on health aspects of air pollution – REVIHAAP*. Project Technical Report.

Bektaş, T. & Laporte, G. (2011). The Pollution-Routing Problem. Transportation Research Part B: Methodological. *Supply chain disruption and risk management 45,* 1232–1250. doi:10.1016/j.trb.2011.02.004

Berger, J., & Barkaoui, M. (2004). A parallel hybrid genetic algorithm for the vehicle routing problem with time windows. *Computers & Operations Research, 31*(12), 2037–2053. doi:10.1016/S0305-0548(03)00163-1

Cheng, Z., Zhao, L., Wang, G., Li, H., & Hu, Q. (2021). Selection of consolidation center locations for China railway express to reduce greenhouse gas emission. *Journal of Cleaner Production, 305,* 126872. doi:10.1016/j.jclepro.2021.126872

Coello, C. C., Lamont, G. B., & van Veldhuizen, D. A. (2007). Evolutionary Algorithms for Solving Multi-Objective Problems. Springer, New York.

Deb, K. (2001). *Multiobjective Optimization Using Evolutionary Algorithms.*

Deb, K., Pratap, A., Agarwal, S., & Meyarivan, T. (2002). A fast and elitist multiobjective genetic algorithm: NSGA-II. *IEEE Transactions on Evolutionary Computation, 6*(2), 182–197. doi:10.1109/4235.996017

Dhaenens, C., Lemesre, J., & Talbi, E. G. (2010). K-PPM: A new exact method to solve multi-objective combinatorial optimization problems. *European Journal of Operational Research, 200*(1), 45–53. doi:10.1016/j.ejor.2008.12.034

Dong, B., Christiansen, M., Fagerholt, K., & Chandra, S. (2020). Design of a sustainable maritime multi-modal distribution network – Case study from automotive logistics. *Transportation Research Part E, Logistics and Transportation Review, 143,* 102086. doi:10.1016/j.tre.2020.102086

Elhedhli, S., & Merrick, R. (2012). Green supply chain network design to reduce carbon emissions. *Transportation Research Part D, Transport and Environment, 17*(5), 370–379. doi:10.1016/j.trd.2012.02.002

Enmon, S. (2015). Sustainable transport practices. United States of America.

Erdoğan, S., & Miller-Hooks, E. (2012). A Green Vehicle Routing Problem. *Transportation Research Part E: Logistics and Transportation Review, Select Papers from the 19th International Symposium on Transportation and Traffic Theory, (48,* 100–114). 10.1016/j.tre.2011.08.001

Figliozzi, M. (2010). Vehicle Routing Problem for Emissions Minimization. *Transportation Research Record: Journal of the Transportation Research Board, 2197*(1), 1–7. doi:10.3141/2197-01

García Nájera, A., & Bullinaria, J. (2011). An improved multi-objective evolutionary algorithm for the vehicle routing problem with time windows. *Computers & Operations Research, 38*(1), 287–300. doi:10.1016/j.cor.2010.05.004

García-Nájera, A., Bullinaria, J. A., & Gutiérrez-Andrade, M. A. (2015). An evolutionary approach for multi-objective vehicle routing problems with backhauls. *Computers & Industrial Engineering, 81*, 90–108. doi:10.1016/j.cie.2014.12.029

Gharaei, A., Karimi, M., & Hoseini Shekarabi, S. A. (2019). An integrated multi-product, multi-buyer supply chain under penalty, green, and quality control polices and a vendor managed inventory with consignment stock agreement: The outer approximation with equality relaxation and augmented penalty algorithm. *Applied Mathematical Modelling, 69*, 223–254. doi:10.1016/j.apm.2018.11.035

Haddadene, S. R. A., Labadie, N., & Prodhon, C. (2016). NSGAII enhanced with a local search for the vehicle routing problem with time windows and synchronization constraints. *IFAC-PapersOnLine, 8th IFAC Conference on Manufacturing Modelling, Management and Control MIM, 49*, 1198–1203. 10.1016/j.ifacol.2016.07.671

Hickman, J., Hassel, D., Joumard, R., Samaras, Z., & Sorenson, S. (1999). MEET methodology for calculating transport emissions and energy consumption. [Technical Report, European Commission/DG VII Rue de la Loi 200]. Belgium.

Jabali, O., Woensel, T. V., & de Kok, A. G. (2012). Analysis of Travel Times and CO2 Emissions in Time-Dependent Vehicle Routing. *Production and Operations Management, 21*(6), 1060–1074. doi:10.1111/j.1937-5956.2012.01338.x

Jozefowiez, N., Semet, F., & Talbi, E.-G. (2009). An evolutionary algorithm for the vehicle routing problem with route balancing. *European Journal of Operational Research, 195*(3), 761–769. doi:10.1016/j.ejor.2007.06.065

Karakatič, S., & Podgorelec, V. (2015). A survey of genetic algorithms for solving multi depot vehicle routing problem. *Applied Soft Computing, 27*, 519–532. doi:10.1016/j.asoc.2014.11.005

Knowles, J., & Corne, D. (1999). The Pareto archived evolution strategy: a new baseline algorithm for Pareto multiobjective optimization. *Proceedings of the 1999 Congress on Evolutionary Computation-CEC99 (Cat. No. 99TH8406)*. IEEE. 10.1109/CEC.1999.781913

Leng, L., Zhang, C., Zhao, Y., Wang, W., Zhang, J., & Li, G. (2020). Biobjective low-carbon location-routing problem for cold chain logistics: Formulation and heuristic approaches. *Journal of Cleaner Production, 273*, 122801. doi:10.1016/j.jclepro.2020.122801

Lenstra, J. K., & Kan, A. H. G. R. (1981). Complexity of vehicle routing and scheduling problems. *Networks, 11*(2), 221–227. doi:10.1002/net.3230110211

Li, A.-D., & He, Z. (2020). Multiobjective feature selection for key quality characteristic identification in production processes using a nondominated-sorting-based whale optimization algorithm. *Computers & Industrial Engineering, 149*, 106852. doi:10.1016/j.cie.2020.106852

Li, J., Wang, D., & Zhang, J. (2018). Heterogeneous fixed fleet vehicle routing problem based on fuel and carbon emissions. *Journal of Cleaner Production, 201*, 896–908. doi:10.1016/j.jclepro.2018.08.075

Liu, Y., Shen, W., Man, Y., Liu, Z., & Seferlis, P. (2019). Optimal scheduling ratio of recycling waste paper with NSGAII based on deinked-pulp properties prediction. *Computers & Industrial Engineering, 132*, 74–83. doi:10.1016/j.cie.2019.04.021

Long, J., Sun, Z., Pardalos, P. M., Hong, Y., Zhang, S., & Li, C. (2019). A hybrid multi-objective genetic local search algorithm for the prize-collecting vehicle routing problem. *Information Sciences, 478*, 40–61. doi:10.1016/j.ins.2018.11.006

Maden, W., Eglese, R., & Black, D. (2010). Vehicle routing and scheduling with time-varying data: A case study. *The Journal of the Operational Research Society, 61*(3), 515–522. doi:10.1057/jors.2009.116

Malladi, K. T., & Sowlati, T. (2018). Sustainability aspects in Inventory Routing Problem: A review of new trends in the literature. *Journal of Cleaner Production, 197*, 804–814. doi:10.1016/j.jclepro.2018.06.224

Matsumoto, R., Umezawa, N., Karaushi, M., Yonemochi, S.-I., & Sakamoto, K. (2006). Comparison of Ammonium Deposition Flux at Roadside and at an Agricultural Area for Long-Term Monitoring: Emission of Ammonia from Vehicles. *Water, Air, and Soil Pollution, 173*(1-4), 355–371. doi:10.1007/s11270-006-9088-z

Molina, J. C., Eguia, I., Racero, J., & Guerrero, F. 2014. Multi-objective Vehicle Routing Problem with Cost and Emission Functions. *Procedia - Social and Behavioral Sciences, XI Congreso de Ingenieria del Transporte (CIT 2014), 160*, 254–263. 10.1016/j.sbspro.2014.12.137

Naderipour, M., & Alinaghian, M. (2016). Measurement, evaluation and minimization of CO2, NOx, and CO emissions in the open time dependent vehicle routing problem. *Measurement, 90*, 443–452. doi:10.1016/j.measurement.2016.04.043

Niu, Y., Zhang, Y., Cao, Z., Gao, K., Xiao, J., Song, W., & Zhang, F. (2021). MIMOA: A membrane-inspired multi-objective algorithm for green vehicle routing problem with stochastic demands. *Swarm and Evolutionary Computation, 60*, 100767. doi:10.1016/j.swevo.2020.100767

Olgun, B., Koç, Ç., & Altıparmak, F. (2021). A hyper heuristic for the green vehicle routing problem with simultaneous pickup and delivery. *Computers & Industrial Engineering, 153*, 107010. doi:10.1016/j.cie.2020.107010

Osvald, A., & Stirn, L. Z. (2008). A vehicle routing algorithm for the distribution of fresh vegetables and similar perishable food. *Journal of Food Engineering, 85*(2), 285–295. doi:10.1016/j.jfoodeng.2007.07.008

Poonthalir, G., & Nadarajan, R. (2018). A Fuel Efficient Green Vehicle Routing Problem with Varying Speed Constraint (F-GVRP). *Expert Systems with Applications, 100*, 131–144. doi:10.1016/j.eswa.2018.01.052

Pradhananga, R., Taniguchi, E., Yamada, T., & Qureshi, A. G. (2014). Environmental Analysis of Pareto Optimal Routes in Hazardous Material Transportation. *Procedia: Social and Behavioral Sciences, 125*, 506–517. doi:10.1016/j.sbspro.2014.01.1492

Prins, C. (2004). A simple and effective evolutionary algorithm for the vehicle routing problem. *Computers & Operations Research, 31*(12), 1985–2002. doi:10.1016/S0305-0548(03)00158-8

Rauniyar, A., Nath, R., & Muhuri, P. K. (2019). Multi-factorial evolutionary algorithm based novel solution approach for multi-objective pollution-routing problem. *Computers & Industrial Engineering, 130*, 757–771. doi:10.1016/j.cie.2019.02.031

Sim, J. (2017). The influence of new carbon emission abatement goals on the truck-freight transportation sector in South Korea. *Journal of Cleaner Production, 164*, 153–162. doi:10.1016/j.jclepro.2017.06.207

Soysal, M., & Çimen, M. (2017). A Simulation Based Restricted Dynamic Programming approach for the Green Time Dependent Vehicle Routing Problem. *Computers & Operations Research, 88*, 297–305. doi:10.1016/j.cor.2017.06.023

Srinivas, N., & Deb, K. (1994). Muiltiobjective Optimization Using Nondominated Sorting in Genetic Algorithms. *Evolutionary Computation, 2*(3), 221–248. doi:10.1162/evco.1994.2.3.221

Sun, B., & Apland, J. (2019). Operational planning of public transit with economic and environmental goals: Application to the Minneapolis–St. Paul bus system. *Public Transport (Berlin)*, *11*(2), 237–267. doi:10.1007/s12469-019-00199-9

Sun, W., Yu, Y., & Wang, J. (2019). Heterogeneous vehicle pickup and delivery problems: Formulation and exact solution. *Transportation Research Part E, Logistics and Transportation Review*, *125*, 181–202. doi:10.1016/j.tre.2019.03.012

Suzuki, Y., 2011. A new truck-routing approach for reducing fuel consumption and pollutants emission. doi:10.1016/j.trd.2010.08.003

Tan, K. C., Chew, Y. H., & Lee, L. H. (2006). A hybrid multiobjective evolutionary algorithm for solving vehicle routing problem with time windows. *Computational Optimization and Applications*, *34*(1), 115–151. doi:10.1007/s10589-005-3070-3

Tirkolaee, E. B., Goli, A., Faridnia, A., Soltani, M., & Weber, G.-W. (2020). Multi-objective optimization for the reliable pollution-routing problem with cross-dock selection using Pareto-based algorithms. *Journal of Cleaner Production*, *276*, 122927. doi:10.1016/j.jclepro.2020.122927

Xiao, Y., & Konak, A. (2017). A genetic algorithm with exact dynamic programming for the green vehicle routing & scheduling problem. *Journal of Cleaner Production*, *167*, 1450–1463. doi:10.1016/j.jclepro.2016.11.115

Xiao, Y., Zhao, Q., Kaku, I., & Xu, Y. (2012). Development of a fuel consumption optimization model for the capacitated vehicle routing problem. *Computers & Operations Research*, *39*(7), 1419–1431. doi:10.1016/j.cor.2011.08.013

Xu, Z., Elomri, A., Pokharel, S., & Mutlu, F. (2019). A model for capacitated green vehicle routing problem with the time-varying vehicle speed and soft time windows. *Computers & Industrial Engineering*, *137*, 106011. doi:10.1016/j.cie.2019.106011

Zhou, A., Qu, B.-Y., Li, H., Zhao, S.-Z., Suganthan, P. N., & Zhang, Q. (2011). Multiobjective evolutionary algorithms: A survey of the state of the art. *Swarm and Evolutionary Computation*, *1*(1), 32–49. doi:10.1016/j.swevo.2011.03.001

Zhu, K. Q. (2003). A diversity-controlling adaptive genetic algorithm for the vehicle routing problem with time windows. *15th IEEE International Conference on Tools with Artificial Intelligence. Presented at the Proceedings*. IEEE.s 10.1109/TAI.2003.1250187

Chapter 6
Essential Guide to Supply Chain Risk Management With Strategic Prospective Tools

Manel Elmsalmi
(iD) https://orcid.org/0000-0003-1749-9939
Higher Institute of Industrial Management of Sfax, Tunisia

Wafik Hachicha
(iD) https://orcid.org/0000-0002-6561-9141
Higher Institute of Industrial Management of Sfax, Tunisia

ABSTRACT

Although numerous risk mitigation strategies have been developed for specific types of risks in supply chain risk management (SCRM), there is a lack of concrete and generic frameworks for an integrated network SCRM process. Consequently, it is often challenging to trace the process by which conclusions are drawn from previous research studies. The main goal is to create a framework that includes articulating SCRM issues, ranking risk variables, and creating mitigation strategies. Using the "scenario method" offers a comprehensive perspective that is displayed in a single table and helps identify different options. The extended supply chain's potential tools are used to create a unique framework for scenario building in risk mitigation plans in this research. The research demonstrates the importance of the framework and how it may help organizations implement strong strategies based on compelling scenarios through a thorough case study.

DOI: 10.4018/979-8-3693-1418-0.ch006

INTRODUCTION

The future is shaped by a multitude of factors, ranging from natural forces to human growth, social dynamics, economic fluctuations, and political influences. However, it's the choices made by individuals and organizations that progressively steer the course of what lies ahead. Consequently, society holds limited control over the future but retains the capacity to influence the unfolding of history. Thus, the fusion of our needs and feasibility is paramount in navigating the complex terrain of tomorrow.

In the realm of prospective studies, scenario organizers grapple with the intricate challenge of encapsulating a multifaceted world within a predefined set of scenarios. This challenge is of utmost significance in the context of future studies and planning. To address this issue, Bryant and Lempert (2010) have introduced an innovative approach termed "Scenario Discovery," which conceptualizes scenarios as plausible future states of the world capable of shedding light on critical policy vulnerabilities.

The evolution of the scenario method, as employed in prospective studies between 1974 and 1979, was the result of amalgamating the intellectual foundation of the scenario method initiated by DATAR in the early 1970s with system analysis tools, primarily stemming from the United States during the 1950s and 1960s (E. Jantsch, 1967). Since then, this method has found application in diverse sectors (e.g., industry, agriculture, demography, employment) and on various geographic scales (countries, regions, and globally). Concurrently, American researchers have developed relatively formalized methods for constructing scenarios, such as Delphi and cross-impact matrices, rooted in expert consultation.

In practice, there isn't a single scenario method; instead, numerous methodologies exist for constructing scenarios. The rationale behind the increasing focus on potential scenarios, along with the associated challenges and objectives, stems from the escalation of uncertainties, the proliferation of interdependencies, the acceleration of change in certain domains, and the resilience of mutual inertia. Hence, companies must adopt a strategic perspective to ensure the continuity of their operations. This book chapter seeks to explore the nexus between developing a prospective scenario and the formulation of a robust supply chain risk mitigation strategy.

The primary issue at hand is the absence of concrete and generic frameworks for an integrated network Supply Chain Risk Management (SCRM) process. This gap impedes the progression from research to practical application within the field. The principal objective of this research is to establish a comprehensive framework guiding the entirety of the SCRM process, from problem formulation and risk variable identification to prioritization and, ultimately, the development of mitigation strategies.

In summary, this book chapter addresses the pressing problem of the lack of a comprehensive and generic framework for integrated network SCRM. This gap complicates the translation of research findings into practical application. This research endeavors to bridge this gap by introducing an innovative framework through the scenario method and substantiating its value through a real case study.

The significance of this work lies in its contribution to the field of SCRM, providing a systematic and structured approach to risk management within the supply chain, thereby equipping businesses with more robust strategies in the ever-evolving global business environment.

The subsequent sections of this manuscript are organized as follows: the following section provides a definition of strategic prospective analysis and the strategic prospective toolbox. Section 3 offers a comprehensive review of the scenario method and supply chain risk management, exploring their interrelationship. Section 4 presents the detailed proposed approach. Subsequently, the analysis phases of this methodology are illustrated through a case study. Finally, this work concludes with a discussion and summary of the findings in Section 6.

STRATEGIC PROSPECTIVE ANALYSIS

Definition of Prospective

Berger G. et al. (1960) define prospective as follows: "Prospective is neither a doctrine nor a system. It is a reflection on the future, which applies itself to describing the most general structures and seeks to identify the elements of a method applicable to this accelerating world." Godet M. (2007) adds that "Prospective increasingly takes the form of collective reflection, a mobilization of minds in the face of changes in the strategic environment." The purpose of prospective is to explore, create, and test visions of both possible and desirable futures. Future visions can help formulate long-term policies, strategies, and plans. Bradfield R. et al. (2005) consider it as "a formalized approach that uses a combination of qualitative and quantitative tools. The researchers describe it as a mixture of intuitive logic and PMT methodologies (modified probabilistic trends)."

From the present, it is possible to conceive several, in fact, an infinity of possible futures. Jouvenel D.H. (1999) specifies that there are five stages in the prospective approach, namely:

- The definition of the problem and the choice of the horizon,
- The construction of the system and the identification of key variables,
- The collection of data and the development of hypotheses,
- The construction, often in the form of a tree, of possible futures and
- Strategic choices.

Traditionally, four methods can be distinguished in prospective exercises, as quoted by Plassard F. (2004). These methods are: structural analysis, consultation of experts, the cross-impact method, and scenarios. However, "these methods should not be considered as being totally independent from one another since some call, at least in part, on others" (Dillaerts H. 2010).

In the integrated approach, most prospective tools and strategic analysis can be used in a modular or combinatorial fashion and in a logical and sequential manner. However, the choice depends on the nature of the problems, the financial and human resources available, and the time allocated to conducting the study.

Strategic Prospective Toolbox

There is no single method or technique for developing a prospective study. There are as many approaches as there are prospective studies. Each approach is distinguished by the arrangement of a set of techniques developed through experience and the contributions from various disciplines. Godet M. (2006) has formalized a "strategic prospective toolbox" used to:

- Initiate and stimulate the entire process by "Strategic foresight workshops".
- Establish a complete diagnosis of the company / territory vis-à-vis its environment by "Skill trees, Strategic analysis tools and Strategic diagnosis".
- Ask the right questions and identify the key variables by "Structural analysis and the Micmac method".
- Analyze stakeholder strategies by "The Mactor method".
- Sweep the field of possibilities and reduce uncertainty by "Morphological analysis, the Delphi method, Régnier's abacus, Probabilistic cross-impacts and Smic-Prob-Expert".
- Evaluate the choices and strategic options by "Relevance trees and Multipol and multicriteria analysis".

Table 1 summarizes the prospective tools and methods according to (European Commission 2002).

Structural analysis views the selected project as a system. It defines it as a set of interacting elements and enables the identification of variables based on their influences and dependencies. Skill trees are a method of collective reflection that can be used in foresight workshops. They involve retracing the past, present, and future dynamics of a system.

The analysis of actors' strategies, known as MACTOR, aims to shed light on alliances, potential conflicts between the actors, and the possibilities of evolving relations between them. Often, the analysis of actors' games is preceded by a structural

Table 1. Tools and methods used by prospective strategy stage (European Commission 2002)

Stage of strategic prospective	Methods and tools
Environment analysis	- Structural analysis - Skill trees - The MACTOR method -The DELPHI method
Risks anticipation	- The grid of issues - The risk technique
Scenarios elaboration	Morphological analysis

analysis to identify key variables, which is considered crucial for constructing scenarios.

As for the issue grid, it assists in developing preventive actions by anticipating the risks arising from issues and the strategies of various actors. Similarly, the risk technique involves considering risks and potential obstacles to a system to enhance it and address as many challenges as possible. Finally, the development of scenarios is typically carried out using morphological analysis, known as MORPHOL. It seeks to explore possible futures through various combinations and aids in reducing uncertainties.

LITERATURE OVERVIEW

Scenrio Method

Plassard F. (2004) defines the scenario method as follows: "The scenario method aims to highlight, on the one hand, the major trends, which encompass all structures and behaviors unlikely to change during the period under prospective analysis, and, on the other hand, the drivers of change, which encompass various, more or less significant indicators that help identify potential transformations leading to new case." There are two types of scenario goals: (1) Intended to inform a "proactive strategy" (desired scenarios) ; (2) Can have a "pre-active strategy" alert function (feared scenarios).

Hatem F., and al. (1993) present the following definition: "The scenario method can be viewed as a kind of 'guideline' to facilitate forward thinking step by step. This straightforward process essentially serves as a 'checklist' to ensure that nothing important is overlooked when constructing scenarios." A scenario is not an end in itself; it only gains significance through its results and consequences for action. It is often better to limit the scenarios to a few key assumptions, perhaps four or five, as the combinatorial complexity beyond these numbers can overwhelm the human mind.

The scenario method follows a logical path that has been established through numerous prospective studies. A snapshot and a schematic of the scenario method are depicted in Figure 1.

After providing an initial overview of related work, specific prior studies utilizing scenario planning in risk management are mentioned: Vecchiato R (2019) develops scenario planning for cognition and strategic investment decisions in a turbulent environment; Kim Y. and al. (2020) advance scenario planning by integrating urban growth prediction with future flood risk models. Additionally, Klerk Y. and al. (2021) present a comparative analysis of national preparedness in selected countries using scenario planning for an autonomous future. Sahraoui Y. and al. (2021) integrate ecological network modeling in a participatory approach to assess the impacts of planning scenarios on landscape connectivity.

Figure 1. Diagram of Scenrio method (Godet M.2007)

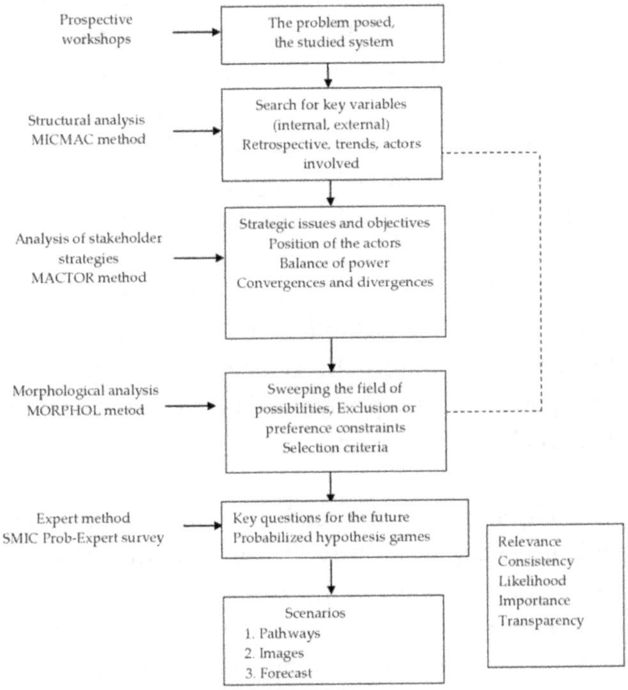

Supply Chain Risk Management

Numerous events that enter the system and affect all product, service, and information exchanges between players in a supply chain network can significantly impact the performance of the supply chain. Supply Chain Risk Management (SCRM) is the term used to describe how these incidents are managed. Essentially, a corporation would be able to effectively implement associated contingency measures when faced with a disruption if it had a well-established, robust supply chain strategy. Consequently, having a solid supply chain strategy may increase a company's resilience.

Zsidisin GA and Ritchie B. (2008) point out that "supply chain risk management is no longer solely a reactive activity focused on improving an organization's capacity to absorb disruptions; it also involves proactive and collaborative efforts to preserve the creation of value in potential circumstances." These two researchers specify that "the natural mission of SCM is to create value throughout the chain, and that of SCRM is to preserve this creation." Norrman A. and Linroth R. (2002) define it as follows: "Supply chain risk management involves collaborating with supply chain partners and applying risk management tools to address risks and uncertainties arising from or affecting logistics-related activities or resources." Artebrand A. and others (2003) add that "The identification and management of risks arise from both within and outside the supply chain, through a coordinated approach involving chain members, with the goal of reducing the vulnerability of the entire chain." Norrman and Jansson (2004) specify that it "can also be represented by a series of procedures and measures taken by certain organizations to deal with various types of risk exposure. It usually includes the identification, measurement, control, and monitoring of risk." The risk management process focuses on understanding the risks and mitigating their effects. Perret et al. (2012) recommend categorizing these different tools based on their compatibility with the ISO 31000 standard.

From the literature, it can be noted that among the conventional risk management tools, none fully aligns with all the principles derived from the ISO 31000 standard, despite it being a benchmark in the field.

- "Risk is generally addressed independently of the project and its environment, whereas it is necessary to identify its causes as well as its consequences to understand it" (Carr, V. and Tah, J., 2001).
- "The tools emphasize individual risk analysis and often fail to consider the complex interactions between different risks" (Baccarini, D., Archer, R., 2001) and (Ward, S., Chapman, C., 2003).

Partial answers have been provided by Tepeli, E. (2014), but they lack sufficiently precise formalism. Breysse, D. and others (2013) suggest that "The vast majority of the tools used are not applicable to the entire risk management process but are often specific to one or even two phases of the process."

Common methods for the identification, analysis, evaluation, and treatment of risks, such as brainstorming, are typically unstructured, reliant on qualitative information, and constrained by user experience (Grimaldi and others, 2012).

Furthermore, the concepts derived from the literature are organized around three phases: identification, evaluation, and mitigation.

Risk Identification

Risk identification is a crucial component of the risk management process. It offers decision-makers a comprehensive view of potential risks within the supply chain by pinpointing the sources or events that could result in disruptions.

Risk Assessment

Risk assessment is a crucial step in aligning control strategies and actions with the risks in the supply chain. It's important to note that, given the challenges of addressing all supply chain risks, prioritization is necessary. In this context, several studies have been conducted on Supply Chain Risk Management (SCRM) with a focus on prioritization, such as those by Diabat, Govindan, and Panicker (2012), Jha and Devaya (2008), and Faisal, Banwet, and Shankar (2006)

Risk Mitigation

The primary objective of this step is to proactively mitigate risks by applying suitable scenarios. Once the risks are identified and quantified, a preventive plan should be established to enhance risk protection for the entire supply chain. This can be accomplished through collaboration with supply chain partners who share strategies and tactics to minimize the impacts of these risks.

In fact, there is a wide variety of research on risk mitigation strategies. T.S. Glickman and H. Khamooshi (2017) have developed a set of mathematical optimization models applicable in such circumstances. These models can help determine the most cost-effective protection or prevention strategy based on estimated mitigation costs. Giovanni Margarido Righetto et al. (2019) have devised an approach and applied it to a real-world stationery company in Brazil. This approach supports decision-making in cash management, dealing with various grace periods, piecewise linear yields, and uncertainty in the exchange rate of external sales. Additionally, Koenig M. and Meissner J. (2017) have introduced a dynamic programming solution that generates policies minimizing the risk of not achieving the target revenue.

Table 2. Proposed strategic prospective toolkit for supply chain risk management

SCRM stage	Tools	Objectives
Identification	Strategic prospective workshops	- Collection of information and identification of all risk variables
Assessment	Structural analysis and Micmac method	- Identify key risk sources and variables
	MACTOR method	- Analyze stakeholder strategies - Development of strategic recommendations
Mitigation	Morphological analysis	- Identify risk reduction scenarios - Sweep the field of possibilities and reduce uncertainty.
	MULTIPOL and multicriteria analysis	- Evaluate strategic choices and options

DETAILED PROPOSED FRAMEWORK

The proposed strategic prospective toolkit for supply chain risk management is given in Table 2.

The detailed proposed framework is given by Figure 2.

Risks Identification With Prospective Workshops

Before embarking on a more substantial exercise in strategic foresight, it is wise to take the time to contemplate the nature of the problem at hand and the approach we intend to use in seeking solutions and measurements. After all, there's no sense in wasting time on false problems, and a well-posed problem is already halfway to being solved.

Forward-looking workshops serve as a means to collaboratively identify and prioritize the key risks for the company within its future, both at the national and international levels.

Upon concluding these workshops, participants can define priorities, objectives, a timeline, and the methodology required to organize the strategic foresight process. The company's managers will take on the responsibility for producing this reflection themselves.

Risks Assessment With Structural Analysis

The proposed approach utilizes a structural modeling tool known as MICMAC (Matrice d'Impacts Croisés Multiplication Appliquée à un Classement, the French acronym). The objective is to define the system and identify the key risk variables,

Figure 2. Detailed proposed framework

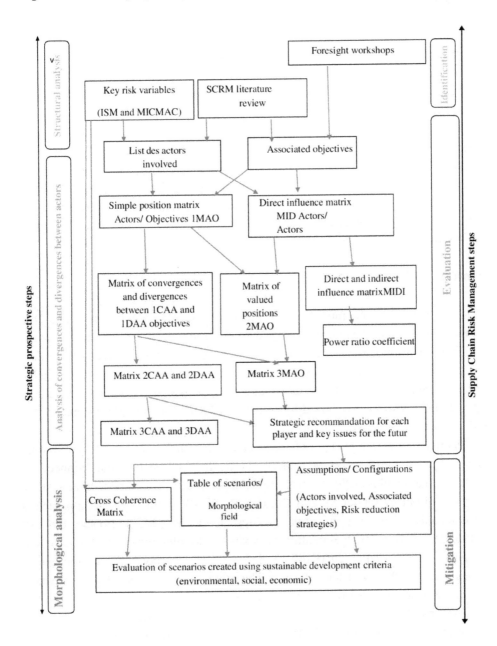

making structural analysis the most suitable method for this task. This method draws inspiration from graph theory and operations research simulations conducted shortly after World War II in the United States, notably at the Rand Corporation for the needs of the U.S. military. It provides a comprehensive representation of the system and aids in reducing its complexity to essential variables. This, in turn, highlights the key variables of the system, whether they are hidden or not, and prompts reflection on the counterintuitive aspects of the system's behavior.

According to Godet M. (2007), structural analysis is "a method for structuring collective reflection, with the chosen project considered as a system defined as a set of interacting elements." Jha K.N. and Devaya M.N. (2008) also note that "structural analysis is a tool for organizing ideas. It describes a system using a matrix that links all its components. Furthermore, it reveals the variables or factors essential to the system by assigning numerical values to their influence and dependence and presenting them on a combined graph.

Inventory of Variables and Structuring of Their Relations

This step is crucial, as emphasized by Plassard F. (2004). He also adds that "the richness of structural analysis, along with its limitations, lies in the choice of variables." The objective is to deconstruct the environment of the system to be studied by first identifying all its components. Then, by structuring them, an exhaustive list of factors representative of the entire system is obtained. This step begins with an open-ended question, as advised by Godet M. (2007), for example: "What are the risk factors in the logistics chain?"

Identifying the components of the system is not sufficient, as the system only becomes meaningful when we understand all the relationships that connect the variables. These relationships constitute the explanatory environment of the system. As pointed out by Godet M. and Durance P. (2008): "In a systemic approach, a variable only exists through its relationships." Godet M. (2007) also specifies that "Structural analysis involves relating variables in a double-entry table (the structural analysis matrix)." This matrix determines whether each column criterion has an influence on each row criterion or not. The group that participated in the variable census is responsible for filling in the matrix.

The first step in supply chain risk management is to assess supply chain risk exposures. Companies must identify not only the direct risks associated with their operations but also the potential causes or sources of those risks at every significant link along the supply chain (Faisal, 2009).

Structuring Relations Between Risk Variables and Their Prioritization With MICMAC Method

To construct a structural analysis matrix, variables need to be listed both in rows and columns, after grouping if it has occurred. The filling of the matrix can be done either row-wise, indicating the influence of each row variable on all other column variables, or column-wise, indicating which column variables influence each row variable.

In simple, non-weighted matrices, a "1" or "0" is placed in the corresponding cell, depending on whether there is a direct relationship between the two variables or not. The concept of a direct relationship is crucial and, together with the number of variables (the number of cells to fill increasing with the square of their quantity), contributes to the complexity and duration of the filling process. Recognizing a relationship between two variables is one thing, while ensuring it is indeed a direct relationship without intermediaries is another.

The initial treatment involves summing the "1" values both row-wise and column-wise, and assigning motoricity and dependency indicators to the various variables. Variables that influence more than others (sums at the end of rows) are referred to as motor variables, while the variables most influenced (sums at the bottom of columns) are referred to as dependent variables.

We can then proceed to an initial classification by listing all the variables in descending order of motoricity, from the most motor or influential variable to the least motor variable (and potentially do the same from most dependent to least dependent).

Some researchers have not organized them in a simple list but rather in a two-axis diagram, influence and dependence. For instance, dividing this diagram into quadrants (4, 8, 16...).

The structural matrices described above inform us about the presence or absence of direct relationships between two variables but not about the intensity of these relationships. One variation involves weighting the intensity of these relationships by assigning them a value (from 1 to 4).

Another development in the matrix approach is assigning signs to direct relationships: - for negative influence, + for positive influence, and n for undetermined or neutral influence, hence the term "NPN matrices" (Negative, Positive, or Neutral).

All of the structural analysis matrices have been established only from direct relationships between variables. However, a variable can also exert its influence on other variables indirectly, either through the intermediary of another variable (a "path" of order 2) or through the intermediary of several others exerting their influence in cascade, creating increasingly longer "paths" that may also loop back on themselves.

The MICMAC analysis is performed using the "Micmac" software developed by the French Institute of IT Innovation for the Enterprise under the supervision of its conceptual creator, LIPSOR (the Laboratory of Innovation of Strategic Prospective and Organization). It calculates the impact of previously identified relationships and, as a result, has the ability to prioritize variables from the structural analysis matrix. [Godet M. (2007)] provides the following definition: "MICMAC, a matrix multiplication program applied to the structural matrix, makes it possible to study the diffusion of impacts through the paths and feedback loops, and consequently to prioritize the variables."

Analysis of the Actors' Game by the MACTOR Method

To address the questions posed by structural analysis, answers must be provided. This is the focus of the first step of the scenario method (MACTOR), which primarily centers on the key variables identified by the structural analysis. It involves identifying the actors involved with these variables, as their past, present, and future actions must be thoroughly studied. In the realm of risk management within the emerging logistics chain sector, the key variables in the system are significantly influenced by the actions of various actors. While evolution hypotheses can be formulated for the general context variables, those dependent on the actions of specific actors are best determined after analyzing their interactions, as the conflicts between different actor positions are often strong. This is where the MACTOR approach becomes valuable.

The MACTOR approach (Matrix of Alliances and Conflicts: Tactics, Objectives, and Recommendations) originates from the work of the French School of "prospective," particularly the formalized scenario planning methodology proposed by Michel Godet. Initially, the MACTOR method was developed in response to the increasing criticism of traditional forecasting methods, which failed to account for the potential disruptive effects of actors involved in a system.

As a result, an actors' strategy analysis has been proposed. Its goal is to assess the impacts of actors' strategies on their environment. The corresponding software is distributed by LIPSOR (Laboratory for Prospective Investigation, Strategy, and Organization, National Conservatory of Arts and Crafts, Paris). The MACTOR method conducts as thorough examination of the strategies and initiatives of potential actors seeking to influence these variables to align them with their own preferences. These methods aim to highlight the most probable scenarios and explore combinations of hypotheses that are to be excluded a priori.

Scan the Field of Possibilities Through Morphological Analysis

Definitions of Morphological Analysis (MA)

The term "morphology" is used in a number of scientific disciplines to refer to the study of structural relationships between different parts or aspects of the object of study. For example, in biology, morphology is the study of the shape and structure of organisms and their specific structural features. In linguistics, it is the branch of grammar that studies the structure of word forms, mainly through the use of the construction of morphemes. Geomorphology is the study of landforms and the processes that shape them. Urban morphology is the study of the shape of human settlements and the process of their formation.

In this context, another definition specifies that "morphological analysis" refers to the analysis of structural relationships within the particular scientific discipline in which this term is used. [Leroy-Therville.S, (2000)] specifies that "Morphological analysis," a well-learned name for a very simple method, is often unknown or forgotten, and it should nevertheless be remembered because it can prove to be very useful for stimulating the imagination, helping identify new products or processes that were hitherto ignored, and for exploring the field of possible scenarios. The inventor of this method, F. Zwicky, wanted precisely, through morphological analysis, to make the invention "a routine," that is to say, a trivial procedure. F. Zwicky, who first imagined dwarf stars, developed this method in the mid-1940s while working for the US military.

It allows for a systematic exploration of the field of possibilities and, consequently, generates a rather large number of possible solutions because of combinatorics. It imposes structured reflection on the components and the configurations to be taken into account to reduce the field of possibilities into a useful morphological subspace, and this is achieved by introducing constraints of selection, exclusion, or preference.

Evaluate Strategic Choices and Options

Although the risk management literature has presented a variety of tools and techniques to assess and manage supply chain risks, there has been limited discussion regarding a comprehensive assessment of the effectiveness of alternative risk mitigation strategies. Such an assessment would assist managers in selecting the most suitable mitigation strategy for improved decision-making.

Recent research defines a robust risk reduction strategy as one that ensures the sustainable development of business operations. Seuring S. et al. (2015) emphasize that "a strategy that is not sustainable cannot be considered a risk reduction strategy." They further contend that "to be sustainable, supply chain risk management (SCRM)

Table 3. List of key risk variables (Hachicha W., Elmsalmi M. (2013)

Key Risks Variable	
R1. Retailer order partially delivered R2. Delayed delivery to retailer R3. Inventory and stock failure R4. Productivity and quality failure R5. insufficient or failed production quality R6. Craft and manual production	R7. Healthy and higiénic products R8. Unique supplier dependency R9. Defect of material quality R10. Forecast error R11. Volatility of retailer demand R12. Seasonal production R13. Poor harvest

must take into account the objectives related to the three dimensions of sustainability: social, environmental, and economic." The sustainability aspect has been the subject of several recent in-depth studies.

CASE STUDY

The objective of this section is to apply the proposed approach to the SC of "Masmoudi Pastry" from the identification of prioritized risk variables to the elaboration of risk mitigation strategies.

A detailed description of the steps is given below:

Step 1: Key risks identification,

Step 2: MACTOR analysis,

Step 3: Morphological analysis,

Step 4: Presentation of results.

Identification of Key Risks Variables

First and foremost, a real case study was conducted on a Tunisian food industry, "Masmoudi Pastry," to demonstrate the application of the proposed approach. The following table illustrates the main risk variables that have been developed using the MICMAC method. For further details on the MICMAC method, please refer to the previous works of Hachicha W. and Elmsalmi M. in 2013, which specify key risk variables for Masmoudi Pastry (Table 3).

MACTOR Analysis

This step involves the identification of the actors involved in the SCRM and the analysis of actors' convergences and divergences in objectives. The MACTOR (Matrix of Alliances and Conflicts: Tactics, Objectives, and Recommendations) was applied

Table 4. List of the identified actors and their associated objectives

Actors	Objectives
A1- Consumer	O1. Ensuring delivery planning
A2- Retailer	O2. Ensuring product safety
A3-Manufacturer	O3. Ensuring the availability of finished product stocks
A4-Suppliers	O4. Ensuring effective communication
A5- Wholesaler	O5. Ensuring a good quality of raw materials
A6- Distributor	O6. Maintaining the quality of finished products
A7- Farmer	O7. Ensuring the availability of raw material stock
A8- State	O8. Establishing appropriate standards and laws O9. Imposing quality labels

to assess the balance of power among the actors in the supply chain. Subsequently, the convergences and divergences of the actors regarding a number of issues and objectives associated with risk management were analyzed. This process led to the formulation of the most appropriate objectives for each actor. Table 6 summarizes the list of actors involved in this system and their respective objectives.

The MACTOR method attempts to study the problem of convergences/divergencies among SC actors against their objectives following a twostep process:

- Interpreting results from Direct Influences Matrix MID,
- Interpreting results from Valued Position Matrix 2MAO

Mactor Inputs

a. First Input: MID: Actors X Actors Direct Influences Matrix

The Actors X Actors Direct Influences Matrix (MID) (Table 7) drawn up from the actors' strategy table describes the direct influences between actors.

The simple statement of the sums of both on-line and on column influences shows that (A6) « Distributor » constitutes, by far, the most influential actor. The « Manufacturer » (A3) is the least armed to reach his objectives and also the most submitted to the pressures of the other actors.

b. Second Input: Valued Position Matrix 2MAO

The valued position matrix is presented in table 8. The 2MAO measures the number of actors agreements and disagreements.

Table 5. Actor/actor influences matrix (MID)

	A_1	A_2	A_3	A_4	A_5	A_6	A_7	A_8	Sum A_j
A_1	0	4	2	0	1	0	0	0	7
A_2	4	0	2	0	2	3	0	0	11
A_3	4	2	0	3	2	3	0	0	14
A_4	2	1	3	0	1	0	0	0	7
A_5	2	4	3	0	0	1	1	0	11
A_6	4	3	4	4	3	0	3	0	**21**
A_7	1	1	4	0	1	3	0	0	10
A_8	1	2	4	4	2	1	4	0	18
Sum A_i	18	17	**22**	11	12	11	8	0	99

Table 6. Valued position matrix (2MAO)

2MAO	O_1	O_2	O_3	O_4	O_5	O_6	O_7	O_8	O_9	Sum
A_1	1	1	4	1	4	4	0	2	2	19
A_2	3	2	3	3	2	2	2	-3	-3	23
A_3	2	4	4	3	3	4	3	-4	-4	31
A_4	3	2	0	3	4	0	4	-3	-3	22
A_5	3	2	3	3	2	2	2	-3	-3	23
A_6	4	3	3	3	0	1	3	-1	-1	19
A_7	3	2	0	3	4	0	4	-3	-3	22
A_8	0	2	0	0	1	1	0	4	4	12
Nb of agreements	19	18	17	19	20	14	18	6	6	
Nb of disagreements	0	0	0	0	0	0	0	-17	-17	
Nb of positions	19	18	17	19	20	14	18	23	23	

Mactor Output

Results from MID

a. MIDI: Direct/Indirect Influences Matrix

The Mactor software measures the direct and indirect influences and dependencies by indicators summing the terms of the MIDI matrix (respectively Ii and Di) (Table 9).

b. Influences/Dependencies Actors' Map

Table 7. Direct/indirect influences matrix (MIDI)

	A_1	A_2	A_3	A_4	A_5	A_6	A_7	A_8	I_i
A_1	7	7	5	2	5	6	1	0	26
A_2	11	11	9	5	8	6	4	0	43
A_3	13	12	12	6	9	6	4	0	50
A_4	7	6	7	3	5	5	1	0	31
A_5	11	10	9	4	7	8	2	0	44
A_6	16	14	17	7	10	10	4	0	68
A_7	10	8	10	6	8	8	4	0	50
A_8	13	10	17	8	10	10	6	0	74
D_i	81	67	74	38	55	49	22	0	386

This plan is calculated from the: MIDI matrix (these are Ii and Di). It allows to visualize on the x-axis the dependence and on the y-axis the influence of the actors between them (Figure 3).

c. Actors' Balance of power

It would be unreasonable to formulate definitive policy recommendations without taking into account the balance of power among the actors, as this factor can influence their positions and implications based on their strategic objectives. The Mactor software provides a scalar that determines the balance of power for each actor, considering their direct influence and dependence. The higher this scalar, the

Figure 3. Influences/ dependencies actors' map

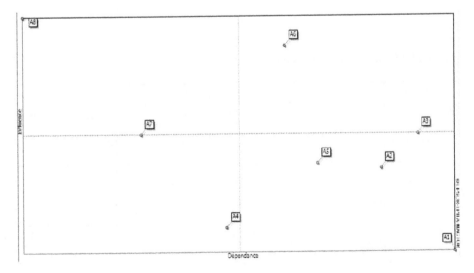

Figure 4. Actors' balance of power relations

Vector of the Actors' power relations		Histogram of Actors' power relations

.	Ri
▶ A1	0,18
A2	0,50
A3	0,61
A4	0,50
A5	0,65
A6	1,34
A7	1,27
A8	2,94

stronger the actor's position. This enables the creation of a power relations histogram directly derived from the corresponding vector (Figure 4).

A balance is also established from the MIDI odds ratio vector. This balance helps identify, for each objective, the favorable and unfavorable players, as well as the dominant trend.

Vector of the Actors' power relations

d. Net balance of influences

The net balance of direct and indirect influences (table 10) measures for each couple of actors the differential of direct and indirect influences.

These values are integers relating to:

Table 8. Net balance of influences

	A_1	A_2	A_3	A_4	A_5	A_6	A_7	A_8	Sum
A_1		-4	-8	-5	-6	-10	-9	-13	-55
A_2	4		-3	-1	-2	-8	-4	-10	-24
A_3	8	3		-1	0	-11	-6	-17	-24
A_4	5	1	1		1	-2	-5	-8	-7
A_5	6	2	0	-1		-2	-6	-10	-11
A_6	10	8	11	2	2		-4	-10	19
A_7	9	4	6	5	6	4		-6	28
A_8	13	10	17	8	10	10	6		74

Table 9. Matrix of simple positions (1MAO)

	O_1	O_2	O_3	O_4	O_5	O_6	O_7	O_8	O_9	Absolute Sum
A_1	1	1	1	1	1	1	0	1	1	8
A_2	1	1	1	1	1	1	1	-1	-1	9
A_3	1	1	1	1	1	1	1	-1	-1	9
A_4	1	1	0	1	1	0	1	-1	-1	7
A_5	1	1	1	1	1	1	1	-1	-1	9
A_6	1	1	1	1	0	1	1	-1	-1	8
A_7	1	1	0	1	1	0	1	-1	-1	7
A_8	0	1	0	0	1	1	0	1	1	5
Nb of agreements	7	8	5	7	7	6	6	2	2	
Nb of disagreements	0	0	0	0	0	0	0	-6	-6	
Nb of positions	7	8	5	7	7	6	6	8	8	

- the (+) sign indicates that the actor exerts more influence than he receives;
- the (-) sign indicates that the actor exerts less influence than he receives.

Results from MAO

e. 1MAO: Matrix of Simple positions

The Matrix of simple positions (1MAO) describes the valence of each actor on each objective (favorable, opposed, neutral or indifferent) (Table 9).

f. 2CAA Matrix

The valued matrix of convergences or valued Convergences Actors X Actors (2CAA) is associated with the Matrix of valued positions Actors X Objectives (2MAO). It identifies for each pair of actors the average intensity of the convergences when the two actors have the same valence (favorable or opposed to the objective) (Table 10).

g. 2CAA Map: Actor/Actor Convergences Graph

Convergence graphs between actors position the actors on a mapping according to their convergences (data in the 1CAA, 2CAA and 3CAA matrix): the closer the actors are to each other (compared to axis 1, the more explanatory), the greater the intensity of their convergences.

Convergence graphs between actors are built from symmetric matrices 1CAA, 2CAA, 3CAA. The nodes of the graph represent the defined actors, and the links the relations expressed in the matrices considered. (Figure 5).

h. 2DAA Graph

Table 10. The valued convergences matrix (2 CAA Matrix)

	O₁	O₂	O₃	O₄	O₅	O₆	O₇	O₈	O₉	Absolute Sum
A₁	1	1	1	1	1	1	0	1	1	8
A₂	1	1	1	1	1	1	1	-1	-1	9
A₃	1	1	1	1	1	1	1	-1	-1	9
A₄	1	1	0	1	1	0	1	-1	-1	7
A₅	1	1	1	1	1	1	1	-1	-1	9
A₆	1	1	1	1	0	1	1	-1	-1	8
A₇	1	1	0	1	1	0	1	-1	-1	70
A₈	0	1	0	0	1	1	0	1	1	5
Nb of agreements	7	8	5	7	7	6	6	2	2	
Nb of disagreements	0	0	0	0	0	0	0	-6	-6	
Nb of positions	7	8	5	7	7	6	6	8	8	

The divergence graphs allow you to easily visualize the divergence relations between the actors. They are built from the 1DAA, 2DAA, 3DAA Matrices. The

Figure 5. Actor/ actor convergences map

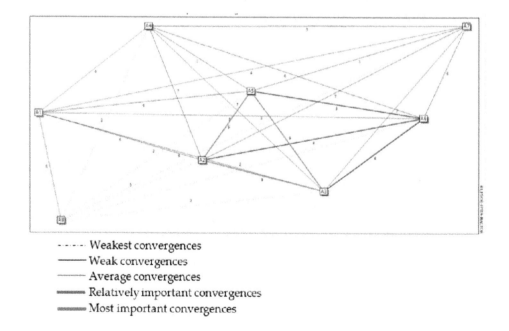

- - - - - Weakest convergences
———— Weak convergences
———— Average convergences
▬▬▬ Relatively important convergences
▬▬▬ Most important convergences

Figure 6. Actor/ actor divergences map

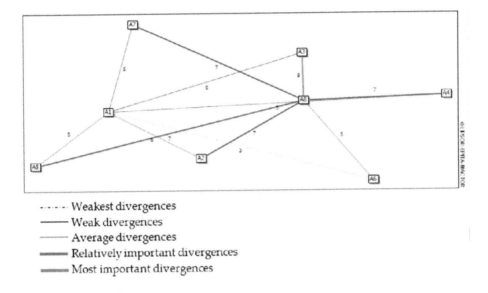

- - - - - - Weakest divergences
——— Weak divergences
————— Average divergences
▬▬▬ Relatively important divergences
▬▬▬ Most important divergences

nodes of the graph represent the defined actors, and the links the relations expressed in the matrices considered (Figure 6).

Identification of Risk Mitigation Strategies and Problem Formulation With Morphological Analysis (MA)

Risk mitigation strategies are derived from Christopher (2006), who outlines robust supply chain strategies for building a resilient supply chain:

- Postponement: refers to a strategy where a company delays the final configuration, assembly, or packaging of products until as late as possible in the production process or the supply chain. The goal of postponement is to increase flexibility and responsiveness to changes in customer demand or market conditions. It works with Generic Production: Initially, a company produces a generic or semi-finished product that can be easily customized or adapted to specific customer requirements or regional variations. This generic product is often referred to as a "base" product.
- Strategic stock: It typically refers to a specific type of inventory or stock that a company maintains for strategic purposes in supply chain management. This inventory is held to address various needs and challenges in the supply chain. The strategic stock may not be directly linked to immediate customer

demand but serves broader business goals It is part of a broader inventory management strategy and is carefully planned to balance the benefits of risk mitigation, cost management, and customer service. Companies aim to strike the right balance by optimizing the level of strategic stock to meet their specific business objectives while minimizing holding costs.

- Flexible supply base: It refers to the adaptability and versatility of a company's network of suppliers and sources. It is a supply chain management strategy that emphasizes the ability to quickly adjust, modify, or reconfigure sources of supply to respond to changing market conditions, customer demands, and disruptions. Having a flexible supply base is particularly valuable in industries where supply chain disruptions and changes in market conditions are common. It enables companies to be more agile and responsive, ensuring a more reliable supply chain even in uncertain and dynamic environments.

- Make and buy: Companies should produce their items in-house and outsource other essential items to their suppliers. This allows firms to quickly shift production.

- Economic supply incentives: Gain flexibility by shifting production among suppliers, where the buyer can provide economic incentives to cultivate additional suppliers. The company can share financial risks with the supplier.

- Flexible transportation: This includes multi-modal transportation, multi-carrier transportation, and multiple routes.

- Revenue management via dynamic pricing and promotion: Enables a firm to quickly influence the demands for different products and increase control of product demand.

- Dynamic assortment: Allows a firm to quickly adjust the demand for different products and maintain control over product demand.

- Silent product rollover: Substitutable products are valuable for managing demand fluctuations in both normal circumstances and during a supply disruption.

In this work, morphological analysis is applied to the case study of "Masmoudi Pastry." After listing the "Key risk variables" and "concerned actors," morphological analysis is used to suggest a list of the most suitable risk mitigation strategies scenarios. Using morphological analysis, managers can choose the appropriate risk mitigation strategies for each risk variable, and then they can develop the final scenario for mitigating the risks across all variables within the system.

This stage involves constructing both the multidimensional matrix and the cross-consistency matrix using all the parameters and configurations defined in stage 1.

In Table 12, the "dimensions" of the system are associated with the "key risk variables" of the supply chain. The configurations consist of "the concerned actors," their "objectives," and "risk mitigation strategies." A scenario is formed by the combination of one "dimension" with one or more "configurations."

Step 1. Constructing the Multidimensional Matrix or Table of Scenarios

The multidimensional matrix enables to visualize the whole problem (key risk variable, actors concerned, actor's objectives, risk mitigation strategies) in the same graph as well as identify the different scenarios created. Two experts defined the choice of the adequate strategies for the supply chain risk management of Masmoudi's Pastry.

Step 2. Cross-Consistency Assessment Matrix

The multidimensional matrix represents the entire morphological field of the system, resulting in $13 * 8 * 9 * 13 = 12,168$ unique configurations. On the other hand, the Cross-Consistency Assessment involves a thorough examination of each pair in the matrix. Cells with an "*" indicate an inconsistent value pair, while open cells indicate that the relevant values are assessed to be consistent.

Morphological analysis facilitates the comparison of two risk variables simultaneously through the scenario table presented below. This table serves as a decision support tool. However, the choice between these strategies must be based on specific criteria according to the preferences of Masmoudi's pastry company. In fact, an interview with company executives confirmed that "sustainability" was their most important strategic option. Moreover, a risk mitigation strategy that does not consider the criteria of "sustainable development" (environmental, social, and economic) is no longer an efficient solution for SCRM. Therefore, this work proposes taking into account the objectives of the actors associated with the key risk variables for a better SCRM. The next step is a multi-criteria analysis of risk mitigation strategies. The final scenario table is presented in Table 13. As clarified in the theoretical section, "a scenario is not an end in itself, but it only makes sense through its results and its consequences for action." Three cases arise in this work:

- The presence of a single risk with a single "RMS" strategy.
- The presence of a single risk with several "RMS" strategies (the actors are in conflict over the choice of the appropriate "RMS" strategy).
- The presence of several risks (more than two) at the same time (the actors choose several "RMS" strategies).

The choice between the "RMS" strategies in the last two cases is most common and follows the same proposed approach. At this stage, the evaluation of the impact

Table 11. Multi-dimensional matrix: Table of scenarios

Key risk variables	Actors concerned	Actor's objectives	Risk mitigation strategies
R1. Retailer order partially delivered	A1. Consumer	O1. Ensuring delivery planning	S1. Postponment
R2. Delayed delivery to retailer	A2. Retailer	O2. Ensuring product safety	S2. Strategic stock
R3. Inventory and stock failure	A3. Manufacturer	O3. Ensuring the availability of finished product stocks	S3. Flexible supplier base
R4.Productivity and quality failure	A4. Suppliers	O4. Ensuring effective communication	S4. Economic incentives for supply
R5. insufficient or failed production quality	A5. Wholesaler	O5. Ensuring a good quality of raw materials	S5. Flexible transport
R6. Craft and manual production	A6. Distributor	O6. Maintaining the quality of finished products	S6. Revenue management
R7. Healthy and higiénic products	A7. Farmer	O7. Ensuring the availability of raw material stock	S7. Assortment planning
R8. Unique supplier dependency	A8. State	O8. Establishing appropriate standards and laws	S8. Traceability
R9. Defect of material quality		O9. Imposing quality labels	S9. Information system
R10. Forecast error			S10. Recovery planning systems
R11. Volatility of retailer demand			S11. Time reduction
R12. Seasonal production			S12. Impose quality labels on finished products
R13.Poor harvest			S13. Support the participative management style

of the strategies in relation to a hierarchy of the organizational objectives of each actor, their power relationship, and a selection based on the robustness of the strategic options for each scenario (using the appropriate sustainable development criteria).

Evaluation of Risks Mitigation Strategies With Sustainable Criteria

According to the literature, conducting a survey to develop optimal risk reduction strategies based on sustainable development criteria within organizations and exploring the interconnections between risk and sustainability would be highly

Table 12. Sets of criterion weights expressing the preferences of the two actors

	Env. Criteria	Eco. Criteria	Social. Criteria	Total
Retailer	3	3	4	10
Distributor	2	5	3	10

Table 13. Distributor policy (A6)

	Env. Criteria	Economique Criteria	Social criteria	Average
S1.	5	5	5	5
S2.	5	5	3	4,4
S3.	5	5	4	4,7

intriguing. The experts at Masmoudi concur on integrating sustainable criteria into the assessment of risk mitigation strategies.

Let's focus on risk "R2," which relates to delayed delivery to the retailer. The primary actors involved are the retailer (A2) and the distributor (A6), who have agreed on specific risk mitigation strategies, namely, "flexible transport, traceability, and information systems." The initial step involves assigning coefficients to each strategy based on the criteria of environmental, economic, and social sustainability. These actors express their preferences by assigning weights to these criteria (Table 12). This research encompasses the policies of both the retailer and the distributor (Table 13 and Table 14)).

According to the literature, conducting a survey to develop optimal risk reduction strategies based on sustainable development criteria within organizations and exploring the interconnections between risk and sustainability would be highly intriguing. The experts at Masmoudi concur on integrating sustainable criteria into the assessment of risk mitigation strategies.

Table 14. Retailer policy (A2)

	Env. Criteria	Economique Criteria	Social criteria	Average
S1.	5	3	5	4.4
S2.	5	5	0	3.0
S3.	5	4	5	4.7

Let's focus on risk "R2," which relates to delayed delivery to the retailer. The primary actors involved are the retailer (A2) and the distributor (A6), who have agreed on specific risk mitigation strategies, namely, "flexible transport, traceability, and information systems." The initial step involves assigning coefficients to each strategy based on the criteria of environmental, economic, and social sustainability. These actors express their preferences by assigning weights to these criteria. This research encompasses the policies of both the retailer and the distributor.

DISCUSSION AND CONCLUSION

The process by which conclusions are drawn in supply chain risk management studies is often challenging to trace. We typically lack a comprehensive audit trail that outlines the progression from the initial problem formulation to specific solutions or conclusions. Without traceability, scientific control over results and reproducibility becomes problematic. Most literature in this field is often related to specific areas of intervention rather than the entire logistics process. Consequently, interactions between various links in the supply chain often go unaccounted for. Furthermore, many risk reduction methods primarily focus on the likelihood of risks occurring, but fail to address unforeseen disasters with negligible probabilities. This led us to explore a "prospective" approach, which involves building the future instead of predicting it.

While prospective analysis methods are relatively straightforward, they require a solid understanding and expertise from the professionals who provide the foundational data. These tools should be used as needed, considering the nature of the problem, time constraints, and available resources. Their benefits include facilitating collective reflections, addressing counterintuitive aspects of system behavior, creating useful models for studying complex, unquantified issues, and utilizing cross-consistency assessment to address vague concepts and terminological differences. The process also creates an audit trail by documenting the formulation and structure process, from the initial problem formulation to specific solutions and conclusions.

In the context of Supply Chain Risk Management (SCRM), the prospective approach offers several advantages. It provides an overview of all components of the logistics chain, including key risk variables, involved actors, their objectives, and risk reduction strategies. This aids decision-making and allows managers to choose the most appropriate strategies for mitigating risk variables. It also helps compare different areas of "Risk Management Strategies" to determine whether strategies for one risk variable conflict with those of others.

However, there are limitations to this approach. Forward-looking strategies are often based on expert opinions, which can be subjective, affecting variable selection and matrix completion. Results of the analysis typically consist of charts and figures that require thorough interpretation.

To enhance supply chain risk management, organizations will need to make more informed decisions while considering potential risks and desired futures. The methods proposed here have demonstrated their effectiveness in numerous applications both in France and abroad.

This book chapter presents a well-defined framework using strategic foresight to formulate risk mitigation strategies in supply chains, demonstrated through a case study of Masmoudi's pastry supply chain. The research involved identifying risk variables, prioritizing them using the MICMAC method, and studying the convergences and divergences of actors' objectives. This was followed by a morphological analysis, resulting in a scenario table encompassing all components of the system, including key risk variables, actors, objectives, and risk mitigation strategies. The last step involved assessing and choosing the most appropriate risk reduction strategies based on the "Environmental, economic, and social" criteria of sustainable development proposed to the company's decision-makers. The strategies and scenarios are specific to this logistics chain, but the approach is general.

In future research, the plan is to expand the evaluation and choice of risk reduction strategies to include other policies, not just sustainable development criteria. Comparing results from different policies will aid in decision-making. Consideration of the MULTIPOL method for this purpose is recommended.

REFERENCES

Álvarez, A., & Ritchey, T. (2015). Applications of general morphological analysis. *Acta Morphologica Generalis*, *4*(1).

Artebrant, A., Jönsson, E., & Nordhemmer, M. (2004). *Risks and Risk Management in the Supply Chain Flow: A Case Study Based on Some of Marsh's Clients.*

Baccarini, D., & Archer, R. (2001). The risk ranking of projects: A methodology. *International Journal of Project Management*, *19*(3), 139–145. doi:10.1016/S0263-7863(99)00074-5

Blanken, L. J. (2012). Reconciling strategic studies... with itself: A common framework for choosing among strategies. *Defense & Security Analysis*, *28*(4), 275–287. doi:10.1080/14751798.2012.730723

Boumaour, A., Grimes, S., Brigand, L., & Larid, M. (2018). Integration process and stakeholders' interactions analysis around a protection project: Case of the National park of Gouraya, Algeria (South-western Mediterranean). *Ocean and Coastal Management, 153*, 215–230. doi:10.1016/j.ocecoaman.2017.12.031

Bradfield, R., Wright, G., Burt, G., Cairns, G., & Van Der Heijden, K. (2005). The origins and evolution of scenario techniques in long range business planning. *Futures, 37*(8), 795–812. doi:10.1016/j.futures.2005.01.003

Breysse, D., Tepeli, E., Khartabil, F., Taillandier, F., Medhizadeh, R., & Morand, D. (2013). Project risk management in construction projects: Developing modelling tools to favor a multidisciplinary approach. *Safety, Reliability, Risk and Life-Cycle Performance of structures and Infrastructures.*

Bryant, B. P., & Lempert, R. J. (2010). Thinking inside the box: A participatory, computer-assisted approach to scenario discovery. *Technological Forecasting and Social Change, 77*(1), 34–49. doi:10.1016/j.techfore.2009.08.002

Carr, V., & Tah, J. H. M. (2001). A fuzzy approach to construction project risk assessment and analysis: Construction project risk management system. *Advances in Engineering Software, 32*(10-11), 847–857. doi:10.1016/S0965-9978(01)00036-9

Chen, K., Ren, Z., Mu, S., Sun, T. Q., & Mu, R. (2020). Integrating the Delphi survey into scenario planning for China's renewable energy development strategy towards 2030. *Technological Forecasting and Social Change, 158*, 120157. doi:10.1016/j.techfore.2020.120157

Dillaerts, H. (2010, November). Analyse prospective du libre accès en France. In *Document numérique et société*. ADSB.

Duczynski, G. (2017). Morphological analysis as an aid to organisational design and transformation. *Futures, 86*, 36–43. doi:10.1016/j.futures.2016.08.001

Elmsalmi, M., & Hachicha, W. (2014, May). Risk mitigation strategies according to the supply actors' objectives through MACTOR method. In *2014 International Conference on Advanced Logistics and Transport (ICALT)* (pp. 362-367). IEEE. 10.1109/ICAdLT.2014.6866339

Elmsalmi, M., Hachicha, W., & Aljuaid, A. M. (2021). Modeling sustainable risks mitigation strategies using a morphological analysis-based approach: A real case study. *Sustainability (Basel), 13*(21), 12210. doi:10.3390/su132112210

European Commission (2002). *Practical guide to territorial foresight in France*. EC.

Fátima Teles, M., & de Sousa, J. F. (2017). A general morphological analysis to support strategic management decisions in public transport companies. *Transportation Research Procedia, 22,* 509–518. doi:10.1016/j.trpro.2017.03.069

Fetoui, M. (2021), Prospects for stakeholder cooperation in effective implementation of enhanced rangeland restoration techniques in southern Tunisia, Rangeland. *Ecology & Management.* https://creativecommons.org/licenses/by-nc-nd/4.0

Godet, M. (1990). Integration of scenarios and strategic management. Butterworth-Heinemann Ltd.

Godet, M. (2006). Creating Futures: Scenario Planning as a strategic management tool (pp. 280). Washington, DC: Economica. Economica Brookings diffusion.

Godet, M. (2007). Manuel de la prospective stratégique: Tome 2. L'Art et la méthode, (pp. 122-159).

Godet, M., & Roubelat, F. (1996). Creating the future: The use and misuse of scenarios. *Long Range Planning, 29*(2), 164–171. doi:10.1016/0024-6301(96)00004-0

Grimaldi, S., Rafele, C., & Cagliano, A. C. (2012). A framework to select techniques supporting project risk management. *Risk Management, 3,* 67–96.

Groves, D. G., & Lempert, R. J. (2007). A new analytic method for finding policy-relevant scenarios. *Global Environmental Change, 17*(1), 73–85. doi:10.1016/j.gloenvcha.2006.11.006

Hachicha, W., & Elmsalmi, M. (2014). An integrated approach based-structural modeling for risk prioritization in supply network management. *Journal of Risk Research, 17*(10), 1301–1324. doi:10.1080/13669877.2013.841734

Hatem F. (1993). *Foresight: Practices and methods.* Paris, Economica.

Huss, W. R., & Honton, E. J. (1987). Scenario planning—What style should you use? *Long Range Planning, 20*(4), 21–29. doi:10.1016/0024-6301(87)90152-X

Jantsch, E. (1967). *Technological forecasting in perspective* (Vol. 3). OECD.

Jha, K. N., & Devaya, M. N. (2008). Modelling the risks faced by Indian construction companies assessing international projects. *Construction Management and Economics, 26*(4), 337–348. doi:10.1080/01446190801953281

Jimenez, H., Stults, I., & Mavris, D. (2009). A morphological approach for proactive risk management in civil aviation security. In *47th AIAA Aerospace Sciences Meeting Including the New Horizons Forum and Aerospace Exposition* (p. 1636). ACM. 10.2514/6.2009-1636

Johansen, I. (2018). Scenario modelling with morphological analysis. *Technological Forecasting and Social Change, 126*, 116–125. doi:10.1016/j.techfore.2017.05.016

Jouvenel, H. (1999). La démarche prospective. Un bref guide méthodologique. *FUTURIBLES-PARIS-*, 47-68.

Keseru, I., Coosemans, T., & Macharis, C. (2021). Stakeholders' preferences for the future of transport in Europe: Participatory evaluation of scenarios combining scenario planning and the multi-actor multi-criteria analysis. *Futures, 127*, 102690. doi:10.1016/j.futures.2020.102690

Kim, Y., & Newman, G. (2020). Advancing scenario planning through integrating urban growth prediction with future flood risk models. *Computers, Environment and Urban Systems, 82*, 101498. doi:10.1016/j.compenvurbsys.2020.101498 PMID:32431469

Kinker, P., Swarnakar, V., Singh, A. R., & Jain, R. (2021). Identifying and evaluating service quality barriers for polytechnic education: An ISM-MICMAC approach. *Materials Today: Proceedings, 46*, 9752–9757. doi:10.1016/j.matpr.2020.09.129

Klerk, Y. (2019). *Scenario planning for an autonomous future: a comparative analysis of national preparedness relating to maritime policy/legislative frameworks, societal readiness and HR development for autonomous vessel operations.*

Kumar, H., Singh, M. K., & Gupta, M. P. (2019). A policy framework for city eligibility analysis: TISM and fuzzy MICMAC-weighted approach to select a city for smart city transformation in India. *Land Use Policy, 82*, 375–390. doi:10.1016/j.landusepol.2018.12.025

Lamé, G., Jouini, O., & Stal-Le Cardinal, J. (2019). Methods and contexts: Challenges of planning with scenarios in a hospital's division. *Futures, 105*, 78–90. doi:10.1016/j.futures.2018.09.005

Nguyen, M. T., & Dunn, M. (2009). *Some Methods for Scenario Analysis in Defence Strategic Planning.*

Norrman, A., & Jansson, U. (2004). Ericsson's proactive supply chain risk management approach after a serious sub-supplier accident. *International Journal of Physical Distribution & Logistics Management, 34*(5), 434–456. doi:10.1108/09600030410545463

Norrman, A., & Linroth, R. (2002). *Supply Chain Risk Management: Purchaser's vs. Planner's Views on sharing capacity investment risks in the Telecom Industry.* Proceedings of the 11th International Annual IPSERA conference, Twente University.

Plassard F. (2004) Retrospective de la prospective. *Travaux de recherche, 20.*

Poskitt, S., Waylen, K. A., & Ainslie, A. (2021). Applying pedagogical theories to understand learning in participatory scenario planning. *Futures, 128,* 102710. doi:10.1016/j.futures.2021.102710

Postma, T. J., & Liebl, F. (2005). How to improve scenario analysis as a strategic management tool? *Technological Forecasting and Social Change, 72*(2), 161–173. doi:10.1016/S0040-1625(03)00152-5

Ritchey, T. (1998). General morphological analysis. In *16th euro conference on operational analysis* (*Vol. 41*).

Roubelat, F. (2000). Scenario planning as a networking process. *Technological Forecasting and Social Change, 65*(1), 99–112. doi:10.1016/S0040-1625(99)00125-0

Sahraoui, Y., Leski, C. D. G., Benot, M. L., Revers, F., Salles, D., van Halder, I., & Carassou, L. (2021). Integrating ecological networks modelling in a participatory approach for assessing impacts of planning scenarios on landscape connectivity. *Landscape and Urban Planning, 209,* 104039. doi:10.1016/j. landurbplan.2021.104039

Strelkovskii, N., Komendantova, N., Sizov, S., & Rovenskaya, E. (2020). Building plausible futures: Scenario-based strategic planning of industrial development of Kyrgyzstan. *Futures, 124,* 102646. doi:10.1016/j.futures.2020.102646

Suresh, M., & Kesav Balajee, T. B. (2021). Modelling of factors influencing on informal learning among school teachers: An ISM-MICMAC approach. Materials today: Proceedings. InPress. doi:10.1016/j.matpr.2020.11.547

Tepeli, E. (2014). *Processus formalis'e et syst'emique de management des risques par des projets de construction complexes et stratégiques.* Université de Bordeaux.

Van der Heijden, K. (2005). *Scenarios. The art of Strategic Thinking* (2nd ed.). John.

Varum, C. A., & Melo, C. (2010). Directions in scenario planning literature–A review of the past decades. *Futures, 42*(4), 355–369. doi:10.1016/j.futures.2009.11.021

Vecchiato, R. (2019). Scenario planning, cognition, and strategic investment decisions in a turbulent environment. *Long Range Planning, 52*(5), 101865. doi:10.1016/j. lrp.2019.01.002

Ward, S., & Chapman, C. (2003). Transforming project risk management into project uncertainty management. *International Journal of Project Management, 21*(2), 97–105. doi:10.1016/S0263-7863(01)00080-1

Witt, T., Dumeier, M., & Geldermann, J. (2020). Combining scenario planning, energy system analysis, and multi-criteria analysis to develop and evaluate energy scenarios. *Journal of Cleaner Production, 242*, 118414. doi:10.1016/j.jclepro.2019.118414

Zsidisin, G. A., & Ritchie, B. (Eds.). (2008). *Supply chain risk: a handbook of assessment, management, and performance* (Vol. 124). Springer Science & Business Media.

Chapter 7

Exploring the Role of Artificial Intelligence in Education

Ghania Khensous

ⓘD https://orcid.org/0000-0003-2735-3300
École Normale Supérieure d'Oran, Algeria

Amal Boumedjout
École Normale Supérieure d'Oran, Algeria

Kaouter Labed
École Normale Supérieure d'Oran, Algeria

ABSTRACT

Artificial intelligence has emerged as a transformative force across numerous sectors, and its impact on education is no exception. In recent years, AI has gained prominence in the field of education; revolutionizing the way we teach, learn, and administer educational processes. From personalized learning experiences to intelligent tutoring systems, AI has the potential to reshape the future of education, making it more accessible, adaptive, and effective than ever before. The future of learning and teaching will be shaped by the convergence of innovative technologies, data-driven methodologies, and personalized learning experiences. Therefore, the authors explore the dynamic landscape of artificial intelligence in education; this book chapter discusses mainly: AIED areas, AIED applications, learning about AI as well as preparing for AI.

DOI: 10.4018/979-8-3693-1418-0.ch007

INTRODUCTION

Education is one of the main fields in the human life. It is the process of teaching and learning methods throughout multiple subjects. If we go all the way back to the primitive man, we observe that knowledge was passed down through oral teaching and storytelling. And it was gained throughout experience while trying to survive nature every day.

Yet as the population increased, it became difficult to carry on handing down knowledge in such inefficient way. From there came the approach of tasking few adults on teaching a large group of kids, more efficient for the society(Cubberley 2005).

However, the first execution to what we consider as school establishment today was the schools in the United States in the 17th century. For example, Boston Latin School, which was founded in 1635, was the first public school and the oldest existing school in the country (Goldin 1999).

These establishments continued to develop in systems and approaches until it became the educational environments, we know today all over the world. And education expanded to become all sorts of institutions such as public schools, private schools, homeschooling as well as languages schools and art schools.

As all other fields, Education is bowed to change due to socio-economic and cultural transformations. And even though, traditional education stood still for centuries, it found itself facing the fast pace of development in IT (Information Technologies) in general and AI (Artificial intelligence) in particular.

Artificial intelligence, sometimes called machine intelligence, is intelligence demonstrated by machines, in contrast to the natural intelligence displayed by humans such as "learning" and "problem solving". It is defined by (Chen, Chen, and Lin 2020) as a field of study and the resulting innovations and developments that have culminated in computers, machines, and other artifacts having human-like intelligence characterized by cognitive abilities, learning, adaptability, and decision-making capabilities.

The application of AI algorithms and systems in education are gaining increased interest year by year. Through AI, educators can personalize instruction to meet the diverse needs of individual students. AI-powered educational games make learning more engaging and interactive. Natural Language Processing (NLP) also enables AI chatbots to assist students with questions and explanations in real-time.

The future of learning and teaching will be shaped by the convergence of innovative technologies, data-driven methodologies and personalized learning experiences. Therefore, we explore the dynamic landscape of artificial intelligence in education; this book chapter discusses mainly: AIED Applications, learning about AI as well as preparing for AI.

LEARNING WITH AI (APPLICATIONS)

AI has been found to be used in higher education because of the tools and services it has. AI is not only transforming higher education but also revolutionizing education across all levels, from early childhood to adult learning. In early childhood education, AI-powered interactive learning tools and educational apps engage young learners in playful and immersive learning experiences, fostering early literacy, numeracy, and critical thinking skills. In adult education and lifelong learning, AI-powered platforms offer flexible learning opportunities, personalized skill development programs, and career guidance services, empowering learners to pursue continuous learning and career advancement.

AI technology has immense potential to improve the standard of education across all levels of study. The key advantages of AI can be summarized as (Kamalov, Santandreu Calonge, and Gurrib 2023): enhanced learning outcomes, time and cost efficiency as well as global access to quality education.

Unfortunately, many educators are ignorant of its significance, extent, and components. Considering the aforementioned issue, this section aims to expand on the exploration of AI applications in education, their scope in teaching and learning.

In general, AIED (Artificial Intelligence in Education) is used in four areas in academic support services, as well as institutional and administrative services, including (Kengam 2020): profiling and prediction (Guan, Mou, and Jiang 2020), assessment and evaluation (Keengwe 2018), adaptive systems (Verdú et al. 2008) and personalization and Intelligent Tutoring Systems (ITS) (Akyuz 2020; Conati et al. 2021).

Another clustering of AIED applications is given by (van der Vorst and Jelicic 2019) noting that AI can be used to: transfer knowledge and skills, to assess knowledge and skills and to inform instructors of students' progress and achievements.

Below we give an overview of the main applications of AI in education:

2.1. Intelligent Tutoring System: AI technology is used by ITS to teach and give feedback to students without having a human teacher, because it can be used for one-on-one lessons. It teaches and illustrates theory through examples. It then asks the students questions. It is capable of understanding the answers provided by students and determining their knowledge, which influences what should be presented to and asked of the student. Additionally, the student can ask questions, and the system is capable of responding to or resolving difficulties within the specified knowledge domain (Fayaz Ahmad et al. 2021).

ITS is an important tool to enable personalized learning and transform teaching methods, curriculum forms and learning environments (Wang et al. 2023).

2.2. Social Robots: Similar to other intelligent systems, social robots monitor social behavior and interact with humans in one way or another. They are now widely used in schooling. They can teach and tutor in addition to other responsibilities in education. Students who lack access to educational institutions and real classrooms have been employing social robots to connect with other students and teachers in real time (Fayaz Ahmad et al. 2021).

Young learners classes in robotics – properly taught – have an impact on the development of mathematical literacy and scientific-technical information and social competences (Smyrnova-Trybulska et al. 2016).

2.3. Adaptive Learning System: Adaptive learning systems are digital learning tools that adapt to the learner to the greatest extent feasible so that the learning process is optimized and/or student performance increases as a result of the learning process (van der Vorst and Jelicic 2019).

In the paper (Peng, Ma, and Spector 2019), the concept of personalized adaptive learning is proposed and used as a new pedagogical approach enabled by SLE (Smart Learning Environment). The authors of the paper provided a clear understanding of personalized adaptive learning.

2.4. Collaborative Learning: At the moment, young people spend an inordinate amount of time on their smartphones or tablets. This allows students to study in their spare time using AI tools. By utilizing Gesture Recognition Technology, AI enables us to ascertain a student's mood or ease throughout lectures (Kengam 2020). It also monitors the speed of a specific individual among the others, primarily through employing advanced analytics, Deep Learning (DL) and Machine Learning (ML) (Kengam 2020). AI can assist each student by providing them with a customized curriculum based on their interests and abilities (Kengam 2020).

Global classrooms are made possible, which benefits students who are unable to attend class due to illness (Kengam 2020). Distance and geography are no longer impediments to education when AI is applied.

Similarly, AI can make it simple for schools and universities to enroll as many students as they require regardless of their location (Fayaz Ahmad et al. 2021).

Besides, AI can gather students into groups that are best suited for specific tasks. This process is referred to as Adaptive Group Formation (Kengam 2020). Students' learning achievements can also be recorded and examined on a regular basis using AI apps. It features algorithms for predicting students' progress, grade chances, and assignment issues with a high degree of certainty (Fayaz Ahmad et al. 2021).

It takes a lot of time for a teacher to mark students' homework and assessments under the traditional school system. When AI is introduced, these duties will be completed quickly. It also aids in the development of strategies for bridging learning gaps (Kengam 2020). In the absence of any outside interference, tasks such as marking, attendance, assignment checking, and so on will be carried out by the intelligent system (Fayaz Ahmad et al. 2021).

2.5. Natural Language Processing: AIED systems equipped with NLP capabilities facilitate language learning by providing interactive exercises, pronunciation feedback, and language comprehension support through conversation-based interactions.

The paper (Litman 2016) has presented a summary of research in the area of NLP for educational applications. Opportunities and challenges for innovative NLP research were highlighted throughout the paper.

Automated Essay Scoring (AES): is a way of evaluating written documents like papers and essays without human interaction. It uses NLP to evaluate a text's substance and style. In automated essay scoring, a model is trained on previously graded texts manually. Following that, machine learning techniques are employed to determine the degree to which new texts relate to or contain elements of the texts used to build the model (van der Vorst and Jelicic 2019).

Educational Recommender Systems (ERS): These AI systems recommend educational resources, such as books, articles, or courses, based on a learner's preferences and needs.

The paper (da Silva et al. 2023) presented a systematic literature review that aims to analyze and synthesize the main trends, limitations and research opportunities related to the teaching and learning support recommender systems area in four dimensions namely: how the recommendations are produced, how the recommendations are presented to the users, how the recommender systems are evaluated and what are the limitations and opportunities for research in the area.

2.6. Augmented Reality (AR), Virtual Reality (VR) and Simulations: Globally, we see increased efforts to combine AI with other digital breakthroughs. AI and augmented reality are being researched in Germany, and smart glasses are being used to make it easier for students to see what they need to do right in front of them at the start of class. Canada, too, is conducting research into how simulations and virtual reality might be used in conjunction with artificial intelligence to enhance the learning experience. Students receive practical instructions from an AI in these simulation environments and can instantly begin working on an issue (van der Vorst and Jelicic 2019).

For instance, learning to fly an airplane cannot be achieved solely from books and instructors. One must gain practical experience of how it feels and functions. Through its virtual environment, Artificial Intelligence Applications (AIA) simulates the required conditions and provides experience with how it operates.

The risk of conducting studies in multiple labs is very high, and doing so on one's own is extremely tough. Artificial intelligence systems in many kinds can conduct such studies without putting humans at danger (Fayaz Ahmad et al. 2021).

Students could be engaged and guided in a game-based environment of learning and reliable virtual reality through the use of intelligent virtual reality, and the work of teachers and facilitators could be performed by virtual agents in remote virtual labs using intelligent virtual reality. For example, AI algorithms develop animations and virtual representations that assist students learn about the human body and organs better than texts.

The paper (Al-Ansi et al. 2023) analyzed the role of AR and VR in education from 2011 to 2022 and explored the main benefits and challenges, mobile applications and platforms, exponential growth during covid-19 pandemic and recent developments. The authors noted that the integration of AR and VR in education is still in the first stages, the potential of these technologies will change the nature of education and bring more benefits for students, teachers and educational institutions.

2.7. Game-Based Learning and Serious Games: AI-driven games and simulations provide engaging and interactive learning experiences. They adapt to learner performance and offer opportunities for hands-on learning.

The study of (Pratama and Setyaningrum 2018) is an attempt to investigate the effect of game-based learning that developed based on problem-solving method, on students cognitive and affective aspects. According to the authors, the results indicated that students who were exposed to the game-based learning within problem-solving method, obtain positive effect on cognitive and affective aspects. They concluded that the use of educational games could support and increase the mathematics learning outcome.

2.8. Educational Data Mining (EDM): EDM involves the use of AI and data analysis techniques to extract insights from educational data. This can inform instructional design, identify learning patterns and predict student performance.

The study (Yağcı 2022) proposed a new model based on ML algorithms to predict the final exam grades of undergraduate students, taking their midterm exam grades as the source data. Using EDM, the study presented a contribution to the early prediction of students at high risk of failure and determined the most effective machine learning methods.

LEARNING ABOUT AI

The use of artificial intelligence to personalize learning represents a significant advancement in the field of education, providing notable benefits to both students and teachers, as well as educational institutions. The use of AI in education gained true momentum during the COVID epidemic. Indeed, the access and improvement of communication between students and teachers began to develop intelligently and very efficiently. In the education industry, the acceptance and implementation of AI are inevitable. Therefore, teachers and educators of future generations must become familiar with artificial intelligence and its educational implications.

To delve deeper into this perspective, various aspects of personalized learning through the use of AI can be described:

Assessment of the learner's strengths and weaknesses: The artificial intelligence can conduct a thorough analysis of each student's past performance. Using sophisticated algorithms, it can discern the areas in which a learner excels and those that require reinforcement. This analysis goes beyond a simple assessment of grades to understand the underlying cognitive processes, enabling more precise personalization. In this context, author of (Anderson 2007) explored the cognitive processes engaged in learning and how AI can replicate these mechanisms to recognize strengths and weaknesses. In (VanLEHN 2011), author offered perspectives on the efficacy of AI within tutoring systems, highlighting its contribution to personalized learning.

In (Berland, Baker, and Blikstein 2014), authors explored the field of educational data mining, illustrating how analytics powered by AI can unveil nuanced insights into the strengths and weaknesses of students.

Adaptation of Educational Content

The integration of artificial intelligence to adapt educational content represents a significant advancement in the field of education. By leveraging a thorough analysis of students' past performances, AI generates personalized recommendations to optimize the learning process. This individualized approach relies on AI's ability to process extensive datasets, drawing insights from previous assessments, learning habits, and individual preferences. With this nuanced understanding, AI identifies specific gaps for each learner, subsequently suggesting targeted educational resources to strengthen areas in need of improvement.

AI recommendations extend beyond traditional materials, encompassing interactive exercises, simulations, and specific projects. For instance, when faced with challenges in mathematics, AI may recommend explanatory videos, online practical exercises, or even educational games to reinforce skills in an engaging manner. This personalized learning allows each student to progress at their own pace. Some may require more time to master certain concepts, while others advance more quickly. AI continually adjusts its recommendations based on each learner's progress, ensuring an educational experience tailored to their individual needs. Moreover, this approach contributes to reducing learning disparities by providing targeted support where it is most needed. Students facing challenges receive additional resources and more in-depth monitoring, while advanced learners are stimulated by more complex challenges.

By implementing the adaptation of educational content through AI, educators gain valuable insights into learning trends within their classrooms. This enables them to adjust their teaching methods and better cater to the specific needs of their students, fostering a more responsive and effective educational environment.

Author in (Conati et al. 2021) presented innovative methods and approaches aimed at personalizing the learning experience based on individual needs, thereby contributing to a deeper understanding of the underlying mechanisms for optimizing learning through intelligent technologies.

In some countries, particularly in the global North, the use of computer programs to assist with teaching and learning has become almost universal. These programs have been utilized to assist with a variety of teaching and learning tasks, ranging from assisting with subject learning to exercise practices and drills to formative and summative examinations. These are currently utilized at all levels of education, from primary to postgraduate, and in a wide variety of courses, not just in the sciences, but also in the arts and humanities (Guilherme 2019).

Ongoing Tracking of Progress

The evolution of artificial intelligence technologies has led to significant advances in the continuous monitoring of students' progress. The work conducted in this field has harnessed sophisticated cognitive tools to establish real-time tracking of academic performance.

Machine learning algorithms, fueled by real-time data and predictive models, play a crucial role. These algorithms instantly assess students' understanding, identifying potential gaps and anticipating their specific educational needs. The judicious use of these techniques enables AI to generate personalized educational recommendations tailored to each student.

The system also relies on in-depth analyses of historical data, allowing AI to contextualize students' progress. By providing instant feedback, this approach promotes reactive learning, thereby reducing gaps in understanding.

This dynamic approach contributes to maintaining students' engagement by creating a stimulating educational environment. By integrating positive feedback for achievements and proposing suitable challenges, AI cultivates a motivating learning experience. Thus, the work in this field represents a major step toward a more personalized, responsive education conducive to students' academic flourishing. In (Azevedo 2005), authors underscored the significance of self-regulation in the learning process, specifically highlighting the mechanisms through which hyperlinks can foster meta cognitive reflection in learners. The article provided practical suggestions for instructional designers, encouraging them to thoughtfully integrate hyperlinks into learning materials to effectively support students' self-regulated learning strategies. In (Zeitlhofer, Zumbach, and Aigner 2023), the study investigated the impact of motivational cues on both learning achievement and motivation within a digital learning setting. To achieve this, the researchers introduced a Pedagogical Agent (PA) into a web-based learning environment to support learners' autonomous motivation. In an experimental setup, learning achievement and motivation were evaluated by comparing environments with and without the presence of the PA or motivational prompting. The findings indicated that learners with the assistance of a PA attain a greater level of knowledge compared to those without such support.

Customizing Learning Trajectories

By analyzing past performance, artificial intelligence can shape individualized learning journeys. It has the capacity to recommend supplementary activities, advanced modules, or specific teaching methods that align with the distinct needs of each learner, ultimately fostering a more efficient and personalized learning experience. In (VanLEHN 2011), authors explored which tutoring methods, including human tutoring, intelligent tutoring systems, and other tutoring systems, prove to be the most effective. The author likely conducted comparative studies to evaluate how these diverse approaches impact the learning process. The article's conclusions likely offered insights into the strengths and limitations of each method, thereby contributing to the ongoing discussion on the roles and effectiveness of various tutoring forms in education.

The outcomes from a teacher education program on artificial intelligence done in schools in southern India indicated that pragmatic efforts at all levels of authority are needed to express the growing necessity for integrating AI into classrooms. It is also to be noted that an educational style that encourages students to use their own creativity, encourages peer-teaching, and utilizes their past knowledge is more effective in boosting students' confidence.

Teachers of foreign languages, for example, are another group that should be considered. The most recent advancements in modern information and communication technology have had a significant impact on the current condition of foreign language instruction.

Multiple books and research articles have addressed preparing teachers for Intelligent Computer Assisted Language Learning (ICALL). The purpose of ICALL teacher training is to educate current and future language educators on AI-powered teaching tools and to provide them with the knowledge and skills necessary to integrate these tools effectively into their classrooms (Pokrivcakova 2019).

PREPARING FOR AI

Preparing for AI involves addressing various challenges and ethical considerations, especially within the field of education. Some of these challenges are discussed in the following sections.

Challenges in AI Applications in Education

AIED has opened new avenues for creating more effective learning activities and technology-enhanced educational environments. However, several challenges block the full integration of these technologies, particularly within the field of education and computer science. Below are some key challenges:

- Technological Reliance and Interdisciplinary Complexity: AIED strongly depends on technology, requiring a cross-disciplinary approach that many find complex. Without a comprehensive understanding of how AI technologies function and their roles within educational contexts, it is challenging for researchers to effectively implement and innovate with AI applications. This concern is discussed in depth by (Timms 2016).
- Theoretical Foundations: Creating the most effective tools, algorithms, and methods for personalized learning experiences requires a solid foundation in cognitive and educational psychology theories. While technologies like Virtual Reality and Augmented Reality offer exciting and innovative approaches, they often fail to incorporate these crucial educational theories into their designs. This lack of integration can compromise their effectiveness in supporting learning (Luan et al. 2020). To effectively utilize virtual reality and augmented reality in educational settings, it is essential to separate the technological aspects from the general human experiences and capabilities.
- Intercultural and Global Considerations: AI applications must adapt to diverse cultural and global contexts, posing challenges in universal design and implementation across varied educational systems.

Other several key challenges can be identified in the field of AIED, including the practical impact of technologies, issues surrounding privacy, the methods of interaction, the scalability of collaboration, the effectiveness across various learning domains, and the overarching role of AIED within educational technology (Pinkwart 2016).

Ethical Issues in the Use of AI in Education

It is essential for developers to recognize the ethical implications of the AI technologies they create. (Borenstein and Howard 2021) highlighted that developers not only play a crucial role in addressing these ethical issues but also have a significant responsibility to do so. Unfortunately, current computer science curricula often lack a focused segment on AI ethics. There is a vital need for education that prepares the next generation of AI engineers to approach their work with a strong ethical mindset, helping them understand and navigate the complexities of ethics in AI development.

According to (Borenstein and Howard 2021; Dignum 2021), it is important to consider the following aspects when developing AI systems:

- Accountability: AI systems need to make decisions that can be explained and justified to users and those impacted. These decisions should also reflect moral values and cultural norms.
- Responsibility: Beyond creating rules for intelligent machines, it is crucial to acknowledge the roles of individuals and institutions in the outcomes from using these systems. They must take responsibility for the consequences of their design and use.
- Transparency: This involves clearly explaining and documenting how AI systems arrive at decisions and how they interact with their environment. It also means being open about the sources of data, the development process, and who the stakeholders are.
- Privacy: As AI becomes more integrated into our lives, privacy issues are increasingly pressing. With vast amounts of personal data online, especially through activities like e-learning registrations, it is crucial to be mindful about the information we share. Knowing who is using AI tools and their purposes is often difficult, yet it is essential for protecting privacy. This understanding helps us navigate the complexities of digital privacy more effectively.

It is important to understand the different uses of AIED, as each application has varying risks. Holding public debates that are informed and include all relevant parties is also key to making collective decisions on how to manage these risks. Skipping such discussions could lead to a loss of trust in the technology, potentially causing a negative reaction and losing the benefits that trustworthy AIED offers. Alternatively, it could lead to the spread of unreliable AIED applications that do not consider the risks they pose, potentially causing irreparable harm (Smuha 2020).

CONCLUSION

The integration of Artificial Intelligence in education represents a transformative force with the potential to revolutionize the learning landscape. The advent of AI technologies has brought forth innovative solutions that cater to individualized learning, adaptive assessments, and personalized feedback, thereby addressing the diverse needs of students. As AI continues to evolve, it holds the promise of enhancing the efficiency of educational processes, automating routine tasks, and enabling educators to focus more on fostering critical thinking and creativity.

Moreover, AI in education has the capacity to democratize access to quality learning resources, breaking down barriers and making education more accessible to a global audience. The adaptive nature of AI-driven platforms ensures that students receive tailored content, adapting to their unique learning styles and pace. This personalized approach not only enhances engagement but also maximizes the potential for knowledge retention.

However, it is crucial to approach the integration of AI in education with a mindful consideration of ethical implications, data privacy, and the need for a human touch in the learning experience. Striking the right balance between technological innovation and human interaction is essential to foster a holistic educational environment.

In the years to come, as AI technologies continue to advance, educators, policymakers, and stakeholders must collaborate to harness the full potential of AI in education. By doing so, we can create a future where AI serves as a powerful ally in cultivating a generation of learners equipped with the skills, adaptability, and critical thinking necessary to thrive in an ever-evolving world.

REFERENCES

Akyuz, Y. (2020, June). Effects of Intelligent Tutoring Systems (ITS) on Personalized Learning (PL). *Creative Education, 11*(6), 6. doi:10.4236/ce.2020.116069

Al-Ansi, A. M., Mohammed, J., Askar, G., & Al-Ansi, A. (2023). Analyzing Augmented Reality (AR) and Virtual Reality (VR) Recent Development in Education. *Social Sciences & Humanities, 8*(1), 100532. doi:10.1016/j.ssaho.2023.100532

Anderson, J. R. (2007). *How Can the Human Mind Occur in the Physical Universe?* Oxford University Press.

Azevedo, R. (2005). Using Hypermedia as a Metacognitive Tool for Enhancing Student Learning? The Role of Self-Regulated Learning. *Educational Psychologist, 40*, 199–209. doi:10.1207/s15326985ep4004_2

Berland, M., Baker, R., & Blikstein, P. (2014). Educational Data Mining and Learning Analytics: Applications to Constructionist Research. *Technology. Knowledge and Learning, 19*. Advance online publication. doi:10.1007/s10758-014-9223-7

Borenstein, J., & Howard, A. (2021). Emerging Challenges in AI and the Need for AI Ethics Education. *AI and Ethics, 1*(1), 61–65. doi:10.1007/s43681-020-00002-7

Chen, L., Chen, P., & Lin, Z. (2020). Artificial Intelligence in Education: A Review. *IEEE Access : Practical Innovations, Open Solutions, 8*, 75264–75278. doi:10.1109/ACCESS.2020.2988510

Conati, C., Barral, O., Putnam, V., & Rieger, L. (2021, September). Toward personalized XAI: A case study in intelligent tutoring systems. *Artificial Intelligence, 298*, 103503. doi:10.1016/j.artint.2021.103503

Cubberley, E. P. (2005). *The History of Education: Educational Practice and Progress Considered as a Phase of the Development and Spread of Western Civilization.*

da Silva, F. L., Slodkowski, B. K., Araújo da Silva, K. K., & Cazella, S. C. (2023). A Systematic Literature Review on Educational Recommender Systems for Teaching and Learning: Research Trends, Limitations and Opportunities. *Education and Information Technologies, 28*(3), 3289–3328. doi:10.1007/s10639-022-11341-9

Dignum, V. (2021). The Role and Challenges of Education for Responsible AI. *London Review of Education, 19*(1), 1–11.

Fayaz Ahmad, S., Rahmat, M., Mubarik, M., Alam, M., & Hyder, S. (2021, November). Artificial Intelligence and Its Role in Education. *Sustainability (Basel), 13*(22), 12902. doi:10.3390/su132212902

Goldin, C. (1999). A Brief History of Education in the United States. h0119. Cambridge, MA: National Bureau of Economic Research. 10.3386/h0119

Guan, C., Mou, J., & Jiang, Z. (2020, December). Artificial intelligence innovation in education: A twenty-year data-driven historical analysis. *International Journal of Innovation Studies, 4*(4), 134–147. doi:10.1016/j.ijis.2020.09.001

Guilherme, A. (2019, March). AI and education: The importance of teacher and student relations. *AI & Society, 34*(1), 47–54. doi:10.1007/s00146-017-0693-8

Kamalov, F., Santandreu Calonge, D., & Gurrib, I. (2023). New Era of Artificial Intelligence in Education: Towards a Sustainable Multifaceted Revolution. *Sustainability, 15*(16), 12451. doi:10.3390/su151612451

Keengwe, J. (Ed.). (2018). *Handbook of research on digital content, mobile learning, and technology integration models in teacher education.* IGI Global. doi:10.4018/978-1-5225-2953-8

Kengam, J. (2020). *Artificial Intelligence In Education.* Research Gate. doi:10.13140/RG.2.2.16375.65445

Litman, D. (2016). Natural Language Processing for Enhancing Teaching and Learning. *Proceedings of the AAAI Conference on Artificial Intelligence, 30*(1). Advance online publication. doi:10.1609/aaai.v30i1.9879

Luan, H., Geczy, P., Lai, H., & ... . (2020). Challenges and Future Directions of Big Data and Artificial Intelligence in Education. *Frontiers in Psychology,* ●●●, 11.

Peng, H., Ma, S., & Spector, J. M. (2019). Personalized Adaptive Learning: An Emerging Pedagogical Approach Enabled by a Smart Learning Environment. *Smart Learning Environments, 6*(1), 9. doi:10.1186/s40561-019-0089-y

Pinkwart, N. (2016). Another 25 Years of AIED? Challenges and Opportunities for Intelligent Educational Technologies of the Future. *International Journal of Artificial Intelligence in Education, 26*(2), 771–783. doi:10.1007/s40593-016-0099-7

Pokrivcakova, S. (2019, December). Preparing teachers for the application of AI-powered technologies in foreign language education. *Journal of Language and Cultural Education, 7*(3), 135–153. doi:10.2478/jolace-2019-0025

Pratama, L. D., & Setyaningrum, W. (2018). Game-Based Learning: The Effects on Student Cognitive and Affective Aspects. *Journal of Physics: Conference Series, 1097*(1), 012123. doi:10.1088/1742-6596/1097/1/012123

Smuha, N. A. 2020. Trustworthy Artificial Intelligence in Education: Pitfalls and Pathways. SSRN Scholarly Paper. 3742421. Rochester, NY: Social Science Research Network. 10.2139/ssrn.3742421

Smyrnova-Trybulska, Eugenia, Nataliia Morze, Piet Kommers, Wojciech Zuziak, and Mariia Gladun. 2016. "EDUCATIONAL ROBOTS IN PRIMARY SCHOOL TEACHERS' AND STUDENTS' OPINION ABOUT STEM EDUCATION FOR YOUNG LEARNERS."

Timms, M. J. (2016). Letting Artificial Intelligence in Education Out of the Box: Educational Cobots and Smart Classrooms. *International Journal of Artificial Intelligence in Education, 26*(2), 701–712. doi:10.1007/s40593-016-0095-y van der Vorst, T., & Jelicic, N. 2019. "Artificial Intelligence in Education: Can AI Bring the Full Potential of Personalized Learning to Education?" *30th European Regional ITS Conference*, Helsinki 2019.

VanLEHN, Kurt. (2011). The Relative Effectiveness of Human Tutoring, Intelligent Tutoring Systems, and Other Tutoring Systems. *Educational Psychologist*, *46*(4), 197–221. doi:10.1080/00461520.2011.611369

Verdú, E., Regueras, L., Verdú, M., De Castro, J. P., & Juárez, M. Á. (2008). *Application of Intelligent Adaptive Systems in a Competitive Learning Environment*, *2*, 275.

Wang, H., Tlili, A., Huang, R., Cai, Z., Li, M., Cheng, Z., Yang, D., Li, M., Zhu, X., & Fei, C. (2023). Examining the Applications of Intelligent Tutoring Systems in Real Educational Contexts: A Systematic Literature Review from the Social Experiment Perspective. *Education and Information Technologies*, *28*(7), 9113–9148. doi:10.1007/s10639-022-11555-x

Yağcı, M. (2022). Educational Data Mining: Prediction of Students' Academic Performance Using Machine Learning Algorithms. *Smart Learning Environments*, *9*(1), 11. doi:10.1186/s40561-022-00192-z

Zeitlhofer, I., Zumbach, J., & Aigner, V. (2023). Effects of Pedagogical Agents on Learners' Knowledge Acquisition and Motivation in Digital Learning Environments. *Knowledge (Beverly Hills, Calif.)*, *3*, 53–67. doi:10.3390/knowledge3010004

Chapter 8

Modelling and Resolution of a Distribution Problem Considering Environmental Criteria:
A Case Study of a Tunisian Company

Jihen Jlassi
Higher Institute of Industrial Management of Sfax, Tunisia

Mohamed Ali Daly Elleuch
(iD) https://orcid.org/0000-0001-5547-6389
Higher Institute of Industrial Management of Sfax, Tunisia

Ines Rekik
Higher Institute of Industrial Management of Sfax, Tunisia

Marwa Mallek
University of Economic Science and Management of Sfax, Tunisia

ABSTRACT

The travelling salesman problem (TSP) is the challenge of finding the shortest yet most efficient route for a person to take given a list of specific destinations. It is an optimization problem in the fields of computer science and operations research. There are obviously a lot of different routes to choose from, but finding the best one the one that will require the least distance or costs, several researchers have spent decades trying to optimize the modeling and the resolution. In some real cases, the classical problem is not able to model the existing problem in a given company. In this paper, we propose models for the TSP, that can be used with linear or quadratic

DOI: 10.4018/979-8-3693-1418-0.ch008

service time functions, and that embeds novel improved lower and upper bounds. With proposed models, the authors consider exponentially many sub-tour eliminations, capacities, and demands constraints, which are separated dynamically. The main purpose is to help the transport manager to select the optimal distribution circuit that optimizes various objectives.

INTRODUCTION

In contemporary enterprises, leaders strive to enhance their performance and maintain competitiveness in the markets. Notably, logistics plays a crucial role in decision-making processes. One of the pivotal activities in corporate logistics management is establishing an efficient distribution network for goods, which serves as the backbone of operations, aiming to deliver a superior level of service while minimizing costs. Consequently, the modeling of distribution logistics systems equips companies with valuable insights to address network design challenges. In numerous logistics scenarios, accurately estimating the distance that vehicles need to cover to fulfill customer demands is vital. Distribution dilemmas emerge as significant concerns for various companies, posing the challenge of effectively delivering goods or services from the company to its customers.

The optimization of Vehicle Routing Problem (VRP) in the logistics distribution is a well-known research widely concerned problem. Companies more and more attach importance to better design and manage their logistics distribution in order to meet higher level quality services at the lowest possible cost effort. The logistics distribution problem is complex and difficult because the network involves various subsystems, activities, relationships and operations (Chandra and Kumar, 2000). Logistics practices include a set of approaches and activities used by a company to effectively integrate supply and demand to improve its supply chain management (Li et al., 2005). Green et al. (2012) suggested that distribution practices should include internal environmental management and cooperation with customers. Lee et al. (2012) noted that logistics practices are composed of corporate and operational strategies aimed at improving environmental sustainability. Laosirihongthong et al. (2013) studied the impacts of reverse logistics practices on the economic and environmental performance of Thai manufacturing companies.

Nowadays, the integration of environmental practices in every node of supply chain and especially in transportation activities becomes the challenge of many researches. This is due to diverse factors. First of all, environmental considerations are required to guarantee the safety, the health and the survival of living beings which are the most important natural resources to take into account. Then, the future decrease in energy systems which are threatened by a serious loss within 2040 according to the 2019 World Energy Outlook report (World Energy Outlook 2019) as well as the pollution caused by unnatural resources induce to search solutions to this major problem such as the reductions in the renewable energy sources and the continuous advances in the new digital technologies. In addition, hazardous effects of such logistic activities especially those of transportation systems which are responsible for 20% of the total Green House Gas (GHG) emissions (European Environment Agency, 2014b), requests for environmental solutions.

In this respect, environmental issues are considered as a performance key in the supply chain of a company so that they contribute not only to the reduction of waste generation, the resource consumption but also to the pollution control which can influence the safety of humanities and also the hazardous impact in the natural environment (Savino and Batbaatar, 2015).

As a result, environment concerns play now a crucial role in logistical decision making such as transport planning, location, raw material sourcing, supplier selection (Wu and Dunn, 1995)… Therefore, the "Green" concept has been added to "logistics" concept in order to obtain eco-friendly systems based on environmental strategies. In this way, green logistics is considered as a supply chain management activities and practices that include environmental measure in any process of the supply chain (Seroka-Stolka, 2014).

Initially, this study will develop a distribution logistics model, starting with a case study of a Tunisian company. The primary goal is to introduce a novel approach aimed at reducing distribution costs. Subsequently, we will introduce a secondary model designed to minimize both distribution costs and environmental impacts associated with the problem. Finally, we will conduct a comparative analysis of the outcomes derived from the two models.

The paper is organized as follows. In the next section, a literature review is presented, focusing on Vehicle Routing Problem. In section 3, the case study is described and the mathematical formulation of the single or multiple objective models is discussed. In section 4, the results are detailed in real case studies. Lastly, in section 5, conclusions and future research directions are presented.

LITERATURE REVIEW

Transportation problems typically involve scheduling the distribution of merchandise from suppliers to destinations with the objective of minimizing overall distribution costs. The distribution problem can be effectively modeled using graph theory, particularly through the utilization of the Traveling Salesman Problem (TSP) and the Vehicle Routing Problem (VRP).

There are a large number of real distribution problems that can be modelled as vehicle routing problems. The VRP constitutes a generalization of the travelling salesman problem (TSP) that consists of determining the shortest circuit or cycle passing through each of n points only once. The TSP and the VRP are both NP-hard. The diversity of research in industry, questions asked, data collected and methods used for distribution modeling, has led to the development of several parallel distribution modeling practices (Araújo et al., 2019). In recent years, many studies have pointed to the effect of the effects of different concepts on TSP and VRP modelling.

Wang, Sun, and Yang (2005) presented a multi-echelon distribution network design problem with transportation and inventory considerations, in addition to the facility location problem. Moreover, Rabbani, Tavakkoli-Moghaddam, and Parsa (2008) formulated a distribution network design problem in a multi-product supply chain system that located production plants and warehouses, and determined the best distribution strategy from plants to warehouses and from warehouses to custemers. Similarly, Ambrosino, Sciomachen, and Grazia Scutellá (2009) studied a distribution network where the company had one depot, a heterogeneous fleet of vehicles, and customers were divided by regions. Their goal was to minimize the distribution costs by placing one depot in each region, assigning some vehicles to each region, and designing the vehicle routes, each starting and ending at the central depot.

Hernández-Pérez et al (2016) aimed to minimize the total travel distance in multi-commodity pickup-anddelivery traveling salesman problem. The authors proposed a hybrid heuristic approach to deal with large instances of a capacitated pickup-and-delivery problem. Then, a numerical example is presented in order to illustrate the proposed approach.

Gámez-Albán et al (2017) propose a mixed-integer multi-period programming model that minimizes logistics network costs for a veterinary products distributor in Colombia. The configuration of the logistics network model considers the cost associated with out-of-stock inventories and opening and closing facilities over the planning horizon defined by the company.

Javier Velásquez et al (2022)developed a distribution logistics model based on a case study, which enabled decision-making to ensure the lowest logistics cost, considering demand, supply, factory capacity, possible sites to build distribution centers, and the stores. The model identified the customer's restrictions and simulated their behavior using data processing using the Gusek tool in such a manner as to establish the optimal solution when the model is run.

According to the literature review, research that addresses real-life case studies involving the vehicle routing problem (VRP) and the traveling salesman problem (TSP) hold significant importance and interest.

Local and regional pollution from road traffic is not a specifically urban problem, nor is it solely a public health problem. The various substances emitted by vehicles traveling on the road network can have harmful consequences for the ecosystems located near the roads. The transport sector constitutes one of the fundamental pillars of modern societies. It interferes at all levels of scale, both from an economic and social point of view as well as with regard to the environment and the structuring of space. The private car is an integral part of the lifestyle of the vast majority of citizens. Road freight transport is the lifeblood of our economy. The issues linked to travel are therefore more and more numerous: public health, environment, living environment, development and economic competitiveness. Public authorities are aware of the increasingly significant tension developing around the transport sector, designated as leading air polluters. The very exposed transit valleys are the first spaces where dysfunctions appear. For the populations, the traffic exceeds the limits of bearable, thus degenerating into social conflict. As social sensitivity on the subject increases, other sites could reach a critical threshold more quickly and join the protest movement. The environmental aspect is often neglected in the classic process of distributing a product. Economic development has led to facing the challenges of climate change. It is generally accepted that the impacts of resource use on the environment. This is the concept of sustainable development, a term commonly used to describe the attempt to achieve profitable economic activities without causing damage to the environment for future generations. In the context of logistics activities, the cost aspect is basically the main factor in any attempt to improve efficiency. Most often, the environmental impact of logistics activities is neglected or relegated to secondary priority. However, attempts to promote the environmental aspect as

Part of the factors for improving logistics performance can be found under the theme of green logistics and is increasingly progressing in developed countries.

Face to the assets of environmental considerations, the application of Green Logistics becomes now the focus of many researches and supply chain managers. In this context, several studies have integrated environmental criteria in supplier selection a (Konys, 2019, Qu et al. 2020), transportation and distribution (Saada, 2020), product lifecycle (Galati et al., 2019), and reverse logistics (Chen et al., 2019).

In this study, we focus on transport activity which is one of the most important issues of green logistic face to its bad impacts on the environment. Since last couple of decades, environmental concerns have been integrated into the traditional supply chain, which have given rise to the concept of Green or Sustainable Supply Chain (Khan, 2018). This concept can be shown essentially in purchasing, manufacturing and distribution (see Figure 1).

Numerous research studies have examined various facets of Green Supply Chain Management (GSCM). However, this paper specifically focuses on the distribution and transportation aspects within the realm of GSCM.

Figure 1. Green supply chain management (GSCM)
(Khan, 2018)

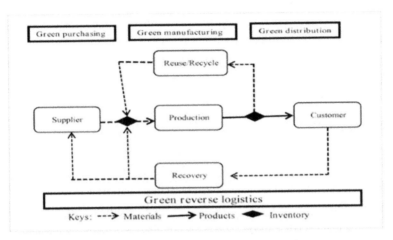

Green distribution plays a crucial role in the reduction of both waste and energy. In this context, diverse transportation problems have been defined based on the objective to reach, the planning process and the constraints to take into consideration such as those of pickup and delivery locations. Vehicle Routing problems are one of the most well-known and important transportation problems. These problems consist on designing the routes traveled by a set of vehicles to serve a given set of customers (Asghari et al., 2020). The objective is to minimize the routing cost.

Research works on vehicle routing are very reach. Some of them treated the Dial-a-ride Problem (DARP) which is a variant of Vehicle Routing Problem (VRP) characterized by a flexible accommodation of customer demands with taking into account the specific desired pickup or delivery time (Cordeau and Laporte, 2007).

For example, Chen et al. (2020) presented a bi-objective model to solve this problem while considering the two perspectives of fluctuation of the travel time and eco-efficiency. They have then proposed a two-step methodology for the resolution of this problem. In a first step, they have developed a revised branch and price algorithm with a large neighbor search (LNS) to solve the classical Dial-a-ride Problem (DARP) aiming the minimization of the travel time. Then, in a second step, they have integrated the environmental criteria and they have applied the weighted sum with the normalization approach to solve the obtained bi-objective problem.

Abdullahi et al. (2020) have adopted the sustainable vehicle routing problem that considers the three dimensions of sustainability which are social, economic and environmental dimensions. In this way, they have presented a multi-objective model that takes into account these dimensions and a hybrid heuristic that combines between the Extended biased randomized savings heuristic with the iterated greedy local search method to solve this problem.

Utama et al. (2020) have treated the distribution node of a supply chain as a green vehicle routing problem (GVRP). To solve this problem, the authors have developed a hybrid butterfly optimization algorithm (HBOA) in order to minimize the distribution costs composed by the vehicle use costs, the fuel costs and the carbon costs and while considering a single distribution center.

Xu et al. (2019) have investigated the capacitated green vehicle routing problem (GVRP) as a multi objective problem aiming to reduce both the traveled time and the fuel consumption. They have proposed a nonlinear mixed integer programming model that incorporates vehicle capacity, vehicle load and time-varying speed to measure the traffic congestion and a Genetic algorithm based approach for the resolution of this problem. They have marked from the obtained results a significant decrease in the consumption of fuel in supply chain without influencing the customer satisfaction.

Foroutan et al. (2018) have treated the collection of returned goods as a vehicle routing with heterogeneous fleet in the context of reverse logistics in order to minimize both operational and environmental costs. They have proposed a mixed integer non-linear programming (MINLP) model in a first way for the formulation of the problem and the application of the two metaheuristics simulating annealing and Genetic Algorithm in a second way for the resolution of this problem.

Peng et al. (2019) have proposed a memetic algorithm for solving the Green Vehicle Routing Problem. They have adopted the green concept by the use of electric vehicles which have a limited autonomy and which are needed to be recharged during their duties. In their proposal approach, they have incorporated an adaptive local search procedure inspired by the reinforcement learning method and based on the mechanism of reward and punishment in order to manage the multiple neighborhood moves.

The literature review conducted in this paper underscores the considerable scope of research in the Green Vehicle Routing Problem (GVRP). Nonetheless, existing studies are beset by certain limitations. For example, there is a lack of consideration of both emission and delivery costs in a context of a distribution problem. Then, there is no research study, as far as the authors' knowledge, integrating certain elements of the distribution cost as the loading and unloading costs and the fixed costs, other than the emission costs. Existing GVRP studies consider only the minimization of the environmental emissions and distances' costs. A series of important decisions are made throughout the distribution modeling process, from problem formulation to model evaluation and use. Identifying objectives and potential constraints at each stage challenges the modeler's knowledge of the object of study, the dataset and the modeling methodology in general. Although the modeler is responsible for providing end users with information about the reliability of the model, the responsibility for the appropriate use of the modeling output lies with the end user. Although attention to reliability in distribution modeling is increasing. Most studies addressing this topic have focused on specific parts of the distribution modeling process, such as the involvement of quantitative and/or qualitative objectives, potential constraints or low spatial resolution in order to improve the quality of the distribution models and to facilitate the interpretation of the models, such a systematic approach should inspect the complexities of the problem throughout the solution process.

The objective of this chapter is to develop a real case study based model for minimizing not only distribution costs but also environmental emissions and while taking into consideration constraints related to the distribution system of the real case study.

CASE STUDY DESCRIPTION

Problem Statement

In this paper, there is an explicit real-life transportation problem to solve. This case analyzed the travelling salesman problem, thereby mostly focusing on the most economical way of delivering goods to customers.

Figure 2. Network of TSP

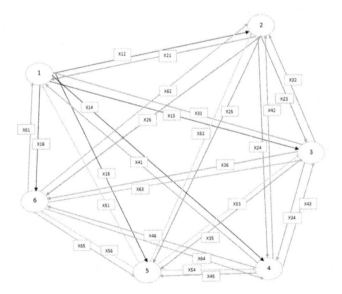

In mathematics, TSP formulations can be expressed as a graph $G = (V,A)$ with $V = \{1, 2, 3, ..., n\}$ denote the set of graph's vertices that shows the location of the city and $A = \{(i,j) \mid i,j \in V, i \neq j\}$ as the set of edges denote connecting roads between cities. Suppose xij is the distance from city i to city j, then the TSP goal is to minimize $z = \sum \sum xi,jnj{=}1\ ni{=}1$.

In this problem, a traveling salesman must visit several cities passing once and only once by each of them and minimizing the total distance traveled. The TSP formulation that we will present below corresponds to the mathematical formulation used in integer linear programming. It reflects the natural modeling of the problem by defining a binary variable Xij equal to 1 if the vehicle travels the arc. Figure 2 represents six cities, each separated by a distance d (i, j). The objective is to find the shortest path passing through all the cities and returning to its starting point (1).

Given a set of cities and the distance between every pair of cities, the problem is to find the shortest possible route that visits every city exactly once and returns to the starting point. To solve this problem, we propose the application of the traveling salesman model with a circuit of 5 customers to end at the end with the presentation of a second model. in which we added other constraints.

Classic Traveling Salesman Model

The travelling salesman problem asks the following question: "Given a list of cities and the distances between each pair of cities, what is the shortest possible route that visits each city exactly once and returns to the origin city?" It is an NP-hard problem in combinatorial optimization, important in theoretical computer science and operations research. In this section, we use a mathematical model based on a set of decision parameters and variables.

Decision Parameters

N : Numbers of cities.
i : Origin
j : Destination
d_ij : Course distance
Y_(i,j) : Edges

Decision variables

Xij: a binary variable that takes the value of 1 if the arc (i, j) is used in the tour and 0 otherwise. We have the following formulation:

$$Min \sum_{i=1}^{n} \sum_{j=1}^{n} d_{ij} x_{ij} \tag{1}$$

Subject to

$$\sum_{i \in X}^{n} x_{ij} = 1, \forall j \in X \tag{2}$$

$$\sum_{j \in X}^{n} x_{ij} = 1, \forall i \in X \tag{3}$$

$$x_{ti} + x_{it} \leq 1, \forall i \in \{1,\ldots,n\} \tag{4}$$

$$x_{ij} \in \{0,1\}; \forall i,j \in X \tag{5}$$

The traveling salesman problem is a widely studied combinatorial optimization problem, which, given a set of cities and a course distance from one city to another, seeks to identify the tour that will allow a salesman to visit each city only once, starting and ending in the same city, at the minimum course distances.

The objective function (1) seeks to minimize the total distance of the circuit covered. Constraints (2) and (3) impose that the traveler enters and exits only once from each node. The elimination of under tours, i.e. paths passing through a subset of nodes without returning to the repository, is ensured by constraint (4) and constraint (5) ensures that all variables must be binary.

Proposed Single-Objective TSP Model

In certain real-life scenarios, the conventional problem-solving approaches may not adequately represent the complexities of the issues faced by a particular company. In this paper, we introduce a novel model for the Traveling Salesman Problem (TSP) that accommodates linear or quadratic service time functions and incorporates enhanced lower and upper bounds. Our model integrates numerous sub-tour elimination constraints, capacity limitations, and demand constraints, all of which are dynamically separated. It relies on a set of decision parameters and variables to formulate an effective solution.

Decision parameters

t : Day
i, j : Customer
$\mathbf{k}$: Truck
Cap_t : Production capacity
D_j : Customer request j
cap_{kt} : Truck capacity k
$\mathbf{N}$: Number of customers

Decision variables

X_{ijkt} : Optimal quantities to be delivered from i to customer j by truck k during period t
Y_{kt} : Binary variable, equal to 1 if truck k will be used during period t
Y_{IJKT} : 1 if arc i, j is used by truck k during day "t" 0 otherwise.

$$Min \sum_i \sum_j d_{ij.} Y_{ijkt} \tag{6}$$

Subject to

$$\sum_j X_{jkt} \le Cap_{kt}.Y_{kt} \, \forall k,t \tag{7}$$

$$\sum_k \sum_t X_{jkt} \ge D_j \, \forall j \tag{8}$$

$$\sum_k Y_{kt} \le N \forall t \tag{9}$$

$$\sum_i Y_{ijkt} = Y_{kt} \forall j,k,t \tag{10}$$

$$\sum_j Y_{ijkt} = Y_{kt} \ \forall j,k,t \tag{11}$$

$$Y_{pi\,kt} + Y_{ipkt} \leq 1 \tag{12}$$

$$Y_{ikt} \in \{0,1\} \tag{13}$$

$$Y_{kt} \in \{0,1\} \tag{14}$$

The objective function (1) seeks to minimize the distance traveled and the travel time. The first constraint (7) makes it possible to respect the delivery capacity. The second constraint (8) ensures customer satisfaction. Constraints (9), (10), and (11) specify the type of each variable. The elimination of sub-tours, ie paths passing through a subset of nodes without returning to the depot, is ensured by the constraint (12). The constraints (13-14) are binary constraints.

Proposed Multi-Objective TSP Model

This multi-objective model is making decisions between conflict objectives, maximizing profit while minimizing fuel consumption and emission of pollutants of a vehicle. In our case, a multi-objective optimization model should be performed, which provides multiple solutions representing the trade-offs among the objective functions.

As described above, the general TSP model tries only to minimize the traveled distance. However, in a real transportation problem, the objective of the decision maker is to minimize the total transportation cost which is composed not only by the traveled distance cost but also by other delivery costs. In this paper, we propose a first modified TSP model which considers the delivery cost. Here, the modification is done only on the objective function and the constraints still the same. As a result, the objective becomes the minimization of the total transportation cost, which is described by Equation (16) and detailed in Equation (17) as follows:

$$Minimize \sum_{i=1}^{n} C_{ei} = \sum_{i=1}^{n} C_{fi} + Q_i C_{vi} \tag{16}$$

Where $C_{fi} = C_{ai} + dC_d$ (17)

Minimize e_{ij} (18)

Where $e_{ij} = d_{ij} X_{ij} \varepsilon(qi_j, \forall i, j \in \{1,...,n\}$ (19)

Equation (16) represents the total delivery cost for all the distribution nodes and that the manager aims to minimize. This cost is composed by the fixed and the variable costs. The variable costs consist on the loading and unloading costs. These costs depend on the delivered quantity (noted as the decision variable Q_i). The fixed costs C_{fi} in node i as shown in Equation (17) are composed by the stopping cost C_{ai} at this node and the traveled distance cost to this node dC_d. In addition, Equation 18 presented the objective to minimize the environmental impact. A previous study is proposed by (Jlassi et al., 2017) in which an integration of environmental criteria in the classical TSP has been developed. In the proposed model, we combine these criteria and the modified TSP model proposed in the previous sub-section. In other words, we focus on minimizing the total distribution costs and while considering the environmental cost. The optimization of the environmental cost is based on the estimation of the environmental emission factor according to the formula detailed in Equation (N°18) and then the calculation of the emission factor described by Equation (N°19).

APPLICATIONS AND DISCUSSIONS

Application of Single-Objective TSP Model

Indeed, transporting large quantities over long and medium distances generates transport costs that can represent a significant percentage of the cost price of the product. Any decrease or increase in transport costs immediately improves or degrades the margin, hence the importance of reducing these costs. As a result, optimizing costs and distances has become a key factor in the success of any business. For this, our choice fell on the transport cost optimization study within the company EL Yousr ISP. The problem of this study is to study the shortest paths by visiting all the cities to ship production units. EL Yousr ISP is a company operating in the chemical sector, and specialized in the manufacture and marketing of paints, varnishes and derivatives. It was created in 1999 by Mr. Kamel Allouch, an engineer with a military academy background. The EL Yousr company, whose customers

Figure 3. Customer requests by regions

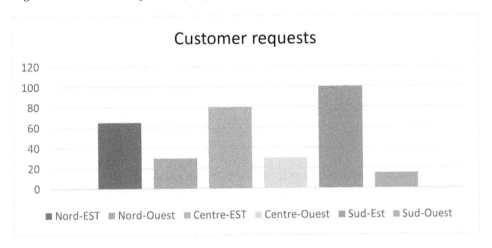

Figure 4. Example of EL Yousr distribution network

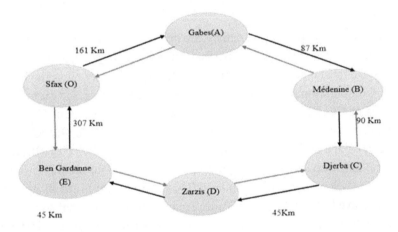

are geographically dispersed, must satisfy all requests under the right conditions. To ensure the supply of its customers at the lowest cost, the company EL YOUSR must consider both the level of production and the link between company-customers. The objectives of this work are:

- Optimization of distribution circuit,
- Customer satisfaction,
- Minimization of transport cost.

Table 1. Summary of business outcomes and optimized outcomes

	Company results	Optimized results	Interpretation
Number of periods	T = 18	T=10	The model has optimized routes that minimize travel distance and travel time.
Distance traveled	17215	15203	
Satisfaction rate	100%	100%	The model fulfilled all orders using only the company's available vehicles.
Number of vehicles	3 + 1 (ST)	3	

Based on data showing customer requests by region during the summer period. We note that this demand is not the same for the different regions of the country. The figure below represents customer demand by region.

From Figure 3, we find that the south of Tunisia is the region that has a high demand for the products. For this reason, the empirical study will focus on customers in this region who are geographically separated. Figure 4 shows the circuit that the company's trucks must follow to meet the demands of customers located in southern Tunisia.

Indeed, the company plans to satisfy the needs of the customers, from where it could ship the quantity transported to 5 main customers. For this, at the level of each destination we must define the quantity to be transported as well as the Kilometers travelled. Computational experiments are performed on real and simulation case instances using CPLEX 10.0 on personal computer Intel® Core 2Duo CPU 2.0 GHZ. The calculations were carried out on a windows cluster. We used ILOG OPL 6.1 as modeling language and the mixed integer solver from CPLEX 10.1 (ILOG, 2007) commercial software for all the variants of the problem. Our algorithms are coded in C++ using Microsoft Visual Studio 6.0. CPU times are given in seconds. The model was solved with CPLEX software package to find optimal solutions of the problem,. Unfortunately this software only works for a reasonable size instances and it does not give optimal solutions for large-scale instances. The numerical results show that the proposed method is robust and efficient, especially for problems with mid-size instance. Table 1 represents the summary of the company's results and the optimized results.

We are investigating a network comprising a factory and five customers, with a fleet of multiple vehicles available at the depot for product delivery. This problem is adaptable and can be addressed with various constraints to achieve specific objectives. Therefore, the primary aim is to provide recommendations regarding the most suitable approach to solving the problem, considering different network options. The optimization model proposed seeks to identify routes that minimize both the distance traveled and/or travel time. Moreover, the model ensures that all

Table 2. Real company vehicle routing network

Xijkt	1	2	3	4	5	6
t=1			2.2 / 1		4	2.8
t=2		3	2			
t=3			2		5	3
t=4			3			7
t=5				7	3	
t=6		4.5	5	2	0.5 / 8	
t=7			3		7	
t=8			2		2	6
t=9		1			7	2

Xijkt	1	2	3	4	5	6
t=10			2			8
t=11				2.5	7	2.5 / 3
t=12			2	4	8 / 1	
t=13				3	7	
t=14		2	3	5		
t=15		3		2		
t=16					8	3
t=17			5	10		
t=18			2 / 3	5		

Vehicle N°1 (Yellow), Vehicle N°2 (Orange), Vehicle N°3 (Red)

Table 3. Optimized vehicle routing network based on single-objective TSP model

Xijkr	1	2	3	4	5	6
t=1		3	2	2		
			2			
				3		
					4	
						4
t=2		3	2	2		
			2			
				3		
					4	
						4
t=3		3	2	2		
			2			
				3		
					4	
						4
t=4		3	2	2		
			2			
				3		
					4	
						4
t=5		3.5	2	2		
			2.5			
				3		
					4	
						4
t=6			3	2	6	
				2		
					3	
						4
t=7			4		6	
				1		
					5	
						4
t=8			5		6	
					5	
						4
t=9			2.4		10	
					2.6	
t=10					5.4	
						2.8

Vehicle N°1 (Yellow), Vehicle N°2 (Orange), Vehicle N°3 (Red)

Table 4. Estimation of the emission factors

Vehicle condition	Charging points in %	Consumption (L/100km)	Fuel conversion factor (kgco2/L)	Emission factor (kg CO2/km)
full load	100	63,214	2,61	1,6498854
High load	50	78,431	2, 61	2,0470491
Low load	25	51,111	2,61	1,3339971
empty	0	41,7054	2,61	1,08851094

Table 5. Calculation of the emission factors

	εqi	Distance(d)	$\varepsilon qi*d$ (10^{-3})
e_{12}	1,6498854	270	4.454
e_{13}	1,6498854	190	3.134
e_{14}	1,6498854	84	1.385
e_{21}	1,6498854	270	2.938
e_{23}	2,0470491	460	9.416
e_{24}	1,3339971	354	4.722
e_{31}	1,6498854	190	2.068
e_{32}	1,3339971	460	6.136
e_{34}	2,0470491	106	2.169
e_{41}	1,6498854	84	9.143
e_{42}	2,0470491	354	7.246
e_{43}	1,3339971	106	1.414

orders are fulfilled exclusively using the company's available vehicles, without relying on subcontractor vehicles (Tables 2 and 3).

The results presented in this study demonstrate a clear advantage of the new model in terms of distance optimization.

Table 6. Distance cost calculation

Circuit	Raw materials (10⁻³)	Vehicle maintenance (oil change, repair, washing) (10⁻³)	Pneumatic (10⁻³)	Driver's salary (10⁻³)	Amortization (10⁻³)	Sum (10⁻³)
Sfax-Tunis	2,783	0	0	0, 2	0,1	3,083
Sfax-Gafsa	3,301	0,2	0	0, 2	0,1	3,501
Sfax-Skhira	1,936	0,1	0	0, 2	0,1	2,036
Tunis-Sfax	1,830	0	3,23	0, 2	0,1	5,060
Gafsa-Sfax	1,222	0	0	0, 2	0,1	1,222
Skhira-Sfax	1, 011	0	0	0, 2	0,1	1,011
Tunis-Gafsa	2,994	0,2	1, 8	0, 2	0,1	4,994
Tunis-Skhira	2,625	0,1	1,8	0, 2	0,1	4, 525
Gafsa-Tunis	3, 528	0, 15	0	0, 2	0,1	3,678
Skhira-Tunis	2,501	0, 1	0	0, 2	0,1	2, 601
Gafsa-Skhira	1,479	0	2,5	0, 2	0,1	3,979
Skhira -Gafsa	2,852	0	0	0, 2	0,1	2,852

Table 7. Delivery cost

Circuit	Quantity transported (Q)	Stop cost (ca)	distance costs (cd)	Distance (d)	fixed costs (Ca+ cd *d)	variable costs	Delivery costs Ce = cf + cv *Q
Sfax-Tunis	80	0, 7	3,083	270	833,198	0,15	845, 198
Sfax-Gafsa	80	0,5	3,501	190	722,733	0,15	734,733
Sfax-Skhira	80	0,3	2,036	84	196,574	0,15	208,574
Tunis-Sfax	VIDE	0,7	5,060	270	1448,132	0	1448,132
Gafsa-Sfax	VIDE	0,5	1,222	190	289,862	0	289,862
Skhira-Sfax	VIDE	0,3	1,011	84	110,433	0	110,433
Tunis-Gafsa	40	0,5	4,994	460	2435,740	0,12	2439,340
Tunis-Skhira	20	0,4	4, 525	354	1708,676	0,12	1711,076
Gafsa-Tunis	20	0,5	3,678	460	1830,541	0,1	1833,541
Skhira-Tunis	40	0,4	2, 601	354	1027,683	0,12	1031,283
Gafsa-Skhira	40	0,4	3,979	106	422,216	0,1	424,216
Skhira-Gafsa	20	0,4	2,852	106	334,526	0,12	338,126

Table 8. Optimized vehicle routing network based on the multi-objective TSP model

Xijkt	1	2	3	4	5	6
t=1		3	2	5		
			2			
					4	
						4
t=2		4	3	2		
			1			
				2		
					4	
						4
t=3		4	3	2		
			1			
				2		
					4	
						4
t=4		4	3	2		
			1			
				2		
					4	
						4
t=5		4	3	2		
			1			
				2		
					4	
						4
t=6			4	3	6	
				1		
					2	
						4
t=7			4		6	
				1		
					5	
						4
t=8			5		6	
					5	
						4
t=9			2,4		10	
					2,6	
t=10					5,4	
						2,8

189

Application of Multi-Objective TSP Model

Transportation activities often lead to significant adverse effects on the environment, including pollution, noise, and congestion. This article delves into the operational-level decisions aimed at mitigating the environmental impact of transportation activities within the EL YOUSR ISP Company. The primary mission of this company is to efficiently distribute customer requests. To this end, we introduce a new model in this subsection to optimize various objectives associated with the problem. The requisite data are provided in the subsequent tables

The proposed integrated model is implemented in a real Tunisian case study of the YOSR Company located in Sfax, responsible for distributing products to various customers across different geographical locations. Table 8 outlines the composition and calculation of the distance cost, which is contingent upon the distance covered. Additionally, Table 7 provides an overview of the delivery cost per trip.

The findings presented herein indicate that the new model offers a distinct advantage in terms of both distance optimization and mitigating negative environmental impacts. Through the implementation of the multi-objective TSP model, which recalibrates and regulates the transport flow, there is a potential reduction in CO_2 emissions anticipated in the forthcoming years. Consequently, this improvement in logistics within the company can be achieved. The optimal unloading sequence comprises stops that include the list and quantity of items to be unloaded.

CONCLUSION

The environmental aspect in product distribution has become increasingly important due to growing concerns about climate change and sustainability. Companies are seeking to minimize the carbon footprint of their distribution operations by optimizing routes, using transportation models to reduce fuel consumption. Companies cooperate with local authorities, environmental organizations and other stakeholders to develop more sustainable distribution solutions and promote good environmental practices. By integrating these environmental considerations into their distribution operations, companies can reduce their impact on the environment while meeting consumers' growing expectations for sustainability. The research presented in this paper is structured into two stages. In the initial phase, the study devised a distribution logistics model grounded in a specific case study. This paper introduces a modified vehicle routing model wherein a mathematical framework is proposed. The objective of this model is to determine routes that minimize both the distance traveled and travel time within the EL YOUSR ISP company, thereby fulfilling customer demands at minimal cost.

A comparison was made with existing tours. The obtained results show the effectiveness of the proposed model. Considering the environmental factors in each node of the supply chain becomes the focus of many researches as well as supply chain managers today in order to guarantee the three pillars of sustainability: social, economic and environmental. In this context, transportation activities and especially vehicle routing presents hazardous impact on both environmental and social issues which can cause a considerable routing cost that should be minimized. So in the second part, this paper added the influence of the environmental measures to the distribution cost. This model is then applied in the EL YOSR ISP company case study. The obtained results show the effectiveness of the proposed model by comparison to the real case current delivery cost. More tests must be done in future works by increasing the size of instances. Also, meta-heuristic algorithms may be considered to compare their performance against current algorithms and improve the quality of the solutions.

REFERENCES

Abdullahia, H., Reyes-Rubianob, L., Ouelhadja, D., Faulinb, J.,A. Juanc, A. (2020). Modelling and Multi-criteria Analysis of the Sustainability Dimensions for the Green Vehicle Routing Problem European. *Journal of Operational Research*.

Araújo, M. B., Anderson, R. P., Barbosa, A. M., Beale, C. M., Dormann, C. F., & Early, R. (2019). Standards for distribution models in biodiversity assessments. *Science Advances*, *5*(1), eaat4858. doi:10.1126/sciadv.aat4858 PMID:30746437

Asghari, M. S., Mohammad, J., & Al-e-hashem, M. (2020). Green vehicle routing problem: A state-of-the-art review. *International Journal of Production Economics*.

Chandra, K., & Kumar, S. (2000). Supply chain management in theory and practice: A passing fad or a fundamental change. *Industrial Management & Data Systems*, *100*(3), 100–113. doi:10.1108/02635570010286168

Chen, A., Ignatius, G., Sun, D., Zhan, S., Zhou, C., Marra, M., & Demirbag, M. (2019). Reverse logistics pricing strategy for a green supply chain: A view of customers' environmental awareness. *International Journal of Production Economics*, *217*, 197–210. doi:10.1016/j.ijpe.2018.08.031

Chen, L. W., Hu, T. Y., & Wu, Y. W. (2020). *A bi-objective model for eco-efficient dial-a-ride problems*. Asia Pacific Management Review.

Cordeau, J. F., & Laporte, G. (2007). The dial-a-ride problem: Models and algorithms. *Annals of Operations Research*, *153*(1), 2. doi:10.1007/s10479-007-0170-8

European Environment Agency. (2014). *Annual European union greenhouse gasinventory 1990–2012 and inventory report 2014.* (Technical report No 09/2014).

Galati, F., Bigliardi, B., Petroni, A., Pinna, C., Rossi, M., & Terz, S. (2019). Sustainable Product Lifecycle: The Role of ICT. *Sustainability (Basel), 11*(24), 7003. doi:10.3390/su11247003

Green, K. W. Jr, Zelbst, P. J., Meacham, J., & Bhadauria, V. S. (2012). Green supply chain management practices: Impact on performance. *Supply Chain Management, 17*(3), 290–305. doi:10.1108/13598541211227126

Khan, S. A. R. (2018). *Introductory Chapter: Introduction of Green Supply Chain Management, Green Practices and Strategies in Supply Chain Management.* IntechOpen. https://www.intechopen.com/chapters/63678 doi:10.5772/intechopen.81088

Konys, A. (2019). Green Supplier Selection Criteria: From a Literature Review to a Comprehensive Knowledge Base. *Sustainability.*

Laosirihongthong, T., Adebanjo, D., & Tan, K. C. (2013). Green supply chain management practices and performance. *Industrial Management & Data Systems, 113*(8), 1088–1109. doi:10.1108/IMDS-04-2013-0164

Lee, S. M., Kim, S. T., & Choi, D. (2012). Green supply chain management and organizational performance. *Industrial Management & Data Systems, 112*(8), 1148–1180. doi:10.1108/02635571211264609

Li, S., Subba Rao, S., Ragu-Nathan, T. S., & Ragu-Nathan, B. (2005). Development and validation of a measurement instrument for studying supply chain management practices. *Journal of Operations Management, 23*(6), 618–641. doi:10.1016/j.jom.2005.01.002

Peng, B., Zhang, Y., Gajpal, Y., & Chen, X. (2019). A Memetic Algorithm for the Green VehicleRouting Problem. *Sustainability (Basel), 11*(21), 6055. doi:10.3390/su11216055

Qu, G., Zhang, Z., Qu, W., & Xu, Z. (2020). Green Supplier Selection Based on Green Practices Evaluated Using Fuzzy Approaches of TOPSIS and ELECTRE with a Case Study in a Chinese Internet Company. *International Journal of Environmental Research and Public Health, 17*(9), 3268. doi:10.3390/ijerph17093268 PMID:32392876

Saada, R. (2020). Green Transportation in Green Supply Chain Management, Green Supply Chain - Competitiveness and Sustainability. *Tamás Bányai and Ireneusz Kaczmar*. IntechOpen, https://www.intechopen.com/chapters/72772 doi:10.5772/intechopen.93113

Savino, M. M., Manzini, R., & Mazza, A. (2015). Environmental and economic assessment of fresh fruit supply chain through value chain analysis. A case study in chestnuts industry. *Production Planning and Control, 26*(1), 1–18. doi:10.1080 /09537287.2013.839066

Seroka-Stolka, O. (2014). The Development of Green Logistics for Implementation Sustainable Development Strategy in Companies. *Procedia: Social and Behavioral Sciences, 151*, 302–309. doi:10.1016/j.sbspro.2014.10.028

Utama, D. M., Widodo, D. S., Ibrahim, M. F., & Dewi, S. K. (2020). A New Hybrid Butterfly Optimization Algorithm for Green Vehicle Routing Problem. *Journal of Advanced Transportation, 2020*, 1–14. doi:10.1155/2020/8834502

World Energy Outlook. (2019). IEA. https://www.iea.org/reports/worldenergy-outlook-2019

Xua, Z., Elomrib, A., Pokharelc, S., & Mutlud, F. (2019). A model for capacitated green vehicle routing problem with the timevaryingvehicle speed and soft time windows. *Computers & Industrial Engineering, 137.*

Chapter 9
Innovating Prosperity:
Intelligent Approaches and Economic Paradigms for Sustainable Futures

Sarâh Benziane

University of Science and Technology of Oran Mohamed-Boudiaf, Algeria

ABSTRACT

This chapter explores the intersection of intelligence, innovation, and sustainability in shaping economic trajectories. It delves into the transformative power of intelligent approaches, guided by technological advancements, data-driven insights, and adaptive policies, to drive economic innovation. The chapter emphasizes the imperative of aligning economic paradigms with sustainability principles, envisioning a future where prosperity is not only economically robust but also environmentally responsible and socially inclusive. Through an examination of case studies, emerging trends, and the role of artificial intelligence, the chapter aims to provide a comprehensive overview of how intelligent economic practices can pave the way for sustainable and resilient futures. It invites readers to consider the critical interplay between intelligence and sustainability in the pursuit of economic prosperity that harmonizes with the needs of both current and future generations.

INTRODUCTION

Background

Brief Overview of the Current Economic Landscape

DOI: 10.4018/979-8-3693-1418-0.ch009

The global economic landscape has been marked by a mix of opportunities and challenges. Please note that economic conditions can evolve, and it's advisable to check more recent sources for the latest information. Here's a brief overview:

- **Global Economic Growth:**

Pre-2020, the world experienced a period of moderate economic growth, though with variations among different regions. The COVID-19 pandemic significantly impacted global economies in 2020, leading to a contraction in many sectors.

- **Technological Advancements:**

Technology continued to play a pivotal role in shaping economic activities, with trends like artificial intelligence, blockchain, and automation influencing various industries. The digital economy saw substantial growth, with e-commerce, remote work, and digital services becoming increasingly prevalent.

- **Environmental and Social Considerations:**

Sustainability and social responsibility gained prominence, with businesses and governments focusing on environmental issues, climate change, and social justice. ESG (Environmental, Social, Governance) considerations became integral to investment and business decisions.

- **Trade Tensions:**

Trade tensions and geopolitical uncertainties persisted, with ongoing negotiations and disputes affecting global trade relationships. Protectionist measures in some regions created challenges for international commerce.

- **Monetary Policies:**

Central banks in various countries implemented accommodative monetary policies to stimulate economic recovery. Interest rates remained generally low, and unconventional measures were used to address economic challenges.

- **Inequality Concerns:**

Economic inequality and disparities in income and wealth distribution garnered increased attention. Discussions around inclusive growth and social safety nets gained momentum.

- **Shifts in Consumer Behavior:**

Changing consumer preferences and behaviors, accelerated by the pandemic, influenced industries such as retail, travel, and entertainment. Online and contactless services saw increased adoption.

- **Global Supply Chain Challenges:**

Supply chain disruptions were observed, partly due to the pandemic, highlighting vulnerabilities in global supply networks. Efforts were made to reassess and strengthen supply chain resilience.

- **Government Stimulus Programs:**

Governments around the world introduced stimulus packages to support businesses and individuals affected by the pandemic, contributing to increased public debt in many cases.

- **Challenges and Opportunities Post-Pandemic:**

The post-pandemic recovery presented both challenges and opportunities, with efforts focused on rebuilding economies in a more resilient and sustainable manner.

The current economic landscape is characterized by a shift in the geographical scale of economic relationships, with a growing emphasis on integration and risk management (Babcock-Lumish, 2005). Despite the global economic recovery following the 2008 financial crisis, there are still concerns about the impact of the crisis on the global economic outlook (Ceyhun, 2017). This is further complicated by the intensifying crisis of the world economy, which calls for a reorientation of the economy and a transition to quantitative economic growth (Evstigneeva, 2014). In this context, there is a need for policy options to improve global economic performance, with a focus on fiscal and monetary policies (Buiter, 1987).

Recognition of the Need for Sustainable Development

The recognition of the need for sustainable development has become a global imperative driven by a growing awareness of environmental, social, and economic challenges. Here are key factors contributing to the acknowledgment of the necessity for sustainable development:

- **Environmental Concerns:**

Climate Change: Increasing evidence of climate change and its adverse effects on ecosystems, weather patterns, and sea levels has underscored the urgency of adopting sustainable practices.

Biodiversity Loss: The rapid decline in biodiversity, including the extinction of species, has raised alarms about the interconnectedness of ecosystems and the consequences for human well-being.

- **Resource Scarcity:**

Depletion of Natural Resources: The realization that finite resources such as fossil fuels, clean water, and arable land are being depleted at an unsustainable rate has prompted a reevaluation of consumption patterns.

Waste Management: The environmental impact of waste generation and the challenges associated with disposal and recycling have emphasized the need for circular economy models.

- **Social Equity and Inclusion:**

Poverty Alleviation: Sustainable development aims to address poverty and promote social inclusion, recognizing that economic growth should be inclusive and benefit all segments of society.

Access to Basic Needs: Ensuring equitable access to education, healthcare, clean water, and sanitation is integral to sustainable development goals.

- **Global Interconnectedness:**

Globalization: Increased interconnectedness through trade, communication, and travel has highlighted the shared responsibility of nations and businesses to address global challenges collectively.

Pandemic Response: The COVID-19 pandemic underscored the importance of global cooperation in addressing health crises and the interconnectedness of health, economy, and the environment.

- **Corporate Social Responsibility (CSR):**

Stakeholder Expectations: Stakeholders, including consumers, investors, and employees, are increasingly demanding that businesses operate ethically, transparently, and with a commitment to sustainability.

Long-Term Viability: Companies recognize that integrating sustainability into their operations is not just a moral imperative but also crucial for long-term business viability.

- **Government Policy and International Agreements:**

Policy Frameworks: Governments around the world have been adopting policy measures to promote sustainable development, including regulations, incentives, and targets.

International Agreements: Agreements such as the Paris Agreement on climate change and the United Nations Sustainable Development Goals (SDGs) provide a global framework for addressing sustainability challenges.

- **Public Awareness and Activism:**

Civil Society Engagement: Increased awareness and activism by civil society, including environmental organizations and grassroots movements, have contributed to the mainstreaming of sustainable development principles.

Educational Initiatives: Educational programs and awareness campaigns have played a role in informing the public about the interconnected nature of environmental, social, and economic issues.

The collective recognition of the need for sustainable development reflects a shift in mindset toward a more holistic and responsible approach to addressing the complex challenges facing the planet and its inhabitants. This acknowledgment is a crucial step in fostering a sustainable and resilient future for generations to come.

The concept of sustainable development, which encompasses economic, social, and environmental factors, has gained recognition over the past few decades (Sathaye, 2007). This recognition has led to a focus on the integration of these factors, particularly in the context of higher education (Barth, 2011). However, the achievement of sustainable development is hindered by political and economic constraints, as well as the need for significant social changes (Blowers, 1995). Redclift (1993) further highlights the contradictions within the concept of sustainable development, suggesting a need for a new vision that questions the authority of science and technology and emphasizes cultural diversity.

Purpose of the Chapter

✓ Setting the stage for exploring innovative economic approaches

Setting the stage for exploring innovative economic approaches involves creating a context that highlights the need for change, introduces the key challenges faced by traditional economic models, and emphasizes the importance of adopting novel and intelligent strategies. Here's a framework for setting the stage:

THE IMPERATIVE FOR CHANGE

Introduction to Current Economic Realities

Briefly outline the existing economic landscape, acknowledging achievements, but emphasizing challenges and vulnerabilities.

Highlight the interconnected nature of environmental, social, and economic issues.

Recognition of Limitations in Traditional Models

Discuss the shortcomings of traditional economic paradigms in addressing sustainability and inclusivity.

Address concerns related to GDP-centric growth, resource depletion, and inequality.

THE CALL FOR INNOVATION

Shifting Perspectives

Discuss the evolving mindset towards sustainability, emphasizing the need for a transition to more responsible and future-oriented economic practices.

Explore how societal values and expectations are changing.

Global Commitments to Sustainable Development

Highlight international agreements and commitments, such as the United Nations Sustainable Development Goals (SDGs) and climate accords, as indicators of a global push toward sustainability.

Explore the role of governments, businesses, and civil society in these global initiatives.

EMERGENCE OF INTELLIGENT APPROACHES

The Role of Technology

Introduce the transformative impact of technology, particularly artificial intelligence, in reshaping economic landscapes.

Provide examples of how technology is influencing decision-making, resource management, and innovation.

From Profit-Centric to Purpose-Driven

Discuss the growing trend of businesses incorporating purpose-driven strategies, where profit is aligned with societal and environmental goals.

Showcase examples of companies successfully balancing profit and purpose.

THE COMPLEXITY OF SUSTAINABLE DEVELOPMENT

Recognizing Interconnected Challenges

Emphasize the complex and interrelated nature of sustainability challenges, requiring holistic and integrated solutions.

Illustrate the linkages between environmental conservation, social equity, and economic prosperity.

Need for Adaptive Strategies

Discuss the dynamic nature of challenges, including emerging issues like climate change, and highlight the importance of adaptive and innovative strategies.

PREVIEW OF INTELLIGENT ECONOMIC APPROACHES

Overview of Intelligent Economic Approaches

Provide a preview of the forthcoming chapters, outlining key themes such as AI in economic decision-making, sustainable technologies, and innovative policy frameworks.

Convey the potential benefits and transformative impact of these intelligent approaches.

Conclusion

This introductory framework aims to capture the reader's attention, convey the urgency for change, and build anticipation for the exploration of innovative economic approaches. It lays the foundation for understanding why traditional models fall short and why intelligent, sustainable strategies are essential for shaping prosperous and resilient futures.

✓ **Highlighting the role of intelligence in shaping sustainable futures**

Highlighting the role of intelligence in shaping sustainable futures involves emphasizing the use of cognitive abilities, advanced technologies, and strategic decision-making to address complex challenges. Here's a structured approach to underscore the significance of intelligence in promoting sustainability:

THE INTELLIGENCE IMPERATIVE

Defining Intelligence in the Context of Sustainability

Clarify that intelligence extends beyond human cognitive abilities to encompass technological, data-driven, and strategic intelligence.

Introduce the concept of smart, adaptive systems that can contribute to sustainable development.

The Adaptive Intelligence Advantage

Discuss the importance of adaptive intelligence in understanding and responding to changing environmental, social, and economic dynamics.

Highlight how learning systems and data analytics contribute to adaptability.

ARTIFICIAL INTELLIGENCE IN SUSTAINABLE DEVELOPMENT

AI as a Decision-Making Tool

Explore how artificial intelligence can enhance decision-making processes in economic, environmental, and social domains.

Provide examples of AI applications in optimizing resource allocation, risk assessment, and policy formulation.

Predictive Analytics for Sustainable Planning

Illustrate how predictive analytics powered by AI can help anticipate environmental changes, market trends, and societal needs.

Emphasize the role of forecasting in developing proactive and sustainable strategies.

HARNESSING DATA FOR SUSTAINABLE SOLUTIONS

Big Data and Environmental Monitoring

Highlight the role of big data in monitoring and understanding environmental changes.

Discuss how data-driven insights contribute to more effective conservation, resource management, and pollution control.

Data-Driven Efficiency in Resource Management

Showcase examples of intelligent resource management systems that optimize energy consumption, water usage, and waste reduction.

Demonstrate how data-driven efficiency contributes to economic and environmental sustainability.

INTELLIGENT TECHNOLOGIES FOR SUSTAINABILITY

Automation in Sustainable Practices

Discuss how automation and robotics contribute to sustainable practices in manufacturing, agriculture, and logistics.

Explore the efficiency gains and environmental benefits of intelligent automation.

Smart Infrastructure for Resilient Cities

Explore the concept of smart cities and how intelligent infrastructure enhances urban sustainability.

Discuss the integration of technology for energy efficiency, waste management, and transportation.

COLLABORATIVE INTELLIGENCE AND INNOVATION

Cross-Sector Collaboration

Emphasize the importance of collaborative intelligence, where diverse stakeholders work together towards common sustainability goals.

Showcase examples of successful collaborations between governments, businesses, and non-profit organizations.

Innovation Ecosystems

Discuss the role of innovation ecosystems in fostering intelligent solutions for sustainability.

Highlight the synergy between research institutions, startups, and established companies in driving sustainable innovation.

ETHICAL CONSIDERATIONS AND HUMAN-CENTRIC INTELLIGENCE

Ethical Use of Technology

Acknowledge the ethical considerations surrounding the use of intelligent technologies for sustainability.

Discuss the importance of responsible AI and the protection of human rights.

Human-Centric Intelligence

Highlight the complementary role of human intelligence in guiding and overseeing intelligent systems.

Emphasize the need for values-driven decision-making in sustainable development.

Conclusion

Summarize the key points highlighting the role of intelligence in shaping sustainable futures.

Reinforce the idea that intelligent approaches, including AI, data analytics, and strategic decision-making, are essential for addressing the complexity of sustainability challenges.

This structured approach aims to showcase the multifaceted role of intelligence in driving sustainable development, from advanced technologies to collaborative and ethical decision-making. It underscores the transformative impact of intelligence in shaping a future that is both prosperous and environmentally and socially sustainable.

THE EVOLUTION OF ECONOMIC PARADIGMS

Traditional Economic Models

Overview of Classical Economic Theories

Classical economic theories form the foundation of modern economic thought and have significantly influenced the development of economic principles. Here's an overview of some key classical economic theories:

1. Classical Economics:
    - **Key Figures:** Adam Smith, David Ricardo, John Stuart Mill
    - **Time Period:** Late 18th to mid-19th century
    - **Central Tenets:**
        - **Laissez-Faire:** Advocated for minimal government intervention in the economy, emphasizing the efficiency of free markets.
        - **Invisible Hand:** Coined by Adam Smith, this concept suggests that individuals pursuing self-interest unintentionally contribute to the overall well-being of society.
        - **Labor Theory of Value:** Suggested by thinkers like David Ricardo, this theory posits that the value of a good or service is determined by the amount of labor required for its production.
2. Mercantilism:
    - **Key Ideas:**
        - **Balance of Trade:** Emphasized the importance of maintaining a surplus in the balance of trade to accumulate gold and silver.
        - **Government Intervention:** Supported government involvement in economic affairs to ensure national economic strength.
    - **Critiques:** Classical economists criticized mercantilist policies for hindering free trade and advocating protectionist measures.
3. Say's Law:
    - **Theorist:** Jean-Baptiste Say
    - **Key Idea:** "Supply creates its own demand." According to Say, the production of goods and services generates income, which is then used

to purchase other goods and services, ensuring a natural equilibrium in the economy.

4. Quantity Theory of Money:
   ◦ **Theorists:** John Locke, David Hume
   ◦ **Key Idea:** States that the general price level in an economy is directly proportional to the quantity of money in circulation. This theory laid the groundwork for later developments in monetary economics.
5. Ricardian Equivalence:
   ◦ **Theorist:** David Ricardo
   ◦ **Key Idea:** Suggested that individuals are forward-looking and will anticipate future taxes, leading them to adjust their behavior in response to expected future government policies. This concept challenges the effectiveness of certain fiscal policies.
6. Classical Dichotomy:
   ◦ **Key Idea:** Separates real and nominal variables in the economy. According to classical economists, changes in the money supply affect only nominal variables (like prices) and not real variables (like output and employment).
7. Neo-Classical Economics:
   ◦ **Key Figures:** Alfred Marshall, Leon Walras
   ◦ **Key Ideas:**
      ▪ **Marginalism:** Emphasized the importance of marginal utility in determining the value of goods and services.
      ▪ **Perfect Competition:** Developed the concept of perfect competition as an ideal market structure.
      ▪ **Equilibrium Analysis:** Focused on the analysis of market equilibrium and the allocation of resources.

While classical economic theories laid the groundwork for many contemporary economic concepts, they have also been subject to criticism and have evolved over time with the introduction of new theories and empirical evidence. Later schools of thought, such as Keynesian economics and neoclassical synthesis, built upon or challenged classical ideas, contributing to the dynamic nature of economic thought.

Critiques and Limitations in Addressing Sustainability

While classical economic theories have greatly contributed to our understanding of economic systems, they face several critiques and limitations when applied to the context of sustainability. Here are some key critiques:

- **Limited Consideration of Environmental Externalities:**
  - ○ **Critique:** Classical economics often neglects the environmental impact of economic activities, treating natural resources as infinite and not accounting for externalities such as pollution and resource depletion.
  - ○ **Limitation:** In a world facing environmental challenges, this oversight undermines the ability to address issues like climate change and biodiversity loss.
- **Short-Term Focus and Discounting the Future:**
  - ○ **Critique:** Classical economic models tend to prioritize short-term gains and may not adequately account for the long-term consequences of resource exploitation or environmental degradation.
  - ○ **Limitation:** Sustainability, by definition, requires consideration of intergenerational equity and the impact of present actions on future generations.
- **Assumption of Rational Economic Agents:**
  - ○ **Critique:** Classical economics often assumes that individuals and firms make decisions based on rational self-interest, without considering the complexities of human behavior, bounded rationality, and the role of emotions in decision-making.
  - ○ **Limitation:** This simplification can lead to an underestimation of the challenges associated with changing behavior for sustainable outcomes.
- **Inadequate Treatment of Social Equity:**
  - ○ **Critique:** Traditional economic models may not sufficiently address issues of social equity and distribution of resources, often assuming that market mechanisms will naturally lead to fair outcomes.
  - ○ **Limitation:** This oversight can perpetuate or exacerbate existing inequalities, hindering efforts to achieve sustainable development goals.
- **Lack of Inclusivity in Economic Growth:**
  - ○ **Critique:** Classical economics tends to focus on aggregate economic growth (e.g., GDP) without necessarily ensuring that this growth is inclusive and benefits all segments of society.
  - ○ **Limitation:** Sustainable development requires not only economic growth but also social inclusivity and improved quality of life for all.
- **Overemphasis on Market Mechanisms:**
  - ○ **Critique:** Classical economics relies heavily on market mechanisms and may underappreciate the role of government intervention, regulation, and non-market institutions in addressing sustainability challenges.
  - ○ **Limitation:** Some environmental and social issues may require collective action, public goods provision, and regulatory frameworks beyond what markets alone can achieve.

- **Failure to Incorporate Complexity and System Dynamics:**
  - ○ **Critique:** Classical economic models often simplify the complexity of real-world systems, ignoring feedback loops, nonlinear dynamics, and the interconnectedness of economic, social, and environmental systems.
  - ○ **Limitation:** Sustainability challenges are inherently complex and require models that can capture and respond to dynamic, interconnected systems.
- **Resistance to Change and Innovation:**
  - ○ **Critique:** Classical economic thought can be resistant to embracing innovative, non-traditional approaches that challenge established norms and practices.
  - ○ **Limitation:** In the face of rapidly evolving sustainability challenges, a reluctance to adapt may hinder progress toward more sustainable economic systems.
- **Neglect of Cultural and Ethical Dimensions:**
  - ○ **Critique:** Classical economics often downplays the role of cultural values and ethical considerations in shaping economic behavior.
  - ○ **Limitation:** Achieving sustainability requires a broader understanding that incorporates diverse cultural perspectives and ethical considerations.

Addressing these critiques often involves integrating insights from fields such as ecological economics, behavioral economics, and institutional economics, which provide frameworks better suited to understanding and addressing sustainability challenges. Embracing a multidisciplinary approach that considers environmental, social, and economic dimensions is essential for advancing sustainable development.

Shifting Towards Sustainability

Emerging Trends in Sustainable Economics

Here are some key emerging trends in sustainable economics:

- **Circular Economy:**
  - ○ **Concept:** A circular economy focuses on minimizing waste and making the most of resources by designing products for longevity, recycling, and reuse.
  - ○ **Impact:** Promotes sustainability by reducing resource extraction, minimizing environmental impact, and fostering a closed-loop system.
- **Impact Investing:**

- **Concept:** Impact investing involves making investments with the intention of generating positive, measurable social and environmental impact alongside financial returns.
- **Impact:** Aligns financial resources with sustainability goals, addressing societal and environmental challenges.
- **Regenerative Agriculture:**
  - **Concept:** Regenerative agriculture goes beyond sustainable farming by emphasizing practices that restore soil health, enhance biodiversity, and sequester carbon.
  - **Impact:** Supports sustainable food production while addressing climate change and promoting ecosystem health.
- **Green Finance:**
  - **Concept:** Green finance involves using financial mechanisms to fund environmentally sustainable projects and activities.
  - **Impact:** Mobilizes capital towards projects that contribute to climate resilience, renewable energy, and other sustainability objectives.
- **Eco-friendly Technologies:**
  - **Concept:** Advancements in clean energy, sustainable transportation, and eco-friendly technologies are driving economic growth while reducing environmental impact.
  - **Impact:** Promotes innovation and supports the transition to a low-carbon and resource-efficient economy.
- **Corporate Sustainability and ESG:**
  - **Concept:** Environmental, Social, and Governance (ESG) criteria are increasingly used by investors to evaluate the sustainability performance of companies.
  - **Impact:** Encourages corporate responsibility, ethical practices, and consideration of environmental and social factors in business operations.
- **Digitalization for Sustainability:**
  - **Concept:** Leveraging digital technologies such as IoT, AI, and blockchain to enhance sustainability efforts, from supply chain transparency to energy efficiency.
  - **Impact:** Improves resource management, reduces environmental impact, and enhances the efficiency of sustainable practices.
- **Sustainable and Resilient Infrastructure:**
  - **Concept:** Focus on developing infrastructure that is not only environmentally sustainable but also resilient to the impacts of climate change.
  - **Impact:** Enhances long-term infrastructure viability while contributing to climate adaptation and mitigation.

- **Nature-Based Solutions:**
  - ◦ **Concept:** Utilizing natural ecosystems and biodiversity to address environmental challenges, such as reforestation, wetland restoration, and sustainable land management.
  - ◦ **Impact:** Offers cost-effective and sustainable solutions for climate change mitigation and adaptation.
- **Stakeholder Capitalism:**
  - ◦ **Concept:** Shift towards a model where businesses consider the interests of all stakeholders, including employees, communities, and the environment, rather than solely focusing on shareholder value.
  - ◦ **Impact:** Encourages responsible business practices and aligns corporate strategies with broader societal goals.
- **Community-Based Economics:**
  - ◦ **Concept:** Emphasizes localized, community-driven economic models that prioritize social well-being, environmental sustainability, and local resilience.
  - ◦ **Impact:** Fosters inclusive and participatory economic development, reducing dependence on global supply chains.
- **Behavioral Economics for Sustainability:**
  - ◦ **Concept:** Applying insights from behavioral economics to encourage pro-environmental behaviors and sustainable decision-making.
  - ◦ **Impact:** Addresses psychological factors influencing consumer choices and promotes the adoption of sustainable practices.

These emerging trends reflect a growing recognition of the interconnectedness between economic activities, social well-being, and environmental health. They represent efforts to create more holistic and sustainable approaches to economic development and resource management. Keep in mind that the field of sustainable economics is continually evolving, and staying informed about the latest developments is essential for understanding the current landscape.

The Role of Technology and Global Awareness

The role of technology and global awareness is instrumental in shaping sustainable economics and fostering positive change at a global scale. These two aspects are interlinked and play a crucial role in addressing environmental challenges, promoting social equity, and driving economic development. Here's an exploration of their roles:

- **Technology in Sustainable Economics:**
  - a.   Renewable Energy and Clean Technologies:

- *Solar, Wind, and Hydro Power:* Advances in renewable energy technologies contribute to a shift away from fossil fuels, reducing carbon emissions and promoting sustainable energy sources.
- *Energy Storage Solutions:* Developments in energy storage enhance the reliability and efficiency of renewable energy systems.

b. Smart Cities and Infrastructure:
- *Urban Planning:* Technology facilitates the creation of smart, sustainable cities with efficient transportation, waste management, and energy systems.
- *IoT Integration:* Internet of Things (IoT) technologies enable real-time data collection for optimizing resource use and improving city services.

c. Circular Economy and Sustainable Manufacturing:
- *Advanced Recycling Technologies:* Innovations in recycling technologies support the transition towards a circular economy by minimizing waste and promoting resource efficiency.
- *Additive Manufacturing (3D Printing):* Reduces material waste and energy consumption in manufacturing processes.

d. Precision Agriculture:
- *Remote Sensing and AI:* Technologies such as satellite imagery and artificial intelligence enhance precision agriculture, optimizing resource use, reducing waste, and minimizing environmental impact.

e. Blockchain for Supply Chain Transparency:
- *Supply Chain Traceability:* Blockchain technology provides transparent and traceable supply chains, ensuring ethical sourcing, reducing environmental impact, and preventing illegal practices.

f. Carbon Capture and Storage (CCS):
- *Technological Solutions:* CCS technologies help capture and store carbon emissions from industries, mitigating the impact of greenhouse gases on climate change.

- **Global Awareness in Sustainable Economics:**
a. Environmental Awareness:
- *Climate Change Awareness:* Global awareness of climate change challenges prompts individuals, businesses, and governments to adopt sustainable practices and support climate action.
- *Biodiversity Conservation:* Increased awareness of biodiversity loss leads to conservation efforts and sustainable practices to protect ecosystems.

b. Social Responsibility and Equity:

- *Consumer Awareness:* Informed consumers drive demand for sustainable products and ethical business practices, influencing companies to adopt socially responsible policies.
- *Fair Trade Movements:* Global awareness of fair trade principles promotes equitable business practices and supports the well-being of workers in developing regions.

c. Global Cooperation and Partnerships:
- *International Collaboration:* Shared awareness of global challenges fosters international cooperation and partnerships for addressing issues like climate change, poverty, and health crises.
- *Multilateral Agreements:* Global awareness encourages the creation and adherence to agreements and frameworks such as the Paris Agreement and Sustainable Development Goals.

d. Social Media and Information Sharing:
- *Digital Platforms:* Social media and online platforms facilitate the rapid spread of information, enabling the global population to stay informed about sustainability issues and initiatives.
- *Activism and Advocacy:* Global awareness amplifies activism and advocacy efforts, influencing policies and encouraging responsible corporate behavior.

e. Educational Initiatives:
- *Curriculum Integration:* Global awareness is promoted through educational initiatives that integrate sustainability into school curricula, fostering a sense of responsibility and environmental stewardship in future generations.

The integration of technology and global awareness in sustainable economics is a powerful force for positive change. Technology provides the tools and solutions needed to address environmental and social challenges, while global awareness ensures that individuals, businesses, and governments are informed and motivated to adopt sustainable practices. The synergy between technological innovation and widespread awareness is essential for creating a more sustainable, equitable, and resilient global economy.

The role of technology in fostering global awareness is a key theme in the literature. Crawford (2008) emphasizes the importance of technology in social studies teaching, as it can help students understand the interrelationships of peoples worldwide. Seçken (2005) further explores this relationship, finding that computer-aided education can significantly increase students' attitudes towards technology and global environmental awareness. Kholdarvovna (2021) underscores the need for information and communication technologies in addressing global issues, such as information security. Lastly, Wyk (2020) calls for a universal definition of technology and a methodology for measuring technological advance to enhance technological awareness and wisdom. These studies collectively highlight the potential of technology in promoting global awareness and understanding.

INTELLIGENCE IN ECONOMIC DECISION-MAKING

Artificial Intelligence (AI) and Economic Analysis

Exploring How AI is Transforming Economic Forecasting

Artificial Intelligence (AI) is transforming economic forecasting by leveraging advanced algorithms, data analytics, and machine learning techniques to analyze large datasets, identify patterns, and make predictions. This has significant implications for decision-making, policy formulation, and risk management in the economic domain. Here's an exploration of how AI is reshaping economic forecasting:

- **Data Processing and Analysis:**
  - **Big Data Handling:** AI systems can efficiently process vast amounts of structured and unstructured data from diverse sources, including economic indicators, financial markets, and social trends.
  - **Pattern Recognition:** Machine learning algorithms excel at identifying complex patterns and correlations within datasets, allowing for more nuanced and accurate analyses.
- **Improved Predictive Modeling:**
  - **Machine Learning Models:** AI enables the development of sophisticated predictive models, such as neural networks and ensemble methods, that outperform traditional econometric models in capturing nonlinear relationships.
  - **Dynamic Modeling:** AI models can adapt to changing economic conditions and incorporate new data in real-time, providing more dynamic and responsive forecasts.
- **Forecasting Unstructured Data:**
  - **Sentiment Analysis:** AI tools can analyze unstructured data, including news articles, social media, and online discussions, to gauge public sentiment and incorporate qualitative insights into economic forecasts.
  - **Natural Language Processing (NLP):** NLP algorithms enable the extraction of valuable information from textual data, aiding in the assessment of economic sentiment and policy impacts.

- **Financial Market Predictions:**
  - **Algorithmic Trading:** AI-powered algorithms are increasingly used in algorithmic trading to forecast market trends, analyze trading patterns, and optimize investment strategies.
  - **Risk Management:** AI models enhance risk assessment by predicting market volatility, identifying potential financial crises, and offering insights into systemic risks.
- **Macroeconomic Indicator Predictions:**
  - **Labor Market Trends:** AI can analyze labor market data to predict employment trends, wage growth, and demographic shifts, providing insights into the overall health of an economy.
  - **Inflation and Price Index Forecasts:** AI models can predict inflation rates and price indices by analyzing factors such as consumer behavior, supply chain dynamics, and global economic indicators.
- **Policy Impact Analysis:**
  - **Scenario Analysis:** AI enables the modeling of different economic scenarios to assess the potential impact of policy changes, geopolitical events, and external shocks.
  - **Policy Recommendation Systems:** AI systems can offer data-driven policy recommendations by analyzing historical data and predicting the likely outcomes of different policy interventions.
- **Real-Time Monitoring and Early Warning Systems:**
  - **Continuous Monitoring:** AI facilitates real-time monitoring of economic indicators, allowing for timely adjustments to forecasts and responses to emerging trends.
  - **Early Warning Signals:** AI algorithms can identify early warning signals of economic downturns, financial instability, or emerging risks, enabling proactive measures.
- **Challenges and Considerations:**
  - **Data Bias and Quality:** AI models are susceptible to biases in training data, and the quality of predictions depends on the accuracy and representativeness of the data.
  - **Interpretability:** Some AI models, particularly deep neural networks, are considered "black boxes," making it challenging to interpret the reasoning behind specific predictions.
  - **Ethical Considerations:** As AI becomes integral to economic decision-making, ethical considerations related to transparency, accountability, and fairness need careful attention.

AI's transformation of economic forecasting represents a paradigm shift, offering the potential for more accurate, dynamic, and nuanced predictions. However, challenges related to data quality, interpretability, and ethical considerations necessitate careful integration and oversight. As AI technologies continue to advance, their role in economic forecasting is likely to evolve, contributing to more informed and resilient economic decision-making.

The integration of AI and big data analytics is transforming economic forecasting, leading to more accurate and comprehensive predictions (Wang, 2022). This is particularly evident in the financial sector, where AI-based techniques have been found to outperform traditional methods (Nair, 2015). However, the high cost and vulnerability to cyber-attacks are potential challenges in the widespread adoption of AI in forecasting (Annor-Antwi, 2019). Despite these challenges, the future of business and the global economy is increasingly reliant on accurate forecasting (Annor-Antwi, 2019).

Case Studies of Successful AI Applications in Economic Decision-Making

several case studies illustrate successful applications of artificial intelligence (AI) in economic decision-making. Keep in mind that developments in this field are dynamic, and there may be additional cases or updates since then. Here are a few notable examples:

- **Alibaba's City Brain:**
  - **Application:** City Brain is an AI-driven urban traffic management system developed by Alibaba Cloud. It has been implemented in cities like Hangzhou, China.
  - **Impact:** The system uses real-time data from various sources, including cameras and sensors, to optimize traffic flow, reduce congestion, and enhance overall urban management. It demonstrates the potential of AI in improving efficiency in city operations and infrastructure planning.
- **Federal Reserve Bank of New York's DSGE Model with Machine Learning:**
  - **Application:** Researchers at the Federal Reserve Bank of New York integrated machine learning techniques into a standard Dynamic Stochastic General Equilibrium (DSGE) model.
  - **Impact:** The incorporation of machine learning allows for a more nuanced understanding of complex economic relationships, enabling better forecasting accuracy and policy analysis.
- **Singapore's AI-Powered Economic Planning:**

- ○ **Application:** Singapore has employed AI in its economic planning and development efforts. The nation has implemented AI-driven systems for data analysis, trend prediction, and scenario planning.
- ○ **Impact:** These applications help policymakers make informed decisions by providing insights into economic trends, potential challenges, and policy implications. Singapore's approach highlights the integration of AI into broader economic governance strategies.

- **IBM Watson for Financial Services:**
  - ○ **Application:** IBM Watson for Financial Services is an AI-powered platform designed to assist financial institutions in making data-driven decisions, managing risks, and enhancing customer experiences.
  - ○ **Impact:** The platform analyzes vast amounts of financial data, regulatory information, and market trends to provide insights that aid in strategic decision-making, compliance, and risk management.

- **Zillow's Home Value Prediction with AI:**
  - ○ **Application:** Zillow, a real estate company, uses AI algorithms to predict home values. The Zestimate, Zillow's home value estimation tool, incorporates machine learning to analyze various factors influencing property values.
  - ○ **Impact:** The AI-driven predictions provide users with estimates of property values, helping homebuyers, sellers, and real estate professionals make informed decisions.

- **European Central Bank's Natural Language Processing (NLP) Applications:**
  - ○ **Application:** The European Central Bank (ECB) has integrated NLP technologies to analyze textual data, including news articles, speeches, and reports.
  - ○ **Impact:** NLP helps the ECB in gauging sentiment, extracting relevant information, and understanding market expectations, contributing to more informed monetary policy decisions.

- **Walmart's AI for Supply Chain Optimization:**
  - ○ **Application:** Walmart utilizes AI in its supply chain management to optimize inventory levels, improve demand forecasting, and enhance overall efficiency.
  - ○ **Impact:** AI algorithms analyze historical sales data, seasonality patterns, and external factors to optimize inventory stocking levels, reduce costs, and minimize stockouts.

- **South Korea's AI in Trade Finance:**

- ○ **Application:** South Korea has implemented AI in trade finance processes, automating document verification and reducing the time required for trade transactions.
- ○ **Impact:** The application of AI streamlines trade finance operations, improves accuracy in document processing, and accelerates the flow of goods and services across borders.

These case studies highlight the diverse applications of AI in economic decision-making, ranging from urban management and monetary policy to financial services and trade. AI's ability to analyze vast datasets, identify patterns, and provide actionable insights has proven valuable in enhancing the efficiency and effectiveness of economic processes. Keep in mind that the field is rapidly evolving, and new developments may have occurred since my last update.

A range of case studies have demonstrated the successful application of AI in economic decision-making. Martin (1991) and Siddique (2018) both highlight the potential of AI to provide consultative advice and improve information processing, with specific examples including credit request processing and customer service improvement. Zhao (2022) and Zhang (2021) further illustrate the effectiveness of AI in economic management and e-commerce fulfillment, respectively, with the former emphasizing the use of a decision support system and the latter focusing on resource orchestration. These studies collectively underscore the transformative impact of AI on economic decision-making processes.

Behavioral Economics and Human Intelligence

Understanding the Psychological Factors Influencing Economic Choices

Understanding economic choices involves considering not only rational decision-making based on objective factors but also the influence of psychological factors. Behavioral economics, a field that combines insights from psychology and economics, explores how individuals deviate from purely rational decision-making and examines the psychological factors that impact economic choices. Here are key psychological factors:

- **Loss Aversion:**
  - ○ **Concept:** People tend to strongly prefer avoiding losses over acquiring equivalent gains. The pain of losing is psychologically more impactful than the pleasure of gaining.

- ○ **Impact on Economic Choices:** Individuals may make decisions to avoid losses even if it means forgoing potential gains, influencing choices in investments, purchases, and risk-taking.
- **Confirmation Bias:**
  - ○ **Concept:** Individuals tend to seek out and give more weight to information that confirms their existing beliefs and preferences.
  - ○ **Impact on Economic Choices:** Confirmation bias can lead to a reluctance to consider alternative viewpoints, affecting decision-making in investments, market predictions, and product choices.
- **Anchoring:**
  - ○ **Concept:** People rely heavily on the first piece of information encountered when making decisions. Subsequent judgments are often based on this initial "anchor."
  - ○ **Impact on Economic Choices:** Anchoring can influence perceptions of value, pricing decisions, and negotiations, as individuals use the initial reference point as a basis for comparisons.
- **Status Quo Bias:**
  - ○ **Concept:** Individuals tend to prefer the current state of affairs and are resistant to change, even when change may lead to better outcomes.
  - ○ **Impact on Economic Choices:** Status quo bias can influence choices related to savings, investments, and adoption of new technologies or financial products.
- **Herding Behavior:**
  - ○ **Concept:** People tend to follow the actions of the majority, assuming that collective behavior provides safety or correctness.
  - ○ **Impact on Economic Choices:** Herding behavior can lead to market trends, bubbles, and mass adoption of certain financial assets or investment strategies.
- **Overconfidence:**
  - ○ **Concept:** Individuals tend to overestimate their own abilities and the precision of their predictions.
  - ○ **Impact on Economic Choices:** Overconfidence can lead to excessive risk-taking, trading frequency, and the failure to adequately account for uncertainties in economic decisions.
- **Present Bias:**
  - ○ **Concept:** People tend to place a higher value on immediate rewards and are often willing to sacrifice long-term benefits for short-term gains.
  - ○ **Impact on Economic Choices:** Present bias can affect decisions related to saving, investing, and debt management, leading to suboptimal outcomes over time.

- **Hyperbolic Discounting:**
  - ○ **Concept:** Individuals prefer smaller, more immediate rewards over larger, delayed rewards, but their preference for immediate rewards diminishes quickly over time.
  - ○ **Impact on Economic Choices:** Hyperbolic discounting influences choices related to intertemporal decision-making, such as savings and retirement planning.
- **Cognitive Biases:**
  - ○ **Concept:** Various cognitive biases, such as availability bias, framing effects, and optimism bias, influence how information is processed and judgments are made.
  - ○ **Impact on Economic Choices:** Cognitive biases can shape perceptions of risk, influence investment decisions, and impact responses to economic information.
- **Social and Cultural Influences:**
  - ○ **Concept:** Social and cultural factors, including norms, values, and peer influences, play a significant role in shaping economic choices.
  - ○ **Impact on Economic Choices:** Cultural expectations and social norms influence spending patterns, savings behavior, and investment decisions.

Understanding these psychological factors is crucial for policymakers, economists, and businesses to design effective interventions, policies, and marketing strategies that account for the complex interplay of rational and irrational elements in economic decision-making. Behavioral economics provides valuable insights into how psychological factors shape choices and offers a more realistic understanding of human behavior in economic contexts.

Psychological factors significantly influence economic decision-making, as highlighted by Publika (2023). These factors include cognitive biases, emotions, and social influences. McNair (2017) further emphasizes the role of psychological dispositions, such as financial attitudes and time orientations, in shaping economic behavior. Hermalin (2000) underscores the impact of current emotional state, particularly positive affect, on decision-making. Lastly, Baddeley (2010) argues for an interdisciplinary approach that considers the interplay of cognitive and emotional factors, and the influence of sociological and psychological forces on economic decision-making.

Designing Intelligent Policies Based on Human Behaviour

Designing intelligent policies based on an understanding of human behavior involves applying insights from behavioral economics and psychology to create interventions that influence behavior positively. Here are key principles and strategies for designing such policies:

- **Nudging:**

  Concept: Nudging involves designing interventions that guide individuals toward making better decisions without restricting their choices. It leverages behavioral insights to influence behavior subtly. **Example:** Opt-out rather than opt-in organ donation systems, default settings for energy-saving options, and personalized feedback on consumption behavior.

- **Framing:**

  Concept: The way information is presented (framed) can significantly impact decision-making. Presenting information in a way that appeals to psychological biases can influence choices. **Example:** Framing healthcare choices in terms of potential losses (e.g., the cost of not having insurance) can encourage enrollment.

- **Incentives and Rewards:**

  Concept: Offering rewards or incentives can motivate desired behaviors. The framing of incentives and their immediacy are crucial factors. **Example:** Cash incentives for completing health screenings, tax credits for energy-efficient home improvements, and loyalty programs for sustainable consumer choices.

- **Feedback Loops:**

  Concept: Providing individuals with timely and relevant feedback about their behavior can create awareness and encourage positive changes. **Example:** Energy consumption reports for households, real-time feedback on fuel efficiency while driving, and personalized financial health dashboards.

- **Social Norms and Influence:**

  Concept: Humans are influenced by social norms and the behavior of others. Policies can leverage social influence to promote positive behavior. **Example:** Publicizing energy conservation efforts in a community, social endorsements for charitable contributions, and highlighting positive social norms for compliance.

- **Default Settings:**

Concept: Setting default options that align with desired outcomes can significantly impact choices, as people tend to stick with default settings. **Example:** Opt-out organ donation registration, default enrollment in retirement savings plans, and default settings for privacy preferences.

- **Simplification:**

Concept: Simplifying choices and reducing complexity can facilitate decision-making and increase the likelihood of desired behaviors. **Example:** Streamlining the enrollment process for government assistance programs, simplifying tax forms, and using clear and concise messaging.

- **Loss Aversion Mitigation:**

Concept: Policies can be designed to mitigate the impact of loss aversion by reframing losses or providing assurances against potential losses. **Example:** Offering trial periods for subscriptions, providing guarantees on product satisfaction, and emphasizing safety measures to reduce perceived risks.

- **Education and Information:**

Concept: Providing clear and relevant information can influence behavior by increasing awareness and understanding of the consequences of choices. **Example:** Health education campaigns, financial literacy programs, and information on the environmental impact of products.

- **Temporal Discounting Consideration:**

Concept: Policies should account for individuals' tendency to discount future rewards and prioritize immediate gains. Designing incentives and consequences with this in mind is crucial. **Example:** Offering immediate rewards for sustainable behavior, creating time-limited promotions, and emphasizing the long-term benefits of healthy habits.

- **Choice Architecture:**

Concept: The way choices are presented (choice architecture) can influence decisions. Designing the environment to guide choices can be a powerful policy tool. **Example:** Placing healthier food options at eye level, organizing menu options to highlight sustainable choices, and structuring retirement plan options for optimal decision-making.

- **Behavioral Trials and Pilots:**

Concept: Testing policy interventions on a small scale allows policymakers to assess their effectiveness and make adjustments before broader implementation. **Example:** Conducting pilot programs for new education policies, healthcare interventions, or environmental initiatives to assess their impact.

Intelligent policies that consider human behavior are rooted in an understanding of psychological factors and behavioral patterns. By applying these insights, policymakers can design interventions that nudge individuals toward choices that align with societal goals, fostering positive outcomes for both individuals and communities. The key is to create policies that acknowledge and work with the way people naturally think and make decisions.

Behavioral economics and insights from human behavior are increasingly being used to inform policy design, with a focus on improving public administration and citizen influence (John, 2015). This approach is particularly relevant in development programs, where it can enhance the reach and effectiveness of policies (Mullainathan, 2014). The use of AI and machine learning methods, such as the AI Economist framework, can further optimize policy design by considering multiple objectives, policy levers, and behavioral responses (Trott, 2021). Finally, a framework for employing behavioral insights in public policy practice has been proposed, emphasizing the need for policy designers to consider the mechanisms driving policy addressees' behaviors (Olejniczak, 2019).

INNOVATIONS IN SUSTAINABLE TECHNOLOGIES

Clean Energy and Green Technologies

Examining the Economic Impact of Renewable Energy

Examining the economic impact of renewable energy involves assessing its effects on various aspects of the economy, including job creation, economic growth, energy costs, and environmental sustainability. Here are key dimensions to consider:

- **Job Creation:**

Positive Impact: The renewable energy sector has the potential to generate substantial employment opportunities. Jobs are created in the installation, operation, and maintenance of renewable energy systems, as well as in the manufacturing of related components. **Example:** Solar photovoltaic (PV) and wind energy projects often require skilled labor for installation and maintenance, contributing to job growth.

- **Economic Growth:**

Positive Impact: Investment in renewable energy projects can stimulate economic growth. The development, construction, and operation of renewable energy infrastructure contribute to economic activity, driving growth in related industries. **Example:** Countries with robust renewable energy policies often experience increased economic activity in sectors like manufacturing, construction, and technology.

- **Energy Cost Stability:**

Positive Impact: Renewable energy can contribute to energy cost stability by providing a more predictable and often lower-cost source of electricity. This stability can benefit consumers, businesses, and industries. **Example:** The declining costs of solar and wind power contribute to the affordability of renewable energy sources, reducing dependence on volatile fossil fuel prices.

- **Diversification of Energy Sources:**

Positive Impact: Transitioning to renewable energy sources reduces dependence on finite and often geopolitically sensitive fossil fuels. Diversification of energy sources enhances energy security and reduces vulnerability to price fluctuations. **Example:** A diversified energy portfolio that includes renewables can mitigate the economic impact of disruptions in fossil fuel supplies.

- **Technological Innovation and Competitiveness:**

Positive Impact: Investment in renewable energy fosters technological innovation, enhancing a country's competitiveness in the global market. Innovation in clean energy technologies can lead to the development of new industries and export opportunities. **Example:** Countries investing in research and development for renewable energy technologies may become leaders in the global clean energy market.

- **Reduction of External Costs:**

Positive Impact: The use of renewable energy can help reduce external costs associated with environmental degradation and public health issues linked to fossil fuel extraction and combustion. **Example:** The avoidance of air and water pollution and the mitigation of climate change contribute to cost savings related to healthcare, agriculture, and disaster management.

- **Infrastructure Investment:**

Positive Impact: The deployment of renewable energy infrastructure requires substantial investment, contributing to economic development. This includes investments in power generation, grid enhancements, and storage technologies. **Example:** Governments and private entities investing in renewable energy projects contribute to infrastructure development, creating economic opportunities.

- **Policy and Regulatory Impacts:**

Positive Impact: Supportive policies and regulations can incentivize the adoption of renewable energy. These may include subsidies, tax incentives, renewable portfolio standards, and feed-in tariffs. **Example:** Policies promoting the use of renewable energy can attract investment, create jobs, and spur economic growth in the clean energy sector.

- **Energy Independence:**

Positive Impact: Increasing reliance on renewable energy sources enhances energy independence, reducing a nation's vulnerability to external energy supply disruptions. **Example:** Countries with abundant renewable resources, such as wind or solar, can reduce dependence on energy imports and strengthen energy security.

- **Challenges and Considerations:**

Intermittency and Reliability: Addressing the intermittency of some renewable sources and ensuring a reliable energy supply. **Initial Costs:** Overcoming the upfront costs of renewable energy infrastructure, which may be higher than traditional energy sources. **Transition Challenges:** Managing the transition from conventional to renewable energy sources without causing economic disruptions in existing industries.

The economic impact of renewable energy is multifaceted, with numerous positive effects, such as job creation, economic growth, and reduced external costs. While challenges exist, continued advancements in technology, supportive policies, and international collaboration can contribute to a more sustainable and economically beneficial energy future.

A number of studies have found a positive and statistically significant relationship between the consumption of renewable energy and economic growth (Inglesi-Lotz, 2016). This is further supported by Zhao (2022), who emphasizes the importance of renewable energy technologies in economic development. Maradin (2017) also highlights the multiplier effect of renewable energy technologies in spurring economic growth. These findings collectively suggest that the promotion and investment in renewable energy can have significant positive impacts on the economy.

Case Studies on Successful Integration of Green Technologies

The successful integration of green technologies is evident in various case studies across different sectors. These examples showcase how businesses, governments, and communities have embraced sustainable practices and green technologies to achieve environmental benefits while often realizing economic advantages. Here are a few notable case studies:

- **Tesla and Electric Vehicles (EVs):**
  - **Overview:** Tesla's success in the electric vehicle market has been transformative for the automotive industry.
  - **Key Features:** Tesla's EVs combine high-performance capabilities with long-range capabilities. The company's investment in battery technology has contributed to increased energy density and reduced costs. Supercharger network deployment facilitates long-distance travel for EV users.
- **Masdar City, Abu Dhabi:**
  - **Overview:** Masdar City is a sustainable urban development project in Abu Dhabi, aiming to be one of the world's most sustainable cities.
  - **Key Features:** Integrates renewable energy sources like solar power for electricity generation. Implements smart city technologies for efficient resource use. Emphasizes pedestrian-friendly designs and electric public transportation.
- **Google's Data Center Efficiency:**
  - **Overview:** Google has implemented various measures to improve the energy efficiency of its data centers.
  - **Key Features:** Advanced cooling technologies, such as using seawater for cooling in its Finland data center. Installation of on-site renewable energy sources, including solar and wind power. Use of machine learning algorithms to optimize data center operations for energy efficiency.

- **Denmark's Wind Energy Success:**
  - ○ **Overview:** Denmark has been a pioneer in wind energy adoption and has successfully integrated wind power into its energy mix.
  - ○ **Key Features:** Strong government support and favorable policies for wind energy development. Investment in research and development to improve wind turbine efficiency. Successful grid integration of wind power, making Denmark a global leader in wind energy.
- **IKEA's Renewable Energy Investments:**
  - ○ **Overview:** IKEA, the furniture retailer, has made significant investments in renewable energy to power its operations.
  - ○ **Key Features:** Installation of solar panels on store rooftops globally. Investment in wind energy projects to offset energy consumption. Commitment to becoming energy-independent and reducing carbon emissions.
- **California's Solar Energy Boom:**
  - ○ **Overview:** California has experienced a significant increase in solar energy capacity, contributing to the state's renewable energy goals.
  - ○ **Key Features:** Policy support, including the California Solar Initiative, incentivizing solar installations. Declining solar panel costs and advances in solar technology. Collaboration between the public and private sectors to expand solar infrastructure.
- **Suzlon's Wind Power Projects in India:**
  - ○ **Overview:** Suzlon Energy, an Indian renewable energy company, has played a crucial role in the development of wind power projects in India.
  - ○ **Key Features:** Suzlon's wind turbines contribute significantly to India's wind energy capacity. The company focuses on both onshore and offshore wind projects. Collaboration with government initiatives to increase the share of renewables in the energy mix.
- **Smart Grid Implementation in South Korea:**
  - ○ **Overview:** South Korea has invested in smart grid technologies to enhance the efficiency and sustainability of its energy infrastructure.
  - ○ **Key Features:** Deployment of advanced metering infrastructure for real-time monitoring. Integration of renewable energy sources into the grid. Implementation of demand response programs for efficient energy use.
- **Costa Rica's Renewable Energy Achievement:**
  - ○ **Overview:** Costa Rica has made significant progress in generating electricity from renewable sources.

○ **Key Features:** A focus on hydropower, geothermal, wind, and solar energy. Consistent policy support for renewable energy development. The country has achieved periods of running on 100% renewable energy.

These case studies highlight diverse examples of successful integration of green technologies across different regions and industries. They demonstrate the feasibility of adopting sustainable practices and showcase the positive impact on the environment, economic efficiency, and long-term viability. Successful integration often involves a combination of technological innovation, supportive policies, and a commitment to sustainability from both public and private stakeholders.

A range of case studies have demonstrated the successful integration of green technologies in various industries. Lee (2011) found that involving key suppliers in green product development can lead to both environmental and commercial success in the semiconductor industry. Similarly, Yeolekar-Kadam (2022) identified the feasibility of integrating green technologies in construction projects, particularly in the domains of energy, materials, and waste management. Bartlett (2010) explored the evolution of green technology projects into eco-innovations in the Russian R&D sector, highlighting the potential for successful integration. Lastly, Nazari (2012) identified factors such as organizational slack, compatibility, and competitive pressure as key influencers in the adoption of green IT, further supporting the successful integration of green technologies.

Circular Economy and Resource Efficiency

Introduction to Circular Economy Principles

The circular economy is an economic model designed to maximize the value of resources while minimizing waste and environmental impact. Unlike the traditional linear economy, which follows a "take, make, dispose" pattern, the circular economy emphasizes sustainability, longevity, and the continuous use of resources. Here's an introduction to the principles of the circular economy:

- **Closed-Loop System:** In a circular economy, the goal is to create closed-loop systems where resources are continually reused, refurbished, remanufactured, and recycled. This reduces the need for extracting new raw materials.
- **Design for Longevity:** Circular economy principles encourage designing products with durability and longevity in mind. This includes creating items that are easy to repair, upgrade, and disassemble to extend their lifespan.

- **Resource Efficiency:** The circular economy emphasizes the efficient use of resources. This involves minimizing waste, optimizing production processes, and using renewable or recyclable materials.
- **Sharing Economy:** Encouraging a sharing economy is a key aspect of the circular model. This involves sharing, renting, or leasing products and services rather than owning them outright. Examples include car-sharing programs or tool libraries.
- **Product as a Service:** Shifting from an ownership model to a service-based model, where consumers pay for the service or utility of a product rather than owning it, can contribute to the circular economy. For instance, companies might offer lighting services instead of selling light bulbs.
- **Reverse Logistics:** Efficient systems for collecting, refurbishing, and recycling products at the end of their life are crucial in a circular economy. This involves the reverse flow of goods from the consumer back to the manufacturer.
- **Waste Reduction:** Minimizing waste is a core principle. This includes reducing both material waste and energy waste throughout the product life cycle.
- **Biological Nutrient Cycles:** The circular economy incorporates the concept of biological nutrient cycles, where organic materials are returned to the soil in a way that supports natural ecosystems.
- **Digital Technology and Innovation:** Embracing digital technologies can enhance the circular economy. For example, the use of the Internet of Things (IoT) can enable better tracking of products throughout their life cycle, facilitating efficient recycling and reusing processes.
- **Collaboration and Stakeholder Engagement:** Circular economy principles encourage collaboration among businesses, governments, communities, and consumers. Engaging all stakeholders is essential for the successful implementation of circular practices.

Adopting circular economy principles is seen as a sustainable solution to address environmental challenges, reduce resource depletion, and create a more resilient and efficient global economy. Many businesses and governments are increasingly recognizing the importance of transitioning to circular models to achieve long-term sustainability goals.

The concept of a sustainable circular economy is a response to the environmental pressures caused by resource extraction and waste generation (Velenturf, 2021). It is characterized by closed supply chains and reverse logistics processes, and is seen as a driver of the fourth industrial revolution (Sedikova, 2019). The circular economy aims to eliminate waste and ensure continual resource use through repair, refurbishment, recycling, and reuse (Bugaian, 2020). It is based on the natural cycle, where waste becomes a new source of resources, and emphasizes the need for resilience, creativity, innovation, and transparency (Gardetti, 2019).

Economic Benefits of Resource-Efficient Practices

Resource-efficient practices offer various economic benefits across different sectors, contributing to sustainable development and long-term prosperity. Here are key economic advantages associated with embracing resource efficiency:

- **Cost Savings:**
  - **Reduced Resource Consumption:** Resource-efficient practices often involve optimizing resource use, leading to lower consumption of raw materials, energy, and water.
  - **Operational Efficiency:** Streamlining production processes and reducing waste contribute to lower operational costs.
- **Increased Productivity and Innovation:**
  - **Efficiency Gains:** Adopting resource-efficient technologies and processes can enhance overall productivity and operational efficiency.
  - **Innovation Opportunities:** The pursuit of resource efficiency often drives innovation in product design, manufacturing processes, and business models.
- **Competitive Advantage:**
  - **Market Differentiation:** Companies that prioritize resource efficiency can differentiate themselves in the market by promoting sustainable and environmentally friendly practices.
  - **Consumer Preference:** Growing consumer awareness and preference for eco-friendly products can translate into increased market share.
- **Risk Mitigation:**
  - **Supply Chain Resilience:** Resource-efficient practices can enhance supply chain resilience by reducing dependence on scarce resources and mitigating the impact of resource price volatility.
  - **Regulatory Compliance:** Adhering to resource efficiency standards and regulations helps businesses avoid potential fines and legal risks.
- **Energy Cost Reduction:**
  - **Energy Efficiency Measures:** Implementing energy-efficient technologies and practices reduces energy consumption, leading to lower energy costs.

- **Renewable Energy Adoption:** Investing in renewable energy sources can provide long-term cost stability and reduce reliance on fluctuating fossil fuel prices.
- **Waste Reduction and Circular Economy:**
  - **Lower Waste Disposal Costs:** Minimizing waste generation reduces costs associated with waste disposal and landfill fees.
  - **Resource Recovery:** Embracing circular economy principles allows for the recovery and reuse of materials, contributing to cost savings.
- **Improved Resource Utilization:**
  - **Optimized Water Use:** Implementing water-efficient practices leads to lower water consumption and associated costs.
  - **Sustainable Agriculture:** Resource-efficient practices in agriculture, such as precision farming, contribute to increased yields and cost-effective production.
- **Long-Term Cost Resilience:**
  - **Future-Proofing:** Businesses that invest in resource efficiency are better positioned to adapt to future resource scarcity and price fluctuations.
  - **Resilience to Environmental Risks:** Reduced dependency on resource-intensive practices enhances resilience to environmental risks, such as climate change impacts.
- **Job Creation and Economic Growth:**
  - **Green Jobs:** The transition to resource-efficient practices often leads to the creation of new job opportunities in industries such as renewable energy, sustainable agriculture, and waste management.
  - **Economic Diversification:** Resource-efficient practices contribute to the growth of industries focused on sustainability and green technologies.
- **Brand Reputation and Market Access:**
  - **Positive Brand Image:** Companies committed to resource efficiency and sustainability build a positive brand image, enhancing customer loyalty and attracting environmentally conscious consumers.
  - **Market Access:** Meeting resource efficiency standards and certifications can open doors to new markets and partnerships.
- **Insurance Against Resource Price Volatility:**
  - **Stable Input Costs:** Resource-efficient practices help businesses manage and mitigate the impact of volatile resource prices, providing more stable input costs.
  - **Supply Chain Stability:** Diversifying and securing supply chains through resource-efficient practices reduce vulnerability to price shocks.
- **Government Incentives and Grants:**

○ **Financial Support:** Governments often provide incentives, grants, and tax breaks to businesses adopting resource-efficient technologies and practices.

○ **Cost-Sharing Programs:** Collaborative initiatives with government agencies can help share the costs of implementing resource-efficient measures.

Resource-efficient practices offer a range of economic benefits, from immediate cost savings to long-term resilience and growth opportunities. Embracing sustainability not only aligns with environmental goals but also positions businesses and economies for success in an increasingly resource-constrained world.

Research consistently shows that resource-efficient practices can lead to significant economic benefits. Bodas-Freitas (2019) found that SMEs that receive external support for resource efficiency adoption experience higher cost savings and profitability. Ekins (2016) further supports this, demonstrating that policies to improve resource efficiency can reduce global resource extraction, boost economic activity, and cut greenhouse gas emissions. The potential for economic growth, employment, and development through resource efficiency is also highlighted. Lastly, Ekins (2005) emphasizes the potential for businesses to increase profitability through eco-efficiency activities. These findings underscore the importance of resource-efficient practices in driving economic benefits.

INTELLIGENT POLICY FRAMEWORKS FOR SUSTAINABLE PROSPERITY

Smart Regulations for Innovation

Balancing Innovation With Regulatory Measures

Balancing innovation with regulatory measures is a complex but crucial task. While innovation drives economic growth, enhances competitiveness, and fosters technological advancements, regulations are necessary to ensure ethical practices, consumer protection, environmental sustainability, and public safety. Finding the right equilibrium between promoting innovation and safeguarding public interests requires a nuanced approach. Here are key considerations for striking this balance:

• **Proactive Regulatory Frameworks:**

Anticipate Emerging Technologies: Regulatory bodies should actively monitor and anticipate the development of emerging technologies to proactively establish frameworks that address potential risks and challenges. **Agile Regulation:** Regulations should be designed to be flexible and adaptable, capable of accommodating advancements without stifling innovation.

- **Risk Assessment and Mitigation:**

Conduct Comprehensive Risk Assessments: Evaluate the potential risks associated with new technologies to understand their implications on safety, security, and ethical considerations. **Implement Risk Mitigation Measures:** Establish regulatory measures to mitigate identified risks, ensuring that innovation occurs within acceptable bounds.

- **Collaboration and Engagement:**

Stakeholder Involvement: Involve stakeholders, including industry experts, innovators, consumers, and advocacy groups, in the regulatory process to gather diverse perspectives. **Public Consultations:** Conduct public consultations to ensure that regulatory decisions reflect the interests and concerns of the broader community.

- **Performance-Based Regulations:**

Focus on Outcomes: Develop regulations that emphasize desired outcomes and performance standards rather than prescribing specific technologies or methods. **Encourage Continuous Improvement:** Provide incentives for continuous improvement in technology and processes to meet evolving standards.

- **Regulatory Sandboxes:**

Create Controlled Environments: Establish regulatory sandboxes or pilot programs that allow innovators to test new technologies in a controlled environment. **Learn and Iterate:** Use insights gained from sandbox experiences to refine regulations, ensuring they are well-informed and practical.

- **Ethical and Privacy Considerations:**

Embed Ethical Standards: Integrate ethical considerations into regulatory frameworks to address issues related to privacy, data security, and potential societal impacts. **Regular Ethical Audits:** Conduct regular audits and assessments of the ethical implications of emerging technologies.

- **International Collaboration:**

Harmonize Standards: Collaborate with international counterparts to harmonize standards and regulations, facilitating a consistent and globally accepted approach to emerging technologies. **Cross-Border Regulatory Cooperation:** Develop mechanisms for cross-border regulatory cooperation to address global challenges associated with innovation.

- **Education and Awareness:**

Educate Stakeholders: Foster awareness and understanding among stakeholders, including businesses, policymakers, and the general public, about the benefits and risks of emerging technologies. **Promote Responsible Innovation:** Encourage responsible innovation by emphasizing the importance of ethical conduct and social responsibility.

- **Regulatory Agility:**

Adapt to Change: Regulatory bodies should be prepared to adapt quickly to technological advancements, revising regulations as needed to address new challenges and opportunities. **Periodic Reviews:** Conduct regular reviews of existing regulations to ensure they remain relevant and effective in a rapidly changing technological landscape.

- **Incentives for Compliance:**

Provide Incentives: Offer incentives for businesses and innovators to comply with regulations voluntarily, such as tax credits, grants, or market advantages. **Recognition for Responsible Practices:** Acknowledge and reward entities that demonstrate exemplary adherence to ethical and regulatory standards.

- **Regulatory Impact Assessments:**

Assess Unintended Consequences: Conduct regulatory impact assessments to evaluate potential unintended consequences and societal impacts of regulations. **Iterative Improvements:** Use the findings to make iterative improvements to regulations and address unforeseen challenges.

- **Public Trust Building:**

Transparent Communication: Maintain transparent communication with the public about regulatory decisions, ensuring clarity and building trust. **Explain the Purpose:** Clearly communicate the purpose and rationale behind regulations, emphasizing their role in ensuring safety, fairness, and ethical practices.

Balancing innovation with regulatory measures is a delicate dance that requires a collaborative, adaptive, and forward-thinking approach. By fostering a regulatory environment that encourages responsible innovation while safeguarding public interests, societies can harness the benefits of technological advancements while minimizing potential risks.

The balance between innovation and regulation is a complex issue, with financial innovations having the potential to both benefit and harm the system (Lumpkin, 2010). Regulation can have a negative impact on innovation, particularly for larger firms, leading to a reduction in the fraction of innovating firms and a decrease in the innovation response to demand shocks (Aghion, 2023). However, the response of companies to regulatory change, particularly in the financial sector, can mediate this relationship, with high flexibility and low complexity in firm response leading to improved innovation performance (Bentzen, 2021).

Creating an Environment Conducive to Sustainable Economic Growth

Creating an environment conducive to sustainable economic growth entails adopting a holistic approach that harmonizes economic development with environmental responsibility and social equity. This involves implementing policies that prioritize renewable energy sources, resource efficiency, and circular economy practices. Additionally, fostering innovation in sustainable technologies, encouraging social entrepreneurship, and promoting inclusive economic growth are crucial components. Robust regulatory frameworks, community engagement, and international collaboration play essential roles in ensuring that growth is resilient, environmentally conscious, and benefits all segments of society. By aligning economic strategies with sustainable development goals, societies can cultivate an environment where prosperity is not only measured in economic terms but also in terms of environmental stewardship and social well-being.

A range of studies emphasize the importance of creating an environment conducive to sustainable economic growth. Zuo (2011) underscores the need for a shift towards renewable energy sources and an optimal balance between environmental protection and energy use. Hirschhorn (2001) and Hilton (2022) both highlight the link between economic growth and quality of life, with the latter emphasizing the role of economic growth in addressing poverty and creating jobs. Smulders (1995) further emphasizes the role of environmental policy in boosting productivity and growth. These studies collectively underscore the need for a holistic approach that balances economic growth with environmental protection and quality of life.

Incentivizing Sustainable Practices

Analyzing Successful Incentive Programs

Analyzing successful incentive programs reveals their instrumental role in driving desired behaviors and achieving targeted outcomes. Effective incentive programs are characterized by well-defined objectives, clear communication, and tangible rewards that align with participants' motivations. Whether in business, healthcare, or environmental initiatives, these programs often incorporate a combination of financial rewards, recognition, and intrinsic motivators. Key to their success is flexibility, allowing for customization to the specific context and audience. Periodic evaluations, feedback mechanisms, and data-driven insights ensure continuous improvement, enabling organizations to fine-tune incentives for optimal impact. Ultimately, successful incentive programs not only stimulate positive actions but also foster a culture of engagement and achievement within the participating individuals or entities.

Policy Recommendations for Encouraging Sustainable Business Models

Implementing policy recommendations for encouraging sustainable business models is essential for fostering a green economy. Governments should incentivize sustainable practices through tax breaks, grants, and subsidies, providing financial support for businesses adopting eco-friendly approaches. Regulations mandating environmental reporting and adherence to sustainability standards can ensure transparency and accountability. Establishing partnerships between public and private sectors can facilitate the exchange of knowledge and resources, promoting sustainable innovation. Moreover, creating a regulatory environment that rewards circular economy practices, resource efficiency, and the reduction of carbon footprints can steer businesses towards more sustainable operations. Encouraging sustainable supply chain management and promoting consumer awareness through labeling and certifications are additional strategies to drive businesses towards environmentally responsible practices. By integrating these policies, governments can catalyze a transition to sustainable business models, contributing to both economic prosperity and environmental well-being.

CASE STUDIES IN INTELLIGENT PROSPERITY

Singapore's Smart Nation Initiative

Overview of Singapore's Approach to Intelligent Urban Development

Singapore has emerged as a global leader in intelligent urban development, leveraging technology to create a smart, efficient, and sustainable city-state. Central to this approach is the Smart Nation initiative, a comprehensive strategy that integrates data-driven solutions to enhance various aspects of urban living. From the widespread deployment of sensors for real-time monitoring to the implementation of smart infrastructure and urban mobility solutions, Singapore prioritizes innovation for the benefit of its residents. The city-state embraces digitalization in public services, transportation, and environmental management, contributing to increased efficiency, reduced energy consumption, and improved quality of life. With a focus on connectivity, Singapore's intelligent urban development is a testament to its commitment to harnessing technology to create a future-ready, resilient, and livable urban environment.

Economic Outcomes and Lessons Learned

Economic outcomes and lessons learned from various scenarios offer invaluable insights into the dynamics of markets and policy efficacy. Whether examining the impact of financial crises, global recessions, or unprecedented events, such as the COVID-19 pandemic, these experiences underscore the importance of adaptive policymaking and resilience. The flexibility to adjust monetary and fiscal policies, prioritize social safety nets, and foster innovation emerges as key lessons. Furthermore, the interconnectedness of global economies highlights the need for international cooperation and coordinated responses to economic challenges. Sustainable economic growth often requires a delicate balance between stimulating innovation, ensuring social inclusivity, and maintaining environmental responsibility. The lessons learned from economic outcomes serve as guideposts for shaping robust, inclusive, and adaptable economic frameworks in the face of dynamic global conditions.

Costa Rica's Pura Vida Economy

Examining Costa Rica's Commitment to Environmental Sustainability

Costa Rica stands out globally for its unwavering commitment to environmental sustainability. Renowned for its lush biodiversity, the country has implemented progressive policies that prioritize conservation, renewable energy, and sustainable development. Costa Rica has set ambitious goals, aiming to achieve carbon neutrality by 2050. The nation has heavily invested in renewable energy sources, such as hydropower, wind, and geothermal, which collectively contribute to a significant portion of its energy mix. Conservation efforts are evident in the extensive national park system, protecting diverse ecosystems. Moreover, community involvement and ecotourism initiatives align with Costa Rica's dedication to balancing economic development with environmental stewardship. This small Central American nation serves as a beacon for countries striving to harmonize economic growth with a profound commitment to preserving the planet's ecological integrity.

Economic Benefits of a Green and Sustainable Strategy

Embracing a green and sustainable strategy yields multifaceted economic benefits. Businesses that prioritize sustainability often experience cost savings through energy efficiency, waste reduction, and streamlined operations. Long-term resilience is cultivated as these entities mitigate risks associated with resource scarcity and environmental degradation. Furthermore, such strategies open new revenue streams, as eco-conscious consumers increasingly prefer sustainable products and services. Governments supporting green initiatives stimulate economic growth, foster innovation, and create job opportunities in burgeoning sectors such as renewable energy and environmental technologies. Overall, a commitment to sustainability not only safeguards the environment but also generates economic advantages, positioning businesses and nations for a more resilient and prosperous future.

CONCLUSION

In conclusion, the importance of intelligent approaches in economic innovation cannot be overstated. As we navigate complex global challenges, embracing intelligence in economic strategies becomes imperative. Intelligent approaches, informed by data-driven insights, technological advancements, and adaptive policies, hold the key to unlocking sustainable, inclusive, and resilient economic growth. Whether in the context of smart urban development, sustainable business models, or harnessing artificial intelligence for economic forecasting, these intelligent approaches offer solutions that address contemporary complexities. By prioritizing innovation guided by intelligence, societies can not only navigate the uncertainties of the future but also forge a path towards economic prosperity that is environmentally responsible, socially inclusive, and technologically advanced. The integration of intelligence in economic paradigms is not merely a choice but a necessity for building a robust foundation for the well-being of both present and future generations.

Emphasizing the role of sustainability in shaping future prosperity is not just an ethical imperative but a strategic necessity. As we confront the challenges of a rapidly changing world, sustainability emerges as the cornerstone for enduring economic success. A commitment to sustainable practices, whether in business models, urban development, or resource management, is an investment in resilience, innovation, and long-term viability. The profound interconnection between ecological health, social equity, and economic well-being cannot be overlooked. By prioritizing sustainability, societies pave the way for a future where economic prosperity is not achieved at the expense of the environment or marginalized communities. It is a call to action, urging businesses, governments, and individuals to be conscientious stewards of resources, embrace circular economy principles, and foster a collective responsibility toward a prosperous and sustainable future. In essence, sustainability is not just a choice; it is the blueprint for building a world where prosperity is enduring, inclusive, and harmoniously balanced with the planet we call home.

The imperative for intelligent and sustainable economic practices necessitates a call for continued research and collaborative efforts. As we navigate a complex landscape of challenges and opportunities, the fusion of intelligence and sustainability emerges as a potent force for positive change. Encouraging further research in artificial intelligence, green technologies, and innovative economic models is pivotal for uncovering new insights and refining existing paradigms. Collaboration between governments, businesses, academia, and communities is equally vital to drive the implementation of intelligent and sustainable practices on a global scale. By fostering a culture of continuous inquiry and shared knowledge, we can collectively shape a future where economic innovation is synonymous with environmental stewardship and societal well-being. The journey toward intelligent and sustainable economic practices is ongoing, and through sustained research and collaboration, we can forge a path to a more prosperous, equitable, and resilient world.

REFERENCES

Aghion, P., Bergeaud, A., & Van Reenen, J. (2023). The impact of regulation on innovation. *American Economic Review, 113*(11), 2894-2936.

Annor Antwi, A., & Al-Dherasi, A. A. M. (2019). Application of Artificial Intelligence in Forecasting: A Systematic Review. *Available at* SSRN *3483313.*

Babcock-Lumish, T. L., & Clark, G. L. (2005). Pricing the economic landscape: financial markets and the communities and institutions of risk management. *Prospects for Cities in the 21st Century.*

Baddeley, M. (2010). Herding, social influence and economic decision-making: socio-psychological and neuroscientific analyses. *Philosophical Transactions of the Royal Society B: Biological Sciences, 365*(1538), 281-290.

Tilbury, D. (2011). Higher education for sustainability: a global overview of commitment and progress. *Higher education in the world, 4*(1), 18-28.

Bartlett, D., & Trifilova, A. (2010). Green technology and eco-innovation: Seven case-studies from a Russian manufacturing context. *Journal of Manufacturing Technology Management, 21*(8), 910-929.

Bentzen, E., Freij, Å., & Varnes, C. J. (2021). The role of flexibility and complexity in response to regulatory change: a case study of innovation in a major Danish financial institution. *The International Journal of Entrepreneurship and Innovation, 22*(4), 229-239.

Blowers, A., & Glasbergen, P. (1995). 7 The search for sustainable development. In *Environmental Policy in an International Context* (Vol. 1, pp. 163-183). Butterworth-Heinemann.

Bodas-Freitas, I.-M., & Corrocher, N.Bodas-Freitas. (2019). Bodas-Freitas, I. M., & Corrocher, N. (2019). The use of external support and the benefits of the adoption of resource efficiency practices: An empirical analysis of european SMEs. *Energy Policy, 132*, 75–82. doi:10.1016/j.enpol.2019.05.019

Popović, A., & Radivojević, V. (2022). The circular economy: Principles, strategies and goals. *Economics of sustainable development, 6*(1), 45-56.

Buiter, W. H. (1987). *The current global economic situation, outlook and policy options, with special emphasis on fiscal policy issues* (No. 210). CEPR Discussion Papers.

Ceyhun, G. Ç. (2017). Global Economic Outlook. *Risk Management, Strategic Thinking and Leadership in the Financial Services Industry: A Proactive Approach to Strategic Thinking*, 3-10.

Crawford, E. O., & Kirby, M. M. (2008). Fostering students' global awareness: Technology applications in social studies teaching and learning. *Journal of Curriculum and Instruction, 2*(1), 56-73.

Ekins, P. (2005). Eco-efficiency: motives, drivers and economic implications. *Journal of Industrial Economy, 9*(4), 12-14.

Ekins, P., Hughes, N., Brigenzu, S., Arden Clark, C., Fischer-Kowalski, M., Graedel, T., ... & Westhowk, H. (2016). Resource efficiency: Potential and economic implications.

Evstigneeva, L., & Evstigneev, R. (2014). The Contours of a New Economic Space. *VOPROSY ECONOMIKI, 11.*

Gardetti, M. A. (2019). Introduction and the concept of circular economy. In *Circular economy in textiles and apparel* (pp. 1-11). Woodhead Publishing.

Hermalin, B. E., & Isen, A. M. (2000). The effect of affect on economic and strategic decision making. *Available at* SSRN *200295.*

Hilton, G. (2022). The role of economic growth in sustainable development. *Review of Public Administration and Management, 10*(2), 1-2.

Hirschhorn, J. S. (2001). Environment, quality of life, and urban growth in the new economy. *Environmental quality management, 10*(3), 1-8.

Inglesi-Lotz, R. (2016). Inglesi-Lotz, R. (2016). The impact of renewable energy consumption to economic growth: A panel data application. *Energy Economics, 53,* 58–63. doi:10.1016/j.eneco.2015.01.003

John, P. (2016). Behavioral approaches: How nudges lead to more intelligent policy design. *Contemporary approaches to public policy: Theories, controversies and perspectives*, 113-131.

Kholdarvovna. (2021) The role of information and communication technologies for environmental sustainability: evidence from a large panel data analysis. *Journal of environmental management, 293*, 112889.

Lastly, W. (2020). Van Wyk, R. J. (2020). Towards technological awareness and wisdom. *South African Journal of Industrial Engineering, 31*(4), 1–8.

Lee, K. H., & Kim, J. W. (2011). Integrating suppliers into green product innovation development: an empirical case study in the semiconductor industry. *Business Strategy and the Environment, 20*(8), 527-538.

Lumpkin, S. (2010). Regulatory issues related to financial innovation. *OECD Journal: Financial Market Trends,* (2), 1–31.

Maradin, D., Cerović, L., & Mjeda, T. (2017). Economic effects of renewable energy technologies. *Naše gospodarstvo/Our economy, 63*(2), 49-59.

Martin, W. S., Jones, W. T., McWilliams, E., & Nabors, M. V. (1991). Developing artificial intelligence applications: a small business development center case study. *Journal of Small Business Management, 29*(4), 28.

Mcnair, S., & Ray Crozier, W. (2017). Assessing psychological dispositions and states that can influence economic behaviour. *Economic psychology*, 69-87.

Datta, S., & Mullainathan, S. (2014). Behavioral design: a new approach to development policy. *Review of Income and Wealth, 60*(1), 7-35.

Nair, B. B., & Mohandas, V. P. (2015). Artificial intelligence applications in financial forecasting–a survey and some empirical results. *Intelligent Decision Technologies, 9*(2), 99-140.

Nazari, G., & Karim, H. (2012, May). Green IT adoption: The impact of IT on environment: A case study on Green IT adoption and underlying factors influencing it. In *2012 Proceedings of 17th Conference on Electrical Power Distribution* (pp. 1-7). IEEE.

Olejniczak, K., Śliwowski, P., & Roszczyńska-Kurasińska, M. (2019). Behaviour architects: a framework for employing behavioural insights in public policy practice. *Zarządzanie Publiczne/Public Governance,* (1 (47), 18-32.

Sofi, M. A., Reshi, I. A., & Sudha, T. (2023). HOW PSYCHOLOGICAL FACTORS INFLUENCE ECONOMIC DECISION-MAKING, AND THE IMPLICATIONS FOR POLICY. *Journal of Accounting Research, Utility Finance and Digital Assets, 1*(4), 370-375.

Redclift, M. (1993). Sustainable development: needs, values, rights. *Environmental values, 2*(1), 3-20.

Sathaye, J., Najam, A., Cocklin, C., Heller, T., Lecocq, F., Llanes-Regueiro, J., ... & Winkler, H. (2007). Sustainable development and mitigation. In *Climate change 2007: Mitigation of climate change* (pp. 691-743). Cambridge University Press.

Seçken, N. (2005). The Relations between Global Environmental Awareness and Technology. *Turkish Online Journal of Educational Technology-TOJET, 4*(1), 57–67.

Sedikova, I. (2019). Development of conceptual principles of the circular economy. *Економіка харчової промисловості*, (11, Вип. 2), 47-53.

Siddique, S. S. (2018). *The road to enterprise artificial intelligence: a case studies driven exploration* [Doctoral dissertation, Massachusetts Institute of Technology].

Smulders, S. (1995). Environmental policy and sustainable economic growth: an endogenous growth perspective. *De Economist, 143*(2), 163-195.

Trott, A., Srinivasa, S., van der Wal, D., Haneuse, S., & Zheng, S. (2021). Building a foundation for data-driven, interpretable, and robust policy design using the ai economist. *arXiv preprint arXiv:2108.02904.*

Velenturf, A. P., & Purnell, P. (2021). Principles for a sustainable circular economy. *Sustainable Production and Consumption, 27*, 1437-1457.

Wang, L., & Zhao, L. (2022). Digital Economy Meets Artificial Intelligence: Forecasting Economic Conditions Based on Big Data Analytics. *Mobile Information Systems.*

Yeolekar-Kadam, B., & Sudarsan, J. S. (2022). Feasibility Study on Integration of Green Technologies in Prospective Construction Projects: A Case of Vishakhapatnam. *International Journal of Management* [IJMTS]. *Technology and Social Sciences, 7*(1), 210–223.

Zhang, D., Pee, L. G., & Cui, L. (2021). Artificial intelligence in E-commerce fulfillment: A case study of resource orchestration at Alibaba's Smart Warehouse. *International Journal of Information Management, 57*, 102304.

Zhao, E., Chen, L., Cui, H., & Zhu, Z. (2022). Assessing the Economic Impact of Renewable Energy from a Technology Perspective. *Advances in Economics and Management Research, 1*(1), 35-35.

Zhao, Y. (2022). Decision support system for economic management of large enterprises based on artificial intelligence. *Wireless Communications and Mobile Computing*, 1–11.

Zuo, H., & Ai, D. (2011). Environment, energy and sustainable economic growth. *Procedia Engineering, 21*, 513-519.

Chapter 10

Introducing the Ultimate NOUN Dataset for Online Handwritten Alphabet Recognition

Khadidja ElKobra Belbachir
University of Science and Technology of Oran Mohamed-Boudiaf, Algeria

Redouane Tlemsani
University of Science and Technology of Oran Mohamed-Boudiaf, Algeria

ABSTRACT

For decades, researchers in the field of machine learning have been trying to raise the features of systems and develop methods and approaches, but they often suffer from a scarcity of data in various machine learning fields. For this and due to the urgent need in our research that we have developed in the field of online handwriting recognition, we had to create a special data set for the Arabic language characters written simultaneously on a graphical tablet. In this work, we created a data set called "Noon" in university neighbourhood laboratories and used its first version in research work that was published in international refereed journals. The construction details have gone through phases, which will be presented in the following sections in this chapter.

DOI: 10.4018/979-8-3693-1418-0.ch010

INTRODUCTION

Even if computers are invading the world of communication, writing and speech remain two privileged modes of communication. On a more or less distant horizon, many works and prospective seek to make the computer disappear from the user's environment. Nevertheless, this one without feeling the constraints will be connected to the information systems by natural interfaces: a hand gesture, a look, speech ... and of course handwriting. From the old utopian concept of the paperless office, we arrive at the paradigm of the office without a perceptible computer.

Today, it is still very often the human who makes the adaptation efforts. The mini-keyboards of mobile phones are an example of this. Their ergonomics are quite limited when we try, for example, to compose a small message. However, the trend is clear; important progress has been made to bring the digital world closer to that of handwriting. The appearance of personal assistants (PDAs), tablet PCs, smart phones, these latest generation phones that combine a multitude of features -personal diaries, notepads, video games, camera and camera... - confirm this situation.

Very significant progress has also been recorded in the comfort of use of digital pens. Today they have become very comparable to conventional pens: their weight and volume have been halved in three years. It is thus possible to write with an almost ordinary pen, on paper, and to process this information in real time, possibly anywhere on the planet. In parallel with all these material advances, it remains to better master the interpretation of these written traces which will proliferate on multiple devices. It is within the framework of these online handwriting input applications with limited capabilities that our work is part of.

Five thousand years after its invention, five hundred fifty years after its automation, writing is still at the heart of human communication. In an age of increasingly sophisticated and efficient interactions between human and machine using "buttons", microphones or cameras, it is natural to seek to understand handwriting automatically. Since the first attempts, address reading systems for automatic mail processing or for reading checks have undergone significant development and are now widely used. However, the comprehension of writing by a computer is still far from fully satisfactory. The reason is that the study of handwriting recognition is a very broad field in terms of both its applications and its techniques.(Sharma & Jayagopi, 2021)

Substantial texts corpora are available for language analysis and recognition. In the field of automatic online handwriting recognition, on the other hand, there are fewer annotated databases. Unlike the Arabic manuscript, the Latin manuscript has known several data sets have been developed such as UNIPEN which is an international project for the collection of online data and examples for online writing, in which a large number of universities and of companies. The project had a closed stage, in which around 40 donors wanted to carry out testing and learning trials. Several companies and universities provided online writing samples of UNIPEN. The first set of UNIPEN's online manuscript database is a "training package", containing enough data to extract test and training configurations. UNIPEN is a large database, widely used in the performance evaluation of various online Latin handwriting recognition systems. (Ratzlaff, 2003)The UNIPEN database is the reference base for the development and comparison of handwriting recognition systems. This database contains traces of more than 200 writers. The difficulty of this database is mainly due to the number of writers and therefore to the many allographs they employ. The R01 / V06 version is often used in the field.(Parizeau et al., 2001).

The IRONOFF database (IReste ON / OFF database) is a dual on-line and off-line database collected and distributed by LORIA. It contains many isolated characters, numbers and words in French and English in UNIPEN format. This database was created in such a way that an inline point can be projected to its corresponding position in the scanned image, and conversely every element of the offline plot can be temporally indexed. (Poisson, 2005) This base was acquired with a Wacom UltraPad tablet, the typical spatial resolution is on the order of 300 dots per inch while the data sampling rate is on the order of 100 dots per second. It was collected from around 700 different writers. The following table shows a sub-corpus of the database containing: isolated numbers, lowercase letters, uppercase letters.(Rabhi et al., 2021)

The ADAB (Arabic DAtaBase) database is developed to enhance the research and development of online Arabic handwritten text recognition systems. This database is developed in cooperation between the Institute of Communication Technologies (Institute for Communications Technology IfN) and the National School of Engineers of Sfax (ENIS), the research group (Research Group on Intelligent Machines REGIM), Sfax, Tunis. (El Abed et al., 2009) The database in version 1.0 contains 15,158 Arabic words written by 130 different writers, most of them selected from the National School of Engineers of Sfax (ENIS). The written text contains 937 names of Tunisian towns and villages. Special tools have been developed for data acquisition and verification. These tools provide the ability to record online written data and other information about writers. This database is broken down into 3 sub-corpora.(Dhieb et al., 2020)

When it comes to writing styles, the differences are also significant. Thus, most of the systems presented during the ICDAR 2007 competition (El Abed & Margner, 2008), trained on Tunisian data, show a drop-in performance of 10 to 15 points between the results obtained on a test set from Tunisia, and another. test set from United Arab Emirates. The proportion of vertical ligatures is higher among Middle Eastern writers, and the variability in writing styles is also greater. Chain adaptations and retraining seem necessary. It should also be noted that Farsi (Persian), used mainly in Iran and Afghanistan, shares many points in common with the Arabic script. This aspect is outside the scope of this chapter: we restrict ourselves here to the study of handwritten Arabic writing on data from Tunisian scriptwriters. Unless otherwise stated, the data used come from the IFN / ENIT database (Pechwitz et al., 2002), a database of names of Tunisian cities.

Here are some examples of computer applications using handwriting recognition systems:

1- take notes with an electronic pen directly on the screen of your PDA or tablet PC and be able to edit them with a word processing software.
2- write messages or emails using a pen on the screen of his Smartphone.
3- enter mathematical formulas on the screen of his tablet PC.
4- retro convert paper documents: for example, to scan a handwritten document with a scanner and transform it into an editable document with a word processing software.
5- indexing archival documents: these are often damaged documents that are not accessible to the public, digitizing them and recognizing certain parts of the document (for example the name on a civil status sheet) makes it easier to search.
6- automatically sort the mail by automatically analysing postal addresses on envelopes.
7- process forms completed by hand: for example, a survey, an order form or a check.

These different examples correspond to the analysis of more or less complex documents containing handwriting. Depending on the case, recognition consists of recognizing complete documents, words or only characters in part of the documents.

THE ARABIC LANGUAGE PRESENTATION

Arabic, one of the six official languages of the United Nations, is the mother tongue of more than 300 million people. One possible hypothesis states that the Arabic manuscript evolved from the Nabataean Aramaic manuscript. It has been used since the 4th century AD, but the oldest document, an Arabic, Syriac and Greek inscription, dated to 512 BD. The Aramaic language has fewer consonants than Arabic, so during the 7th new century Arabic letters were created by adding dots to existing letters to avoid ambiguities. Other diacritics indicating short vowels have been presented, but were only used to ensure the Qur'an were read aloud without errors.

Literal Arabic, modern unified Arabic or classical Arabic is the name given to a variant of the Arabic language, used as an official language in all Arab countries, and as a common language between Arab countries. It is also used in most writings and, orally, in official or formal situations (religious, political speeches, television news).

Literal Arabic is thus distinguished from dialectal Arabic, which is the vernacular language spoken on a daily basis and has been since the expansion of Islam. This variety of language covers several local dialects that can vary quite greatly from one country to another. In all Arab countries, a national dialect composed by several local dialects is spoken. None of these dialects is completely identical to classical or literary Arabic.

The Arab world consists of twenty-two countries stretching from Mauritania in the west to the Sultanate of Oman in the east. Its population is estimated at 355 million people. It is divided into Mashreq in the east, and Maghreb in the west (the border between Mashreq and Maghreb is the Nile). Understanding is possible, even easy, between speakers of the dialectal Arabic variants of Mashreq, as is it between speakers of the dialectal Arabic variants of North Africa, but it is more difficult between speakers of Mashreq and Maghreb.

In the reality of linguistic exchanges, there is no sealed separation between literal Arabic and dialectal Arabic, but rather a continuum where mixed forms dominate. Nevertheless, geographical and historical specificities influence the different versions of dialectal Arabic. For example, let's cite:

- the influence of Berber for the Maghreb dialects
- the influence of the ancient Egyptian for the Egyptian
- the influence of Phoenician for Syrian-Lebanese-Palestinian, Tunisian, Algerian and Maltese
- the influence of italics for Maltese
- french, Italian and Castilian loans for the Maghreb dialects and Lebanese
- Turkish loans for the Syrian-Lebanese-Palestinian.

When it comes to writing styles, the differences are also important. Thus, most of the systems presented during the ICDAR 2007 competition(Märgner & El Abed, 2012), trained on Tunisian data, show a drop in performance of 10 to 15 points between the results obtained on a test set from Tunisia, and another test set from the United Arab Emirates. The proportion of vertical ligatures is higher among Middle Eastern scriptwriters, and the variability of writing styles is also greater. Chain adaptations and retraining seem necessary. It should also be noted that Farsi (Persian), used mainly in Iran and Afghanistan, shares a large number of common points with the Arabic script. This aspect is outside the scope of this thesis: we restrict ourselves here to the study of Arabic handwriting on data from Tunisian scripters. Unless otherwise stated, the data used come from the IFN/ENIT database, a database of Tunisian city names.

The Arabic script is semi-cursive both in its printed and handwritten form. The characters of the same string (or pseudo-word) are ligated horizontally and sometimes vertically (in some fonts two, three and even four characters can be ligated vertically), thus obscuring any attempt to segmentation into characters. In addition, the shape of a character differs according to its position in the pseudo-word and even in some cases, according to the phonetic context. In addition, more than half of the Arabic characters include diacritical points (1,2 or 3) in their form. These points can be located above or below the character, but never at the top and bottom simultaneously. Several characters may have the same body but a different number and/or position of diacritical points. On the other hand, the Arabic character has a vowel cursive form requiring, for the majority of letters, matrices of significant dimensions. This leaves so far, the computerized forms of Arabic characters not yet standardized.

The Arabic word has no fixed length, it can comprise one or more pseudo-words each including an often-different number of characters. The study of the morphology of pseudo-words shows that the Arabic script presents variations in more or less complex horizontal bands depending on the calligraphy of the characters contained in the pseudo-word (Amara et al., 1998). The central band is generally the most loaded from the point of view of information density in pixels. It corresponds to the places of horizontal ligatures, centered characters (without extensions), loops... .

For more information on the morphological characteristics of Arabic, we refer the reader to the following references: (Miled, 1998).

Moreover, the various works elaborated in AOCR, show that the cursiveness of the Arabic script, the complexity of the morphology of the characters, the elongations of the horizontal ligatures as well as the vertical combinations of certain characters, constitute the major problems related to the treatment of this script. Indeed, these problems generate a strong inertia at different levels, in particular in:

- The choice of relevant primitives describing the variability of the morphology of the characters, knowing that certain topological characteristics are sensitive to degradation, in particular the diacritical points and the loops.
- The method of segmentation into characters or even pseudo-words (which can overlap especially in the case of the manuscript).

All these problems and many others are accentuated in the case of the manuscript where other factors intervene (intra- and inter-scripter variability, writing conditions, fusion of diacritical points, overlapping pseudo-words, unevenly proportioned graphics...).

Faced with these problems, the need for a robust modeling is imposed, the classical methods of statistical, structural, neural type, etc. being ineffective to take into account all the morphological variations of Arabic.

ONLINE HANDWRITING

This chapter is placed in the context of handwriting and more particularly in that of isolated characters, typed online on peripherals such as Tablet PCs.

The main difference between the two fields of online and offline handwriting, often treated separately, lies in the nature of the data to be processed (temporal or spatial) and the relevant information that can be extracted for recognition purposes.

The user writes naturally using a stylus on a slate or a screen or a digital pen. Recognition software interprets written characters or words to turn them into numeric characters. Three properties characterize online recognition: the notion of writing order (temporal chaining of lines), the dynamics of the line (speed, acceleration, lifting of the pen) and skeleton of the line (no line thickness).

The first commercial handwriting recognition software were integrated into electronic organizers equipped with a stylus allowing the entry of characters or even words and sentences today and sometimes equipped with a keyboard. Apart from this important market of small personal assistants, other applications have developed from graphic tablets and recently digital pens:

Unlike paper documents which are scanned in the form of images, documents entered online (and more specifically characters and gestures) are stored in the form of electronic ink. Online documents can be entered using several types of devices:

- the mouse of a desktop computer;
- a graphic tablet without visual feedback;
- a touch screen on which we draw with the finger or a passive pencil (ATM, PDA, smartphone...) ;
- a sensitive screen used with a specific pen (Tablet PC...) ;
- a pen recording its absolute position (like the Anoto pen using a camera on a specific paper);

These different peripherals mean that the recorded electronic ink can be of different nature and quality. The application areas are just as wide, from writing texts to entering diagrams, filling out forms or editing documents.

But the main difficulty encountered when recognizing handwriting is the variability of writing styles. Indeed, the shape of the handwritten characters varies enormously from one scripter to another and even for a given scripter depending on the context of the character (its position in the word, the neighbouring letters...). This variability is even a source of ambiguity between the characters since the same plot can have different meanings depending on the context or according to the scripter. These properties make handwriting recognition a field of application for pattern recognition very rich in difficulties and challenges.

248

In the medical environment, for entering and storing information at the bedside, for entering medical prescriptions.(Carbune et al., 2020)

In the world of education, to support teaching in its task of learning to write which can only monitor one child at a time during his gesture of writing production. Both in the school and in the medical environment, to quickly detect the various causes linked to mental and motor disorders (Parkinson's, sclerosis, etc.) and school failures (dyslexia).

And in the world of meetings, with the possibility of taking notes, annotations, conservation of all written and oral records of the various participants in the meeting.

The main lines of research around online recognition can be summarized as follows:(Singh et al., 2021)

- recognition of words, sentences, texts using contextual knowledge (document specific, linguistic, etc.);
- automatic adaptation to the writing of a writer from a generic recognition system;
- presentation of recognition results, ergonomics of the pen interface, editing of a document;
- educational tools to help with learning to write, the detection of writing-related disorders;
- writer authentication, signature recognition.

Here are some examples of computer applications using handwriting recognition systems:(Castro et al., 2018)

- take notes with an electronic pen directly on the screen of your PDA or tablet PC and be able to edit them with word processing software.
- write messages or emails using a pen on the screen of your smartphone.
- enter mathematical formulas on the screen of your tablet PC.
- reverse convert paper documents: for example, to digitize a handwritten document using a scanner and transform it into an editable document with word processing software.
- index archival documents: these are often damaged documents that are not easily accessible to the public, digitizing them and recognizing certain parts of the document (for example the name on a civil status form) makes it easier to search.
- automatically sort mail by automatically analysing postal addresses on envelopes.
- process forms filled in by hand: such as a survey, an order form or a check.

These different examples correspond to the analysis of complex documents containing handwriting. Depending on the case, recognition consists in recognizing complete documents, words or only characters in part of the documents.

The user writes naturally using a stylus on a slate or a screen or a digital pen. The recognition software interprets the characters or the written words to transform them into digital characters.

Three properties characterize online recognition: the notion of writing order (temporal sequence of strokes), the dynamics of the trace (speed, acceleration, lifting of the pen) and skeleton of the trace (no line thickness).

The first commercial handwriting recognition software was integrated into electronic organizers equipped with a stylus allowing the entry of characters or even words and sentences today and sometimes equipped with a keyboard. A part from this important market of small personal assistants, other applications have developed from graphic tablets and recently digital pens:

In the medical field, for the entry and storage of information near the sickbed, for the entry of medical prescriptions. (Roy et al., 2017)

In the world of education, to support teaching in its task of learning to write which can only monitor one child at a time during its writing production gesture. Both in the school and medical environment, to quickly detect the various causes related to mental and motor disorders (Parkinson's, sclerosis ...) and school failures (dyslexia).(Limpo & Graham, 2020)

And in the world of meetings, with the possibilities of note-taking, annotations, preservation of all written and oral traces of the various speakers of the meeting. (Liwicki et al., 2008)

The main lines of research around online recognition can be summarized as follows:

- the recognition of words, sentences, texts using contextual knowledge (document-specific, linguistic, etc.) ;
- automatic adaptation to the writing of a scripter from a geo-numeric recognition system;
- the presentation of the recognition results, the ergonomics of the pen interface, the editing of a document;
- educational tools to help learning to write, the detection of writing-related disorders ;
- the scripter's authentication, signature recognition.

Over a few last years, much work has been done based on online handwriting. On different manuscripts types (Latin, Chinese, Arabic and others), (Keysers et al., 2016) and using several recognition approaches. Among these works we may mention a work (Caillault, 2005) which is based on a hybrid online recognition system Neuro-Markovian dealing with the Latin manuscript. A spiking system applied to the recognition of arabic characters in Line was proposed by(Ltaief et al., 2016). Authors in (Saabni & El-Sana, 2009) treated recognition of the Arabic manuscript online by detailed hierarchical approach. The work of (Ahmed, 2017) was carried out to develop a

Two Stages Neuro-Fuzzy System for Isolated Arabic Handwritten Character Recognition. In the thesis (Mezghani et al., 2006), a Bayesian method of on-line recognition of Arab characters has been described where class probability densities are estimated by the principle of maximum entropy. Authors in (Biadsy et al., 2006) present a system based on Hidden Markov Models to provide solutions for most of the difficulties. A combination of context-dependent bidirectional long short-term memory classifiers for robust offline handwriting recognition has been used in (Chherawala et al., 2017).

The letters connectivity, characters forms and dependence on their positions and stroke segmentation delays are inherent characteristics of the Arabic manuscript.

For Indian scripts (Keysers et al., 2016), only Bangla has this additional difficulty of tackling mixed cursiveness of its handwriting. BLSTM neural networks are a special kind of RNN and have recently attracted special attention in solving sequence labeling problems.

The use of statistical approaches permitted a huge progress in the handwriting recognition domain. Among the approaches that have been put to contribute, the connection-based approaches (neural networks) that possess a strong discriminating power and a capacity to construct decisions borders in big dimension spaces. Another way, is the modeling based on the HMMs (Abdelaziz et al., 2016) which uses a parametric approach to model the observation sequences generated by stochastic processes (handwritten scripts, for example), that are more obvious when it is about word recognition. The HMMs (Choudhury et al., 2016) have the capability to model the observations distribution for every shape class to recognize. (Sarno & Sungkono, 2016).

HARDWARE TOOLS

The emergence of new input devices such as digital pens coupled to paper supports, makes it possible to produce documents online in a very efficient way. Real documents can be produced thanks to these devices, they can consist as well of note-taking, lectures, exam copies, article redactions, etc. This expands the fields of application of on-line handwriting often confined to small terminals (PDA, smartphone) where only character recognition was justified.

Establishing an interface where anyone can write words and have them identified online automatically gives a certain advantage and increased ease today. Indeed, the recent development of electronic diaries, the appearance of new types of devices such as electronic tablets and pens and the appearance of electronic ink software, increase the need for this type of system.

The development of mobile terminals such as Notebooks, mobile phones and computers, books and the electronic brochure, etc., creates a need for new types of interfaces. The manufacturers of these interfaces have proposed a certain number of pen interfaces based in the literature for these devices. All these interfaces allow the user to write text and/ or control the terminal, the pen is used as a device of choice and clicking to operate buttons, menus, and select characters in a programmable keyboard.

Our main motivation in this field is to study the Arabic manuscript via vis-à-vis online technology, in other words, the online writing signal acquired from an electronic tablet to be digitized especially since few online Arabic writing applications have emerged.

For carrying out the experiments, a desktop computer was used and for construction of data set, a WACOM BAMBOO tablet was used and illustrated in the following figure:

The tablet has a wireless and battery-less stylus, helps get the job done by activating its digital inking functions. The stylus is a pressure sensitive freehand tool. There are four basic things you can do with the stylus: point, click, double-click, and drag. Figure 2 shows the components of this stylus and the setting of parameters. (Belbachir & Tlemsani, 2019)

You must hold the stylus like a regular pencil. The stylus can be tilted to work.

The stylus buttons are positioned so they can be easily pressed with your thumb or forefinger. (See Figure 3). Before using the tablet, organize the workspace so that you can work comfortably. The tablet, stylus and keyboard should be positioned so that they are easily accessible. The monitor should also be positioned so that it can be viewed with minimal eye strain. For best use, the tablet should be oriented so that the screen cursor moves in the same direction as the writer's hand. (See Figure 4)

CONSTRUCTION

Scriptwriter Handwriting Sheet

The Arabic alphabet is made up of 28 letters with their isolated shapes. The writer is invited to enter the entire alphabet a number N of occurrences. It must comply with the sheet mentioned in the following figure:

Figure 1. Features of the WACOM tablet

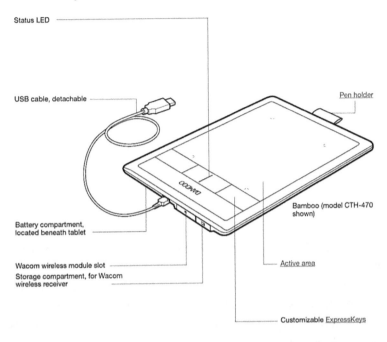

The interface for constructing samples of isolated Arabic characters is as follows:

The writer must enter his name, first name and the date of entry in the "Writer Information" tab mentioned on the left in the interface. In blue, the two buttons: "Write" and "points" are reserved for entering the character and the points of

Figure 2. Stylus components and parameter settings

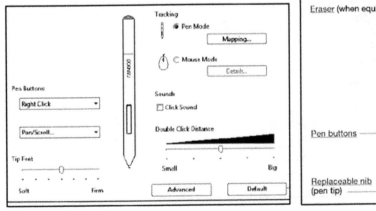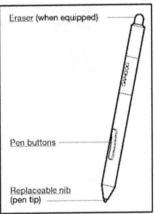

Figure 3. Stylus positioning

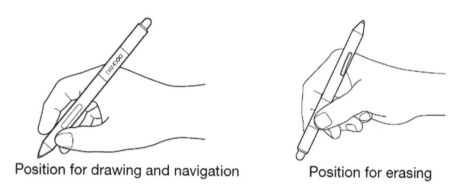

Position for drawing and navigation   Position for erasing

characters respectively. The writer must select which character to enter and which occurrence without the "character" tab.

The "controls" tab on the right is used to apply some useful controls for constructing samples. In green, the "save" button for saving, in yellow the "initialize" button for resetting all the information on the interface. In gray for viewing the saved character and in red to exit the interface.

Noun Data Set Samples

Our study concerns online handwriting, acquired dynamically using a graphics tablet to be digitized. This has a precise and sampled resolution at a chosen write

Figure 4. Work area on tablet

Figure 5. Alphabet entered by the writer

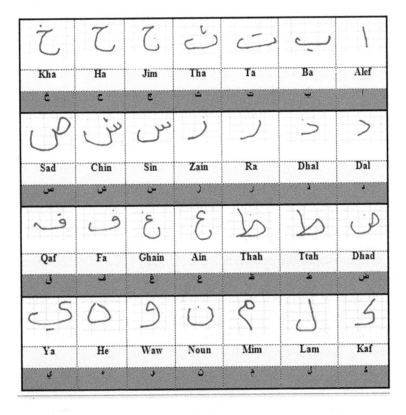

Figure 6. Acquisition interface

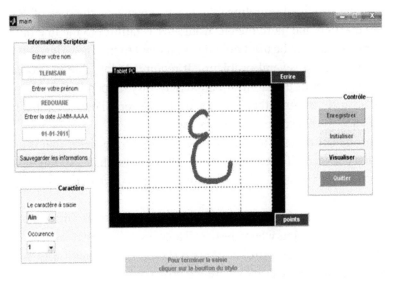

speed. An adaptation time is necessary for the writer to be able to write correctly. (Tlemsani & Belbachir, 2018) (Tlemsani et al., 2017)

The input of a classifier is a form that corresponds to an observation of the environment outside the system. This form is acquired by means of a sensor and presented as a signal (temporal or static). In our context, this raw signal is called electronic ink. It can be presented directly to the classifier or it can first undergo a set of modifications ranging from simple pre-processing to feature extraction. (Pawar et al., 2017)

Electronic ink describes a handwritten path acquired through a device recording various parameters over time. The content of this time signal therefore depends on the equipment used. In general, electronic ink is defined by a discrete parametric function p (t) giving the position of the pencil and various additional information. It is therefore a vector of at least two dimensions that can represent at time t:

- the coordinates of the pencil, noted x (t) and y (t), in an absolute coordinate system;
- the pressure of the pencil on the surface, zero (or negative) if the pencil does not touch the surface;
- the inclination of the pencil relative to the surface (specified by two angles);
- a drawing mode (some pencils have a button or an eraser);
- ...

Depending on the type of application, different information can be selected. On the other hand, new information can be calculated from this such as the instantaneous speed or the curvature of the track. The time between two points is generally constant and determines the signal sampling rate which depends on the type of device used. The higher this rate, the more the electronic ink is faithful to the line drawn by the user. This raw signal can be used directly as an input to the classifier. But this mode of operation can pose several problems. It requires being able to process signals in which the amount of useful information may vary (depending on the size of the shape, the acquisition time, the accuracy of the sensor). Therefore, this raw signal very often undergoes a series of pre-processing.

The objective of these is to obtain a description of the shape that is as stable as possible, that between different acquisitions of the same shape, the signals obtained must be as similar as possible. These treatments strongly depend on the application framework.

We use from the original signal only the points of the trace which have a strictly positive pressure, the points where the pencil touches the sensitive surface. For certain characters written in several strokes, there is therefore a discontinuity in the signal. Each line is separated by a point where the pressure is zero and is called a trace. A

Table 1. Size of the noun database

Base	Classes	Total	Training	Test
Digits	10	1 000	750	250
Alphabets	28	2 800	2 100	700

route is therefore made up of one or more traces. Then only the coordinates of the points are used to define the electronic ink, so we have:

$$p(t) = \begin{bmatrix} x(t) \\ y(t) \end{bmatrix} \tag{1}$$

But this signal is not used directly at the input of the classifier, in fact a certain number of characteristics are extracted from the electronic ink.(Kim, 2019)

In the context of on-line recognition, the ink sample is made up of a set of time-ordered coordinates. It is thus possible to follow the route, to know the posed and raised of the pen and possibly the inclination and the speed. Obviously, specific equipment is needed to enter such a sample, this is particularly the case with digital pens or styluses on electronic diaries or on Tablet PCs.

Online recognition is generally much more efficient than offline recognition because the samples are much more informative. On the other hand, it requires much more expensive equipment and imposes strong constraints on the writer since the ink capture must be done at the time of capture (synchronous capture) and not posteriori (asynchronous capture).

The NOUN data set in its first version is developed to initiate research and develop online Arabic manuscript recognition systems. It contains 2800 isolated characters, in Arabic. It was collected from around 25 different writers, each of whom wrote the letters of the Arabic alphabet five times. This database was developed between the SIMPA laboratory (Signal Image Parole) at the University of Sciences and Technology of Oran USTO-MB and the LaRATIC laboratory (Laboratory of Applied Research and ICTs) at the Institute National Telecommunications and Information and Communication Technologies INTTIC.

This dataset presents a data number itemized in the following table:

Spatial Sampling

During the construction of our database we used the WACOM tablet, the raw data of the writing signal contain significant variations according to the writing speed

Figure 7. Spatial sampling algorithm

Definition of the line a sequence of points between a "pen up" and a "pen down"
N: number of sampling points
Reserving memory space for the following vectors: X, Y, PenUpDown
\ Calculation of the total length of the signal If a single line
Length = Length + distance between points
If several traits
Length = Length + Length between lines
\\ Calculation of sampling distance Dist-echa = Length \ (N-I)
    Determination of N-I points by interpolation

Figure 8. Character "noun" before and after spatial sampling

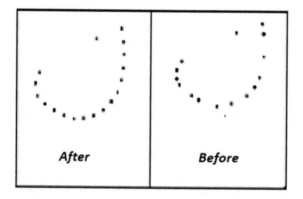

After   **Before**

resulting in a different number of dots forming the letter. Training a neural network with such data can lead to very low performance, which can reach an error rate of up to 70%. Spatial sampling significantly improves the performance rate.

The spatial sampling step is a very important step which makes it possible to eliminate the redundant information symbolized by the repetition of points while retaining the useful information of the signal. Indeed, the writing signal varies and that for the same writer, the time of formation of a character as well as its form can vary appreciably from one writer to another, and from one occurrence to another.

Spatial sampling consists in representing a sequence of points whose coordinates [X (n), Y (n)] (n being the number of the point), spaced by an identical distance according to the length of the line by fixing the number of points. By experimentation, we set the number of dots to 17 for each character.

Segmentation of Isolated Characters

Our study concerns online scripts, that is to say acquired dynamically using a graphic tablet to be digitized. This has a precise resolution and sampled at a chosen writing speed. An adaptation time is necessary for the scripter to be able to write almost correctly. Nevertheless, for its processing, the character will have to be segmented into plots, that is to say into elementary strokes.

The following figure shows the various changes implemented and applied, for example, on three chosen characters:

To further facilitate the use of computers, new approaches have been proposed and created. They no longer use the keyboard or the mouse but a stylus connected to an electronic tablet. Studying a problem of recognition of the Arabic manuscript is a particular challenge especially via online technology, knowing that few works marketed in this direction have emerged. The Arabic letters have specificities linked to this manuscript which is dated by several centuries and consequently its treatment was not an easy task. The research carried out has led us to discover many problems in the field of handwriting recognition, one of which we have tried to solve, one of several. That is, the construction of our own NOUN database.(Tlemsani & Benyettou, 2012)

Figure 9. Processing and segmentation of the characters "Ba", "Ain" and "Sad"

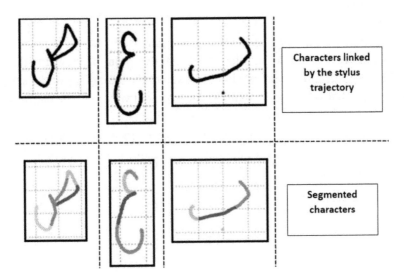

Characters linked
by the stylus
trajectory

Segmented
characters

CONCLUSION

The data science world lives at the rate of the emergence of personal assistants (PDA), tablet PCs and smart-phones, these devices have a multitude of functions. To further facilitate formerly complicated tasks, new approaches have been proposed and created. They no longer use the keyboard or mouse, but a stylus connected to an electronic tablet.(Long et al., 1997)

Studying an issue of Arabic manuscript recognition is a challenge, especially via online technology, knowing that few works marketed in this direction have emerged and that the treatment of the Arabic manuscript remains a problem not at all obvious.

Our research has led us to discover many problems in the field of handwriting recognition, one of several of which we have tried to solve. The construction of our own NOUN database. (Chin & Kim, 2002)

The world of telecommunications is living at the pace of the emergence of personal assistants (PDAs), tablet PCs and smart phones, these devices possessing a multitude of functionalities. To further facilitate previously complicated tasks, new approaches have been proposed and created. They no longer use the keyboard or the mouse but a stylus connected to an electronic tablet.

Studying a problem of recognition of the Arabic manuscript is a particular challenge especially via online technology, knowing that few commercialized works in this direction have emerged and that the treatment of the Arabic manuscript remains a problem not at all obvious.

The research carried out has led us to discover many problems in the field of handwriting recognition, one of which we have tried to solve among several. That is to say, the construction of our own NOUN database represents a necessary step for the processing of isolated characters which in order to be able to proceed to the recognition of words or phrases.

Finally, the purpose of handwriting recognition is to be able to use this representation in a computer application. From this point of view, the difficulties of handwriting recognition are obviously linked to the variability of the scripts, but also to the fact that we do not yet know how to model very well the enormous mass of knowledge and information useful for recognition.

As future work, the passage to the second stage in processing words and sentences is interesting especially with a guaranteed enrichment of our new online Arabic handwriting dataset.

REFERENCES

Abdelaziz, I., Abdou, S., & Al-Barhamtoshy, H. (2016). A large vocabulary system for Arabic online handwriting recognition. *Pattern Analysis & Applications*, *19*(4), 1129–1141. doi:10.1007/s10044-015-0526-7

Ahmed, O. B. A. (2017). *Two Stages Neuro-Fuzzy System for Isolated Arabic Handwritten Character Recognition* [PhD Thesis, Sudan University of Science and Technology].

Amara, N. B., Belaïd, A., & Ellouze, N. (1998). Modélisation pseudo bidimensionnelle pour la reconnaissance de chaînes de caractères arabes imprimés. *Conférence Internationale Francophone sur l'Écrit et les Documents*, 131-140. https://members.loria.fr/ABelaid/publis/Cifed98.pdf

Belbachir, K., & Tlemsani, R. (2019). Temporal neural system applied to arabic online characters recognition. *The International Arab Journal of Information Technology*, *16*(3A), 514–524.

BiadsyF.El-SanaJ.HabashN. Y. (2006). *Online Arabic Handwriting Recognition Using Hidden Markov Models*. doi:10.7916/D8NZ8H35

Caillault, E. (2005). *Architecture et Apprentissage d'un Système Hybride Neuro-Markovien pour la Reconnaissance de l'Écriture Manuscrite En-Ligne* [PhD Thesis, Université de Nantes]. https://theses.hal.science/tel-00084061

Carbune, V., Gonnet, P., Deselaers, T., Rowley, H. A., Daryin, A., Calvo, M., Wang, L.-L., Keysers, D., Feuz, S., & Gervais, P. (2020). Fast multi-language LSTM-based online handwriting recognition. [IJDAR]. *International Journal on Document Analysis and Recognition*, 1–14.

Castro, D., Bezerra, B. L., & Valenca, M. (2018). Boosting the deep multidimensional long-short-term memory network for handwritten recognition systems. *2018 16th international conference on frontiers in handwriting recognition (ICFHR)*, 127-132.

Chherawala, Y., Roy, P. P., & Cheriet, M. (2017). Combination of context-dependent bidirectional long short-term memory classifiers for robust offline handwriting recognition. *Pattern Recognition Letters*, *90*, 58–64. doi:10.1016/j.patrec.2017.03.012

Chin, W., & Kim, K.-D. (2002). On-line Handwriting Chinese Character Recognition for PDA Using a Unit Reconstruction Method. *Journal of the Institute of Electronics Engineers of Korea SP*, *39*(1), 97–107.

Choudhury, H., Mandal, S., & Prasanna, S. M. (2016). Optimization of HMM parameters for online handwriting synthesis. *2016 IEEE Region 10 Conference (TENCON)*, (pp. 277-281). IEEE. https://ieeexplore.ieee.org/abstract/document/7848006/

Dhieb, T., Njah, S., Boubaker, H., Ouarda, W., Ayed, M. B., & Alimi, A. M. (2020). Towards a novel biometric system for forensic document examination. *Computers & Security, 97*, 101973. doi:10.1016/j.cose.2020.101973

El Abed, H., & Margner, V. (2008). Arabic text recognition systems-state of the art and future trends. *2008 International Conference on Innovations in Information Technology*, (pp. 692-696). IEEE. 10.1109/INNOVATIONS.2008.4781781

El Abed, H., Märgner, V., Kherallah, M., & Alimi, A. M. (2009). Icdar 2009 online arabic handwriting recognition competition. *2009 10th International Conference on Document Analysis and Recognition*, 1388-1392.

Keysers, D., Deselaers, T., Rowley, H. A., Wang, L.-L., & Carbune, V. (2016). Multi-language online handwriting recognition. *IEEE Transactions on Pattern Analysis and Machine Intelligence, 39*(6), 1180–1194. doi:10.1109/TPAMI.2016.2572693 PMID:27244718

Kim, S. (2019). Electronic Ink Formulation for Drop-on-Demand (DoD) Inkjet Printing Fabrication Process. *2019 34th International Technical Conference on Circuits/Systems, Computers and Communications (ITC-CSCC)*, (pp. 1-2). IEEE.

Limpo, T., & Graham, S. (2020). THE ROLE OF HANDWRITING INSTRUCTION IN WRITERS' EDUCATION. *British Journal of Educational Studies, 68*(3), 311–329. doi:10.1080/00071005.2019.1692127

Liwicki, M., Schlapbach, A., & Bunke, H. (2008). Writer-dependent recognition of handwritten whiteboard notes in smart meeting room environments. *2008 The Eighth IAPR International Workshop on Document Analysis Systems*, 151-157. https://ieeexplore.ieee.org/abstract/document/4669956/

Long, A. C., Landay, J. A., & Rowe, L. A. (1997). *PDA and gesture use in practice : Insights for designers of pen-based user interfaces.* Computer Science Division, University of California. https://www.researchgate.net/profile/Lawrence-Rowe/publication/2506125_PDA_and_Gesture_Use_in_Practice_Insights_for_Designers_of_Pen-based_User_Interfaces/links/0912f511294c672dd1000000/PDA-and-Gesture-Use-in-Practice-Insights-for-Designers-of-Pen-based-User-Interfaces.pdf

Ltaief, M., Bezine, H., & Alimi, A. M. (2016). A spiking neural network model for complex handwriting movements generation. *International Journal of Computer Science and Information Security, 14*(7), 319.

Märgner, V., & El Abed, H. (2012). Arabic Handwriting Recognition Competitions. In V. Märgner & H. El Abed (Eds.), *Guide to OCR for Arabic Scripts* (pp. 395–422). Springer London., doi:10.1007/978-1-4471-4072-6_17

Mezghani, N., Mitiche, A., & Cheriet, M. (2006). *Estimation de densité de probabilité par maximum d'entropie et reconnaissance bayesienne de caractères Arabes en-ligne.* https://espace2.etsmtl.ca/id/eprint/5395/

Miled, H. (1998). *Stratégies de résolution en reconnaissance de l'écriture semi-cursive : Application aux mots manuscrits arabes* [PhD Thesis, Rouen]. https://www.theses.fr/1998ROUES050

Parizeau, M., Lemieux, A., & Gagné, C. (2001). Character recognition experiments using UNIPEN data. *Proceedings of Sixth International Conference on Document Analysis and Recognition*, (pp. 481-485). IEEE. 10.1109/ICDAR.2001.953836

Pawar, M., Kadam, S., & Late, D. J. (2017). High-Performance Sensing Behavior Using Electronic Ink of 2D SnSe2 Nanosheets. *ChemistrySelect, 2*(14), 4068–4075. doi:10.1002/slct.201700261

Pechwitz, M., Maddouri, S. S., Märgner, V., Ellouze, N., & Amiri, H. (2002). IFN/ENIT-database of handwritten Arabic words. *Proc. of CIFED, 2*, 127-136.

Poisson, E. (2005). *Architecture et apprentissage d'un systeme hybride neuro-markovien pour la reconnaissance de l'écriture manuscrite en-ligne.* [Thesis, Ecole polytechnique de l'université de Nantes].

Rabhi, B., Elbaati, A., Boubaker, H., Hamdi, Y., Hussain, A., & Alimi, A. (2021). *Temporal Order and Pen Velocity Recovery for Character Handwriting Based on Sequence-to-Sequence with Attention Mode.*

Ratzlaff, E. H. (2003). Methods, reports and survey for the comparison of diverse isolated character recognition results on the UNIPEN database. *Seventh International Conference on Document Analysis and Recognition, 2003. Proceedings.*, (pp. 623-628). IEEE. 10.1109/ICDAR.2003.1227737

Roy, P. P., Bhunia, A. K., Das, A., Dhar, P., & Pal, U. (2017). Keyword spotting in doctor's handwriting on medical prescriptions. *Expert Systems with Applications, 76*, 113–128. doi:10.1016/j.eswa.2017.01.027

Saabni, R., & El-Sana, J. (2009). Hierarchical on-line arabic handwriting recognition. *2009 10th International Conference on Document Analysis and Recognition*, (pp. 867-871). IEEE. https://ieeexplore.ieee.org/abstract/document/5277534/

Sarno, R., & Sungkono, K. R. (2016). Hidden markov model for process mining of parallel business processes. [IRECOS]. *International Review on Computers and Software, 11*(4), 290–300. doi:10.15866/irecos.v11i4.8700

Sharma, A., & Jayagopi, D. B. (2021). Towards efficient unconstrained handwriting recognition using Dilated Temporal Convolution Network. *Expert Systems with Applications, 164*, 114004. doi:10.1016/j.eswa.2020.114004

Singh, H., Sharma, R. K., & Singh, V. P. (2021). Online handwriting recognition systems for Indic and non-Indic scripts : A review. *Artificial Intelligence Review, 54*(2), 1525–1579. doi:10.1007/s10462-020-09886-7

Tlemsani, R., & Belbachir, K. (2018). An Improved Arabic On-Line Characters Recognition System. *2018 International Arab Conference on Information Technology (ACIT)*, (pp. 1-10). IEEE. 10.1109/ACIT.2018.8672673

Tlemsani, R., Benbakreti, S., & Benyettou, A. (2017). On-line Arabic characters recognition using enhanced time delay neural networks. [IRECAP]. *International Journal on Communications Antenna and Propagation, 7*(4), 254. doi:10.15866/irecap.v7i4.13204

Tlemsani, R., & Benyettou, A. (2012). Arabic on line characters recognition using improved dynamic Bayesian Networks. *2012 International Conference on Multimedia Computing and Systems*, (pp. 290-295). IEEE. https://ieeexplore.ieee.org/abstract/document/6320148/

Compilation of References

Abdelaziz, I., Abdou, S., & Al-Barhamtoshy, H. (2016). A large vocabulary system for Arabic online handwriting recognition. *Pattern Analysis & Applications*, *19*(4), 1129–1141. doi:10.1007/s10044-015-0526-7

Abdullahia, H., Reyes-Rubianob, L., Ouelhadja, D., Faulinb, J.,A. Juanc, A. (2020). Modelling and Multi-criteria Analysis of the Sustainability Dimensions for the Green Vehicle Routing Problem European. *Journal of Operational Research*.

Abdullahi, H., Reyes-Rubiano, L., Ouelhadj, D., Faulin, J., & Juan, A. A. (2021). Modelling and multi-criteria analysis of the sustainability dimensions for the green vehicle routing problem. *European Journal of Operational Research*, *292*(1), 143–154. doi:10.1016/j.ejor.2020.10.028

Aftab, S., Shah, A., Nisar, J., Ashiq, M. N., Akhter, M. S., & Shah, A. H. (2020). Marketability Prospects of Microbial Fuel Cells for Sustainable Energy Generation. *Energy & Fuels*, *34*(8), 9108–9136. doi:10.1021/acs.energyfuels.0c01766

Aghababaie, M., Farhadian, M., Jeihanipour, A., & Biria, D. (2015). Effective factors on the performance of microbial fuel cells in wastewater treatment–a review. *Environmental Technology Reviews*, *4*(1), 71–89. doi:10.1080/09593330.2015.1077896

Aghion, P., Bergeaud, A., & Van Reenen, J. (2023). The impact of regulation on innovation. *American Economic Review, 113*(11), 2894-2936.

Ahmed, O. B. A. (2017). *Two Stages Neuro-Fuzzy System for Isolated Arabic Handwritten Character Recognition* [PhD Thesis, Sudan University of Science and Technology].

Ahring, B. K. (2003). Perspectives for anaerobic digestion. *Advances in Biochemical Engineering/Biotechnology*, *81*, 1–30. doi:10.1007/3-540-45839-5_1 PMID:12747559

Akarsu, B., & Genç, M. S. (2022). Optimization of electricity and hydrogen production with hybrid renewable energy systems. *Fuel*, *324*, 124465. doi:10.1016/j.fuel.2022.124465

Akhtari, M. R., & Baneshi, M. (2019). Techno-economic assessment and optimization of a hybrid renewable co-supply of electricity, heat and hydrogen system to enhance performance by recovering excess electricity for a large energy consumer. *Energy Conversion and Management*, *188*, 131–141. doi:10.1016/j.enconman.2019.03.067

Akyuz, Y. (2020, June). Effects of Intelligent Tutoring Systems (ITS) on Personalized Learning (PL). *Creative Education*, *11*(6), 6. doi:10.4236/ce.2020.116069

Álvarez, A., & Ritchey, T. (2015). Applications of general morphological analysis. *Acta Morphologica Generalis*, *4*(1).

Amara, N. B., Belaïd, A., & Ellouze, N. (1998). Modélisation pseudo bidimensionnelle pour la reconnaissance de chaînes de caractères arabes imprimés. *Conférence Internationale Francophone sur l'Écrit et les Documents*, 131-140. https://members.loria.fr/ABelaid/publis/Cifed98.pdf

Angelidaki, I., Ellegaard, L., & Ahring, B. K. (2003). Applications of the anaerobic digestion process. *Advances in Biochemical Engineering/Biotechnology*, *82*, 1–33. doi:10.1007/3-540-45838-7_1 PMID:12747564

Anitha, C., Komala, C. R., Vivekanand, C. V., Lalitha, S. D., Boopathi, S., & Revathi, R. (2023, February). Artificial Intelligence driven security model for Internet of Medical Things (IoMT). *Proceedings of 2023 3rd International Conference on Innovative Practices in Technology and Management, ICIPTM 2023*. IEEE. 10.1109/ICIPTM57143.2023.10117713

Annor Antwi, A., & Al-Dherasi, A. A. M. (2019). Application of Artificial Intelligence in Forecasting: A Systematic Review. *Available at* SSRN *3483313*.

Araújo, M. B., Anderson, R. P., Barbosa, A. M., Beale, C. M., Dormann, C. F., & Early, R. (2019). Standards for distribution models in biodiversity assessments. *Science Advances*, *5*(1), eaat4858. doi:10.1126/sciadv.aat4858 PMID:30746437

Artebrant, A., Jönsson, E., & Nordhemmer, M. (2004). *Risks and Risk Management in the Supply Chain Flow: A Case Study Based on Some of Marsh's Clients*.

Asghari, M. S., Mohammad, J., & Al-e-hashem, M. (2020). Green vehicle routing problem: A state-of-the-art review. *International Journal of Production Economics*.

Atkinson, R., Barregård, L., Bellander, T., Burnett, R., Cassee, F., De Oliveira Fernandes, E., Forastiere, F., & Forsberg, B. (2013). *Review of evidence on health aspects of air pollution – REVIHAAP*. Project Technical Report.

Azad, A., & Shateri, H. (2023). Design and optimization of an entirely hybrid renewable energy system (WT/PV/BW/HS/TES/EVPL) to supply electrical and thermal loads with considering uncertainties in generation and consumption. *Applied Energy*, *336*, 120782. doi:10.1016/j.apenergy.2023.120782

Babcock-Lumish, T. L., & Clark, G. L. (2005). Pricing the economic landscape: financial markets and the communities and institutions of risk management. *Prospects for Cities in the 21st Century*.

Babu, B. S., Kamalakannan, J., Meenatchi, N., M, S. K. S., S, K., & Boopathi, S. (2023). Economic impacts and reliability evaluation of battery by adopting Electric Vehicle. *IEEE Explore*, 1–6. doi:10.1109/ICPECTS56089.2022.10046786

Baccarini, D., & Archer, R. (2001). The risk ranking of projects: A methodology. *International Journal of Project Management, 19*(3), 139–145. doi:10.1016/S0263-7863(99)00074-5

Bachmann, O. (2023). Large scale low-cost green hydrogen production using thermal energy storage and polymer electrolyte membrane electrolysis systems. *IET Renewable Power Generation, 17*(4), pp.775-793. (Bachmann, 2023)

Baddeley, M. (2010). Herding, social influence and economic decision-making: socio-psychological and neuroscientific analyses. *Philosophical Transactions of the Royal Society B: Biological Sciences, 365*(1538), 281-290.

Bartlett, D., & Trifilova, A. (2010). Green technology and eco-innovation: Seven case-studies from a Russian manufacturing context. *Journal of Manufacturing Technology Management, 21*(8), 910-929.

Batstone, D. J., Keller, J., Angelidaki, I., Kalyuzhnyi, S. V., Pavlostathis, S. G., Rozzi, A., Sanders, W. T., Siegrist, H., & Vavilin, V. A. (2002). The IWA Anaerobic Digestion Model No 1 (ADM1). *Water Science and Technology : A Journal of the International Association on Water Pollution Research, 45*(10), 65–73. doi:10.2166/wst.2002.0292

Behzadi, A., Alirahmi, S. M., Yu, H., & Sadrizadeh, S. (2023). An efficient renewable hybridization based on hydrogen storage for peak demand reduction: A rule-based energy control and optimization using machine learning techniques. *Journal of Energy Storage, 57*, 106168. doi:10.1016/j.est.2022.106168

Bektaş, T. & Laporte, G. (2011). The Pollution-Routing Problem. Transportation Research Part B: Methodological. *Supply chain disruption and risk management 45*, 1232–1250. doi:10.1016/j.trb.2011.02.004

Belbachir, K., & Tlemsani, R. (2019). Temporal neural system applied to arabic online characters recognition. *The International Arab Journal of Information Technology, 16*(3A), 514–524.

Bentzen, E., Freij, Å., & Varnes, C. J. (2021). The role of flexibility and complexity in response to regulatory change: a case study of innovation in a major Danish financial institution. *The International Journal of Entrepreneurship and Innovation, 22*(4), 229-239.

Berger, J., & Barkaoui, M. (2004). A parallel hybrid genetic algorithm for the vehicle routing problem with time windows. *Computers & Operations Research, 31*(12), 2037–2053. doi:10.1016/S0305-0548(03)00163-1

BiadsyF.El-SanaJ.HabashN. Y. (2006). *Online Arabic Handwriting Recognition Using Hidden Markov Models.* doi:10.7916/D8NZ8H35

Blanken, L. J. (2012). Reconciling strategic studies… with itself: A common framework for choosing among strategies. *Defense & Security Analysis, 28*(4), 275–287. doi:10.1080/14751798.2012.730723

Blowers, A., & Glasbergen, P. (1995). 7 The search for sustainable development. In *Environmental Policy in an International Context* (Vol. 1, pp. 163-183). Butterworth-Heinemann.

Bodas-Freitas, I.-M., & Corrocher, N.Bodas-Freitas. (2019). Bodas-Freitas, I. M., & Corrocher, N. (2019). The use of external support and the benefits of the adoption of resource efficiency practices: An empirical analysis of european SMEs. *Energy Policy*, *132*, 75–82. doi:10.1016/j.enpol.2019.05.019

Boopathi, S. (2021). Improving of Green Sand-Mould Quality using Taguchi Technique. *Journal of Engineering Research*. doi:10.36909/jer.14079

Boopathi, S. (2023b). Deep Learning Techniques Applied for Automatic Sentence Generation. In Promoting Diversity, Equity, and Inclusion in Language Learning Environments (pp. 255–273). IGI Global. doi:10.4018/978-1-6684-3632-5.ch016

Boopathi, S., Arigela, S. H., Raman, R., Indhumathi, C., Kavitha, V., & Bhatt, B. C. (2023). Prominent Rule Control-based Internet of Things: Poultry Farm Management System. *IEEE Explore*, (pp. 1–6). IEEE. doi:10.1109/ICPECTS56089.2022.10047039

Boopathi, S., Siva Kumar, P. K., & Meena, R. S. J., S. I., P., S. K., & Sudhakar, M. (2023). Sustainable Developments of Modern Soil-Less Agro-Cultivation Systems. In Human Agro-Energy Optimization for Business and Industry (pp. 69–87). IGI Global. doi:10.4018/978-1-6684-4118-3.ch004

Boopathi, S. (2019). Experimental investigation and parameter analysis of LPG refrigeration system using Taguchi method. *SN Applied Sciences*, *1*(8), 892. doi:10.1007/s42452-019-0925-2

Boopathi, S. (2022a). An experimental investigation of Quench Polish Quench (QPQ) coating on AISI 4150 steel. *Engineering Research Express*, *4*(4), 45009. doi:10.1088/2631-8695/ac9ddd

Boopathi, S. (2022b). Cryogenically treated and untreated stainless steel grade 317 in sustainable wire electrical discharge machining process: A comparative study. *Environmental Science and Pollution Research International*, *30*(44), 1–10. doi:10.1007/s11356-022-22843-x PMID:36057706

Boopathi, S. (2022c). Experimental investigation and multi-objective optimization of cryogenic Friction-stir-welding of AA2014 and AZ31B alloys using MOORA technique. *Materials Today. Communications*, *33*, 104937. doi:10.1016/j.mtcomm.2022.104937

Boopathi, S. (2022d). Performance Improvement of Eco-Friendly Near-Dry Wire-Cut Electrical Discharge Machining Process Using Coconut Oil-Mist Dielectric Fluid. *Journal of Advanced Manufacturing Systems*. doi:10.1142/S0219686723500178

Boopathi, S. (2023a). An Investigation on Friction Stir Processing of Aluminum Alloy-Boron Carbide Surface Composite. In *Materials Horizons: From Nature to Nanomaterials* (pp. 249–257). Springer. doi:10.1007/978-981-19-7146-4_14

Boopathi, S. (2023c). Internet of Things-Integrated Remote Patient Monitoring System: Healthcare Application. In *Dynamics of Swarm Intelligence Health Analysis for the Next Generation* (pp. 137–161). IGI Global. doi:10.4018/978-1-6684-6894-4.ch008

Boopathi, S., Balasubramani, V., & Sanjeev Kumar, R. (2023). Influences of various natural fibers on the mechanical and drilling characteristics of coir-fiber-based hybrid epoxy composites. *Engineering Research Express, 5*(1), 15002. doi:10.1088/2631-8695/acb132

Boopathi, S., & Myilsamy, S. (2021). Material removal rate and surface roughness study on Near-dry wire electrical discharge Machining process. *Materials Today: Proceedings, 45*(9), 8149–8156. doi:10.1016/j.matpr.2021.02.267

Boumaour, A., Grimes, S., Brigand, L., & Larid, M. (2018). Integration process and stakeholders' interactions analysis around a protection project: Case of the National park of Gouraya, Algeria (South-western Mediterranean). *Ocean and Coastal Management, 153*, 215–230. doi:10.1016/j.ocecoaman.2017.12.031

Bradfield, R., Wright, G., Burt, G., Cairns, G., & Van Der Heijden, K. (2005). The origins and evolution of scenario techniques in long range business planning. *Futures, 37*(8), 795–812. doi:10.1016/j.futures.2005.01.003

Brenner, W., Zarnekow, R., & Wittig, H. (1998). Fundamental Concepts of Intelligent Software Agents. Springer. doi:10.1007/978-3-642-80484-7

Breysse, D., Tepeli, E., Khartabil, F., Taillandier, F., Medhizadeh, R., & Morand, D. (2013). Project risk management in construction projects: Developing modelling tools to favor a multidisciplinary approach. *Safety, Reliability, Risk and Life-Cycle Performance of structures and Infrastructures*.

Bryan, J., Meek, A., Dana, S., Sakir, M. S. I., & Wang, H. (2023). Modeling and design optimization of carbon-free hybrid energy systems with thermal and hydrogen storage. *International Journal of Hydrogen Energy, 48*(99), 39097–39111. doi:10.1016/j.ijhydene.2023.03.135

Bryant, B. P., & Lempert, R. J. (2010). Thinking inside the box: A participatory, computer-assisted approach to scenario discovery. *Technological Forecasting and Social Change, 77*(1), 34–49. doi:10.1016/j.techfore.2009.08.002

Buiter, W. H. (1987). *The current global economic situation, outlook and policy options, with special emphasis on fiscal policy issues* (No. 210). CEPR Discussion Papers.

Caillault, E. (2005). *Architecture et Apprentissage d'un Système Hybride Neuro-Markovien pour la Reconnaissance de l'Écriture Manuscrite En-Ligne* [PhD Thesis, Université de Nantes]. https://theses.hal.science/tel-00084061

Carbune, V., Gonnet, P., Deselaers, T., Rowley, H. A., Daryin, A., Calvo, M., Wang, L.-L., Keysers, D., Feuz, S., & Gervais, P. (2020). Fast multi-language LSTM-based online handwriting recognition. [IJDAR]. *International Journal on Document Analysis and Recognition*, 1–14.

Carr, V., & Tah, J. H. M. (2001). A fuzzy approach to construction project risk assessment and analysis: Construction project risk management system. *Advances in Engineering Software, 32*(10-11), 847–857. doi:10.1016/S0965-9978(01)00036-9

Castro, D., Bezerra, B. L., & Valenca, M. (2018). Boosting the deep multidimensional long-short-term memory network for handwritten recognition systems. *2018 16th international conference on frontiers in handwriting recognition (ICFHR)*, 127-132.

Ceyhun, G. Ç. (2017). Global Economic Outlook. *Risk Management, Strategic Thinking and Leadership in the Financial Services Industry: A Proactive Approach to Strategic Thinking*, 3-10.

Chandra, K., & Kumar, S. (2000). Supply chain management in theory and practice: A passing fad or a fundamental change. *Industrial Management & Data Systems*, *100*(3), 100–113. doi:10.1108/02635570010286168

Chandrasekhar, K., Kumar, G., Venkata Mohan, S., Pandey, A., Jeon, B. H., Jang, M., & Kim, S. H. (2020). Microbial Electro-Remediation (MER) of hazardous waste in aid of sustainable energy generation and resource recovery. *Environmental Technology & Innovation*, *19*, 100997. doi:10.1016/j.eti.2020.100997

Chen, A., Ignatius, G., Sun, D., Zhan, S., Zhou, C., Marra, M., & Demirbag, M. (2019). Reverse logistics pricing strategy for a green supply chain: A view of customers' environmental awareness. *International Journal of Production Economics*, *217*, 197–210. doi:10.1016/j.ijpe.2018.08.031

Cheng, Z., Zhao, L., Wang, G., Li, H., & Hu, Q. (2021). Selection of consolidation center locations for China railway express to reduce greenhouse gas emission. *Journal of Cleaner Production*, *305*, 126872. doi:10.1016/j.jclepro.2021.126872

Chen, K., Ren, Z., Mu, S., Sun, T. Q., & Mu, R. (2020). Integrating the Delphi survey into scenario planning for China's renewable energy development strategy towards 2030. *Technological Forecasting and Social Change*, *158*, 120157. doi:10.1016/j.techfore.2020.120157

Chen, L. W., Hu, T. Y., & Wu, Y. W. (2020). *A bi-objective model for eco-efficient dial-a-ride problems*. Asia Pacific Management Review.

Chen, Y., Cheng, J. J., & Creamer, K. S. (2008). Inhibition of anaerobic digestion process: A review. *Bioresource Technology*, *99*(10), 4044–4064. doi:10.1016/j.biortech.2007.01.057 PMID:17399981

Cheung, K. (2014). *Petri Nets*.

Chherawala, Y., Roy, P. P., & Cheriet, M. (2017). Combination of context-dependent bidirectional long short-term memory classifiers for robust offline handwriting recognition. *Pattern Recognition Letters*, *90*, 58–64. doi:10.1016/j.patrec.2017.03.012

Chin, W., & Kim, K.-D. (2002). On-line Handwriting Chinese Character Recognition for PDA Using a Unit Reconstruction Method. *Journal of the Institute of Electronics Engineers of Korea SP*, *39*(1), 97–107.

Chiu, M. C., & Kremer, G. E. O. (2013). An investigation on centralized and decentralized supply chain scenarios at the product design stage to increase performance. *IEEE Transactions on Engineering Management*, *61*(1), 114–128. doi:10.1109/TEM.2013.2246569

Choudhury, H., Mandal, S., & Prasanna, S. M. (2016). Optimization of HMM parameters for online handwriting synthesis. *2016 IEEE Region 10 Conference (TENCON)*, (pp. 277-281). IEEE. https://ieeexplore.ieee.org/abstract/document/7848006/

Chowdhary, P. (2020). *Fundamentals of Artificial Intelligence*. Springer. doi:10.1007/978-81-322-3972-7

Chrifi, H., Echchatbi, A., & Cherkaoui, A. (2015). Modélisation de la chaîne logistique pharmaceutique marocaine: vers l'intégration du facteur risque. Xème Conférence Internationale, Tanger, Maroc.

Coello, C. C., Lamont, G. B., & van Veldhuizen, D. A. (2007). Evolutionary Algorithms for Solving Multi-Objective Problems. Springer, New York.

Conati, C., Barral, O., Putnam, V., & Rieger, L. (2021, September). Toward personalized XAI: A case study in intelligent tutoring systems. *Artificial Intelligence*, *298*, 103503. doi:10.1016/j.artint.2021.103503

Cordeau, J. F., & Laporte, G. (2007). The dial-a-ride problem: Models and algorithms. *Annals of Operations Research*, *153*(1), 2. doi:10.1007/s10479-007-0170-8

Crawford, E. O., & Kirby, M. M. (2008). Fostering students' global awareness: Technology applications in social studies teaching and learning. *Journal of Curriculum and Instruction*, *2*(1), 56-73.

Cui-hong, H. (2011). *Automated negotiation model of supply chain management based on multi-agent* (p. 180).

Datta, S., & Mullainathan, S. (2014). Behavioral design: a new approach to development policy. *Review of Income and Wealth*, *60*(1), 7-35.

Deb, K. (2001). *Multiobjective Optimization Using Evolutionary Algorithms*.

Deb, K., Pratap, A., Agarwal, S., & Meyarivan, T. (2002). A fast and elitist multiobjective genetic algorithm: NSGA-II. *IEEE Transactions on Evolutionary Computation*, *6*(2), 182–197. doi:10.1109/4235.996017

Dhaenens, C., Lemesre, J., & Talbi, E. G. (2010). K-PPM: A new exact method to solve multi-objective combinatorial optimization problems. *European Journal of Operational Research*, *200*(1), 45–53. doi:10.1016/j.ejor.2008.12.034

Dhieb, T., Njah, S., Boubaker, H., Ouarda, W., Ayed, M. B., & Alimi, A. M. (2020). Towards a novel biometric system for forensic document examination. *Computers & Security*, *97*, 101973. doi:10.1016/j.cose.2020.101973

Di Micco, S., Romano, F., Jannelli, E., Perna, A., & Minutillo, M. (2023). Techno-economic analysis of a multi-energy system for the co-production of green hydrogen, renewable electricity and heat. *International Journal of Hydrogen Energy*, *48*(81), 31457–31467. doi:10.1016/j.ijhydene.2023.04.269

Dillaerts, H. (2010, November). Analyse prospective du libre accès en France. In *Document numérique et société*. ADSB.

Divsalar, M., Ahmadi, M., & Nemati, Y. (2020). A SCOR-based model to evaluate LARG supplychain performance using a hybrid MADM method. *IEEE Transactions on Engineering Management*, *69*(4), 1101–1120. doi:10.1109/TEM.2020.2974030

Dominguez, H., & Lashkari, R. S. (2004). Model for integrating the supply chain of an appliance company: A value of information approach. *International Journal of Production Research*, *42*(11), 2113–2140. doi:10.1080/00207540410001666297

Dong, B., Christiansen, M., Fagerholt, K., & Chandra, S. (2020). Design of a sustainable maritime multi-modal distribution network – Case study from automotive logistics. *Transportation Research Part E, Logistics and Transportation Review*, *143*, 102086. doi:10.1016/j.tre.2020.102086

Duczynski, G. (2017). Morphological analysis as an aid to organisational design and transformation. *Futures*, *86*, 36–43. doi:10.1016/j.futures.2016.08.001

Econstor. (2022). https://www.econstor.eu/bitstream/10419/205222/1/van-der-Vorst-Jelicic.pdf

Eisapour, A. H., Jafarpur, K., & Farjah, E. (2021). Feasibility study of a smart hybrid renewable energy system to supply the electricity and heat demand of Eram Campus, Shiraz University; simulation, optimization, and sensitivity analysis. *Energy Conversion and Management*, *248*, 114779. doi:10.1016/j.enconman.2021.114779

Ekins, P. (2005). Eco-efficiency: motives, drivers and economic implications. *Journal of Industrial Economy*, *9*(4), 12-14.

Ekins, P., Hughes, N., Brigenzu, S., Arden Clark, C., Fischer-Kowalski, M., Graedel, T., ... & Westhowk, H. (2016). Resource efficiency: Potential and economic implications.

El Abed, H., Märgner, V., Kherallah, M., & Alimi, A. M. (2009). Icdar 2009 online arabic handwriting recognition competition. *2009 10th International Conference on Document Analysis and Recognition*, 1388-1392.

El Abed, H., & Margner, V. (2008). Arabic text recognition systems-state of the art and future trends. *2008 International Conference on Innovations in Information Technology*, (pp. 692-696). IEEE. 10.1109/INNOVATIONS.2008.4781781

Elhedhli, S., & Merrick, R. (2012). Green supply chain network design to reduce carbon emissions. *Transportation Research Part D, Transport and Environment*, *17*(5), 370–379. doi:10.1016/j.trd.2012.02.002

Elmsalmi, M., & Hachicha, W. (2014, May). Risk mitigation strategies according to the supply actors' objectives through MACTOR method. In *2014 International Conference on Advanced Logistics and Transport (ICALT)* (pp. 362-367). IEEE. 10.1109/ICAdLT.2014.6866339

Elmsalmi, M., Hachicha, W., & Aljuaid, A. M. (2021). Modeling sustainable risks mitigation strategies using a morphological analysis-based approach: A real case study. *Sustainability (Basel), 13*(21), 12210. doi:10.3390/su132112210

Enmon, S. (2015). Sustainable transport practices. United States of America.

Erdoğan, S., & Miller-Hooks, E. (2012). A Green Vehicle Routing Problem. *Transportation Research Part E: Logistics and Transportation Review, Select Papers from the 19th International Symposium on Transportation and Traffic Theory, (48,* 100–114). 10.1016/j.tre.2011.08.001

European Commission (2002). *Practical guide to territorial foresight in France*. EC.

European Environment Agency. (2014). *Annual European union greenhouse gasinventory 1990–2012 and inventory report 2014*. (Technical report No 09/2014).

Evstigneeva, L., & Evstigneev, R. (2014). The Contours of a New Economic Space. *VOPROSY ECONOMIKI, 11.*

Fan, G., Liu, Z., Liu, X., Shi, Y., Wu, D., Guo, J., Zhang, S., Yang, X., & Zhang, Y. (2022). Two-layer collaborative optimization for a renewable energy system combining electricity storage, hydrogen storage, and heat storage. *Energy, 259,* 125047. doi:10.1016/j.energy.2022.125047

Fátima Teles, M., & de Sousa, J. F. (2017). A general morphological analysis to support strategic management decisions in public transport companies. *Transportation Research Procedia, 22,* 509–518. doi:10.1016/j.trpro.2017.03.069

Fayaz Ahmad, S., Rahmat, M., Mubarik, M., Alam, M., & Hyder, S. (2021, November). Artificial Intelligence and Its Role in Education. *Sustainability (Basel), 13*(22), 12902. doi:10.3390/su132212902

Fetoui, M. (2021), Prospects for stakeholder cooperation in effective implementation of enhanced rangeland restoration techniques in southern Tunisia, Rangeland. *Ecology & Management.* https://creativecommons.org/licenses/by-nc-nd/4.0

Figliozzi, M. (2010). Vehicle Routing Problem for Emissions Minimization. *Transportation Research Record: Journal of the Transportation Research Board, 2197*(1), 1–7. doi:10.3141/2197-01

Galati, F., Bigliardi, B., Petroni, A., Pinna, C., Rossi, M., & Terz, S. (2019). Sustainable Product Lifecycle: The Role of ICT. *Sustainability (Basel), 11*(24), 7003. doi:10.3390/su11247003

García Nájera, A., & Bullinaria, J. (2011). An improved multi-objective evolutionary algorithm for the vehicle routing problem with time windows. *Computers & Operations Research, 38*(1), 287–300. doi:10.1016/j.cor.2010.05.004

García-Nájera, A., Bullinaria, J. A., & Gutiérrez-Andrade, M. A. (2015). An evolutionary approach for multi-objective vehicle routing problems with backhauls. *Computers & Industrial Engineering, 81,* 90–108. doi:10.1016/j.cie.2014.12.029

Gardetti, M. A. (2019). Introduction and the concept of circular economy. In *Circular economy in textiles and apparel* (pp. 1-11). Woodhead Publishing.

Gharaei, A., Karimi, M., & Hoseini Shekarabi, S. A. (2019). An integrated multi-product, multi-buyer supply chain under penalty, green, and quality control polices and a vendor managed inventory with consignment stock agreement: The outer approximation with equality relaxation and augmented penalty algorithm. *Applied Mathematical Modelling, 69*, 223–254. doi:10.1016/j.apm.2018.11.035

Godet, M. (1990). Integration of scenarios and strategic management. Butterworth-Heinemann Ltd.

Godet, M. (2006). Creating Futures: Scenario Planning as a strategic management tool (pp. 280). Washington, DC: Economica. Economica Brookings diffusion.

Godet, M. (2007). Manuel de la prospective stratégique: Tome 2. L'Art et la méthode, (pp. 122-159).

Godet, M., & Roubelat, F. (1996). Creating the future: The use and misuse of scenarios. *Long Range Planning, 29*(2), 164–171. doi:10.1016/0024-6301(96)00004-0

Goosen, M., Mahmoudi, H., & Ghaffour, N. (2010). Water Desalination using geothermal energy. *Energies, 3*(8), 1423–1442. doi:10.3390/en3081423

Govindan, K., Kadzi´nski, M., Ehling, R., & Miebs, G. (2019). Selection of a sustainable third-party reverse logistics provider based on the robustness analysis of an outranking graph kernel conducted with ELECTRE I and SMAA. *Omega, 85*, 1–15. doi:10.1016/j.omega.2018.05.007

Gowri, N. V., Dwivedi, J. N., Krishnaveni, K., Boopathi, S., Palaniappan, M., & Medikondu, N. R. (2023). Experimental investigation and multi-objective optimization of eco-friendly near-dry electrical discharge machining of shape memory alloy using Cu/SiC/Gr composite electrode. *Environmental Science and Pollution Research International, 0123456789*(49), 1–19. doi:10.1007/s11356-023-26983-6 PMID:37126160

Green, K. W. Jr, Zelbst, P. J., Meacham, J., & Bhadauria, V. S. (2012). Green supply chain management practices: Impact on performance. *Supply Chain Management, 17*(3), 290–305. doi:10.1108/13598541211227126

Grimaldi, S., Rafele, C., & Cagliano, A. C. (2012). A framework to select techniques supporting project risk management. *Risk Management, 3*, 67–96.

Groves, D. G., & Lempert, R. J. (2007). A new analytic method for finding policy-relevant scenarios. *Global Environmental Change, 17*(1), 73–85. doi:10.1016/j.gloenvcha.2006.11.006

Guan, C., Mou, J., & Jiang, Z. (2020, December). Artificial intelligence innovation in education: A twenty-year data-driven historical analysis. *International Journal of Innovation Studies, 4*(4), 134–147. doi:10.1016/j.ijis.2020.09.001

Gude, V. G. (2018). Geothermal Source for Water Desalination-Challenges and Opportunities. *Renewable Energy Powered Desalination Handbook: Application and Thermodynamics, 141*–176. doi:10.1016/B978-0-12-815244-7.00004-0

Gude, V. G. (2016). Geothermal source potential for water desalination - Current status and future perspective. *Renewable & Sustainable Energy Reviews, 57*, 1038–1065. doi:10.1016/j.rser.2015.12.186

Guilherme, A. (2019, March). AI and education: The importance of teacher and student relations. *AI & Society, 34*(1), 47–54. doi:10.1007/s00146-017-0693-8

Gujer, W., & Zehnder, A. J. B. (1983). Conversion processes in anaerobic digestion. *Water Science and Technology, 15*(8–9), 127–167. doi:10.2166/wst.1983.0164

Guo, Z., Sun, Y., Pan, S. Y., & Chiang, P. C. (2019). Integration of green energy and advanced energy-efficient technologies for municipal wastewater treatment plants. *International Journal of Environmental Research and Public Health, 16*(7), 1282. doi:10.3390/ijerph16071282 PMID:30974807

Hachicha, W., & Elmsalmi, M. (2014). An integrated approach based-structural modeling for risk prioritization in supply network management. *Journal of Risk Research, 17*(10), 1301–1324. doi:10.1080/13669877.2013.841734

Haddadene, S. R. A., Labadie, N., & Prodhon, C. (2016). NSGAII enhanced with a local search for the vehicle routing problem with time windows and synchronization constraints. *IFAC-PapersOnLine, 8th IFAC Conference on Manufacturing Modelling, Management and Control MIM, 49*, 1198–1203. 10.1016/j.ifacol.2016.07.671

Hai, T., El-Shafay, A. S., Alizadeh, A. A., Dhahad, H. A., Chauhan, B. S., Almojil, S. F., Almohana, A. I., & Alali, A. F. (2023). Comparison analysis of hydrogen addition into both anode and afterburner of fuel cell incorporated with hybrid renewable energy driven SOFC: An application of techno-environmental horizon and multi-objective optimization. *International Journal of Hydrogen Energy.*

Hald, K. S., & Mouritsen, J. (2018). The evolution of performance measurement systems in a supply chain: A longitudinal case study on the role of interorganisational factors. *International Journal of Production Economics, 205*, 256–271. doi:10.1016/j.ijpe.2018.09.021

Hamidi, N., & Bouzembrak, A. (2020). *La chaine logistique et la gestion des stocks d'une entreprise Cas: ENIEM* [Doctoral dissertation, Université Mouloud Mammeri].

Han, F., Zeng, J., Lin, J., & Gao, C. (2023). Multi-stage distributionally robust optimization for hybrid energy storage in regional integrated energy system considering robustness and nonanticipativity. *Energy, 277*, 127729. doi:10.1016/j.energy.2023.127729

Haribalaji, V., Boopathi, S., & Asif, M. M. (2021). Optimization of friction stir welding process to join dissimilar AA2014 and AA7075 aluminum alloys. *Materials Today: Proceedings, 50*, 2227–2234. doi:10.1016/j.matpr.2021.09.499

Harikaran, M., Boopathi, S., Gokulakannan, S., & Poonguzhali, M. (2023). Study on the Source of E-Waste Management and Disposal Methods. In *Sustainable Approaches and Strategies for E-Waste Management and Utilization* (pp. 39–60). IGI Global. doi:10.4018/978-1-6684-7573-7.ch003

HassanzadehFard, H., Tooryan, F., & Dargahi, V. (2023). Standalone hybrid system energy management optimization for remote village considering methane production from livestock manure. *International Journal of Hydrogen Energy*, *48*(29), 10778–10796. doi:10.1016/j.ijhydene.2022.12.085

Hatem F. (1993). *Foresight: Practices and methods*. Paris, Economica.

He, J., Wu, Y., Wu, M., Xu, M., & Liu, F. (2022a). Two-stage configuration optimization of a novel standalone renewable integrated energy system coupled with hydrogen refueling. *Energy Conversion and Management*, *251*, 114953. doi:10.1016/j.enconman.2021.114953

He, J., Wu, Y., Yong, X., Tan, Q., & Liu, F. (2022b). Bi-level optimization of a near-zero-emission integrated energy system considering electricity-hydrogen-gas nexus: A two-stage framework aiming at economic and environmental benefits. *Energy Conversion and Management*, *274*, 116434. doi:10.1016/j.enconman.2022.116434

Hermalin, B. E., & Isen, A. M. (2000). The effect of affect on economic and strategic decision making. *Available at* SSRN *200295*.

Hickman, J., Hassel, D., Joumard, R., Samaras, Z., & Sorenson, S. (1999). MEET methodology for calculating transport emissions and energy consumption. [Technical Report, European Commission/DG VII Rue de la Loi 200]. Belgium.

Hilton, G. (2022). The role of economic growth in sustainable development. *Review of Public Administration and Management, 10*(2), 1-2.

Hirschhorn, J. S. (2001). Environment, quality of life, and urban growth in the new economy. *Environmental quality management, 10*(3), 1-8.

Huangfu, Y., Tian, C., Zhuo, S., Xu, L., Li, P., Quan, S., Zhang, Y., & Ma, R. (2023). An optimal energy management strategy with subsection bi-objective optimization dynamic programming for photovoltaic/battery/hydrogen hybrid energy system. *International Journal of Hydrogen Energy*, *48*(8), 3154–3170. doi:10.1016/j.ijhydene.2022.10.133

Huss, W. R., & Honton, E. J. (1987). Scenario planning—What style should you use? *Long Range Planning*, *20*(4), 21–29. doi:10.1016/0024-6301(87)90152-X

Inglesi-Lotz, R. (2016). Inglesi-Lotz, R. (2016). The impact of renewable energy consumption to economic growth: A panel data application. *Energy Economics*, *53*, 58–63. doi:10.1016/j.eneco.2015.01.003

Ishizaka, A., Khan, S. A., Kheybari, S., & Zaman, S. I. (2023). Supplier selection in closed loop pharma supply chain: A novel BWM–GAIA framework. *Annals of Operations Research*, *324*(1-2), 13–36. doi:10.1007/s10479-022-04710-7

Jabali, O., Woensel, T. V., & de Kok, A. G. (2012). Analysis of Travel Times and CO2 Emissions in Time-Dependent Vehicle Routing. *Production and Operations Management, 21*(6), 1060–1074. doi:10.1111/j.1937-5956.2012.01338.x

Jabeur, N., Al-Belushi, T., Mbarki, M., & Gharrad, H. (2017). Toward Leveraging Smart Logistics Collaboration with a Multi-Agent System Based Solution. *Procedia Computer Science, 109,* 672–679. doi:10.1016/j.procs.2017.05.374

Jaimez-González, C., & Luna-Ramírez, W.-A. (2012). *Towards a Multi-Agent System Architecture for Supply Chain Management., 58,* 207–219.

Janardhana, K., Anushkannan, N. K., Dinakaran, K. P., Puse, R. K., & Boopathi, S. (2023). Experimental Investigation on Microhardness, Surface Roughness, and White Layer Thickness of Dry EDM. *Engineering Research Express, 5*(2), 025022. doi:10.1088/2631-8695/acce8f

Jantsch, E. (1967). *Technological forecasting in perspective* (Vol. 3). OECD.

Jeevanantham, Y. A., A, S., V, V., J, S. I., Boopathi, S., & Kumar, D. P. (2023). Implementation of Internet-of Things (IoT) in Soil Irrigation System. *IEEE Explore*, (pp. 1–5). IEEE. doi:10.1109/ICPECTS56089.2022.10047185

Jha, K. N., & Devaya, M. N. (2008). Modelling the risks faced by Indian construction companies assessing international projects. *Construction Management and Economics, 26*(4), 337–348. doi:10.1080/01446190801953281

Jia, K., Liu, C., Li, S., & Jiang, D. (2023). Modeling and optimization of a hybrid renewable energy system integrated with gas turbine and energy storage. *Energy Conversion and Management, 279,* 116763. doi:10.1016/j.enconman.2023.116763

Jimenez, H., Stults, I., & Mavris, D. (2009). A morphological approach for proactive risk management in civil aviation security. In *47th AIAA Aerospace Sciences Meeting Including the New Horizons Forum and Aerospace Exposition* (p. 1636). ACM. 10.2514/6.2009-1636

Johansen, I. (2018). Scenario modelling with morphological analysis. *Technological Forecasting and Social Change, 126,* 116–125. doi:10.1016/j.techfore.2017.05.016

John, P. (2016). Behavioral approaches: How nudges lead to more intelligent policy design. *Contemporary approaches to public policy: Theories, controversies and perspectives,* 113-131.

Jouvenel, H. (1999). La démarche prospective. Un bref guide méthodologique. *FUTURIBLES-PARIS-,* 47-68.

Jozefowiez, N., Semet, F., & Talbi, E.-G. (2009). An evolutionary algorithm for the vehicle routing problem with route balancing. *European Journal of Operational Research, 195*(3), 761–769. doi:10.1016/j.ejor.2007.06.065

Jurado, F., Mezrhab, A., Moussaoui, M. A., & Vera, D. (2023). Cost and size optimization of hybrid solar and hydrogen subsystem using HomerPro software. *International Journal of Hydrogen Energy.*

Kaczmarczyk, M., Tomaszewska, B., & Bujakowski, W. (2022). Innovative desalination of geothermal wastewater supported by electricity generated from low-enthalpy geothermal resources. *Desalination*, *524*, 115450. doi:10.1016/j.desal.2021.115450

Karakatič, S., & Podgorelec, V. (2015). A survey of genetic algorithms for solving multi depot vehicle routing problem. *Applied Soft Computing*, *27*, 519–532. doi:10.1016/j.asoc.2014.11.005

Karn, A. L., Pandya, S., Mehbodniya, A., Arslan, F., Sharma, D. K., Phasinam, K., Aftab, M. N., Rajan, R., Bommisetti, R. K., & Sengan, S. (2021). An integrated approach for sustainable development of wastewater treatment and management system using IoT in smart cities. *Soft Computing*, 1–17. doi:10.1007/s00500-021-06244-9

Karunananda, A., & Perera, L. C. M. (2016). Using a multi-agent system for supply chain management. *International Journal of Design & Nature and Ecodynamics*, *11*(2), 107–115. doi:10.2495/DNE-V11-N2-107-115

Keengwe, J. (Ed.). (2018). *Handbook of research on digital content, mobile learning, and technology integration models in teacher education*. IGI Global. doi:10.4018/978-1-5225-2953-8

Kengam, J. (2020). *Artificial Intelligence In Education*. Research Gate. doi:10.13140/RG.2.2.16375.65445

Keseru, I., Coosemans, T., & Macharis, C. (2021). Stakeholders' preferences for the future of transport in Europe: Participatory evaluation of scenarios combining scenario planning and the multi-actor multi-criteria analysis. *Futures*, *127*, 102690. doi:10.1016/j.futures.2020.102690

Keysers, D., Deselaers, T., Rowley, H. A., Wang, L.-L., & Carbune, V. (2016). Multi-language online handwriting recognition. *IEEE Transactions on Pattern Analysis and Machine Intelligence*, *39*(6), 1180–1194. doi:10.1109/TPAMI.2016.2572693 PMID:27244718

Khan, S. A. R. (2018). *Introductory Chapter: Introduction of Green Supply Chain Management, Green Practices and Strategies in Supply Chain Management*. IntechOpen. https://www.intechopen.com/chapters/63678 doi:10.5772/intechopen.81088

Khan, S. A., Gupta, H., Gunasekaran, A., Mubarik, M. S., & Lawal, J. (2023). A hybrid multi-criteria decision-making approach to evaluate interrelationships and impacts of supply chain performance factors on pharmaceutical industry. *Journal of Multi-Criteria Decision Analysis*, *30*(1-2), 62–90. doi:10.1002/mcda.1800

Khan, T., Yu, M., & Waseem, M. (2022). Review on recent optimization strategies for hybrid renewable energy system with hydrogen technologies: State of the art, trends and future directions. *International Journal of Hydrogen Energy*, *47*(60), 25155–25201. doi:10.1016/j.ijhydene.2022.05.263

Kholdarvovna. (2021) The role of information and communication technologies for environmental sustainability: evidence from a large panel data analysis. *Journal of environmental management*, *293*, 112889.

Khosravifar, S. (2013). Modeling Multi Agent Communication Activities with Petri Nets. *International Journal of Information and Education Technology (IJIET)*, 310–314. doi:10.7763/IJIET.2013.V3.287

Kiaghadi, A., Sobel, R. S., & Rifai, H. S. (2017). Modeling geothermal energy efficiency from abandoned oil and gas wells to desalinate produced water. *Desalination*, *414*, 51–62. doi:10.1016/j.desal.2017.03.024

Kilic, M., & Altun, A. F. (2022). Dynamic modelling and multi-objective optimization of off-grid hybrid energy systems by using battery or hydrogen storage for different climates. *International Journal of Hydrogen Energy*.

Kim, S. (2019). Electronic Ink Formulation for Drop-on-Demand (DoD) Inkjet Printing Fabrication Process. *2019 34th International Technical Conference on Circuits/Systems, Computers and Communications (ITC-CSCC)*, (pp. 1-2). IEEE.

Kim, Y., & Newman, G. (2020). Advancing scenario planning through integrating urban growth prediction with future flood risk models. *Computers, Environment and Urban Systems*, *82*, 101498. doi:10.1016/j.compenvurbsys.2020.101498 PMID:32431469

Kinker, P., Swarnakar, V., Singh, A. R., & Jain, R. (2021). Identifying and evaluating service quality barriers for polytechnic education: An ISM-MICMAC approach. *Materials Today: Proceedings*, *46*, 9752–9757. doi:10.1016/j.matpr.2020.09.129

Klerk, Y. (2019). *Scenario planning for an autonomous future: a comparative analysis of national preparedness relating to maritime policy/legislative frameworks, societal readiness and HR development for autonomous vessel operations.*

Knowles, J., & Corne, D. (1999). The Pareto archived evolution strategy: a new baseline algorithm for Pareto multiobjective optimization. *Proceedings of the 1999 Congress on Evolutionary Computation-CEC99 (Cat. No. 99TH8406)*. IEEE. 10.1109/CEC.1999.781913

Konys, A. (2019). Green Supplier Selection Criteria: From a Literature Review to a Comprehensive Knowledge Base. *Sustainability*.

Koshariya, A. K., Kalaiyarasi, D., Jovith, A. A., Sivakami, T., Hasan, D. S., & Boopathi, S. (2023a). AI-Enabled IoT and WSN-Integrated Smart Agriculture System. In *Artificial Intelligence Tools and Technologies for Smart Farming and Agriculture Practices* (pp. 200–218). IGI Global. doi:10.4018/978-1-6684-8516-3.ch011

Kumara, V., Mohanaprakash, T. A., Fairooz, S., Jamal, K., Babu, T., & B., S. (2023). Experimental Study on a Reliable Smart Hydroponics System. In *Human Agro-Energy Optimization for Business and Industry* (pp. 27–45). IGI Global. doi:10.4018/978-1-6684-4118-3.ch002

Kumar, H., Singh, M. K., & Gupta, M. P. (2019). A policy framework for city eligibility analysis: TISM and fuzzy MICMAC-weighted approach to select a city for smart city transformation in India. *Land Use Policy*, *82*, 375–390. doi:10.1016/j.landusepol.2018.12.025

La Londe, B. J., & Masters, J. M. (1994). Emerging logistics strategies: Blueprints for the next century. *International Journal of Physical Distribution & Logistics Management*, 24(7), 35–47. doi:10.1108/09600039410070975

Lamé, G., Jouini, O., & Stal-Le Cardinal, J. (2019). Methods and contexts: Challenges of planning with scenarios in a hospital's division. *Futures*, 105, 78–90. doi:10.1016/j.futures.2018.09.005

Laosirihongthong, T., Adebanjo, D., & Tan, K. C. (2013). Green supply chain management practices and performance. *Industrial Management & Data Systems*, 113(8), 1088–1109. doi:10.1108/IMDS-04-2013-0164

Lastly, W. (2020). Van Wyk, R. J. (2020). Towards technological awareness and wisdom. *South African Journal of Industrial Engineering*, 31(4), 1–8.

Lee, K. H., & Kim, J. W. (2011). Integrating suppliers into green product innovation development: an empirical case study in the semiconductor industry. *Business Strategy and the Environment*, 20(8), 527-538.

Lee, H. L., & Billington, C. (1993). Material Management in Decentralized Supply Chains. *Operations Research*, 41(5), 835–847. doi:10.1287/opre.41.5.835

Lee, S. M., Kim, S. T., & Choi, D. (2012). Green supply chain management and organizational performance. *Industrial Management & Data Systems*, 112(8), 1148–1180. doi:10.1108/02635571211264609

Leng, L., Zhang, C., Zhao, Y., Wang, W., Zhang, J., & Li, G. (2020). Biobjective low-carbon location-routing problem for cold chain logistics: Formulation and heuristic approaches. *Journal of Cleaner Production*, 273, 122801. doi:10.1016/j.jclepro.2020.122801

Lenstra, J. K., & Kan, A. H. G. R. (1981). Complexity of vehicle routing and scheduling problems. *Networks*, 11(2), 221–227. doi:10.1002/net.3230110211

Li, A.-D., & He, Z. (2020). Multiobjective feature selection for key quality characteristic identification in production processes using a nondominated-sorting-based whale optimization algorithm. *Computers & Industrial Engineering*, 149, 106852. doi:10.1016/j.cie.2020.106852

Li, J., Li, G., Ma, S., Liang, Z., Li, Y., & Zeng, W. (2022). Modeling and Simulation of Hydrogen Energy Storage System for Power-to-Gas and Gas-to-Power Systems. *Journal of Modern Power Systems and Clean Energy*.

Li, J., Wang, D., & Zhang, J. (2018). Heterogeneous fixed fleet vehicle routing problem based on fuel and carbon emissions. *Journal of Cleaner Production*, 201, 896–908. doi:10.1016/j.jclepro.2018.08.075

Limpo, T., & Graham, S. (2020). THE ROLE OF HANDWRITING INSTRUCTION IN WRITERS' EDUCATION. *British Journal of Educational Studies*, 68(3), 311–329. doi:10.10 80/00071005.2019.1692127

Li, S., & Kokar, M. (2013). *Agent Communication Language*. doi:10.1007/978-1-4614-0968-7_5

Li, S., Subba Rao, S., Ragu-Nathan, T. S., & Ragu-Nathan, B. (2005). Development and validation of a measurement instrument for studying supply chain management practices. *Journal of Operations Management*, *23*(6), 618–641. doi:10.1016/j.jom.2005.01.002

Liu, J., Zhou, Y., Yang, H., & Wu, H. (2022). Net-zero energy management and optimization of commercial building sectors with hybrid renewable energy systems integrated with energy storage of pumped hydro and hydrogen taxis. *Applied Energy*, *321*, 119312. doi:10.1016/j.apenergy.2022.119312

Liu, Y., Liu, H., Wang, C., Hou, S. X., & Yang, N. (2013). Sustainable energy recovery in wastewater treatment by microbial fuel cells: Stable power generation with nitrogen-doped graphene cathode. *Environmental Science & Technology*, *47*(23), 13889–13895. doi:10.1021/es4032216 PMID:24219223

Liu, Y., Shen, W., Man, Y., Liu, Z., & Seferlis, P. (2019). Optimal scheduling ratio of recycling waste paper with NSGAII based on deinked-pulp properties prediction. *Computers & Industrial Engineering*, *132*, 74–83. doi:10.1016/j.cie.2019.04.021

Liwicki, M., Schlapbach, A., & Bunke, H. (2008). Writer-dependent recognition of handwritten whiteboard notes in smart meeting room environments. *2008 The Eighth IAPR International Workshop on Document Analysis Systems*, 151-157. https://ieeexplore.ieee.org/abstract/document/4669956/

Llácer-Iglesias, R. M., López-Jiménez, P. A., & Pérez-Sánchez, M. (2021). Hydropower technology for sustainable energy generation in wastewater systems: Learning from the experience. *Water (Basel)*, *13*(22), 3259. doi:10.3390/w13223259

Long, A. C., Landay, J. A., & Rowe, L. A. (1997). *PDA and gesture use in practice : Insights for designers of pen-based user interfaces*. Computer Science Division, University of California. https://www.researchgate.net/profile/Lawrence-Rowe/publication/2506125_PDA_and_Gesture_Use_in_Practice_Insights_for_Designers_of_Pen-based_User_Interfaces/links/0912f511294c672dd1000000/PDA-and-Gesture-Use-in-Practice-Insights-for-Designers-of-Pen-based-User-Interfaces.pdf

Long, J., Sun, Z., Pardalos, P. M., Hong, Y., Zhang, S., & Li, C. (2019). A hybrid multi-objective genetic local search algorithm for the prize-collecting vehicle routing problem. *Information Sciences*, *478*, 40–61. doi:10.1016/j.ins.2018.11.006

Ltaief, M., Bezine, H., & Alimi, A. M. (2016). A spiking neural network model for complex handwriting movements generation. *International Journal of Computer Science and Information Security*, *14*(7), 319.

Lu, D. (2011). *Fundamentals of supply chain management*. Ventus Publishing Aps.

Lumpkin, S. (2010). Regulatory issues related to financial innovation. *OECD Journal: Financial Market Trends*, (2), 1–31.

Luo, L., Cristofari, C., & Levrey, S. (2023). Cogeneration: Another way to increase energy efficiency of hybrid renewable energy hydrogen chain–A review of systems operating in cogeneration and of the energy efficiency assessment through exergy analysis. *Journal of Energy Storage, 66,* 107433. doi:10.1016/j.est.2023.107433

Maden, W., Eglese, R., & Black, D. (2010). Vehicle routing and scheduling with time-varying data: A case study. *The Journal of the Operational Research Society, 61*(3), 515–522. doi:10.1057/jors.2009.116

Maestre, V. M., Ortiz, A., & Ortiz, I. (2022). Transition to a low-carbon building stock. Techno-economic and spatial optimization of renewables-hydrogen strategies in Spain. *Journal of Energy Storage, 56,* 105889. doi:10.1016/j.est.2022.105889

Makridakis, S., Petropoulos, F., & Kang, Y. (2023). Large Language Models: Their Success and Impact. *Forecasting, 5*(3), 536–549. doi:10.3390/forecast5030030

Malladi, K. T., & Sowlati, T. (2018). Sustainability aspects in Inventory Routing Problem: A review of new trends in the literature. *Journal of Cleaner Production, 197,* 804–814. doi:10.1016/j.jclepro.2018.06.224

Maradin, D., Cerović, L., & Mjeda, T. (2017). Economic effects of renewable energy technologies. *Naše gospodarstvo/Our economy, 63*(2), 49-59.

Märgner, V., & El Abed, H. (2012). Arabic Handwriting Recognition Competitions. In V. Märgner & H. El Abed (Eds.), *Guide to OCR for Arabic Scripts* (pp. 395–422). Springer London., doi:10.1007/978-1-4471-4072-6_17

Martin, W. S., Jones, W. T., McWilliams, E., & Nabors, M. V. (1991). Developing artificial intelligence applications: a small business development center case study. *Journal of Small Business Management, 29*(4), 28.

Matsumoto, R., Umezawa, N., Karaushi, M., Yonemochi, S.-I., & Sakamoto, K. (2006). Comparison of Ammonium Deposition Flux at Roadside and at an Agricultural Area for Long-Term Monitoring: Emission of Ammonia from Vehicles. *Water, Air, and Soil Pollution, 173*(1-4), 355–371. doi:10.1007/s11270-006-9088-z

Mcnair, S., & Ray Crozier, W. (2017). Assessing psychological dispositions and states that can influence economic behaviour. *Economic psychology,* 69-87.

Meneses-Jácome, A., Diaz-Chavez, R., Velásquez-Arredondo, H. I., Cárdenas-Chávez, D. L., Parra, R., & Ruiz-Colorado, A. A. (2016). Sustainable Energy from agro-industrial wastewaters in Latin-America. *Renewable & Sustainable Energy Reviews, 56,* 1249–1262. doi:10.1016/j.rser.2015.12.036

Mezghani, N., Mitiche, A., & Cheriet, M. (2006). *Estimation de densité de probabilité par maximum d'entropie et reconnaissance bayesienne de caractères Arabes en-ligne.* https://espace2.etsmtl.ca/id/eprint/5395/

Miled, H. (1998). *Stratégies de résolution en reconnaissance de l'écriture semi-cursive : Application aux mots manuscrits arabes* [PhD Thesis, Rouen]. https://www.theses.fr/1998ROUES050

Mille, F. (2008). Systèmes de détection des interactions médicamenteuses: points faibles & propositions d'améliorations (Doctoral dissertation, Université Pierre et Marie Curie-Paris VI).

Ministry of New and Renewable Energy. (2023). *India rolls out green hydrogen production standards*. Live Mint. https://www.livemint.com/industry/energy/india-rolls-out-green-hydrogen-production-standards-11692426710928.html

Ministry of Science & Technology. (2023). *National Green Hydrogen Mission*. MST. https://www.india.gov.in/spotlight/national-green-hydrogen-mission

Mohanakrishna, G., Srikanth, S., & Pant, D. (2016). Bioprocesses for waste and wastewater remediation for sustainable energy. In *Bioremediation and Bioeconomy* (pp. 537–565). Elsevier. doi:10.1016/B978-0-12-802830-8.00021-6

Molina, J. C., Eguia, I., Racero, J., & Guerrero, F. 2014. Multi-objective Vehicle Routing Problem with Cost and Emission Functions. *Procedia - Social and Behavioral Sciences, XI Congreso de Ingenieria del Transporte (CIT 2014), 160,* 254–263. 10.1016/j.sbspro.2014.12.137

Mujkić, Z., Qorri, A., & Kraslawski, A. (2018). Sustainability and Optimization of Supply Chains: A Literature Review. *Operations and Supply Chain Management: An International Journal, 11,* 186–199. doi:10.31387/oscm0350213

Naderipour, M., & Alinaghian, M. (2016). Measurement, evaluation and minimization of CO_2, NO_x, and CO emissions in the open time dependent vehicle routing problem. *Measurement, 90,* 443–452. doi:10.1016/j.measurement.2016.04.043

Nair, B. B., & Mohandas, V. P. (2015). Artificial intelligence applications in financial forecasting–a survey and some empirical results. *Intelligent Decision Technologies, 9*(2), 99-140.

Nathalie Sampieri-Teissier. (2004). *Enjeux et limites d'une amélioration des pratiques logistiques dans les hôpitaux publics français. Logistique & management.* Taylor & Francis.

Nazari, G., & Karim, H. (2012, May). Green IT adoption: The impact of IT on environment: A case study on Green IT adoption and underlying factors influencing it. In *2012 Proceedings of 17th Conference on Electrical Power Distribution* (pp. 1-7). IEEE.

Nguyen, M. T., & Dunn, M. (2009). *Some Methods for Scenario Analysis in Defence Strategic Planning*.

Nicolas, P., & Charles, D. (2013). *Le contrôle de gestion logistique hospitalier. Comptabilité sans frontières.* The French Connection.

Niu, Y., Zhang, Y., Cao, Z., Gao, K., Xiao, J., Song, W., & Zhang, F. (2021). MIMOA: A membrane-inspired multi-objective algorithm for green vehicle routing problem with stochastic demands. *Swarm and Evolutionary Computation, 60,* 100767. doi:10.1016/j.swevo.2020.100767

Norrman, A., & Linroth, R. (2002). *Supply Chain Risk Management: Purchaser's vs. Planner's Views on sharing capacity investment risks in the Telecom Industry.* Proceedings of the 11th International Annual IPSERA conference, Twente University.

Norrman, A., & Jansson, U. (2004). Ericsson's proactive supply chain risk management approach after a serious sub-supplier accident. *International Journal of Physical Distribution & Logistics Management, 34*(5), 434–456. doi:10.1108/09600030410545463

Olejniczak, K., Śliwowski, P., & Roszczyńska-Kurasińska, M. (2019). Behaviour architects: a framework for employing behavioural insights in public policy practice. *Zarządzanie Publiczne/ Public Governance*, (1 (47), 18-32.

Olgun, B., Koç, Ç., & Altıparmak, F. (2021). A hyper heuristic for the green vehicle routing problem with simultaneous pickup and delivery. *Computers & Industrial Engineering, 153*, 107010. doi:10.1016/j.cie.2020.107010

Osman, A. I., Mehta, N., Elgarahy, A. M., Hefny, M., Al-Hinai, A., Al-Muhtaseb, A. A. H., & Rooney, D. W. (2022). Hydrogen production, storage, utilisation and environmental impacts: A review. *Environmental Chemistry Letters, 20*(1), 1–36. doi:10.1007/s10311-021-01322-8

Osvald, A., & Stirn, L. Z. (2008). A vehicle routing algorithm for the distribution of fresh vegetables and similar perishable food. *Journal of Food Engineering, 85*(2), 285–295. doi:10.1016/j.jfoodeng.2007.07.008

Palaniappan, M., Tirlangi, S., Mohamed, M. J. S., Moorthy, R. M. S., Valeti, S. V., & Boopathi, S. (2023). Fused Deposition Modelling of Polylactic Acid (PLA)-Based Polymer Composites. In Development, Properties, and Industrial Applications of 3D Printed Polymer Composites (pp. 66–85). IGI Global. doi:10.4018/978-1-6684-6009-2.ch005

Pant, D., Singh, A., Van Bogaert, G., Irving Olsen, S., Singh Nigam, P., Diels, L., & Vanbroekhoven, K. (2012). Bioelectrochemical systems (BES) for sustainable energy production and product recovery from organic wastes and industrial wastewaters. *RSC Advances, 2*(4), 1248–1263. doi:10.1039/C1RA00839K

Pant, D., Van Bogaert, G., Diels, L., & Vanbroekhoven, K. (2010). A review of the substrates used in microbial fuel cells (MFCs) for sustainable energy production. *Bioresource Technology, 101*(6), 1533–1543. doi:10.1016/j.biortech.2009.10.017 PMID:19892549

Parizeau, M., Lemieux, A., & Gagné, C. (2001). Character recognition experiments using UNIPEN data. *Proceedings of Sixth International Conference on Document Analysis and Recognition*, (pp. 481-485). IEEE. 10.1109/ICDAR.2001.953836

Pawar, M., Kadam, S., & Late, D. J. (2017). High-Performance Sensing Behavior Using Electronic Ink of 2D SnSe2 Nanosheets. *ChemistrySelect, 2*(14), 4068–4075. doi:10.1002/slct.201700261

Pechwitz, M., Maddouri, S. S., Märgner, V., Ellouze, N., & Amiri, H. (2002). IFN/ENIT-database of handwritten Arabic words. *Proc. of CIFED, 2*, 127-136.

Peng, B., Zhang, Y., Gajpal, Y., & Chen, X. (2019). A Memetic Algorithm for the Green VehicleRouting Problem. *Sustainability (Basel)*, *11*(21), 6055. doi:10.3390/su11216055

Plassard F. (2004) Retrospective de la prospective. *Travaux de recherche, 20.*

Poisson, E. (2005). *Architecture et apprentissage d'un systeme hybride neuro-markovien pour la reconnaissance de l'écriture manuscrite en-ligne*. [Thesis, Ecole polytechnique de l'université de Nantes].

Pokrivcakova, S. (2019, December). Preparing teachers for the application of AI-powered technologies in foreign language education. *Journal of Language and Cultural Education*, *7*(3), 135–153. doi:10.2478/jolace-2019-0025

Poonthalir, G., & Nadarajan, R. (2018). A Fuel Efficient Green Vehicle Routing Problem with Varying Speed Constraint (F-GVRP). *Expert Systems with Applications*, *100*, 131–144. doi:10.1016/j.eswa.2018.01.052

Popović, A., & Radivojević, V. (2022). The circular economy: Principles, strategies and goals. *Economics of sustainable development, 6*(1), 45-56.

Poskitt, S., Waylen, K. A., & Ainslie, A. (2021). Applying pedagogical theories to understand learning in participatory scenario planning. *Futures*, *128*, 102710. doi:10.1016/j.futures.2021.102710

Postma, T. J., & Liebl, F. (2005). How to improve scenario analysis as a strategic management tool? *Technological Forecasting and Social Change*, *72*(2), 161–173. doi:10.1016/S0040-1625(03)00152-5

Pradhananga, R., Taniguchi, E., Yamada, T., & Qureshi, A. G. (2014). Environmental Analysis of Pareto Optimal Routes in Hazardous Material Transportation. *Procedia: Social and Behavioral Sciences*, *125*, 506–517. doi:10.1016/j.sbspro.2014.01.1492

Prins, C. (2004). A simple and effective evolutionary algorithm for the vehicle routing problem. *Computers & Operations Research*, *31*(12), 1985–2002. doi:10.1016/S0305-0548(03)00158-8

PwC. (2023). *The green hydrogen economy: Predicting the decarbonisation agenda of tomorrow.* PwC. https://www.pwc.com/gx/en/industries/energy-utilities-resources/future-energy/green-hydrogen-cost.html

Qu, G., Zhang, Z., Qu, W., & Xu, Z. (2020). Green Supplier Selection Based on Green Practices Evaluated Using Fuzzy Approaches of TOPSIS and ELECTRE with a Case Study in a Chinese Internet Company. *International Journal of Environmental Research and Public Health*, *17*(9), 3268. doi:10.3390/ijerph17093268 PMID:32392876

Rabhi, B., Elbaati, A., Boubaker, H., Hamdi, Y., Hussain, A., & Alimi, A. (2021). *Temporal Order and Pen Velocity Recovery for Character Handwriting Based on Sequence-to-Sequence with Attention Mode.*

Radeef, A. Y., & Ismail, Z. Z. (2021). Bioelectrochemical treatment of actual carwash wastewater associated with sustainable energy generation in three-dimensional microbial fuel cell. *Bioelectrochemistry (Amsterdam, Netherlands)*, *142*, 107925. doi:10.1016/j.bioelechem.2021.107925 PMID:34392137

Ramezankhani, M. J., Torabi, S. A., & Vahidi, F. (2018). Supply chain performance measurement and evaluation: A mixed sustainability and resilience approach. *Computers & Industrial Engineering*, *126*, 531–548. doi:10.1016/j.cie.2018.09.054

Ratzlaff, E. H. (2003). Methods, reports and survey for the comparison of diverse isolated character recognition results on the UNIPEN database. *Seventh International Conference on Document Analysis and Recognition, 2003. Proceedings.*, (pp. 623-628). IEEE. 10.1109/ICDAR.2003.1227737

Rauniyar, A., Nath, R., & Muhuri, P. K. (2019). Multi-factorial evolutionary algorithm based novel solution approach for multi-objective pollution-routing problem. *Computers & Industrial Engineering*, *130*, 757–771. doi:10.1016/j.cie.2019.02.031

Redclift, M. (1993). Sustainable development: needs, values, rights. *Environmental values, 2*(1), 3-20.

Reddy, M. A., Reddy, B. M., Mukund, C. S., Venneti, K., Preethi, D. M. D., & Boopathi, S. (2023). Social Health Protection During the COVID-Pandemic Using IoT. In *The COVID-19 Pandemic and the Digitalization of Diplomacy* (pp. 204–235). IGI Global. doi:10.4018/978-1-7998-8394-4.ch009

Ritchey, T. (1998). General morphological analysis. In *16th euro conference on operational analysis* (*Vol. 41*).

Rota-Frantz, K., Thierry, C., & Bel, G. (2001). Gestion des flux dans les chaînes logistiques (Supply Chain Management). *Performances Industrielles et Gestion Des Flux*. Hermes Science-Lavoisier Paris.

Roubelat, F. (2000). Scenario planning as a networking process. *Technological Forecasting and Social Change*, *65*(1), 99–112. doi:10.1016/S0040-1625(99)00125-0

Roy, P. P., Bhunia, A. K., Das, A., Dhar, P., & Pal, U. (2017). Keyword spotting in doctor's handwriting on medical prescriptions. *Expert Systems with Applications*, *76*, 113–128. doi:10.1016/j.eswa.2017.01.027

Russell, S. J., & Norvig, P. (2010). *Artificial intelligence a modern approach*.

Saabni, R., & El-Sana, J. (2009). Hierarchical on-line arabic handwriting recognition. *2009 10th International Conference on Document Analysis and Recognition*, (pp. 867-871). IEEE. https://ieeexplore.ieee.org/abstract/document/5277534/

Saada, R. (2020). Green Transportation in Green Supply Chain Management, Green Supply Chain - Competitiveness and Sustainability. *Tamás Bányai and Ireneusz Kaczmar*. IntechOpen, https://www.intechopen.com/chapters/72772 doi:10.5772/intechopen.93113

Saberi, S., & Makatsoris, H. (2008). *Multi agent system for negotiation in supply chain management.*

Sabouhi, F., Pishvaee, M. S., & Jabalameli, M. S. (2018). Resilient supply chain design under operational and disruption risks considering quantity discount: A case study of pharmaceutical supply chain. *Computers & Industrial Engineering, 126,* 657–672. doi:10.1016/j.cie.2018.10.001

Sahraoui, Y., Leski, C. D. G., Benot, M. L., Revers, F., Salles, D., van Halder, I., & Carassou, L. (2021). Integrating ecological networks modelling in a participatory approach for assessing impacts of planning scenarios on landscape connectivity. *Landscape and Urban Planning, 209,* 104039. doi:10.1016/j.landurbplan.2021.104039

Samikannu, R., Koshariya, A. K., Poornima, E., Ramesh, S., Kumar, A., & Boopathi, S. (2023). Sustainable Development in Modern Aquaponics Cultivation Systems Using IoT Technologies. In *Human Agro-Energy Optimization for Business and Industry* (pp. 105–127). IGI Global. doi:10.4018/978-1-6684-4118-3.ch006

Sampath, B., Pandian, M., Deepa, D., & Subbiah, R. (2022). Operating parameters prediction of liquefied petroleum gas refrigerator using simulated annealing algorithm. *AIP Conference Proceedings, 2460*(1), 70003. doi:10.1063/5.0095601

Sarigil, Ş., & Koklu, M. (2022). *NATURAL LANGUAGE PROCESSING TECHNIQUES.*

Sarno, R., & Sungkono, K. R. (2016). Hidden markov model for process mining of parallel business processes. [IRECOS]. *International Review on Computers and Software, 11*(4), 290–300. doi:10.15866/irecos.v11i4.8700

Sathaye, J., Najam, A., Cocklin, C., Heller, T., Lecocq, F., Llanes-Regueiro, J., ... & Winkler, H. (2007). Sustainable development and mitigation. In *Climate change 2007: Mitigation of climate change* (pp. 691-743). Cambridge University Press.

Sathish, T., Sunagar, P., Singh, V., Boopathi, S., Sathyamurthy, R., Al-Enizi, A. M., Pandit, B., Gupta, M., & Sehgal, S. S. (2023). Characteristics estimation of natural fibre reinforced plastic composites using deep multi-layer perceptron (MLP) technique. *Chemosphere, 337*(June), 139346. doi:10.1016/j.chemosphere.2023.139346 PMID:37379988

Savino, M. M., Manzini, R., & Mazza, A. (2015). Environmental and economic assessment of fresh fruit supply chain through value chain analysis. A case study in chestnuts industry. *Production Planning and Control, 26*(1), 1–18. doi:10.1080/09537287.2013.839066

Seçken, N. (2005). The Relations between Global Environmental Awareness and Technology. *Turkish Online Journal of Educational Technology-TOJET, 4*(1), 57–67.

Sedikova, I. (2019). Development of conceptual principles of the circular economy. *Економіка харчової промисловості*, (11, Вип. 2), 47-53.

Selvakumar, S., Adithe, S., Isaac, J. S., Pradhan, R., Venkatesh, V., & Sampath, B. (2023). A Study of the Printed Circuit Board (PCB) E-Waste Recycling Process. In Sustainable Approaches and Strategies for E-Waste Management and Utilization (pp. 159–184). IGI Global.

Seroka-Stolka, O. (2014). The Development of Green Logistics for Implementation Sustainable Development Strategy in Companies. *Procedia: Social and Behavioral Sciences, 151*, 302–309. doi:10.1016/j.sbspro.2014.10.028

Seuring, S. (2013). A review of modeling approaches for sustainable supply chain management. *Decision Support Systems, 54*(4), 1513–1520. doi:10.1016/j.dss.2012.05.053

Shahverdian, M. H., Sedayevatan, S., Hosseini, M., Sohani, A., Javadijam, R., & Sayyaadi, H. (2023). Multi-objective technoeconomic optimization of an off-grid solar-ground-source driven cycle with hydrogen storage for power and fresh water production. *International Journal of Hydrogen Energy, 48*(52), 19772–19791. doi:10.1016/j.ijhydene.2023.02.062

Sharma, A., & Jayagopi, D. B. (2021). Towards efficient unconstrained handwriting recognition using Dilated Temporal Convolution Network. *Expert Systems with Applications, 164*, 114004. doi:10.1016/j.eswa.2020.114004

Siddique, S. S. (2018). *The road to enterprise artificial intelligence: a case studies driven exploration* [Doctoral dissertation, Massachusetts Institute of Technology].

Sierra, C., Botti, V., & Ossowski, S. (2011). Agreement Computing. *Kunstliche Intelligenz, 25*(1), 57–61. doi:10.1007/s13218-010-0070-y

Sim, J. (2017). The influence of new carbon emission abatement goals on the truck-freight transportation sector in South Korea. *Journal of Cleaner Production, 164*, 153–162. doi:10.1016/j.jclepro.2017.06.207

Singh, H., Sharma, R. K., & Singh, V. P. (2021). Online handwriting recognition systems for Indic and non-Indic scripts : A review. *Artificial Intelligence Review, 54*(2), 1525–1579. doi:10.1007/s10462-020-09886-7

Sinta, T. (2021). *Tunisia: the ambitions of the pharmaceutical industry*. African News Agency. https://www.africanewsagency.fr/tunisie-les-ambitions-du-secteurpharmaceutique/?lang=en

Smulders, S. (1995). Environmental policy and sustainable economic growth: an endogenous growth perspective. *De Economist, 143*(2), 163-195.

Sofi, M. A., Reshi, I. A., & Sudha, T. (2023). HOW PSYCHOLOGICAL FACTORS INFLUENCE ECONOMIC DECISION-MAKING, AND THE IMPLICATIONS FOR POLICY. *Journal of Accounting Research, Utility Finance and Digital Assets, 1*(4), 370-375.

Soysal, M., & Çimen, M. (2017). A Simulation Based Restricted Dynamic Programming approach for the Green Time Dependent Vehicle Routing Problem. *Computers & Operations Research, 88*, 297–305. doi:10.1016/j.cor.2017.06.023

Srinivas, N., & Deb, K. (1994). Muiltiobjective Optimization Using Nondominated Sorting in Genetic Algorithms. *Evolutionary Computation, 2*(3), 221–248. doi:10.1162/evco.1994.2.3.221

Strelkovskii, N., Komendantova, N., Sizov, S., & Rovenskaya, E. (2020). Building plausible futures: Scenario-based strategic planning of industrial development of Kyrgyzstan. *Futures*, *124*, 102646. doi:10.1016/j.futures.2020.102646

Subha, S., Inbamalar, T. M., Komala, C. R., Suresh, L. R., Boopathi, S., & Alaskar, K. (2023, February). A Remote Health Care Monitoring system using internet of medical things (IoMT). *Proceedings of 2023 3rd International Conference on Innovative Practices in Technology and Management, ICIPTM 2023*. IEEE. 10.1109/ICIPTM57143.2023.10118103

Su, C. M., Horng, D. J., Tseng, M. L., Chiu, A. S. F., Wu, K.-J., & Chen, H.-P. (2016). Improving sustainable supply chain management using a novel hierarchical grey-DEMATEL approach. *Journal of Cleaner Production*, *134*, 469–481. doi:10.1016/j.jclepro.2015.05.080

Sun, B., & Apland, J. (2019). Operational planning of public transit with economic and environmental goals: Application to the Minneapolis–St. Paul bus system. *Public Transport (Berlin)*, *11*(2), 237–267. doi:10.1007/s12469-019-00199-9

Sun, W., Yu, Y., & Wang, J. (2019). Heterogeneous vehicle pickup and delivery problems: Formulation and exact solution. *Transportation Research Part E, Logistics and Transportation Review*, *125*, 181–202. doi:10.1016/j.tre.2019.03.012

Suresh, M., & Kesav Balajee, T. B. (2021). Modelling of factors influencing on informal learning among school teachers: An ISM-MICMAC approach. Materials today: Proceedings. InPress. doi:10.1016/j.matpr.2020.11.547

Suzuki, Y., 2011. A new truck-routing approach for reducing fuel consumption and pollutants emission. doi:10.1016/j.trd.2010.08.003

Talebirad, Y., & Nadiri, A. (2023). *Multi-Agent Collaboration: Harnessing the Power of Intelligent LLM Agents*.

Tan, K. (2003). *Sur l'évaluation de performances des chaînes logistiques* [Doctoral dissertation, Institut National Polytechnique de Grenoble-INPG].

Tan, K. C., Chew, Y. H., & Lee, L. H. (2006). A hybrid multiobjective evolutionary algorithm for solving vehicle routing problem with time windows. *Computational Optimization and Applications*, *34*(1), 115–151. doi:10.1007/s10589-005-3070-3

Tayur S., Ganeshan R., & Magazine M. (1999). *Quantitative models for supply chain management*. Kluwer AcademicPublishers.

Tepeli, E. (2014). *Processus formalis'e et syst'emique de management des risques par des projets de construction complexes et stratégiques*. Université de Bordeaux.

Terrada, L., El Khaili, M., & Hassan, O. (2020). Multi-Agents System Implementation for Supply Chain Management Making-Decision. *Procedia Computer Science*, *177*, 624–630. doi:10.1016/j.procs.2020.10.089

Thanh, N. V., & Lan, N. T. K. (2022). A new hybrid triple bottom line metrics and fuzzy MCDM model: Sustainable supplier selection in the food-processing industry. *Axioms*, *11*(2), 57. doi:10.3390/axioms11020057

Thomas, D. J., & Griffin, P. M. (1996). Coordinated supply chain management. *European Journal of Operational Research*, *94*(1), 1–15. doi:10.1016/0377-2217(96)00098-7

Tilbury, D. (2011). Higher education for sustainability: a global overview of commitment and progress. *Higher education in the world, 4*(1), 18-28.

Tirkolaee, E. B., Goli, A., Faridnia, A., Soltani, M., & Weber, G.-W. (2020). Multi-objective optimization for the reliable pollution-routing problem with cross-dock selection using Pareto-based algorithms. *Journal of Cleaner Production*, *276*, 122927. doi:10.1016/j.jclepro.2020.122927

Tlemsani, R., & Benyettou, A. (2012). Arabic on line characters recognition using improved dynamic Bayesian Networks. *2012 International Conference on Multimedia Computing and Systems*, (pp. 290-295). IEEE. https://ieeexplore.ieee.org/abstract/document/6320148/

Tlemsani, R., & Belbachir, K. (2018). An Improved Arabic On-Line Characters Recognition System. *2018 International Arab Conference on Information Technology (ACIT)*, (pp. 1-10). IEEE. 10.1109/ACIT.2018.8672673

Tlemsani, R., Benbakreti, S., & Benyettou, A. (2017). On-line Arabic characters recognition using enhanced time delay neural networks. [IRECAP]. *International Journal on Communications Antenna and Propagation*, *7*(4), 254. doi:10.15866/irecap.v7i4.13204

Trott, A., Srinivasa, S., van der Wal, D., Haneuse, S., & Zheng, S. (2021). Building a foundation for data-driven, interpretable, and robust policy design using the ai economist. *arXiv preprint arXiv:2108.02904*.

Utama, D. M., Widodo, D. S., Ibrahim, M. F., & Dewi, S. K. (2020). ANewHybrid Butterfly Optimization Algorithm for Green VehicleRouting Problem. *Journal of Advanced Transportation*, *2020*, 1–14. doi:10.1155/2020/8834502

Van der Heijden, K. (2005). *Scenarios. The art of Strategic Thinking* (2nd ed.). John.

Van Lier, J. B., Tilche, A., Ahring, B. K., Macarie, H., Moletta, R., Dohanyos, M., Hulshoff Pol, L. W., Lens, P., & Verstraete, W. (2001). New perspectives in anaerobic digestion. *Water Science and Technology*, *43*(1), 1–18. doi:10.2166/wst.2001.0001 PMID:11379079

Vanitha, S. K. R., & Boopathi, S. (2023). Artificial Intelligence Techniques in Water Purification and Utilization. In *Human Agro-Energy Optimization for Business and Industry* (pp. 202–218). IGI Global. doi:10.4018/978-1-6684-4118-3.ch010

Varum, C. A., & Melo, C. (2010). Directions in scenario planning literature–A review of the past decades. *Futures*, *42*(4), 355–369. doi:10.1016/j.futures.2009.11.021

Vazhayil, A., Shetty, R., Bhavani, R. R., & Akshay, N. (2019). Focusing on Teacher Education to Introduce AI in Schools: Perspectives and Illustrative Findings. *2019 IEEE Tenth International Conference on Technology for Education (T4E)*, (pp. 71–77). IEEE. 10.1109/T4E.2019.00021

Vecchiato, R. (2019). Scenario planning, cognition, and strategic investment decisions in a turbulent environment. *Long Range Planning*, *52*(5), 101865. doi:10.1016/j.lrp.2019.01.002

Velenturf, A. P., & Purnell, P. (2021). Principles for a sustainable circular economy. *Sustainable Production and Consumption, 27*, 1437-1457.

Verdú, E., Regueras, L., Verdú, M., De Castro, J. P., & Juárez, M. Á. (2008). *Application of Intelligent Adaptive Systems in a Competitive Learning Environment*, *2*, 275.

Wang, L., & Zhao, L. (2022). Digital Economy Meets Artificial Intelligence: Forecasting Economic Conditions Based on Big Data Analytics. *Mobile Information Systems*.

Wang, Y., Song, M., Jia, M., Li, B., Fei, H., Zhang, Y., & Wang, X. (2023). Multi-objective distributionally robust optimization for hydrogen-involved total renewable energy CCHP planning under source-load uncertainties. *Applied Energy*, *342*, 121212. doi:10.1016/j.apenergy.2023.121212

Ward, A. J., Hobbs, P. J., Holliman, P. J., & Jones, D. L. (2008). Optimisation of the anaerobic digestion of agricultural resources. *Bioresource Technology*, *99*(17), 7928–7940. doi:10.1016/j.biortech.2008.02.044 PMID:18406612

Ward, S., & Chapman, C. (2003). Transforming project risk management into project uncertainty management. *International Journal of Project Management*, *21*(2), 97–105. doi:10.1016/S0263-7863(01)00080-1

Witt, T., Dumeier, M., & Geldermann, J. (2020). Combining scenario planning, energy system analysis, and multi-criteria analysis to develop and evaluate energy scenarios. *Journal of Cleaner Production*, *242*, 118414. doi:10.1016/j.jclepro.2019.118414

World Energy Outlook. (2019). IEA. https://www.iea.org/reports/worldenergy-outlook-2019

Xiao, Y., & Konak, A. (2017). A genetic algorithm with exact dynamic programming for the green vehicle routing & scheduling problem. *Journal of Cleaner Production*, *167*, 1450–1463. doi:10.1016/j.jclepro.2016.11.115

Xiao, Y., Zhao, Q., Kaku, I., & Xu, Y. (2012). Development of a fuel consumption optimization model for the capacitated vehicle routing problem. *Computers & Operations Research*, *39*(7), 1419–1431. doi:10.1016/j.cor.2011.08.013

Xua, Z., Elomrib, A., Pokharelc, S., & Mutlud, F. (2019). A model for capacitated green vehicle routing problem with the timevaryingvehicle speed and soft time windows. *Computers & Industrial Engineering*, 137.

Xu, B., Ge, Z., & He, Z. (2015). Sediment microbial fuel cells for wastewater treatment: Challenges and opportunities. *Environmental Science. Water Research & Technology*, *1*(3), 279–284. doi:10.1039/C5EW00020C

Xu, Z., Elomri, A., Pokharel, S., & Mutlu, F. (2019). A model for capacitated green vehicle routing problem with the time-varying vehicle speed and soft time windows. *Computers & Industrial Engineering, 137*, 106011. doi:10.1016/j.cie.2019.106011

Yang, G., Zhang, H., Wang, W., Liu, B., Lyu, C., & Yang, D. (2023). Capacity optimization and economic analysis of PV–hydrogen hybrid systems with physical solar power curve modeling. *Energy Conversion and Management, 288*, 117128. doi:10.1016/j.enconman.2023.117128

Yan, R., Wang, J., Huo, S., Qin, Y., Zhang, J., Tang, S., Wang, Y., Liu, Y., & Zhou, L. (2023). Flexibility improvement and stochastic multi-scenario hybrid optimization for an integrated energy system with high-proportion renewable energy. *Energy, 263*, 125779. doi:10.1016/j.energy.2022.125779

Yaqoob, A. A., Ibrahim, M. N. M., Umar, K., Parveen, T., Ahmad, A., Lokhat, D., & Setapar, S. H. M. (2021). A glimpse into the microbial fuel cells for wastewater treatment with energy generation. *Desalination and Water Treatment, 214*, 379–389. doi:10.5004/dwt.2021.26737

Yeolekar-Kadam, B., & Sudarsan, J. S. (2022). Feasibility Study on Integration of Green Technologies in Prospective Construction Projects: A Case of Vishakhapatnam. *International Journal of Management* [IJMTS]. *Technology and Social Sciences, 7*(1), 210–223.

Yousefi, S., Shabanpour, H., Fisher, R., & Saen, R. F. (2016). Evaluating and ranking sustainable suppliers by robust dynamic data envelopment analysis. *Measurement, 83*, 72–85. doi:10.1016/j.measurement.2016.01.032

Yu, F., Xue, L., Sun, C., & Zhang, C. (2016). Product transportation distance-based supplier selection in sustainable supply chain network. *Journal of Cleaner Production, 137*, 29–39. doi:10.1016/j.jclepro.2016.07.046

Yupapin, P., Trabelsi, Y., Nattappan, A., & Boopathi, S. (2023). Performance Improvement of Wire-Cut Electrical Discharge Machining Process Using Cryogenically Treated Super-Conductive State of Monel-K500 Alloy. *Iranian Journal of Science and Technology. Transaction of Mechanical Engineering, 47*(1), 267–283. doi:10.1007/s40997-022-00513-0

Zhang, D., Pee, L. G., & Cui, L. (2021). Artificial intelligence in E-commerce fulfillment: A case study of resource orchestration at Alibaba's Smart Warehouse. *International Journal of Information Management, 57*, 102304.

Zhang, H., Du, W., Shan, J., Zhou, Q., Du, Y., Tenenbaum, J. B., Shu, T., & Gan, C. (2023). *Building Cooperative Embodied Agents Modularly with Large Language Models* (arXiv:2307.02485). arXiv.

Zhang, H., Wang, J., Zhao, X., Yang, J., & Bu sinnah, Z. A. (2023). Modeling a hydrogen-based sustainable multi-carrier energy system using a multi-objective optimization considering embedded joint chance constraints. *Energy, 278*, 127643. doi:10.1016/j.energy.2023.127643

Zhang, K., Zhou, B., Or, S. W., Li, C., Chung, C. Y., & Voropai, N. (2021). Optimal coordinated control of multi-renewable-to-hydrogen production system for hydrogen fueling stations. *IEEE Transactions on Industry Applications, 58*(2), 2728–2739. doi:10.1109/TIA.2021.3093841

Zhang, Y., Hua, Q. S., Sun, L., & Liu, Q. (2020). Life cycle optimization of renewable energy systems configuration with hybrid battery/hydrogen storage: A comparative study. *Journal of Energy Storage, 30*, 101470. doi:10.1016/j.est.2020.101470

Zhao, E., Chen, L., Cui, H., & Zhu, Z. (2022). Assessing the Economic Impact of Renewable Energy from a Technology Perspective. *Advances in Economics and Management Research, 1*(1), 35-35.

Zhao, Y. (2022). Decision support system for economic management of large enterprises based on artificial intelligence. *Wireless Communications and Mobile Computing*, 1–11.

Zhao, P., Gu, C., Hu, Z., Xie, D., Hernando-Gil, I., & Shen, Y. (2020). Distributionally robust hydrogen optimization with ensured security and multi-energy couplings. *IEEE Transactions on Power Systems, 36*(1), 504–513. doi:10.1109/TPWRS.2020.3005991

Zhou, A., Qu, B.-Y., Li, H., Zhao, S.-Z., Suganthan, P. N., & Zhang, Q. (2011). Multiobjective evolutionary algorithms: A survey of the state of the art. *Swarm and Evolutionary Computation, 1*(1), 32–49. doi:10.1016/j.swevo.2011.03.001

Zhu, K. Q. (2003). A diversity-controlling adaptive genetic algorithm for the vehicle routing problem with time windows. *15th IEEE International Conference on Tools with Artificial Intelligence. Presented at the Proceedings.* IEEE.s 10.1109/TAI.2003.1250187

Zsidisin, G. A., & Ritchie, B. (Eds.). (2008). *Supply chain risk: a handbook of assessment, management, and performance* (Vol. 124). Springer Science & Business Media.

Zuo, H., & Ai, D. (2011). Environment, energy and sustainable economic growth. *Procedia Engineering, 21*, 513-519.

Related References

To continue our tradition of advancing information science and technology research, we have compiled a list of recommended IGI Global readings. These references will provide additional information and guidance to further enrich your knowledge and assist you with your own research and future publications.

Abdul Razak, R., & Mansor, N. A. (2021). Instagram Influencers in Social Media-Induced Tourism: Rethinking Tourist Trust Towards Tourism Destination. In M. Dinis, L. Bonixe, S. Lamy, & Z. Breda (Eds.), *Impact of New Media in Tourism* (pp. 135-144). IGI Global. https://doi.org/10.4018/978-1-7998-7095-1.ch009

Abir, T., & Khan, M. Y. (2022). Importance of ICT Advancement and Culture of Adaptation in the Tourism and Hospitality Industry for Developing Countries. In C. Ramos, S. Quinteiro, & A. Gonçalves (Eds.), *ICT as Innovator Between Tourism and Culture* (pp. 30–41). IGI Global. https://doi.org/10.4018/978-1-7998-8165-0.ch003

Abir, T., & Khan, M. Y. (2022). Importance of ICT Advancement and Culture of Adaptation in the Tourism and Hospitality Industry for Developing Countries. In C. Ramos, S. Quinteiro, & A. Gonçalves (Eds.), *ICT as Innovator Between Tourism and Culture* (pp. 30–41). IGI Global. https://doi.org/10.4018/978-1-7998-8165-0.ch003

Abtahi, M. S., Behboudi, L., & Hasanabad, H. M. (2017). Factors Affecting Internet Advertising Adoption in Ad Agencies. *International Journal of Innovation in the Digital Economy*, 8(4), 18–29. doi:10.4018/IJIDE.2017100102

Afenyo-Agbe, E., & Mensah, I. (2022). Principles, Benefits, and Barriers to Community-Based Tourism: Implications for Management. In I. Mensah & E. Afenyo-Agbe (Eds.), *Prospects and Challenges of Community-Based Tourism and Changing Demographics* (pp. 1–29). IGI Global. doi:10.4018/978-1-7998-7335-8.ch001

Agbo, V. M. (2022). Distributive Justice Issues in Community-Based Tourism. In I. Mensah & E. Afenyo-Agbe (Eds.), *Prospects and Challenges of Community-Based Tourism and Changing Demographics* (pp. 107–129). IGI Global. https://doi.org/10.4018/978-1-7998-7335-8.ch005

Agrawal, S. (2017). The Impact of Emerging Technologies and Social Media on Different Business(es): Marketing and Management. In O. Rishi & A. Sharma (Eds.), *Maximizing Business Performance and Efficiency Through Intelligent Systems* (pp. 37–49). Hershey, PA: IGI Global. doi:10.4018/978-1-5225-2234-8.ch002

Ahmad, A., & Johari, S. (2022). Georgetown as a Gastronomy Tourism Destination: Visitor Awareness Towards Revisit Intention of Nasi Kandar Restaurant. In M. Valeri (Ed.), *New Governance and Management in Touristic Destinations* (pp. 71–83). IGI Global. https://doi.org/10.4018/978-1-6684-3889-3.ch005

Alkhatib, G., & Bayouq, S. T. (2021). A TAM-Based Model of Technological Factors Affecting Use of E-Tourism. *International Journal of Tourism and Hospitality Management in the Digital Age*, 5(2), 50–67. https://doi.org/10.4018/IJTHMDA.20210701.oa1

Altinay Ozdemir, M. (2021). Virtual Reality (VR) and Augmented Reality (AR) Technologies for Accessibility and Marketing in the Tourism Industry. In C. Eusébio, L. Teixeira, & M. Carneiro (Eds.), *ICT Tools and Applications for Accessible Tourism* (pp. 277-301). IGI Global. https://doi.org/10.4018/978-1-7998-6428-8.ch013

Anantharaman, R. N., Rajeswari, K. S., Angusamy, A., & Kuppusamy, J. (2017). Role of Self-Efficacy and Collective Efficacy as Moderators of Occupational Stress Among Software Development Professionals. *International Journal of Human Capital and Information Technology Professionals*, 8(2), 45–58. doi:10.4018/IJHCITP.2017040103

Aninze, F., El-Gohary, H., & Hussain, J. (2018). The Role of Microfinance to Empower Women: The Case of Developing Countries. *International Journal of Customer Relationship Marketing and Management*, 9(1), 54–78. doi:10.4018/IJCRMM.2018010104

Antosova, G., Sabogal-Salamanca, M., & Krizova, E. (2021). Human Capital in Tourism: A Practical Model of Endogenous and Exogenous Territorial Tourism Planning in Bahía Solano, Colombia. In V. Costa, A. Moura, & M. Mira (Eds.), *Handbook of Research on Human Capital and People Management in the Tourism Industry* (pp. 282–302). IGI Global. https://doi.org/10.4018/978-1-7998-4318-4.ch014

Arsenijević, O. M., Orčić, D., & Kastratović, E. (2017). Development of an Optimization Tool for Intangibles in SMEs: A Case Study from Serbia with a Pilot Research in the Prestige by Milka Company. In M. Vemić (Ed.), *Optimal Management Strategies in Small and Medium Enterprises* (pp. 320–347). Hershey, PA: IGI Global. doi:10.4018/978-1-5225-1949-2.ch015

Aryanto, V. D., Wismantoro, Y., & Widyatmoko, K. (2018). Implementing Eco-Innovation by Utilizing the Internet to Enhance Firm's Marketing Performance: Study of Green Batik Small and Medium Enterprises in Indonesia. *International Journal of E-Business Research*, 14(1), 21–36. doi:10.4018/IJEBR.2018010102

Asero, V., & Billi, S. (2022). New Perspective of Networking in the DMO Model. In M. Valeri (Ed.), *New Governance and Management in Touristic Destinations* (pp. 105–118). IGI Global. https://doi.org/10.4018/978-1-6684-3889-3.ch007

Atiku, S. O., & Fields, Z. (2017). Multicultural Orientations for 21st Century Global Leadership. In N. Baporikar (Ed.), *Management Education for Global Leadership* (pp. 28–51). Hershey, PA: IGI Global. doi:10.4018/978-1-5225-1013-0.ch002

Atiku, S. O., & Fields, Z. (2018). Organisational Learning Dimensions and Talent Retention Strategies for the Service Industries. In N. Baporikar (Ed.), *Global Practices in Knowledge Management for Societal and Organizational Development* (pp. 358–381). Hershey, PA: IGI Global. doi:10.4018/978-1-5225-3009-1.ch017

Atsa'am, D. D., & Kuset Bodur, E. (2021). Pattern Mining on How Organizational Tenure Affects the Psychological Capital of Employees Within the Hospitality and Tourism Industry: Linking Employees' Organizational Tenure With PsyCap. *International Journal of Tourism and Hospitality Management in the Digital Age*, 5(2), 17–28. https://doi.org/10.4018/IJTHMDA.2021070102

Ávila, L., & Teixeira, L. (2018). The Main Concepts Behind the Dematerialization of Business Processes. In M. Khosrow-Pour, D.B.A. (Ed.), Encyclopedia of Information Science and Technology, Fourth Edition (pp. 888-898). Hershey, PA: IGI Global. https://doi.org/ doi:10.4018/978-1-5225-2255-3.ch076

Ayorekire, J., Mugizi, F., Obua, J., & Ampaire, G. (2022). Community-Based Tourism and Local People's Perceptions Towards Conservation: The Case of Queen Elizabeth Conservation Area, Uganda. In I. Mensah & E. Afenyo-Agbe (Eds.), *Prospects and Challenges of Community-Based Tourism and Changing Demographics* (pp. 56–82). IGI Global. https://doi.org/10.4018/978-1-7998-7335-8.ch003

Baleiro, R. (2022). Tourist Literature and the Architecture of Travel in Olga Tokarczuk and Patti Smith. In R. Baleiro & R. Pereira (Eds.), *Global Perspectives on Literary Tourism and Film-Induced Tourism* (pp. 202-216). IGI Global. https://doi.org/10.4018/978-1-7998-8262-6.ch011

Barat, S. (2021). Looking at the Future of Medical Tourism in Asia. *International Journal of Tourism and Hospitality Management in the Digital Age*, 5(1), 19–33. https://doi.org/10.4018/IJTHMDA.2021010102

Barbosa, C. A., Magalhães, M., & Nunes, M. R. (2021). Travel Instagramability: A Way of Choosing a Destination? In M. Dinis, L. Bonixe, S. Lamy, & Z. Breda (Eds.), *Impact of New Media in Tourism* (pp. 173-190). IGI Global. https://doi.org/10.4018/978-1-7998-7095-1.ch011

Bari, M. W., & Khan, Q. (2021). Pakistan as a Destination of Religious Tourism. In E. Alaverdov & M. Bari (Eds.), *Global Development of Religious Tourism* (pp. 1-10). IGI Global. https://doi.org/10.4018/978-1-7998-5792-1.ch001

Bartens, Y., Chunpir, H. I., Schulte, F., & Voß, S. (2017). Business/IT Alignment in Two-Sided Markets: A COBIT 5 Analysis for Media Streaming Business Models. In S. De Haes & W. Van Grembergen (Eds.), *Strategic IT Governance and Alignment in Business Settings* (pp. 82–111). Hershey, PA: IGI Global. doi:10.4018/978-1-5225-0861-8.ch004

Bashayreh, A. M. (2018). Organizational Culture and Organizational Performance. In W. Lee & F. Sabetzadeh (Eds.), *Contemporary Knowledge and Systems Science* (pp. 50–69). Hershey, PA: IGI Global. doi:10.4018/978-1-5225-5655-8.ch003

Bechthold, L., Lude, M., & Prügl, R. (2021). Crisis Favors the Prepared Firm: How Organizational Ambidexterity Relates to Perceptions of Organizational Resilience. In A. Zehrer, G. Glowka, K. Schwaiger, & V. Ranacher-Lackner (Eds.), *Resiliency Models and Addressing Future Risks for Family Firms in the Tourism Industry* (pp. 178–205). IGI Global. https://doi.org/10.4018/978-1-7998-7352-5.ch008

Bedford, D. A. (2018). Sustainable Knowledge Management Strategies: Aligning Business Capabilities and Knowledge Management Goals. In N. Baporikar (Ed.), *Global Practices in Knowledge Management for Societal and Organizational Development* (pp. 46–73). Hershey, PA: IGI Global. doi:10.4018/978-1-5225-3009-1.ch003

Bekjanov, D., & Matyusupov, B. (2021). Influence of Innovative Processes in the Competitiveness of Tourist Destination. In J. Soares (Ed.), *Innovation and Entrepreneurial Opportunities in Community Tourism* (pp. 243–263). IGI Global. https://doi.org/10.4018/978-1-7998-4855-4.ch014

Bharwani, S., & Musunuri, D. (2018). Reflection as a Process From Theory to Practice. In M. Khosrow-Pour, D.B.A. (Ed.), Encyclopedia of Information Science and Technology, Fourth Edition (pp. 1529-1539). Hershey, PA: IGI Global. doi:10.4018/978-1-5225-2255-3.ch132

Bhatt, G. D., Wang, Z., & Rodger, J. A. (2017). Information Systems Capabilities and Their Effects on Competitive Advantages: A Study of Chinese Companies. *Information Resources Management Journal, 30*(3), 41–57. doi:10.4018/IRMJ.2017070103

Bhushan, M., & Yadav, A. (2017). Concept of Cloud Computing in ESB. In R. Bhadoria, N. Chaudhari, G. Tomar, & S. Singh (Eds.), *Exploring Enterprise Service Bus in the Service-Oriented Architecture Paradigm* (pp. 116–127). Hershey, PA: IGI Global. doi:10.4018/978-1-5225-2157-0.ch008

Bhushan, S. (2017). System Dynamics Base-Model of Humanitarian Supply Chain (HSCM) in Disaster Prone Eco-Communities of India: A Discussion on Simulation and Scenario Results. *International Journal of System Dynamics Applications, 6*(3), 20–37. doi:10.4018/IJSDA.2017070102

Binder, D., & Miller, J. W. (2021). A Generations' Perspective on Employer Branding in Tourism. In V. Costa, A. Moura, & M. Mira (Eds.), *Handbook of Research on Human Capital and People Management in the Tourism Industry* (pp. 152–174). IGI Global. https://doi.org/10.4018/978-1-7998-4318-4.ch008

Birch Freeman, A. A., Mensah, I., & Antwi, K. B. (2022). Smiling vs. Frowning Faces: Community Participation for Sustainable Tourism in Ghanaian Communities. In I. Mensah & E. Afenyo-Agbe (Eds.), *Prospects and Challenges of Community-Based Tourism and Changing Demographics* (pp. 83–106). IGI Global. https://doi.org/10.4018/978-1-7998-7335-8.ch004

Biswas, A., & De, A. K. (2017). On Development of a Fuzzy Stochastic Programming Model with Its Application to Business Management. In S. Trivedi, S. Dey, A. Kumar, & T. Panda (Eds.), *Handbook of Research on Advanced Data Mining Techniques and Applications for Business Intelligence* (pp. 353–378). Hershey, PA: IGI Global. doi:10.4018/978-1-5225-2031-3.ch021

Boragnio, A., & Faracce Macia, C. (2021). "Taking Care of Yourself at Home": Use of E-Commerce About Food and Care During the COVID-19 Pandemic in the City of Buenos Aires. In M. Korstanje (Ed.), *Socio-Economic Effects and Recovery Efforts for the Rental Industry: Post-COVID-19 Strategies* (pp. 45–71). IGI Global. https://doi.org/10.4018/978-1-7998-7287-0.ch003

Borges, V. D. (2021). Happiness: The Basis for Public Policy in Tourism. In A. Perinotto, V. Mayer, & J. Soares (Eds.), *Rebuilding and Restructuring the Tourism Industry: Infusion of Happiness and Quality of Life* (pp. 1–25). IGI Global. https://doi.org/10.4018/978-1-7998-7239-9.ch001

Bücker, J., & Ernste, K. (2018). Use of Brand Heroes in Strategic Reputation Management: The Case of Bacardi, Adidas, and Daimler. In A. Erdemir (Ed.), *Reputation Management Techniques in Public Relations* (pp. 126–150). Hershey, PA: IGI Global. doi:10.4018/978-1-5225-3619-2.ch007

Buluk Eşitti, B. (2021). COVID-19 and Alternative Tourism: New Destinations and New Tourism Products. In M. Demir, A. Dalgıç, & F. Ergen (Eds.), *Handbook of Research on the Impacts and Implications of COVID-19 on the Tourism Industry* (pp. 786–805). IGI Global. https://doi.org/10.4018/978-1-7998-8231-2.ch038

Bureš, V. (2018). Industry 4.0 From the Systems Engineering Perspective: Alternative Holistic Framework Development. In R. Brunet-Thornton & F. Martinez (Eds.), *Analyzing the Impacts of Industry 4.0 in Modern Business Environments* (pp. 199–223). Hershey, PA: IGI Global. doi:10.4018/978-1-5225-3468-6.ch011

Buzady, Z. (2017). Resolving the Magic Cube of Effective Case Teaching: Benchmarking Case Teaching Practices in Emerging Markets – Insights from the Central European University Business School, Hungary. In D. Latusek (Ed.), *Case Studies as a Teaching Tool in Management Education* (pp. 79–103). Hershey, PA: IGI Global. doi:10.4018/978-1-5225-0770-3.ch005

Camillo, A. (2021). *Legal Matters, Risk Management, and Risk Prevention: From Forming a Business to Legal Representation.* IGI Global. doi:10.4018/978-1-7998-4342-9.ch004

Căpusneanu, S., & Topor, D. I. (2018). Business Ethics and Cost Management in SMEs: Theories of Business Ethics and Cost Management Ethos. In I. Oncioiu (Ed.), *Ethics and Decision-Making for Sustainable Business Practices* (pp. 109–127). Hershey, PA: IGI Global. doi:10.4018/978-1-5225-3773-1.ch007

Chan, R. L., Mo, P. L., & Moon, K. K. (2018). Strategic and Tactical Measures in Managing Enterprise Risks: A Study of the Textile and Apparel Industry. In K. Strang, M. Korstanje, & N. Vajjhala (Eds.), *Research, Practices, and Innovations in Global Risk and Contingency Management* (pp. 1–19). Hershey, PA: IGI Global. doi:10.4018/978-1-5225-4754-9.ch001

Charlier, S. D., Burke-Smalley, L. A., & Fisher, S. L. (2018). Undergraduate Programs in the U.S: A Contextual and Content-Based Analysis. In J. Mendy (Ed.), *Teaching Human Resources and Organizational Behavior at the College Level* (pp. 26–57). Hershey, PA: IGI Global. doi:10.4018/978-1-5225-2820-3.ch002

Chumillas, J., Güell, M., & Quer, P. (2022). The Use of ICT in Tourist and Educational Literary Routes: The Role of the Guide. In C. Ramos, S. Quinteiro, & A. Gonçalves (Eds.), *ICT as Innovator Between Tourism and Culture* (pp. 15–29). IGI Global. https://doi.org/10.4018/978-1-7998-8165-0.ch002

Dahlberg, T., Kivijärvi, H., & Saarinen, T. (2017). IT Investment Consistency and Other Factors Influencing the Success of IT Performance. In S. De Haes & W. Van Grembergen (Eds.), *Strategic IT Governance and Alignment in Business Settings* (pp. 176–208). Hershey, PA: IGI Global. doi:10.4018/978-1-5225-0861-8.ch007

Damnjanović, A. M. (2017). Knowledge Management Optimization through IT and E-Business Utilization: A Qualitative Study on Serbian SMEs. In M. Vemić (Ed.), *Optimal Management Strategies in Small and Medium Enterprises* (pp. 249–267). Hershey, PA: IGI Global. doi:10.4018/978-1-5225-1949-2.ch012

Daneshpour, H. (2017). Integrating Sustainable Development into Project Portfolio Management through Application of Open Innovation. In M. Vemić (Ed.), *Optimal Management Strategies in Small and Medium Enterprises* (pp. 370–387). Hershey, PA: IGI Global. doi:10.4018/978-1-5225-1949-2.ch017

Daniel, A. D., & Reis de Castro, V. (2018). Entrepreneurship Education: How to Measure the Impact on Nascent Entrepreneurs. In A. Carrizo Moreira, J. Guilherme Leitão Dantas, & F. Manuel Valente (Eds.), *Nascent Entrepreneurship and Successful New Venture Creation* (pp. 85–110). Hershey, PA: IGI Global. doi:10.4018/978-1-5225-2936-1.ch004

David, R., Swami, B. N., & Tangirala, S. (2018). Ethics Impact on Knowledge Management in Organizational Development: A Case Study. In N. Baporikar (Ed.), *Global Practices in Knowledge Management for Societal and Organizational Development* (pp. 19–45). Hershey, PA: IGI Global. doi:10.4018/978-1-5225-3009-1.ch002

De Uña-Álvarez, E., & Villarino-Pérez, M. (2022). Fostering Ecocultural Resources, Identity, and Tourism in Inland Territories (Galicia, NW Spain). In G. Fernandes (Ed.), *Challenges and New Opportunities for Tourism in Inland Territories: Ecocultural Resources and Sustainable Initiatives* (pp. 1-16). IGI Global. https://doi.org/10.4018/978-1-7998-7339-6.ch001

Delias, P., & Lakiotaki, K. (2018). Discovering Process Horizontal Boundaries to Facilitate Process Comprehension. *International Journal of Operations Research and Information Systems*, *9*(2), 1–31. doi:10.4018/IJORIS.2018040101

Denholm, J., & Lee-Davies, L. (2018). Success Factors for Games in Business and Project Management. In *Enhancing Education and Training Initiatives Through Serious Games* (pp. 34–68). Hershey, PA: IGI Global. doi:10.4018/978-1-5225-3689-5.ch002

Deshpande, M. (2017). Best Practices in Management Institutions for Global Leadership: Policy Aspects. In N. Baporikar (Ed.), *Management Education for Global Leadership* (pp. 1–27). Hershey, PA: IGI Global. doi:10.4018/978-1-5225-1013-0.ch001

Deshpande, M. (2018). Policy Perspectives for SMEs Knowledge Management. In N. Baporikar (Ed.), *Knowledge Integration Strategies for Entrepreneurship and Sustainability* (pp. 23–46). Hershey, PA: IGI Global. doi:10.4018/978-1-5225-5115-7.ch002

Dezdar, S. (2017). ERP Implementation Projects in Asian Countries: A Comparative Study on Iran and China. *International Journal of Information Technology Project Management*, *8*(3), 52–68. doi:10.4018/IJITPM.2017070104

Domingos, D., Respício, A., & Martinho, R. (2017). Reliability of IoT-Aware BPMN Healthcare Processes. In C. Reis & M. Maximiano (Eds.), *Internet of Things and Advanced Application in Healthcare* (pp. 214–248). Hershey, PA: IGI Global. doi:10.4018/978-1-5225-1820-4.ch008

Dosumu, O., Hussain, J., & El-Gohary, H. (2017). An Exploratory Study of the Impact of Government Policies on the Development of Small and Medium Enterprises in Developing Countries: The Case of Nigeria. *International Journal of Customer Relationship Marketing and Management*, *8*(4), 51–62. doi:10.4018/IJCRMM.2017100104

Durst, S., Bruns, G., & Edvardsson, I. R. (2017). Retaining Knowledge in Smaller Building and Construction Firms. *International Journal of Knowledge and Systems Science*, *8*(3), 1–12. doi:10.4018/IJKSS.2017070101

Edvardsson, I. R., & Durst, S. (2017). Outsourcing, Knowledge, and Learning: A Critical Review. *International Journal of Knowledge-Based Organizations*, *7*(2), 13–26. doi:10.4018/IJKBO.2017040102

Edwards, J. S. (2018). Integrating Knowledge Management and Business Processes. In M. Khosrow-Pour, D.B.A. (Ed.), Encyclopedia of Information Science and Technology, Fourth Edition (pp. 5046-5055). Hershey, PA: IGI Global. doi:10.4018/978-1-5225-2255-3.ch437

Eichelberger, S., & Peters, M. (2021). Family Firm Management in Turbulent Times: Opportunities for Responsible Tourism. In A. Zehrer, G. Glowka, K. Schwaiger, & V. Ranacher-Lackner (Eds.), *Resiliency Models and Addressing Future Risks for Family Firms in the Tourism Industry* (pp. 103–124). IGI Global. https://doi.org/10.4018/978-1-7998-7352-5.ch005

Eide, D., Hjalager, A., & Hansen, M. (2022). Innovative Certifications in Adventure Tourism: Attributes and Diffusion. In R. Augusto Costa, F. Brandão, Z. Breda, & C. Costa (Eds.), *Planning and Managing the Experience Economy in Tourism* (pp. 161-175). IGI Global. https://doi.org/10.4018/978-1-7998-8775-1.ch009

Ejiogu, A. O. (2018). Economics of Farm Management. In *Agricultural Finance and Opportunities for Investment and Expansion* (pp. 56–72). Hershey, PA: IGI Global. doi:10.4018/978-1-5225-3059-6.ch003

Ekanem, I., & Abiade, G. E. (2018). Factors Influencing the Use of E-Commerce by Small Enterprises in Nigeria. *International Journal of ICT Research in Africa and the Middle East*, 7(1), 37–53. doi:10.4018/IJICTRAME.2018010103

Ekanem, I., & Alrossais, L. A. (2017). Succession Challenges Facing Family Businesses in Saudi Arabia. In P. Zgheib (Ed.), *Entrepreneurship and Business Innovation in the Middle East* (pp. 122–146). Hershey, PA: IGI Global. doi:10.4018/978-1-5225-2066-5.ch007

El Faquih, L., & Fredj, M. (2017). Ontology-Based Framework for Quality in Configurable Process Models. *Journal of Electronic Commerce in Organizations*, 15(2), 48–60. doi:10.4018/JECO.2017040104

Faisal, M. N., & Talib, F. (2017). Building Ambidextrous Supply Chains in SMEs: How to Tackle the Barriers? *International Journal of Information Systems and Supply Chain Management*, 10(4), 80–100. doi:10.4018/IJISSCM.2017100105

Fernandes, T. M., Gomes, J., & Romão, M. (2017). Investments in E-Government: A Benefit Management Case Study. *International Journal of Electronic Government Research*, 13(3), 1–17. doi:10.4018/IJEGR.2017070101

Figueira, L. M., Honrado, G. R., & Dionísio, M. S. (2021). Human Capital Management in the Tourism Industry in Portugal. In V. Costa, A. Moura, & M. Mira (Eds.), *Handbook of Research on Human Capital and People Management in the Tourism Industry* (pp. 1–19). IGI Global. doi:10.4018/978-1-7998-4318-4.ch001

Gao, S. S., Oreal, S., & Zhang, J. (2018). Contemporary Financial Risk Management Perceptions and Practices of Small-Sized Chinese Businesses. In I. Management Association (Ed.), Global Business Expansion: Concepts, Methodologies, Tools, and Applications (pp. 917-931). Hershey, PA: IGI Global. doi:10.4018/978-1-5225-5481-3.ch041

Garg, R., & Berning, S. C. (2017). Indigenous Chinese Management Philosophies: Key Concepts and Relevance for Modern Chinese Firms. In B. Christiansen & G. Koc (Eds.), *Transcontinental Strategies for Industrial Development and Economic Growth* (pp. 43–57). Hershey, PA: IGI Global. doi:10.4018/978-1-5225-2160-0.ch003

Gencer, Y. G. (2017). Supply Chain Management in Retailing Business. In U. Akkucuk (Ed.), *Ethics and Sustainability in Global Supply Chain Management* (pp. 197–210). Hershey, PA: IGI Global. doi:10.4018/978-1-5225-2036-8.ch011

Gera, R., Arora, S., & Malik, S. (2021). Emotional Labor in the Tourism Industry: Strategies, Antecedents, and Outcomes. In V. Costa, A. Moura, & M. Mira (Eds.), *Handbook of Research on Human Capital and People Management in the Tourism Industry* (pp. 73–91). IGI Global. https://doi.org/10.4018/978-1-7998-4318-4.ch004

Giacosa, E. (2018). The Increasing of the Regional Development Thanks to the Luxury Business Innovation. In L. Carvalho (Ed.), *Handbook of Research on Entrepreneurial Ecosystems and Social Dynamics in a Globalized World* (pp. 260–273). Hershey, PA: IGI Global. doi:10.4018/978-1-5225-3525-6.ch011

Glowka, G., Tusch, M., & Zehrer, A. (2021). The Risk Perception of Family Business Owner-Manager in the Tourism Industry: A Qualitative Comparison of the Intra-Firm Senior and Junior Generation. In A. Zehrer, G. Glowka, K. Schwaiger, & V. Ranacher-Lackner (Eds.), *Resiliency Models and Addressing Future Risks for Family Firms in the Tourism Industry* (pp. 126–153). IGI Global. https://doi.org/10.4018/978-1-7998-7352-5.ch006

Glykas, M., & George, J. (2017). Quality and Process Management Systems in the UAE Maritime Industry. *International Journal of Productivity Management and Assessment Technologies*, 5(1), 20–39. doi:10.4018/IJPMAT.2017010102

Glykas, M., Valiris, G., Kokkinaki, A., & Koutsoukou, Z. (2018). Banking Business Process Management Implementation. *International Journal of Productivity Management and Assessment Technologies, 6*(1), 50–69. doi:10.4018/IJPMAT.2018010104

Gomes, J., & Romão, M. (2017). The Balanced Scorecard: Keeping Updated and Aligned with Today's Business Trends. *International Journal of Productivity Management and Assessment Technologies, 5*(2), 1–15. doi:10.4018/IJPMAT.2017070101

Gomes, J., & Romão, M. (2017). Aligning Information Systems and Technology with Benefit Management and Balanced Scorecard. In S. De Haes & W. Van Grembergen (Eds.), *Strategic IT Governance and Alignment in Business Settings* (pp. 112–131). Hershey, PA: IGI Global. doi:10.4018/978-1-5225-0861-8.ch005

Goyal, A. (2021). Communicating and Building Destination Brands With New Media. In M. Dinis, L. Bonixe, S. Lamy, & Z. Breda (Eds.), *Impact of New Media in Tourism* (pp. 1-20). IGI Global. https://doi.org/10.4018/978-1-7998-7095-1.ch001

Grefen, P., & Turetken, O. (2017). Advanced Business Process Management in Networked E-Business Scenarios. *International Journal of E-Business Research, 13*(4), 70–104. doi:10.4018/IJEBR.2017100105

Guasca, M., Van Broeck, A. M., & Vanneste, D. (2021). Tourism and the Social Reintegration of Colombian Ex-Combatants. In J. da Silva, Z. Breda, & F. Carbone (Eds.), *Role and Impact of Tourism in Peacebuilding and Conflict Transformation* (pp. 66-86). IGI Global. https://doi.org/10.4018/978-1-7998-5053-3.ch005

Haider, A., & Saetang, S. (2017). Strategic IT Alignment in Service Sector. In S. Rozenes & Y. Cohen (Eds.), *Handbook of Research on Strategic Alliances and Value Co-Creation in the Service Industry* (pp. 231–258). Hershey, PA: IGI Global. doi:10.4018/978-1-5225-2084-9.ch012

Hajilari, A. B., Ghadaksaz, M., & Fasghandis, G. S. (2017). Assessing Organizational Readiness for Implementing ERP System Using Fuzzy Expert System Approach. *International Journal of Enterprise Information Systems, 13*(1), 67–85. doi:10.4018/IJEIS.2017010105

Haldorai, A., Ramu, A., & Murugan, S. (2018). Social Aware Cognitive Radio Networks: Effectiveness of Social Networks as a Strategic Tool for Organizational Business Management. In H. Bansal, G. Shrivastava, G. Nguyen, & L. Stanciu (Eds.), *Social Network Analytics for Contemporary Business Organizations* (pp. 188–202). Hershey, PA: IGI Global. doi:10.4018/978-1-5225-5097-6.ch010

Hall, O. P. Jr. (2017). Social Media Driven Management Education. *International Journal of Knowledge-Based Organizations, 7*(2), 43–59. doi:10.4018/IJKBO.2017040104

Hanifah, H., Halim, H. A., Ahmad, N. H., & Vafaei-Zadeh, A. (2017). Innovation Culture as a Mediator Between Specific Human Capital and Innovation Performance Among Bumiputera SMEs in Malaysia. In N. Ahmad, T. Ramayah, H. Halim, & S. Rahman (Eds.), *Handbook of Research on Small and Medium Enterprises in Developing Countries* (pp. 261–279). Hershey, PA: IGI Global. doi:10.4018/978-1-5225-2165-5.ch012

Hartlieb, S., & Silvius, G. (2017). Handling Uncertainty in Project Management and Business Development: Similarities and Differences. In Y. Raydugin (Ed.), *Handbook of Research on Leveraging Risk and Uncertainties for Effective Project Management* (pp. 337–362). Hershey, PA: IGI Global. doi:10.4018/978-1-5225-1790-0.ch016

Hass, K. B. (2017). Living on the Edge: Managing Project Complexity. In Y. Raydugin (Ed.), *Handbook of Research on Leveraging Risk and Uncertainties for Effective Project Management* (pp. 177–201). Hershey, PA: IGI Global. doi:10.4018/978-1-5225-1790-0.ch009

Hawking, P., & Carmine Sellitto, C. (2017). Developing an Effective Strategy for Organizational Business Intelligence. In M. Tavana (Ed.), *Enterprise Information Systems and the Digitalization of Business Functions* (pp. 222–237). Hershey, PA: IGI Global. doi:10.4018/978-1-5225-2382-6.ch010

Hawking, P., & Sellitto, C. (2017). A Fast-Moving Consumer Goods Company and Business Intelligence Strategy Development. *International Journal of Enterprise Information Systems, 13*(2), 22–33. doi:10.4018/IJEIS.2017040102

Hawking, P., & Sellitto, C. (2017). Business Intelligence Strategy: Two Case Studies. *International Journal of Business Intelligence Research, 8*(2), 17–30. doi:10.4018/IJBIR.2017070102

Hee, W. J., Jalleh, G., Lai, H., & Lin, C. (2017). E-Commerce and IT Projects: Evaluation and Management Issues in Australian and Taiwanese Hospitals. *International Journal of Public Health Management and Ethics, 2*(1), 69–90. doi:10.4018/IJPHME.2017010104

Hernandez, A. A. (2018). Exploring the Factors to Green IT Adoption of SMEs in the Philippines. *Journal of Cases on Information Technology, 20*(2), 49–66. doi:10.4018/JCIT.2018040104

Hollman, A., Bickford, S., & Hollman, T. (2017). Cyber InSecurity: A Post-Mortem Attempt to Assess Cyber Problems from IT and Business Management Perspectives. *Journal of Cases on Information Technology, 19*(3), 42–70. doi:10.4018/JCIT.2017070104

Ibrahim, F., & Zainin, N. M. (2021). Exploring the Technological Impacts: The Case of Museums in Brunei Darussalam. *International Journal of Tourism and Hospitality Management in the Digital Age, 5*(1), 1–18. https://doi.org/10.4018/IJTHMDA.2021010101

Igbinakhase, I. (2017). Responsible and Sustainable Management Practices in Developing and Developed Business Environments. In Z. Fields (Ed.), *Collective Creativity for Responsible and Sustainable Business Practice* (pp. 180–207). Hershey, PA: IGI Global. doi:10.4018/978-1-5225-1823-5.ch010

Iwata, J. J., & Hoskins, R. G. (2017). Managing Indigenous Knowledge in Tanzania: A Business Perspective. In P. Jain & N. Mnjama (Eds.), *Managing Knowledge Resources and Records in Modern Organizations* (pp. 198–214). Hershey, PA: IGI Global. doi:10.4018/978-1-5225-1965-2.ch012

Jain, P. (2017). Ethical and Legal Issues in Knowledge Management Life-Cycle in Business. In P. Jain & N. Mnjama (Eds.), *Managing Knowledge Resources and Records in Modern Organizations* (pp. 82–101). Hershey, PA: IGI Global. doi:10.4018/978-1-5225-1965-2.ch006

James, S., & Hauli, E. (2017). Holistic Management Education at Tanzanian Rural Development Planning Institute. In N. Baporikar (Ed.), *Management Education for Global Leadership* (pp. 112–136). Hershey, PA: IGI Global. doi:10.4018/978-1-5225-1013-0.ch006

Janošková, M., Csikósová, A., & Čulková, K. (2018). Measurement of Company Performance as Part of Its Strategic Management. In R. Leon (Ed.), *Managerial Strategies for Business Sustainability During Turbulent Times* (pp. 309–335). Hershey, PA: IGI Global. doi:10.4018/978-1-5225-2716-9.ch017

Jean-Vasile, A., & Alecu, A. (2017). Theoretical and Practical Approaches in Understanding the Influences of Cost-Productivity-Profit Trinomial in Contemporary Enterprises. In A. Jean Vasile & D. Nicolò (Eds.), *Sustainable Entrepreneurship and Investments in the Green Economy* (pp. 28–62). Hershey, PA: IGI Global. doi:10.4018/978-1-5225-2075-7.ch002

Joia, L. A., & Correia, J. C. (2018). CIO Competencies From the IT Professional Perspective: Insights From Brazil. *Journal of Global Information Management, 26*(2), 74–103. doi:10.4018/JGIM.2018040104

Juma, A., & Mzera, N. (2017). Knowledge Management and Records Management and Competitive Advantage in Business. In P. Jain & N. Mnjama (Eds.), *Managing Knowledge Resources and Records in Modern Organizations* (pp. 15–28). Hershey, PA: IGI Global. doi:10.4018/978-1-5225-1965-2.ch002

K., I., & A, V. (2018). Monitoring and Auditing in the Cloud. In K. Munir (Ed.), *Cloud Computing Technologies for Green Enterprises* (pp. 318-350). Hershey, PA: IGI Global. https://doi.org/ doi:10.4018/978-1-5225-3038-1.ch013

Kabra, G., Ghosh, V., & Ramesh, A. (2018). Enterprise Integrated Business Process Management and Business Intelligence Framework for Business Process Sustainability. In A. Paul, D. Bhattacharyya, & S. Anand (Eds.), *Green Initiatives for Business Sustainability and Value Creation* (pp. 228–238). Hershey, PA: IGI Global. doi:10.4018/978-1-5225-2662-9.ch010

Kaoud, M. (2017). Investigation of Customer Knowledge Management: A Case Study Research. *International Journal of Service Science, Management, Engineering, and Technology*, 8(2), 12–22. doi:10.4018/IJSSMET.2017040102

Katuu, S. (2018). A Comparative Assessment of Enterprise Content Management Maturity Models. In N. Gwangwava & M. Mutingi (Eds.), *E-Manufacturing and E-Service Strategies in Contemporary Organizations* (pp. 93–118). Hershey, PA: IGI Global. doi:10.4018/978-1-5225-3628-4.ch005

Khan, M. Y., & Abir, T. (2022). The Role of Social Media Marketing in the Tourism and Hospitality Industry: A Conceptual Study on Bangladesh. In C. Ramos, S. Quinteiro, & A. Gonçalves (Eds.), *ICT as Innovator Between Tourism and Culture* (pp. 213–229). IGI Global. https://doi.org/10.4018/978-1-7998-8165-0.ch013

Kinnunen, S., Ylä-Kujala, A., Marttonen-Arola, S., Kärri, T., & Baglee, D. (2018). Internet of Things in Asset Management: Insights from Industrial Professionals and Academia. *International Journal of Service Science, Management, Engineering, and Technology*, 9(2), 104–119. doi:10.4018/IJSSMET.2018040105

Klein, A. Z., Sabino de Freitas, A., Machado, L., Freitas, J. C. Jr, Graziola, P. G. Jr, & Schlemmer, E. (2017). Virtual Worlds Applications for Management Education. In L. Tomei (Ed.), *Exploring the New Era of Technology-Infused Education* (pp. 279–299). Hershey, PA: IGI Global. doi:10.4018/978-1-5225-1709-2.ch017

Kővári, E., Saleh, M., & Steinbachné Hajmásy, G. (2022). The Impact of Corporate Digital Responsibility (CDR) on Internal Stakeholders' Satisfaction in Hungarian Upscale Hotels. In M. Valeri (Ed.), *New Governance and Management in Touristic Destinations* (pp. 35–51). IGI Global. https://doi.org/10.4018/978-1-6684-3889-3.ch003

Kożuch, B., & Jabłoński, A. (2017). Adopting the Concept of Business Models in Public Management. In M. Lewandowski & B. Kożuch (Eds.), *Public Sector Entrepreneurship and the Integration of Innovative Business Models* (pp. 10–46). Hershey, PA: IGI Global. doi:10.4018/978-1-5225-2215-7.ch002

Kumar, J., Adhikary, A., & Jha, A. (2017). Small Active Investors' Perceptions and Preferences Towards Tax Saving Mutual Fund Schemes in Eastern India: An Empirical Note. *International Journal of Asian Business and Information Management*, 8(2), 35–45. doi:10.4018/IJABIM.2017040103

Latusi, S., & Fissore, M. (2021). Pilgrimage Routes to Happiness: Comparing the Camino de Santiago and Via Francigena. In A. Perinotto, V. Mayer, & J. Soares (Eds.), *Rebuilding and Restructuring the Tourism Industry: Infusion of Happiness and Quality of Life* (pp. 157–182). IGI Global. https://doi.org/10.4018/978-1-7998-7239-9.ch008

Lavassani, K. M., & Movahedi, B. (2017). Applications Driven Information Systems: Beyond Networks toward Business Ecosystems. *International Journal of Innovation in the Digital Economy*, 8(1), 61–75. doi:10.4018/IJIDE.2017010104

Lazzareschi, V. H., & Brito, M. S. (2017). Strategic Information Management: Proposal of Business Project Model. In G. Jamil, A. Soares, & C. Pessoa (Eds.), *Handbook of Research on Information Management for Effective Logistics and Supply Chains* (pp. 59–88). Hershey, PA: IGI Global. doi:10.4018/978-1-5225-0973-8.ch004

Lechuga Sancho, M. P., & Martín Navarro, A. (2022). Evolution of the Literature on Social Responsibility in the Tourism Sector: A Systematic Literature Review. In G. Fernandes (Ed.), *Challenges and New Opportunities for Tourism in Inland Territories: Ecocultural Resources and Sustainable Initiatives* (pp. 169–186). IGI Global. https://doi.org/10.4018/978-1-7998-7339-6.ch010

Lederer, M., Kurz, M., & Lazarov, P. (2017). Usage and Suitability of Methods for Strategic Business Process Initiatives: A Multi Case Study Research. *International Journal of Productivity Management and Assessment Technologies*, 5(1), 40–51. doi:10.4018/IJPMAT.2017010103

Lee, I. (2017). A Social Enterprise Business Model and a Case Study of Pacific Community Ventures (PCV). In V. Potocan, M. Üngan, & Z. Nedelko (Eds.), *Handbook of Research on Managerial Solutions in Non-Profit Organizations* (pp. 182–204). Hershey, PA: IGI Global. doi:10.4018/978-1-5225-0731-4.ch009

Leon, L. A., Seal, K. C., Przasnyski, Z. H., & Wiedenman, I. (2017). Skills and Competencies Required for Jobs in Business Analytics: A Content Analysis of Job Advertisements Using Text Mining. *International Journal of Business Intelligence Research*, 8(1), 1–25. doi:10.4018/IJBIR.2017010101

Levy, C. L., & Elias, N. I. (2017). SOHO Users' Perceptions of Reliability and Continuity of Cloud-Based Services. In M. Moore (Ed.), *Cybersecurity Breaches and Issues Surrounding Online Threat Protection* (pp. 248–287). Hershey, PA: IGI Global. doi:10.4018/978-1-5225-1941-6.ch011

Levy, M. (2018). Change Management Serving Knowledge Management and Organizational Development: Reflections and Review. In N. Baporikar (Ed.), *Global Practices in Knowledge Management for Societal and Organizational Development* (pp. 256–270). Hershey, PA: IGI Global. doi:10.4018/978-1-5225-3009-1.ch012

Lewandowski, M. (2017). Public Organizations and Business Model Innovation: The Role of Public Service Design. In M. Lewandowski & B. Kożuch (Eds.), *Public Sector Entrepreneurship and the Integration of Innovative Business Models* (pp. 47–72). Hershey, PA: IGI Global. doi:10.4018/978-1-5225-2215-7.ch003

Lhannaoui, H., Kabbaj, M. I., & Bakkoury, Z. (2017). A Survey of Risk-Aware Business Process Modelling. *International Journal of Risk and Contingency Management*, 6(3), 14–26. doi:10.4018/IJRCM.2017070102

Li, J., Sun, W., Jiang, W., Yang, H., & Zhang, L. (2017). How the Nature of Exogenous Shocks and Crises Impact Company Performance?: The Effects of Industry Characteristics. *International Journal of Risk and Contingency Management*, 6(4), 40–55. doi:10.4018/IJRCM.2017100103

Lopez-Fernandez, M., Perez-Perez, M., Serrano-Bedia, A., & Cobo-Gonzalez, A. (2021). Small and Medium Tourism Enterprise Survival in Times of Crisis: "El Capricho de Gaudí. In D. Toubes & N. Araújo-Vila (Eds.), *Risk, Crisis, and Disaster Management in Small and Medium-Sized Tourism Enterprises* (pp. 103–129). IGI Global. doi:10.4018/978-1-7998-6996-2.ch005

Mahajan, A., Maidullah, S., & Hossain, M. R. (2022). Experience Toward Smart Tour Guide Apps in Travelling: An Analysis of Users' Reviews on Audio Odigos and Trip My Way. In R. Augusto Costa, F. Brandão, Z. Breda, & C. Costa (Eds.), *Planning and Managing the Experience Economy in Tourism* (pp. 255-273). IGI Global. https://doi.org/10.4018/978-1-7998-8775-1.ch014

Malega, P. (2017). Small and Medium Enterprises in the Slovak Republic: Status and Competitiveness of SMEs in the Global Markets and Possibilities of Optimization. In M. Vemić (Ed.), *Optimal Management Strategies in Small and Medium Enterprises* (pp. 102–124). Hershey, PA: IGI Global. doi:10.4018/978-1-5225-1949-2.ch006

Malewska, K. M. (2017). Intuition in Decision-Making on the Example of a Non-Profit Organization. In V. Potocan, M. Üngan, & Z. Nedelko (Eds.), *Handbook of Research on Managerial Solutions in Non-Profit Organizations* (pp. 378–399). Hershey, PA: IGI Global. doi:10.4018/978-1-5225-0731-4.ch018

Maroofi, F. (2017). Entrepreneurial Orientation and Organizational Learning Ability Analysis for Innovation and Firm Performance. In N. Baporikar (Ed.), *Innovation and Shifting Perspectives in Management Education* (pp. 144–165). Hershey, PA: IGI Global. doi:10.4018/978-1-5225-1019-2.ch007

Marques, M., Moleiro, D., Brito, T. M., & Marques, T. (2021). Customer Relationship Management as an Important Relationship Marketing Tool: The Case of the Hospitality Industry in Estoril Coast. In M. Dinis, L. Bonixe, S. Lamy, & Z. Breda (Eds.), Impact of New Media in Tourism (pp. 39-56). IGI Global. https://doi.org/doi:10.4018/978-1-7998-7095-1.ch003

Martins, P. V., & Zacarias, M. (2017). A Web-based Tool for Business Process Improvement. *International Journal of Web Portals*, *9*(2), 68–84. doi:10.4018/IJWP.2017070104

Matthies, B., & Coners, A. (2017). Exploring the Conceptual Nature of e-Business Projects. *Journal of Electronic Commerce in Organizations*, *15*(3), 33–63. doi:10.4018/JECO.2017070103

Mayer, V. F., Fraga, C. C., & Silva, L. C. (2021). Contributions of Neurosciences to Studies of Well-Being in Tourism. In A. Perinotto, V. Mayer, & J. Soares (Eds.), *Rebuilding and Restructuring the Tourism Industry: Infusion of Happiness and Quality of Life* (pp. 108–128). IGI Global. https://doi.org/10.4018/978-1-7998-7239-9.ch006

McKee, J. (2018). Architecture as a Tool to Solve Business Planning Problems. In M. Khosrow-Pour, D.B.A. (Ed.), Encyclopedia of Information Science and Technology, Fourth Edition (pp. 573-586). Hershey, PA: IGI Global. doi:10.4018/978-1-5225-2255-3.ch050

McMurray, A. J., Cross, J., & Caponecchia, C. (2018). The Risk Management Profession in Australia: Business Continuity Plan Practices. In N. Bajgoric (Ed.), *Always-On Enterprise Information Systems for Modern Organizations* (pp. 112–129). Hershey, PA: IGI Global. doi:10.4018/978-1-5225-3704-5.ch006

Meddah, I. H., & Belkadi, K. (2018). Mining Patterns Using Business Process Management. In R. Hamou (Ed.), *Handbook of Research on Biomimicry in Information Retrieval and Knowledge Management* (pp. 78–89). Hershey, PA: IGI Global. doi:10.4018/978-1-5225-3004-6.ch005

Melian, A. G., & Camprubí, R. (2021). The Accessibility of Museum Websites: The Case of Barcelona. In C. Eusébio, L. Teixeira, & M. Carneiro (Eds.), *ICT Tools and Applications for Accessible Tourism* (pp. 234–255). IGI Global. https://doi.org/10.4018/978-1-7998-6428-8.ch011

Mendes, L. (2017). TQM and Knowledge Management: An Integrated Approach Towards Tacit Knowledge Management. In D. Jaziri-Bouagina & G. Jamil (Eds.), *Handbook of Research on Tacit Knowledge Management for Organizational Success* (pp. 236–263). Hershey, PA: IGI Global. doi:10.4018/978-1-5225-2394-9.ch009

Menezes, V. D., & Cavagnaro, E. (2021). Communicating Sustainable Initiatives in the Hotel Industry: The Case of the Hotel Jakarta Amsterdam. In F. Brandão, Z. Breda, R. Costa, & C. Costa (Eds.), *Handbook of Research on the Role of Tourism in Achieving Sustainable Development Goals* (pp. 224-234). IGI Global. https://doi.org/10.4018/978-1-7998-5691-7.ch013

Menezes, V. D., & Cavagnaro, E. (2021). Communicating Sustainable Initiatives in the Hotel Industry: The Case of the Hotel Jakarta Amsterdam. In F. Brandão, Z. Breda, R. Costa, & C. Costa (Eds.), *Handbook of Research on the Role of Tourism in Achieving Sustainable Development Goals* (pp. 224-234). IGI Global. https://doi.org/10.4018/978-1-7998-5691-7.ch013

Mitas, O., Bastiaansen, M., & Boode, W. (2022). If You're Happy, I'm Happy: Emotion Contagion at a Tourist Information Center. In R. Augusto Costa, F. Brandão, Z. Breda, & C. Costa (Eds.), *Planning and Managing the Experience Economy in Tourism* (pp. 122-140). IGI Global. https://doi.org/10.4018/978-1-7998-8775-1.ch007

Mnjama, N. M. (2017). Preservation of Recorded Information in Public and Private Sector Organizations. In P. Jain & N. Mnjama (Eds.), *Managing Knowledge Resources and Records in Modern Organizations* (pp. 149–167). Hershey, PA: IGI Global. doi:10.4018/978-1-5225-1965-2.ch009

Mokoqama, M., & Fields, Z. (2017). Principles of Responsible Management Education (PRME): Call for Responsible Management Education. In Z. Fields (Ed.), *Collective Creativity for Responsible and Sustainable Business Practice* (pp. 229–241). Hershey, PA: IGI Global. doi:10.4018/978-1-5225-1823-5.ch012

Monteiro, A., Lopes, S., & Carbone, F. (2021). Academic Mobility: Bridging Tourism and Peace Education. In J. da Silva, Z. Breda, & F. Carbone (Eds.), *Role and Impact of Tourism in Peacebuilding and Conflict Transformation* (pp. 275-301). IGI Global. https://doi.org/10.4018/978-1-7998-5053-3.ch016

Muniapan, B. (2017). Philosophy and Management: The Relevance of Vedanta in Management. In P. Ordóñez de Pablos (Ed.), *Managerial Strategies and Solutions for Business Success in Asia* (pp. 124–139). Hershey, PA: IGI Global. doi:10.4018/978-1-5225-1886-0.ch007

Murad, S. E., & Dowaji, S. (2017). Using Value-Based Approach for Managing Cloud-Based Services. In A. Turuk, B. Sahoo, & S. Addya (Eds.), *Resource Management and Efficiency in Cloud Computing Environments* (pp. 33–60). Hershey, PA: IGI Global. doi:10.4018/978-1-5225-1721-4.ch002

Mutahar, A. M., Daud, N. M., Thurasamy, R., Isaac, O., & Abdulsalam, R. (2018). The Mediating of Perceived Usefulness and Perceived Ease of Use: The Case of Mobile Banking in Yemen. *International Journal of Technology Diffusion*, *9*(2), 21–40. doi:10.4018/IJTD.2018040102

Naidoo, V. (2017). E-Learning and Management Education at African Universities. In N. Baporikar (Ed.), *Management Education for Global Leadership* (pp. 181–201). Hershey, PA: IGI Global. doi:10.4018/978-1-5225-1013-0.ch009

Naidoo, V., & Igbinakhase, I. (2018). Opportunities and Challenges of Knowledge Retention in SMEs. In N. Baporikar (Ed.), *Knowledge Integration Strategies for Entrepreneurship and Sustainability* (pp. 70–94). Hershey, PA: IGI Global. doi:10.4018/978-1-5225-5115-7.ch004

Naumov, N., & Costandachi, G. (2021). Creativity and Entrepreneurship: Gastronomic Tourism in Mexico. In J. Soares (Ed.), *Innovation and Entrepreneurial Opportunities in Community Tourism* (pp. 90–108). IGI Global. https://doi.org/10.4018/978-1-7998-4855-4.ch006

Nayak, S., & Prabhu, N. (2017). Paradigm Shift in Management Education: Need for a Cross Functional Perspective. In N. Baporikar (Ed.), *Management Education for Global Leadership* (pp. 241–255). Hershey, PA: IGI Global. doi:10.4018/978-1-5225-1013-0.ch012

Nedelko, Z., & Potocan, V. (2017). Management Solutions in Non-Profit Organizations: Case of Slovenia. In V. Potocan, M. Üngan, & Z. Nedelko (Eds.), *Handbook of Research on Managerial Solutions in Non-Profit Organizations* (pp. 1–22). Hershey, PA: IGI Global. doi:10.4018/978-1-5225-0731-4.ch001

Nedelko, Z., & Potocan, V. (2017). Priority of Management Tools Utilization among Managers: International Comparison. In V. Wang (Ed.), *Encyclopedia of Strategic Leadership and Management* (pp. 1083–1094). Hershey, PA: IGI Global. doi:10.4018/978-1-5225-1049-9.ch075

Nedelko, Z., Raudeliūnienė, J., & Črešnar, R. (2018). Knowledge Dynamics in Supply Chain Management. In N. Baporikar (Ed.), *Knowledge Integration Strategies for Entrepreneurship and Sustainability* (pp. 150–166). Hershey, PA: IGI Global. doi:10.4018/978-1-5225-5115-7.ch008

Nguyen, H. T., & Hipsher, S. A. (2018). Innovation and Creativity Used by Private Sector Firms in a Resources-Constrained Environment. In S. Hipsher (Ed.), *Examining the Private Sector's Role in Wealth Creation and Poverty Reduction* (pp. 219–238). Hershey, PA: IGI Global. doi:10.4018/978-1-5225-3117-3.ch010

Obicci, P. A. (2017). Risk Sharing in a Partnership. In *Risk Management Strategies in Public-Private Partnerships* (pp. 115–152). Hershey, PA: IGI Global. doi:10.4018/978-1-5225-2503-5.ch004

Obidallah, W. J., & Raahemi, B. (2017). Managing Changes in Service Oriented Virtual Organizations: A Structural and Procedural Framework to Facilitate the Process of Change. *Journal of Electronic Commerce in Organizations*, *15*(1), 59–83. doi:10.4018/JECO.2017010104

Ojo, O. (2017). Impact of Innovation on the Entrepreneurial Success in Selected Business Enterprises in South-West Nigeria. *International Journal of Innovation in the Digital Economy*, *8*(2), 29–38. doi:10.4018/IJIDE.2017040103

Okdinawati, L., Simatupang, T. M., & Sunitiyoso, Y. (2017). Multi-Agent Reinforcement Learning for Value Co-Creation of Collaborative Transportation Management (CTM). *International Journal of Information Systems and Supply Chain Management*, *10*(3), 84–95. doi:10.4018/IJISSCM.2017070105

Olivera, V. A., & Carrillo, I. M. (2021). Organizational Culture: A Key Element for the Development of Mexican Micro and Small Tourist Companies. In J. Soares (Ed.), *Innovation and Entrepreneurial Opportunities in Community Tourism* (pp. 227–242). IGI Global. doi:10.4018/978-1-7998-4855-4.ch013

Ossorio, M. (2022). Corporate Museum Experiences in Enogastronomic Tourism. In R. Augusto Costa, F. Brandão, Z. Breda, & C. Costa (Eds.), Planning and Managing the Experience Economy in Tourism (pp. 107-121). IGI Global. https://doi.org/doi:10.4018/978-1-7998-8775-1.ch006

Ossorio, M. (2022). Enogastronomic Tourism in Times of Pandemic. In G. Fernandes (Ed.), *Challenges and New Opportunities for Tourism in Inland Territories: Ecocultural Resources and Sustainable Initiatives* (pp. 241–255). IGI Global. https://doi.org/10.4018/978-1-7998-7339-6.ch014

Özekici, Y. K. (2022). ICT as an Acculturative Agent and Its Role in the Tourism Context: Introduction, Acculturation Theory, Progress of the Acculturation Theory in Extant Literature. In C. Ramos, S. Quinteiro, & A. Gonçalves (Eds.), *ICT as Innovator Between Tourism and Culture* (pp. 42–66). IGI Global. https://doi.org/10.4018/978-1-7998-8165-0.ch004

Pal, K. (2018). Building High Quality Big Data-Based Applications in Supply Chains. In A. Kumar & S. Saurav (Eds.), *Supply Chain Management Strategies and Risk Assessment in Retail Environments* (pp. 1–24). Hershey, PA: IGI Global. doi:10.4018/978-1-5225-3056-5.ch001

Palos-Sanchez, P. R., & Correia, M. B. (2018). Perspectives of the Adoption of Cloud Computing in the Tourism Sector. In J. Rodrigues, C. Ramos, P. Cardoso, & C. Henriques (Eds.), *Handbook of Research on Technological Developments for Cultural Heritage and eTourism Applications* (pp. 377–400). Hershey, PA: IGI Global. doi:10.4018/978-1-5225-2927-9.ch018

Papadopoulou, G. (2021). Promoting Gender Equality and Women Empowerment in the Tourism Sector. In F. Brandão, Z. Breda, R. Costa, & C. Costa (Eds.), Handbook of Research on the Role of Tourism in Achieving Sustainable Development Goals (pp. 152-174). IGI Global. https://doi.org/ doi:10.4018/978-1-7998-5691-7.ch009

Papp-Váry, Á. F., & Tóth, T. Z. (2022). Analysis of Budapest as a Film Tourism Destination. In R. Baleiro & R. Pereira (Eds.), *Global Perspectives on Literary Tourism and Film-Induced Tourism* (pp. 257-279). IGI Global. https://doi.org/10.4018/978-1-7998-8262-6.ch014

Patiño, B. E. (2017). New Generation Management by Convergence and Individual Identity: A Systemic and Human-Oriented Approach. In N. Baporikar (Ed.), *Innovation and Shifting Perspectives in Management Education* (pp. 119–143). Hershey, PA: IGI Global. doi:10.4018/978-1-5225-1019-2.ch006

Patro, C. S. (2021). Digital Tourism: Influence of E-Marketing Technology. In M. Dinis, L. Bonixe, S. Lamy, & Z. Breda (Eds.), *Impact of New Media in Tourism* (pp. 234-254). IGI Global. https://doi.org/10.4018/978-1-7998-7095-1.ch014

Pawliczek, A., & Rössler, M. (2017). Knowledge of Management Tools and Systems in SMEs: Knowledge Transfer in Management. In A. Bencsik (Ed.), *Knowledge Management Initiatives and Strategies in Small and Medium Enterprises* (pp. 180–203). Hershey, PA: IGI Global. doi:10.4018/978-1-5225-1642-2.ch009

Pejic-Bach, M., Omazic, M. A., Aleksic, A., & Zoroja, J. (2018). Knowledge-Based Decision Making: A Multi-Case Analysis. In R. Leon (Ed.), *Managerial Strategies for Business Sustainability During Turbulent Times* (pp. 160–184). Hershey, PA: IGI Global. doi:10.4018/978-1-5225-2716-9.ch009

Perano, M., Hysa, X., & Calabrese, M. (2018). Strategic Planning, Cultural Context, and Business Continuity Management: Business Cases in the City of Shkoder. In A. Presenza & L. Sheehan (Eds.), *Geopolitics and Strategic Management in the Global Economy* (pp. 57–77). Hershey, PA: IGI Global. doi:10.4018/978-1-5225-2673-5.ch004

Pereira, R., Mira da Silva, M., & Lapão, L. V. (2017). IT Governance Maturity Patterns in Portuguese Healthcare. In S. De Haes & W. Van Grembergen (Eds.), *Strategic IT Governance and Alignment in Business Settings* (pp. 24–52). Hershey, PA: IGI Global. doi:10.4018/978-1-5225-0861-8.ch002

Pérez-Uribe, R. I., Torres, D. A., Jurado, S. P., & Prada, D. M. (2018). Cloud Tools for the Development of Project Management in SMEs. In R. Perez-Uribe, C. Salcedo-Perez, & D. Ocampo-Guzman (Eds.), *Handbook of Research on Intrapreneurship and Organizational Sustainability in SMEs* (pp. 95–120). Hershey, PA: IGI Global. doi:10.4018/978-1-5225-3543-0.ch005

Petrisor, I., & Cozmiuc, D. (2017). Global Supply Chain Management Organization at Siemens in the Advent of Industry 4.0. In L. Saglietto & C. Cezanne (Eds.), *Global Intermediation and Logistics Service Providers* (pp. 123–142). Hershey, PA: IGI Global. doi:10.4018/978-1-5225-2133-4.ch007

Pierce, J. M., Velliaris, D. M., & Edwards, J. (2017). A Living Case Study: A Journey Not a Destination. In N. Silton (Ed.), *Exploring the Benefits of Creativity in Education, Media, and the Arts* (pp. 158–178). Hershey, PA: IGI Global. doi:10.4018/978-1-5225-0504-4.ch008

Pipia, S., & Pipia, S. (2021). Challenges of Religious Tourism in the Conflict Region: An Example of Jerusalem. In E. Alaverdov & M. Bari (Eds.), *Global Development of Religious Tourism* (pp. 135-148). IGI Global. https://doi.org/10.4018/978-1-7998-5792-1.ch009

Poulaki, P., Kritikos, A., Vasilakis, N., & Valeri, M. (2022). The Contribution of Female Creativity to the Development of Gastronomic Tourism in Greece: The Case of the Island of Naxos in the South Aegean Region. In M. Valeri (Ed.), *New Governance and Management in Touristic Destinations* (pp. 246–258). IGI Global. https://doi.org/10.4018/978-1-6684-3889-3.ch015

Radosavljevic, M., & Andjelkovic, A. (2017). Multi-Criteria Decision Making Approach for Choosing Business Process for the Improvement: Upgrading of the Six Sigma Methodology. In J. Stanković, P. Delias, S. Marinković, & S. Rochhia (Eds.), *Tools and Techniques for Economic Decision Analysis* (pp. 225–247). Hershey, PA: IGI Global. doi:10.4018/978-1-5225-0959-2.ch011

Radovic, V. M. (2017). Corporate Sustainability and Responsibility and Disaster Risk Reduction: A Serbian Overview. In M. Camilleri (Ed.), *CSR 2.0 and the New Era of Corporate Citizenship* (pp. 147–164). Hershey, PA: IGI Global. doi:10.4018/978-1-5225-1842-6.ch008

Raghunath, K. M., Devi, S. L., & Patro, C. S. (2018). Impact of Risk Assessment Models on Risk Factors: A Holistic Outlook. In K. Strang, M. Korstanje, & N. Vajjhala (Eds.), *Research, Practices, and Innovations in Global Risk and Contingency Management* (pp. 134–153). Hershey, PA: IGI Global. doi:10.4018/978-1-5225-4754-9.ch008

Raman, A., & Goyal, D. P. (2017). Extending IMPLEMENT Framework for Enterprise Information Systems Implementation to Information System Innovation. In M. Tavana (Ed.), *Enterprise Information Systems and the Digitalization of Business Functions* (pp. 137–177). Hershey, PA: IGI Global. doi:10.4018/978-1-5225-2382-6.ch007

Rao, Y., & Zhang, Y. (2017). The Construction and Development of Academic Library Digital Special Subject Databases. In L. Ruan, Q. Zhu, & Y. Ye (Eds.), *Academic Library Development and Administration in China* (pp. 163–183). Hershey, PA: IGI Global. doi:10.4018/978-1-5225-0550-1.ch010

Ravasan, A. Z., Mohammadi, M. M., & Hamidi, H. (2018). An Investigation Into the Critical Success Factors of Implementing Information Technology Service Management Frameworks. In K. Jakobs (Ed.), *Corporate and Global Standardization Initiatives in Contemporary Society* (pp. 200–218). Hershey, PA: IGI Global. doi:10.4018/978-1-5225-5320-5.ch009

Rezaie, S., Mirabedini, S. J., & Abtahi, A. (2018). Designing a Model for Implementation of Business Intelligence in the Banking Industry. *International Journal of Enterprise Information Systems*, *14*(1), 77–103. doi:10.4018/IJEIS.2018010105

Richards, V., Matthews, N., Williams, O. J., & Khan, Z. (2021). The Challenges of Accessible Tourism Information Systems for Tourists With Vision Impairment: Sensory Communications Beyond the Screen. In C. Eusébio, L. Teixeira, & M. Carneiro (Eds.), *ICT Tools and Applications for Accessible Tourism* (pp. 26–54). IGI Global. https://doi.org/10.4018/978-1-7998-6428-8.ch002

Rodrigues de Souza Neto, V., & Marques, O. (2021). Rural Tourism Fostering Welfare Through Sustainable Development: A Conceptual Approach. In A. Perinotto, V. Mayer, & J. Soares (Eds.), *Rebuilding and Restructuring the Tourism Industry: Infusion of Happiness and Quality of Life* (pp. 38–57). IGI Global. https://doi.org/10.4018/978-1-7998-7239-9.ch003

Romano, L., Grimaldi, R., & Colasuonno, F. S. (2017). Demand Management as a Success Factor in Project Portfolio Management. In L. Romano (Ed.), *Project Portfolio Management Strategies for Effective Organizational Operations* (pp. 202–219). Hershey, PA: IGI Global. doi:10.4018/978-1-5225-2151-8.ch008

Rubio-Escuderos, L., & García-Andreu, H. (2021). Competitiveness Factors of Accessible Tourism E-Travel Agencies. In C. Eusébio, L. Teixeira, & M. Carneiro (Eds.), *ICT Tools and Applications for Accessible Tourism* (pp. 196–217). IGI Global. https://doi.org/10.4018/978-1-7998-6428-8.ch009

Rucci, A. C., Porto, N., Darcy, S., & Becka, L. (2021). Smart and Accessible Cities?: Not Always – The Case for Accessible Tourism Initiatives in Buenos Aries and Sydney. In C. Eusébio, L. Teixeira, & M. Carneiro (Eds.), *ICT Tools and Applications for Accessible Tourism* (pp. 115–145). IGI Global. https://doi.org/10.4018/978-1-7998-6428-8.ch006

Ruhi, U. (2018). Towards an Interdisciplinary Socio-Technical Definition of Virtual Communities. In M. Khosrow-Pour, D.B.A. (Ed.), Encyclopedia of Information Science and Technology, Fourth Edition (pp. 4278-4295). Hershey, PA: IGI Global. doi:10.4018/978-1-5225-2255-3.ch371

Ryan, L., Catena, M., Ros, P., & Stephens, S. (2021). Designing Entrepreneurial Ecosystems to Support Resource Management in the Tourism Industry. In V. Costa, A. Moura, & M. Mira (Eds.), *Handbook of Research on Human Capital and People Management in the Tourism Industry* (pp. 265–281). IGI Global. https://doi.org/10.4018/978-1-7998-4318-4.ch013

Sabuncu, I. (2021). Understanding Tourist Perceptions and Expectations During Pandemic Through Social Media Big Data. In M. Demir, A. Dalgıç, & F. Ergen (Eds.), *Handbook of Research on the Impacts and Implications of COVID-19 on the Tourism Industry* (pp. 330–350). IGI Global. https://doi.org/10.4018/978-1-7998-8231-2.ch016

Safari, M. R., & Jiang, Q. (2018). The Theory and Practice of IT Governance Maturity and Strategies Alignment: Evidence From Banking Industry. *Journal of Global Information Management, 26*(2), 127–146. doi:10.4018/JGIM.2018040106

Sahoo, J., Pati, B., & Mohanty, B. (2017). Knowledge Management as an Academic Discipline: An Assessment. In B. Gunjal (Ed.), *Managing Knowledge and Scholarly Assets in Academic Libraries* (pp. 99–126). Hershey, PA: IGI Global. doi:10.4018/978-1-5225-1741-2.ch005

Saini, D. (2017). Relevance of Teaching Values and Ethics in Management Education. In N. Baporikar (Ed.), *Management Education for Global Leadership* (pp. 90–111). Hershey, PA: IGI Global. doi:10.4018/978-1-5225-1013-0.ch005

Sambhanthan, A. (2017). Assessing and Benchmarking Sustainability in Organisations: An Integrated Conceptual Model. *International Journal of Systems and Service-Oriented Engineering, 7*(4), 22–43. doi:10.4018/IJSSOE.2017100102

Sambhanthan, A., & Potdar, V. (2017). A Study of the Parameters Impacting Sustainability in Information Technology Organizations. *International Journal of Knowledge-Based Organizations, 7*(3), 27–39. doi:10.4018/IJKBO.2017070103

Sánchez-Fernández, M. D., & Manríquez, M. R. (2018). The Entrepreneurial Spirit Based on Social Values: The Digital Generation. In P. Isaias & L. Carvalho (Eds.), *User Innovation and the Entrepreneurship Phenomenon in the Digital Economy* (pp. 173–193). Hershey, PA: IGI Global. doi:10.4018/978-1-5225-2826-5.ch009

Sanchez-Ruiz, L., & Blanco, B. (2017). Process Management for SMEs: Barriers, Enablers, and Benefits. In M. Vemić (Ed.), *Optimal Management Strategies in Small and Medium Enterprises* (pp. 293–319). Hershey, PA: IGI Global. doi:10.4018/978-1-5225-1949-2.ch014

Sanz, L. F., Gómez-Pérez, J., & Castillo-Martinez, A. (2018). Analysis of the European ICT Competence Frameworks. In V. Ahuja & S. Rathore (Eds.), *Multidisciplinary Perspectives on Human Capital and Information Technology Professionals* (pp. 225–245). Hershey, PA: IGI Global. doi:10.4018/978-1-5225-5297-0.ch012

Sarvepalli, A., & Godin, J. (2017). Business Process Management in the Classroom. *Journal of Cases on Information Technology*, *19*(2), 17–28. doi:10.4018/JCIT.2017040102

Saxena, G. G., & Saxena, A. (2021). Host Community Role in Medical Tourism Development. In M. Singh & S. Kumaran (Eds.), *Growth of the Medical Tourism Industry and Its Impact on Society: Emerging Research and Opportunities* (pp. 105–127). IGI Global. https://doi.org/10.4018/978-1-7998-3427-4.ch006

Saygili, E. E., Ozturkoglu, Y., & Kocakulah, M. C. (2017). End Users' Perceptions of Critical Success Factors in ERP Applications. *International Journal of Enterprise Information Systems*, *13*(4), 58–75. doi:10.4018/IJEIS.2017100104

Saygili, E. E., & Saygili, A. T. (2017). Contemporary Issues in Enterprise Information Systems: A Critical Review of CSFs in ERP Implementations. In M. Tavana (Ed.), *Enterprise Information Systems and the Digitalization of Business Functions* (pp. 120–136). Hershey, PA: IGI Global. doi:10.4018/978-1-5225-2382-6.ch006

Schwaiger, K. M., & Zehrer, A. (2021). The COVID-19 Pandemic and Organizational Resilience in Hospitality Family Firms: A Qualitative Approach. In A. Zehrer, G. Glowka, K. Schwaiger, & V. Ranacher-Lackner (Eds.), *Resiliency Models and Addressing Future Risks for Family Firms in the Tourism Industry* (pp. 32–49). IGI Global. https://doi.org/10.4018/978-1-7998-7352-5.ch002

Scott, N., & Campos, A. C. (2022). Cognitive Science of Tourism Experiences. In R. Augusto Costa, F. Brandão, Z. Breda, & C. Costa (Eds.), Planning and Managing the Experience Economy in Tourism (pp. 1-21). IGI Global. https://doi.org/ doi:10.4018/978-1-7998-8775-1.ch001

Seidenstricker, S., & Antonino, A. (2018). Business Model Innovation-Oriented Technology Management for Emergent Technologies. In M. Khosrow-Pour, D.B.A. (Ed.), Encyclopedia of Information Science and Technology, Fourth Edition (pp. 4560-4569). Hershey, PA: IGI Global. doi:10.4018/978-1-5225-2255-3.ch396

Selvi, M. S. (2021). Changes in Tourism Sales and Marketing Post COVID-19. In M. Demir, A. Dalgıç, & F. Ergen (Eds.), *Handbook of Research on the Impacts and Implications of COVID-19 on the Tourism Industry* (pp. 437–460). IGI Global. doi:10.4018/978-1-7998-8231-2.ch021

Senaratne, S., & Gunarathne, A. D. (2017). Excellence Perspective for Management Education from a Global Accountants' Hub in Asia. In N. Baporikar (Ed.), *Management Education for Global Leadership* (pp. 158–180). Hershey, PA: IGI Global. doi:10.4018/978-1-5225-1013-0.ch008

Sensuse, D. I., & Cahyaningsih, E. (2018). Knowledge Management Models: A Summative Review. *International Journal of Information Systems in the Service Sector*, *10*(1), 71–100. doi:10.4018/IJISSS.2018010105

Seth, M., Goyal, D., & Kiran, R. (2017). Diminution of Impediments in Implementation of Supply Chain Management Information System for Enhancing its Effectiveness in Indian Automobile Industry. *Journal of Global Information Management*, *25*(3), 1–20. doi:10.4018/JGIM.2017070101

Seyal, A. H., & Rahman, M. N. (2017). Investigating Impact of Inter-Organizational Factors in Measuring ERP Systems Success: Bruneian Perspectives. In M. Tavana (Ed.), *Enterprise Information Systems and the Digitalization of Business Functions* (pp. 178–204). Hershey, PA: IGI Global. doi:10.4018/978-1-5225-2382-6.ch008

Shaqrah, A. A. (2018). Analyzing Business Intelligence Systems Based on 7s Model of McKinsey. *International Journal of Business Intelligence Research*, *9*(1), 53–63. doi:10.4018/IJBIR.2018010104

Sharma, A. J. (2017). Enhancing Sustainability through Experiential Learning in Management Education. In N. Baporikar (Ed.), *Management Education for Global Leadership* (pp. 256–274). Hershey, PA: IGI Global. doi:10.4018/978-1-5225-1013-0.ch013

Shetty, K. P. (2017). Responsible Global Leadership: Ethical Challenges in Management Education. In N. Baporikar (Ed.), *Innovation and Shifting Perspectives in Management Education* (pp. 194–223). Hershey, PA: IGI Global. doi:10.4018/978-1-5225-1019-2.ch009

Sinthupundaja, J., & Kohda, Y. (2017). Effects of Corporate Social Responsibility and Creating Shared Value on Sustainability. *International Journal of Sustainable Entrepreneurship and Corporate Social Responsibility*, *2*(1), 27–38. doi:10.4018/IJSECSR.2017010103

Škarica, I., & Hrgović, A. V. (2018). Implementation of Total Quality Management Principles in Public Health Institutes in the Republic of Croatia. *International Journal of Productivity Management and Assessment Technologies*, *6*(1), 1–16. doi:10.4018/IJPMAT.2018010101

Skokic, V. (2021). How Small Hotel Owners Practice Resilience: Longitudinal Study Among Small Family Hotels in Croatia. In A. Zehrer, G. Glowka, K. Schwaiger, & V. Ranacher-Lackner (Eds.), *Resiliency Models and Addressing Future Risks for Family Firms in the Tourism Industry* (pp. 50–73). IGI Global. doi:10.4018/978-1-7998-7352-5.ch003

Smuts, H., Kotzé, P., Van der Merwe, A., & Loock, M. (2017). Framework for Managing Shared Knowledge in an Information Systems Outsourcing Context. *International Journal of Knowledge Management*, *13*(4), 1–30. doi:10.4018/IJKM.2017100101

Sousa, M. J., Cruz, R., Dias, I., & Caracol, C. (2017). Information Management Systems in the Supply Chain. In G. Jamil, A. Soares, & C. Pessoa (Eds.), *Handbook of Research on Information Management for Effective Logistics and Supply Chains* (pp. 469–485). Hershey, PA: IGI Global. doi:10.4018/978-1-5225-0973-8.ch025

Spremic, M., Turulja, L., & Bajgoric, N. (2018). Two Approaches in Assessing Business Continuity Management Attitudes in the Organizational Context. In N. Bajgoric (Ed.), *Always-On Enterprise Information Systems for Modern Organizations* (pp. 159–183). Hershey, PA: IGI Global. doi:10.4018/978-1-5225-3704-5.ch008

Steenkamp, A. L. (2018). Some Insights in Computer Science and Information Technology. In *Examining the Changing Role of Supervision in Doctoral Research Projects: Emerging Research and Opportunities* (pp. 113–133). Hershey, PA: IGI Global. doi:10.4018/978-1-5225-2610-0.ch005

Stipanović, C., Rudan, E., & Zubović, V. (2022). Reaching the New Tourist Through Creativity: Sustainable Development Challenges in Croatian Coastal Towns. In M. Valeri (Ed.), *New Governance and Management in Touristic Destinations* (pp. 231–245). IGI Global. https://doi.org/10.4018/978-1-6684-3889-3.ch014

Tabach, A., & Croteau, A. (2017). Configurations of Information Technology Governance Practices and Business Unit Performance. *International Journal of IT/Business Alignment and Governance*, *8*(2), 1–27. doi:10.4018/IJITBAG.2017070101

Talaue, G. M., & Iqbal, T. (2017). Assessment of e-Business Mode of Selected Private Universities in the Philippines and Pakistan. *International Journal of Online Marketing*, *7*(4), 63–77. doi:10.4018/IJOM.2017100105

Tam, G. C. (2017). Project Manager Sustainability Competence. In *Managerial Strategies and Green Solutions for Project Sustainability* (pp. 178–207). Hershey, PA: IGI Global. doi:10.4018/978-1-5225-2371-0.ch008

Tambo, T. (2018). Fashion Retail Innovation: About Context, Antecedents, and Outcome in Technological Change Projects. In I. Management Association (Ed.), Fashion and Textiles: Breakthroughs in Research and Practice (pp. 233-260). Hershey, PA: IGI Global. https://doi.org/ doi:10.4018/978-1-5225-3432-7.ch010

Tantau, A. D., & Frățilă, L. C. (2018). Information and Management System for Renewable Energy Business. In *Entrepreneurship and Business Development in the Renewable Energy Sector* (pp. 200–244). Hershey, PA: IGI Global. doi:10.4018/978-1-5225-3625-3.ch006

Teixeira, N., Pardal, P. N., & Rafael, B. G. (2018). Internationalization, Financial Performance, and Organizational Challenges: A Success Case in Portugal. In L. Carvalho (Ed.), *Handbook of Research on Entrepreneurial Ecosystems and Social Dynamics in a Globalized World* (pp. 379–423). Hershey, PA: IGI Global. doi:10.4018/978-1-5225-3525-6.ch017

Teixeira, P., Teixeira, L., Eusébio, C., Silva, S., & Teixeira, A. (2021). The Impact of ICTs on Accessible Tourism: Evidence Based on a Systematic Literature Review. In C. Eusébio, L. Teixeira, & M. Carneiro (Eds.), *ICT Tools and Applications for Accessible Tourism* (pp. 1–25). IGI Global. doi:10.4018/978-1-7998-6428-8.ch001

Trad, A., & Kalpić, D. (2018). The Business Transformation Framework, Agile Project and Change Management. In M. Khosrow-Pour, D.B.A. (Ed.), Encyclopedia of Information Science and Technology, Fourth Edition (pp. 620-635). Hershey, PA: IGI Global. https://doi.org/ doi:10.4018/978-1-5225-2255-3.ch054

Trad, A., & Kalpić, D. (2018). The Business Transformation and Enterprise Architecture Framework: The Financial Engineering E-Risk Management and E-Law Integration. In B. Sergi, F. Fidanoski, M. Ziolo, & V. Naumovski (Eds.), *Regaining Global Stability After the Financial Crisis* (pp. 46–65). Hershey, PA: IGI Global. doi:10.4018/978-1-5225-4026-7.ch003

Trengereid, V. (2022). Conditions of Network Engagement: The Quest for a Common Good. In R. Augusto Costa, F. Brandão, Z. Breda, & C. Costa (Eds.), *Planning and Managing the Experience Economy in Tourism* (pp. 69-84). IGI Global. https://doi.org/10.4018/978-1-7998-8775-1.ch004

Turulja, L., & Bajgoric, N. (2018). Business Continuity and Information Systems: A Systematic Literature Review. In N. Bajgoric (Ed.), *Always-On Enterprise Information Systems for Modern Organizations* (pp. 60–87). Hershey, PA: IGI Global. doi:10.4018/978-1-5225-3704-5.ch004

Vargas-Hernández, J. G. (2017). Professional Integrity in Business Management Education. In N. Baporikar (Ed.), *Management Education for Global Leadership* (pp. 70–89). Hershey, PA: IGI Global. doi:10.4018/978-1-5225-1013-0.ch004

Varnacı Uzun, F. (2021). The Destination Preferences of Foreign Tourists During the COVID-19 Pandemic and Attitudes Towards: Marmaris, Turkey. In M. Demir, A. Dalgıç, & F. Ergen (Eds.), *Handbook of Research on the Impacts and Implications of COVID-19 on the Tourism Industry* (pp. 285–306). IGI Global. https://doi. org/10.4018/978-1-7998-8231-2.ch014

Vasista, T. G., & AlAbdullatif, A. M. (2017). Role of Electronic Customer Relationship Management in Demand Chain Management: A Predictive Analytic Approach. *International Journal of Information Systems and Supply Chain Management, 10*(1), 53–67. doi:10.4018/IJISSCM.2017010104

Vieru, D., & Bourdeau, S. (2017). Survival in the Digital Era: A Digital Competence-Based Multi-Case Study in the Canadian SME Clothing Industry. *International Journal of Social and Organizational Dynamics in IT, 6*(1), 17–34. doi:10.4018/ IJSODIT.2017010102

Vijayan, G., & Kamarulzaman, N. H. (2017). An Introduction to Sustainable Supply Chain Management and Business Implications. In M. Khan, M. Hussain, & M. Ajmal (Eds.), *Green Supply Chain Management for Sustainable Business Practice* (pp. 27–50). Hershey, PA: IGI Global. doi:10.4018/978-1-5225-0635-5.ch002

Vlachvei, A., & Notta, O. (2017). Firm Competitiveness: Theories, Evidence, and Measurement. In A. Vlachvei, O. Notta, K. Karantininis, & N. Tsounis (Eds.), *Factors Affecting Firm Competitiveness and Performance in the Modern Business World* (pp. 1–42). Hershey, PA: IGI Global. doi:10.4018/978-1-5225-0843-4.ch001

Wang, C., Schofield, M., Li, X., & Ou, X. (2017). Do Chinese Students in Public and Private Higher Education Institutes Perform at Different Level in One of the Leadership Skills: Critical Thinking?: An Exploratory Comparison. In V. Wang (Ed.), *Encyclopedia of Strategic Leadership and Management* (pp. 160–181). Hershey, PA: IGI Global. doi:10.4018/978-1-5225-1049-9.ch013

Wang, J. (2017). Multi-Agent based Production Management Decision System Modelling for the Textile Enterprise. *Journal of Global Information Management, 25*(4), 1–15. doi:10.4018/JGIM.2017100101

Wiedemann, A., & Gewald, H. (2017). Examining Cross-Domain Alignment: The Correlation of Business Strategy, IT Management, and IT Business Value. *International Journal of IT/Business Alignment and Governance, 8*(1), 17–31. doi:10.4018/IJITBAG.2017010102

Wolf, R., & Thiel, M. (2018). Advancing Global Business Ethics in China: Reducing Poverty Through Human and Social Welfare. In S. Hipsher (Ed.), *Examining the Private Sector's Role in Wealth Creation and Poverty Reduction* (pp. 67–84). Hershey, PA: IGI Global. doi:10.4018/978-1-5225-3117-3.ch004

Yablonsky, S. (2018). Innovation Platforms: Data and Analytics Platforms. In *Multi-Sided Platforms (MSPs) and Sharing Strategies in the Digital Economy: Emerging Research and Opportunities* (pp. 72–95). Hershey, PA: IGI Global. doi:10.4018/978-1-5225-5457-8.ch003

Yaşar, B. (2021). The Impact of COVID-19 on Volatility of Tourism Stocks: Evidence From BIST Tourism Index. In M. Demir, A. Dalgıç, & F. Ergen (Eds.), *Handbook of Research on the Impacts and Implications of COVID-19 on the Tourism Industry* (pp. 23–44). IGI Global. https://doi.org/10.4018/978-1-7998-8231-2.ch002

Yusoff, A., Ahmad, N. H., & Halim, H. A. (2017). Agropreneurship among Gen Y in Malaysia: The Role of Academic Institutions. In N. Ahmad, T. Ramayah, H. Halim, & S. Rahman (Eds.), *Handbook of Research on Small and Medium Enterprises in Developing Countries* (pp. 23–47). Hershey, PA: IGI Global. doi:10.4018/978-1-5225-2165-5.ch002

Zacher, D., & Pechlaner, H. (2021). Resilience as an Opportunity Approach: Challenges and Perspectives for Private Sector Participation on a Community Level. In A. Zehrer, G. Glowka, K. Schwaiger, & V. Ranacher-Lackner (Eds.), *Resiliency Models and Addressing Future Risks for Family Firms in the Tourism Industry* (pp. 75–102). IGI Global. https://doi.org/10.4018/978-1-7998-7352-5.ch004

Zanin, F., Comuzzi, E., & Costantini, A. (2018). The Effect of Business Strategy and Stock Market Listing on the Use of Risk Assessment Tools. In *Management Control Systems in Complex Settings: Emerging Research and Opportunities* (pp. 145–168). Hershey, PA: IGI Global. doi:10.4018/978-1-5225-3987-2.ch007

Zgheib, P. W. (2017). Corporate Innovation and Intrapreneurship in the Middle East. In P. Zgheib (Ed.), *Entrepreneurship and Business Innovation in the Middle East* (pp. 37–56). Hershey, PA: IGI Global. doi:10.4018/978-1-5225-2066-5.ch003

About the Contributors

Latifa Dekhici is an associate professor in computer sciences and vice dean of external relations in mathematics and computer science faculty in the university of sciences and technology of Oran; and a researcher in LDREI, Smart Grid Developement laboratory in the Higher School of Electrical Engineering and Energetic of Oran. Her research interests include power dispatch, power system design, healthcare scheduling and green optimization as well as optimization methods especially meta-heuristic. DEKHICI has been a member of Inside Project (Inclusion of Students With impairements in Distance Education) in 2023 and a Responsable of Digitalisation Strategy Office in her university. As a gamifier and social responsability trainer, she partipated in many sustainability; digitalization; accessibilty and inclusivity activities.

Khaled Guerraiche received his Bachelor degree in Electrical Engineering from the Institute of Electrical Engineering at the University of Science and Technology of Oran (USTOMB) in 2004, his Master degree in Electrical Engineering from the Institute of Electrical Engineering at the University of Science and Technology of Oran (USTO) in 2008, and his Ph.D. from the University of Science and Technology of Oran (USTO) in 2016. He is currently an Assistant Professor at the Higher School of Electrical and Energetic engineering in Oran, Algeria. His research interests include the design,reconfiguration, planning, and economics of electrical energy systems, as well as optimization theory and its applications in smart grids.

Rabia Azzemou is a professor and researcher in the field of management, specializing in lean manufacturing. She obtained her doctorate from the University of Oran Ahmed Ben Ahmed. With over 15 years of experience in higher education, she currently heads the Institute of Applied Sciences and Techniques (ISTA), where she teaches business management to undergraduate students and Lean Management to professional Master's students. Her research focuses on the application of lean manufacturing, a managerial approach aimed at optimizing production processes by eliminating waste and maximizing value for the customer. Her research explores the practical applications of this methodology in the specific context of Algerian businesses, where she seeks to improve operational efficiency and competitiveness in the global market. In addition to her work on lean manufacturing, Pr. Azzemou is also interested in alternative economic models focused on sustainability. Convinced of the growing importance of corporate social and environmental responsibility, she explores potential synergies between these models and lean manufacturing, thereby seeking to promote more environmentally friendly and socially responsible business practices.

Jihène Jlassi Mabrouk is an assistant professor of science in logistics and transport at the Higher Institute of Industrial Management of Sfax (ISGI Sfax_ University of Sfax). She got her PhD in Industrial Engineering from the Paris 8 University. She was also member of scientific committees of many conferences. In addition, she served as a reviewer for several referred conferences and journals in her field. As a member of OLID research lab, her main research interests are logistics and optimization. She has published many papers in international journals and presented several communications.

***

Khadidja Belbachir is a Teacher, Researcher, and Lecturer at the University of Science and Technology of Oran Mohammed Boudiaf in Algeria. With a Doctorate in Computer Science, she has been working in the field of Databases since 2004. Her main areas of research include Spatial Geographic Systems, Distributed Databases, and Text Mining. Dr. Belbachir's work focuses on analyzing, managing, and visualizing geospatial information, enhancing the efficiency of distributed databases, and extracting valuable insights from textual data. She has published extensively and is dedicated to education and mentoring. Her contributions advance the field of computer science and inspire the next generation of researchers

Karima Belmabrouk received her engineering degree in 1998 and her magister degree in 2006 and her Phd degree in 2017 from the University of Science and Technology of Oran, USTO-MB. Since December 2006, she is an associate professor and researcher in the computer science department of the USTO-MB. Her research interests are based on agent-based modeling and simulation, Web services composition, ontology and semantic Web as well as planning in artificial intelligence. Currently, she is working on cybersecurity and supply chain optimization.

Amal Boumedjout earned her Ph.D. degree from USTO-MB University in 2016 in Networking domain. Her researches focused on routing Protocols and Cross layer approach. Currently she focuses her researches on internet of thing; artificial intelligence and CyberSecurity. In addition, she is a head of department and full-time teacher at the National polytechnical School of Oran Maurice Audin (ENPO-MA) in Algeria. Amal Boumedjout is also a Cisco Teacher she create several CCNA Classes in CCNA1: Introduction to Networks., CCNA2: Switching, Routing, and Wireless Essentials, linux essential and Python.

Amel Mounia Djebbar has a PhD in Computer Science from the University of Science and Technology of Oran Mohamed-Boudiaf, Algeria. Presently, she is working as a professor at the Graduate School of Economics of Oran, Algeria. She carries out research in the fields of optimization, artificial intelligence, operational research, big data, and machine learning techniques using C++ and Python.

Wafik Hachicha is a Professor in Industrial Engineering at the Higher Institute of Management of Sfax (ISGIS, Tunisia). He has an Industrial Engineer Diploma from National School of Engineering of Tunis (ENIT, Tunisia) since 1999. After a five-year professional experience in various industries, he was obtained his PhD in Mechanical and Manufacturing Engineering (2009) and his HdR in Logistic and Industrial Engineering (2014) from the University of Sfax (Tunisia). He was a former Head of the Industrial Management Department at the Higher Institute of Management of Sfax (ISGIS, Tunisia) and he is a member of several scientific and technical committees at the Ministry of Higher Education and Research (Tunisia). His specialization is about Applied Quantitative Methods in Quality and Industrial Engineering. His research activities deal principally with three topics includes the following. (1) Quality Engineering and Process Control. (2) Sustainable Development and Supply chain Risk Management (3) Modeling, Optimization, and Simulation of Supply Chain and Manufacturing System. Dr. Wafik Hachicha has generated more than 90 publications including more than 50 journal papers.

Khiloun Imad Eddine is a PhD student at the university of sciences and technology of Oran, Algeria, he is a member of SIMPA Laboratory of the same university, he received his Master degree in 2022 from the University of Djilali Liabes of Sidi Bel Abbès, Algeria, his research interests are related to multi-agent systems, supply chains optimization, deep learning and machine learning methods.

Azizul Islam was born at Asansol, West Bengal, India. He is currently pursuing B.Tech from Asansol Engineering College in Electrical Engineering (2021-2024). His understanding in IOT & Robotics devices and its uses.

Md. Irfan Khan is regional manager-South Asia for IAC Electrical Pvt. Ltd., India. Previously, he was a regional manager for Supreme T&D Co. Ltd., Thailand.

Ghania Khensous received her PhD degree from the USTO-MB University in 2018. She is currently a full time-teacher at Ecole Normale Superieure d'Oran (Algeria). Her research interests include BioInformatics especialy Computational Molecular Docking (CMD), Arificial Intelligence (AI), Optimization and Meta-heuristics, Natural Language Processing (NLP) and Information and Communication Technologies in Education.

Rahul Kumar was born in 2000 at Masaurhi, Bihar, India. He has done his Matriculation from ST. Mary's School Masaurhi Patna, Bihar and Intermediate studies from D.N College Masaurhi Patna, Bihar. Presently, he has pursued Bachelor Degree in Department of Electrical Engineering, Asansol Engineering College, Asansol, West Bengal, India. His research interest is a study on green hydrogen-based isolated microgridusing HOMER.

Kaouter Labed earned her Ph.D. degree from USTO-MB University in 2018, specializing in Artificial Intelligence. Her research focuses deeply on integrating bio-inspired algorithms for complex data analysis and decision-making processes. Currently, she is a full-time teacher at the École Normale Supérieure d'Oran in Algeria. She brings extensive experience in satellite image clustering and has innovatively combined multicriteria analysis with bio-inspired algorithms, particularly in the areas of territorial management and spatial decision support systems. Kaouter LABED also holds an international certificate in Data Science and is actively engaged in various cutting-edge projects in natural language processing (NLP) and image processing.

Sabyasachi Pramanik is a professional IEEE member. He obtained a PhD in Computer Science and Engineering from Sri Satya Sai University of Technology and Medical Sciences, Bhopal, India. Presently, he is an Associate Professor, Department of Computer Science and Engineering, Haldia Institute of Technology, India. He has many publications in various reputed international conferences, journals, and book chapters (Indexed by SCIE, Scopus, ESCI, etc). He is doing research in the fields of Artificial Intelligence, Data Privacy, Cybersecurity, Network Security, and Machine Learning. He also serves on the editorial boards of several international journals. He is a reviewer of journal articles from IEEE, Springer, Elsevier, Inderscience, IET and IGI Global. He has reviewed many conference papers, has been a keynote speaker, session chair, and technical program committee member at many international conferences. He has authored a book on Wireless Sensor Network. He has edited 8 books from IGI Global, CRC Press, Springer and Wiley Publications.

Dharmbir Prasad was born in 1986 at Nalanda, Bihar, India. He received his B.Tech. degree in electrical engineering from Hooghly Engineering & Technology College (under West Bengal University of Technology), Hooghly, India and M.Tech. in Power System from Dr. B.C. Roy Engineering College (under West Bengal University of Technology), Durgapur, India, respectively. Currently, he is working in the capacity of assistant professor in the department of electrical engineering, Asansol Engineering College, Asansol, West Bengal, India. He has pursued Ph.D. degree from Indian School of Mines, Dhanbad, Jharkhand, India. His research interest includes economic operation of power system.

Ranadip Roy received the Ph.D. degree from the Department of Electrical Engineering at the Indian Institute of Technology (Indian School of Mines), Dhanbad, India, in 2022. He is currently associated in the Department of Electrical Engineering as an Associate Professor at Sanaka Eduactional Trust's Group of Institutions, Durgapur, India. His-research interests are in the area of Renewable Energy, Fuel cell, power system optimization.

Zohra Sabrina Delhoum is currently an associate professor of mathematics at the Higher School of Economics in Oran. Her research focuses on optimization. She previously held the position of Quality Assurance Manager and currently serves as the Deputy Director of Postgraduate Studies. In addition to her current roles, Zohra Sabrina DELHOUM has made notable contributions to the field, with two publications in indexed international journals, showcasing her significant impact on optimization research. Furthermore, she has authored a lecture note on probability courses, providing a valuable educational resource. Her commitment to knowledge dissemination is evident through her active participation in numerous conferences and continuous attendance at various training sessions. These experiences underscore her dedication to staying abreast of the latest developments in her expertise.

Rudra Pratap Singh was born in 1983 at Chittaranjan, Burdwan, West Bengal, India. He received his B. Tech. and M. Tech degree in electrical engineering from Asansol Engineering (under the West Bengal University of Technology), Asansol, West Bengal, India and MBA in Power Management from the University of Petroleum and Energy Studies, Dehradun, Uttrakhand, India, respectively. He received his Ph.D. degree from the Indian School of Mines, Dhanbad, Jharkhand, India. Currently, he is working in the capacity of assistant professor in the department of electrical engineering, Asansol Engineering College, Asansol, West Bengal, India. His research interest includes the application of state estimation and optimization techniques in various fields of engineering.

Redouane Tlemsani is an accomplished academic and researcher, currently serving as an Associate Professor since 2017. With a Ph.D. in Data Sciences and Artificial Intelligence, he specializes in data processing and computer sciences. He is affiliated with the University of Sciences and Technologies of Oran USTO in Algeria, where he conducts cutting-edge research in his field. In addition to his research endeavors, he is a dedicated educator, imparting his expertise to students at both the Engineering and LMD levels in computer science and software engineering.

Index

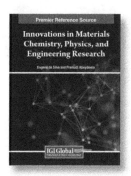
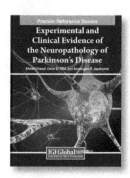

www.igi-global.com

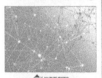